MASTERING THE **STOCK MARKET**:

A COMPREHENSIVE GUIDE TO INVESTING AND TRADING

MASTERING THE **STOCK MARKET**: A COMPREHENSIVE GUIDE TO INVESTING AND TRADING

MIKE IKE

Library of Congress Control Number:		2024923522
ISBN:	Hardcover	979-8-3694-3290-7
	Softcover	979-8-3694-3289-1
	eBook	979-8-3694-3288-4

Print information available on the last page.

Rev. date: 11/07/2024

To order additional copies of this book, contact:
Xlibris
844-714-8691
www.Xlibris.com
Orders@Xlibris.com
863232

CONTENTS

INTRODUCTION TO THE STOCK MARKET

Mastering the Stock Market: A Comprehensive Guide to Investing and Trading is your definitive guide to navigating the intricate world of investing and trading in a landscape where financial markets continually evolve and present opportunities and challenges. This comprehensive resource is designed to empower you with the knowledge, strategies, and tools necessary to succeed, instilling a sense of confidence and capability.

Our journey begins with the 'History of the Stock Market', tracing its evolution from humble beginnings to the robust financial ecosystem we see today. Understanding this history is crucial, as it provides context for current market dynamics and informs us about the strategies employed by investors throughout the ages. This knowledge will make you feel informed and knowledgeable, ready to make sound investment decisions. From the establishment of stock exchanges to the impact of technological advancements, the narrative of the stock market is rich in lessons that can shape your investment decisions.

In the chapter on 'Stock Market Exchange', we delve into the various platforms where securities are traded, illuminating their roles, structures, and operational mechanisms. Knowledge of these exchanges is essential for any investor looking to navigate the complexities of buying and selling securities efficiently.

As we progress to 'Understanding the Basics', we demystify the foundational investing concepts. You will learn essential terminology, trading mechanics, and various financial instruments here. This foundational knowledge serves as a springboard for more advanced topics and strategies, ensuring you are well-prepared for the journey ahead.

In 'Getting Started', we provide practical guidance on setting investment goals, selecting the right brokerage, and executing your first trades. This chapter emphasizes the importance of strategic planning and execution, laying the groundwork for a successful investment journey and making you feel prepared and ready to take action.

'Fundamental Analysis and Technical Analysis' are explored in detail, providing you with the analytical tools to evaluate potential investments. Fundamental analysis allows you to assess a company's intrinsic value, while technical analysis equips you with the skills to interpret market trends and price movements. Mastery of both methods will enhance your ability to make informed investment decisions.

The chapter on 'Trading Strategies' introduces you to diverse approaches, from long-term investing to short-term trading. Understanding various strategies enables you to align your trading style with your financial goals and market conditions, empowering you to navigate the stock market confidently.

'Risk Management and Psychology' are critical components of successful investing. Here, we emphasize the importance of emotional discipline and sound risk mitigation techniques. By recognizing behavioral biases and implementing effective risk management strategies, you can better navigate the inherent volatility of financial markets.

As we delve into 'Advanced Topics,' we explore sophisticated trading strategies and instruments, including options trading strategies, buying and selling stock options, futures, derivatives, leveraged trading and margin accounts, algorithmic trading, high-frequency trading, and artificial intelligence (AI). Understanding these advanced concepts expands your investment toolkit and prepares you for the complexities of modern trading environments.

'The Global Markets and International Investing' chapter highlights the opportunities and challenges of diversifying your investments across borders. Embracing a global perspective allows you to tap into growth potential in emerging markets while mitigating risk through geographic diversification.

In 'Putting It All Together', we synthesize the knowledge gained throughout the guide, reinforcing the interconnectedness of the concepts discussed. This holistic approach empowers you to develop a cohesive investment strategy tailored to your objectives and risk tolerance.

Finally, the 'Financial Ratios and Metrics' chapter equips you with the analytical tools to evaluate a company's financial health. Mastering these metrics will enhance your ability to assess potential investments and make informed decisions.

In conclusion, *Mastering the Stock Market: A Comprehensive Guide to Investing and Trading* is more than just a guide; it is a powerful resource designed to elevate your understanding of investing and trading. By immersing yourself in this comprehensive framework, you will gain the insights, skills, and confidence to navigate the complexities of the stock market and work towards achieving your financial goals. Prepare to embark on a transformative journey that will empower you to master the art and science of investing in today's dynamic financial landscape.

Chapter 1

STOCK MARKET HISTORY

In the late 1400s, Antwerp, situated in what is now modern-day Belgium, emerged as a pivotal force in international trade. Its strategic location at the confluence of the Scheldt and Rupel rivers provided unparalleled access to waterways, making it an ideal nexus for commerce and trade. As a result, Antwerp rapidly transformed into a vibrant hub where merchants and traders gathered to exchange a wealth of goods, including luxurious textiles, exotic spices, and precious metals that were sought after across Europe. The city's thriving port, one of the most advanced of its time, boasted an intricate network of canals and a well-developed infrastructure that facilitated the seamless movement of goods. This unparalleled connectivity attracted a diverse array of traders from various regions, establishing Antwerp as an essential center for trade and the exchange of ideas and culture. The bustling markets became a melting pot of innovation and collaboration, fostering an environment where economic and cultural dynamism flourished. Antwerp's rise as a major international trade center marked the beginning of a transformative era in commerce, solidifying its place in history as a cornerstone of European trade and cultural exchange.

In 1611, Amsterdam, Netherlands, witnessed the birth of organized stock market trading, a groundbreaking moment that would forever alter the finance landscape. The Dutch East India Company (VOC), officially known as the Vereenigde Oost-Indische Compagnie, was at the forefront of this revolutionary development. As the world's first publicly traded company, the VOC boldly issued stocks and bonds, enabling individuals to invest in its ventures and share in the lucrative profits of global trade. This pioneering act introduced the concept of equity investment and laid the groundwork for modern stock trading practices. The establishment of the Amsterdam Stock Exchange marked a new era in financial history, positioning Amsterdam as one of the dominant financial centers of the seventeenth and eighteenth centuries. The exchange became a bustling marketplace where investors could trade shares and bonds, driving unprecedented economic activity and innovation. The remarkable success of the VOC and its ability to attract investment catalyzed the Dutch Republic's emergence as a dominant economic power in Europe, fundamentally shaping the trajectory of capitalism. This pivotal moment in history set the stage for the development of modern stock markets, showcasing the power of collective investment and the importance of transparent trading practices. The legacy of the VOC and the Amsterdam Stock Exchange continues to resonate today, as they exemplify the principles of entrepreneurship, investment, and market efficiency that underpin the global financial system.

In the late 1700s, a pivotal moment in financial history unfolded in New York City when a small group of visionary merchants convened beneath a buttonwood tree to craft the Buttonwood Agreement. This foundational agreement was a landmark initiative that established essential rules governing securities trading, marking the dawn of organized stock trading in America. The merchants, recognizing the need for a structured approach to trading, outlined key provisions that included the payment of commissions on transactions and the implementation of an auction system to determine prices. Named after the tree that served as their meeting place, the Buttonwood Agreement became the precursor to what would eventually evolve into the New York Stock Exchange (NYSE), officially established in

1792. The NYSE quickly rose to prominence, becoming one of the world's oldest and largest stock exchanges. Its formation represented the birth of a trading platform and the emergence of a significant center for stock trading and financial activity, both in the United States and globally. The establishment of the NYSE underpinned the growth of American capitalism and laid the groundwork for modern financial markets. It transformed how securities were traded, fostering an environment of transparency and competition that has driven economic progress. Today, the NYSE stands as a symbol of financial innovation and resilience, continuing to play a crucial role in shaping the global economy. The legacy of the Buttonwood Agreement endures, reminding us of the power of collaboration and vision in creating a robust financial system.

In 1790, the establishment of the Philadelphia Stock Exchange (PHLX) marked a significant milestone in the evolution of financial markets, positioning it as one of the oldest stock exchanges in the United States. Founded by a pioneering group of brokers and traders in Philadelphia, the PHLX was created to facilitate trading stocks, bonds, and other securities. This initiative played a crucial role in developing a more organized and formalized securities market in the nation, setting the stage for the future of American finance. The PHLX distinguished itself as a trailblazer in trading options, emerging as one of the first exchanges in the United States to embrace this innovative financial instrument. It was the inaugural exchange to offer currency options and led the way in trading options on individual stocks, pushing the boundaries of investment possibilities. This forward-thinking approach not only enhanced the sophistication of the financial markets but also empowered investors with more diverse strategies for managing risk and maximizing returns. Today, PHLX's legacy continues under the banner of the Nasdaq Options Market, where it operates as an integral part of the Nasdaq Stock Market. Its historical significance as a pioneer in securities trading and options markets remains a testament to its foundational role in shaping the modern financial landscape. The Philadelphia Stock Exchange's enduring influence highlights the importance of innovation and adaptability in the ever-evolving world of finance, serving as an inspiration for future generations of traders and investors.

In 1896, Charles Dow, a visionary and co-founder of Dow Jones & Company, forever transformed the financial landscape by creating the Dow Jones Industrial Average (DJIA). The DJIA is one of the world's oldest and most closely monitored stock market indices, serving as a barometer for the performance of the American industrial economy. Originally composed of just twelve carefully selected components, Dow intended to create a representative snapshot of the burgeoning industrial sector defining America's economic landscape at the time. The DJIA is structured as a price-weighted index, meaning that stocks with higher prices significantly influence the index's overall movement. This methodology reflects the impact of major corporations on the market, emphasizing the importance of leading firms in shaping economic trends. Over the years, the index has evolved to include thirty blue-chip stocks, each a leader in its respective industry, showcasing the strength and resilience of the U.S. economy. Today, the DJIA is not just a statistical measure but a widely respected benchmark against which the performance of the U.S. stock market and the broader economic landscape is assessed. Its enduring relevance speaks to its foundational role in guiding investor sentiment, shaping economic policy and informing strategic decision-making. As a touchstone for investors, analysts, and policymakers alike, the Dow Jones Industrial Average captures the essence of American enterprise and the dynamic forces that drive financial markets.

In 1923, Henry Varnum Poor's company laid the groundwork for what would become a monumental tool in the financial landscape: the early version of the S&P 500 index, now recognized as S&P Global. Today, the S&P 500 is hailed as a premier stock market index, serving as a critical indicator of the health and performance of the U.S. stock market and economy. Comprising 500 large-cap stocks meticulously selected by Standard & Poor's (S&P), the index embodies a comprehensive snapshot of American corporate performance, reflecting the diversity and dynamism of the nation's economy. As a barometer of the broader U.S. equity market, the S&P 500 is not just a collection of stocks; it is a vital benchmark used by investors, analysts, and financial professionals to evaluate market trends and performance. Its market capitalization-weighted structure ensures that companies with the largest market capitalizations have a proportionately significant impact on the index, emphasizing the influence of major corporations on the overall market dynamics. Today, the S&P 500 is among the most important and closely followed stock market indices globally. It provides invaluable insights into economic health and investor sentiment, serving as a standard against which investment strategies are measured. Its legacy continues to shape financial decision-making, making it an essential tool for understanding the complexities of the modern financial landscape and guiding investors toward informed choices in their pursuit of wealth and growth.

In 1929, the U.S. stock market faced a catastrophic collapse, shattering the illusion of unending prosperity that characterized the Roaring Twenties. This dramatic downturn began on October 24, 1929, infamously known as Black Thursday and heralded the onset of the Great Depression. This devastating economic crisis would grip the nation for more than a decade. The stock market crash resulted from a perfect storm of factors, including rampant speculation, a lack of regulatory oversight, and the overvaluation of stocks. During this period of economic vitality, many investors were lured into the market, often buying stocks on margin—borrowing money to purchase shares in hopes of magnifying their returns. However, when the market began its steep decline, these investors could not meet margin calls, forcing them to sell their stocks at steep losses, further fueling the decline. The repercussions of the crash were immediate and severe. As stock prices plummeted, businesses collapsed into financial ruin, leading to unprecedented unemployment. Banks, unable to withstand the economic strain, failed in staggering numbers, wiping out the savings of countless families and plunging millions into despair. The stock market crash of 1929 and the ensuing Great Depression profoundly transformed the U.S. economy and society. It ignited widespread poverty, social upheaval, and a sense of disillusionment that permeated the nation. The government implemented groundbreaking regulations and policies designed to stabilize the economy and prevent future financial catastrophes in response to the economic devastation. This crisis was a crucial turning point in American financial history, shaping the regulatory landscape and establishing the foundation for the modern monetary system.

In 1941, the landscape of financial information and analysis was transformed with the founding of Standard & Poor's (S&P), a result of the groundbreaking merger between Poor's Publishing, an esteemed provider of financial data since the late 1800s, and Standard Statistics. This union marked a significant milestone in the evolution of financial services, establishing S&P as a powerhouse in the industry. S&P has become synonymous with excellence in financial analytics, providing critical credit ratings, research, and data to investors and financial institutions worldwide. Its credit ratings are highly regarded as authoritative assessments of the creditworthiness of individuals, corporations, and nations, serving as indispensable tools for investors. These ratings empower investors to evaluate the risk associated with securities, guiding their investment decisions with informed confidence. Moreover, S&P is renowned for publishing influential indices, notably the S&P 500, a cornerstone of stock market analysis. This index is widely considered a leading indicator of the U.S. stock market and economic performance, reflecting the health and vitality of the nation's largest companies. The merger of Poor's Publishing and Standard Statistics signaled a new era in financial data and analysis, enabling S&P to leverage its extensive historical knowledge and statistical rigor to become a leading provider of financial insights. Today, S&P Global operates as a publicly traded entity, delivering vital financial market intelligence, data, and analytics to investors and financial institutions across the globe. With its unwavering commitment to quality and integrity, S&P has cemented its reputation as one of the most reputable and influential companies in the financial services sector, continuing

to shape the landscape of investment and economic analysis for generations.

In 1971, the financial landscape underwent a revolutionary transformation with the launch of the National Association of Securities Dealers Automated Quotations (Nasdaq), marking the inception of the first electronic stock market in the United States. This groundbreaking platform utilized advanced computer technology to connect buyers and sellers of securities in real time, fundamentally changing how trading was conducted. Unlike the traditional New York Stock Exchange (NYSE), which relied on floor traders to facilitate transactions, Nasdaq's innovative electronic matching system enabled faster and more efficient trading, setting a new standard for market operations. Originally conceived as an exchange for over-the-counter (OTC) securities, Nasdaq provided a platform for companies that could not meet the stringent listing requirements of established exchanges like the NYSE. Many of these early listings included smaller emerging companies poised for growth, reflecting the dynamic and entrepreneurial spirit of the American economy at the time. Today, Nasdaq is one of the world's largest and most influential stock exchanges, serving as a vital center of technology and innovation within the financial industry. Its reputation for listing high-growth and tech-focused companies, including giants like Apple, Microsoft, and Amazon, underscores its role as a catalyst for modern investment opportunities. The Nasdaq Composite, a key stock market index, encompasses all common stocks and similar securities listed on the Nasdaq, providing a comprehensive overview of the market's performance. This index has become a benchmark for investors, offering insights into the health of the technology sector and the broader market. Nasdaq's pioneering spirit and commitment to innovation continue to shape the trading future, making it an integral part of the global financial ecosystem.

In the late 1980s, several factors contributed to a run-up in stock prices, which peaked on October 19, 1987, also known as Black Monday. One of the main factors was the increased use of corporate buyouts, in which companies used leverage (borrowing money) to purchase other companies. This led to a large amount of debt on corporate balance sheets and an overvaluation of stocks. Another factor was portfolio insurance, a financial product that used derivatives to protect against market declines. The idea was that as the market went down, the portfolio insurance would automatically sell stocks to offset the losses, limiting the damage to an investor's portfolio. However, as the market began to decline on October 19, 1987, many investors tried to sell simultaneously, resulting in a massive sell-off that caused the market to crash. The Dow Jones Industrial Average fell by 22.6% on October 19, 1987, the most significant one-day percentage decline in history. Many other markets around the world also experienced substantial declines. The crash severely impacted the global economy and led to changes in regulations and policies aimed at preventing future market crashes and improving market stability.

In 2008, the stock market plunged, culminating in a catastrophic crash that reverberated across the globe. This upheaval was precipitated by a confluence of factors tied to the housing market's explosive rise and subsequent collapse. The housing market experienced unprecedented growth during the preceding years, buoyed by historically low interest rates and an influx of easy credit. This environment encouraged a surge in mortgage lending, including several subprime loans—mortgages extended to borrowers with poor credit histories and questionable repayment abilities.

As interest rates began to rise and the housing market began to cool, the consequences of this reckless lending became painfully evident. Many subprime borrowers could not meet their mortgage obligations, leading to a devastating wave of defaults and foreclosures. The resulting deluge of foreclosures sent shockwaves through the market, causing the value of mortgage-backed securities to plummet. These complex financial instruments, once deemed secure, became toxic assets as the underlying loans were sourced.

Large financial institutions, heavily entrenched in the housing market, had amassed significant holdings of these mortgage-backed securities. As their values eroded, many of these institutions faced severe financial distress, some even collapsing under the weight of their losses. The ensuing crisis eroded confidence in the entire financial system, triggering a massive withdrawal of capital from the stock market. Gripped by fear and uncertainty, investors pulled their money out, leading to a sharp and dramatic decline in stock prices.

This catastrophic crash marked the onset of the Great Recession, a severe economic downturn significantly impacting the global economy. The fallout was devastating: widespread unemployment, countless business closures, and a steep decline in economic activity became the new reality for millions. The aftermath of the 2008 financial crisis served as a stark reminder of the dangers of unchecked speculation and poor risk management, prompting a reevaluation of financial regulations and practices that would shape the future of the financial landscape.

In conclusion, the history of the stock market, tracing back to the late 1400s, reveals a remarkable evolution from the bustling trade center of Antwerp to the sophisticated financial networks we see today. Antwerp's emergence as a central international trade hub laid the foundational principles of trading and investment that would shape the future of financial markets. The city's innovations in financial transactions and the development of early stock trading mechanisms set the stage for the creation of formal stock exchanges.

As centuries passed, the stock market evolved through various stages, reflecting the dynamic interplay of economic, technological, and regulatory changes. From forming the Amsterdam Stock Exchange in the seventeenth century to establishing major global exchanges like the NYSE and Nasdaq, each milestone in the stock market's history has contributed to its current complexity and significance.

Understanding this historical trajectory highlights the stock market's role as a critical component of the global economy, enabling businesses to raise capital and investors to participate in economic growth. The lessons learned from centuries of market development emphasize the importance of adaptability, innovation, and regulation in ensuring the market's integrity and efficiency. The journey of the stock market from Antwerp to the present day underscores its enduring impact on financial systems worldwide. This rich historical context enhances our appreciation of the market's evolution and equips us with valuable insights for navigating the contemporary investment landscape. The stock market's history is a testament to human ingenuity and its capacity to drive economic progress through changing times.

Chapter 2

STOCK MARKET EXCHANGE

A stock exchange is a marketplace where stocks, bonds, and other securities are bought and sold. It provides a platform for companies to raise capital by issuing shares of stock and for investors to buy and sell these shares. The most well-known stock exchanges include the New York Stock Exchange (NYSE) and Nasdaq in the United States, the London Stock Exchange (LSE) in the United Kingdom, and the Tokyo Stock Exchange (TSE) in Japan.

Stock exchanges have strict listing requirements that companies must meet before their shares can be traded. These requirements can include minimum levels of revenue, net income, assets, and public float, which is the number of shares held by the public. Stock exchanges are regulated by government agencies and are required to follow strict rules and regulations to protect investors and maintain the market's integrity. They also use complex systems to match buyers and sellers and execute trades promptly and efficiently. Stock exchanges are an essential part of the financial system as they provide a way for companies to raise capital and investors to buy and sell securities. They also serve as a barometer of economic activity and can be used to gauge the health of a country's industries and businesses.

There are over 220 stock exchanges worldwide operating in more than 100 countries. These stock exchanges vary in size, with some being large and well-established, such as the New York Stock Exchange (NYSE) and the Nasdaq, and others being smaller and more regional. However, it is essential to note that this number constantly changes as new stock exchanges are created, and others may merge or close down. Additionally, alternative trading systems such as dark pools, electronic communication networks, and other platforms allow the trading of securities, which are not included in this number.

The top ten stock exchanges in the world based on market capitalization are the following:

1. New York Stock Exchange (NYSE) (United States)
2. Nasdaq (United States)
3. Tokyo Stock Exchange (TSE) (Japan)
4. Shanghai Stock Exchange (SSE) (China)
5. Hong Kong Stock Exchange (HKEX) (Hong Kong)
6. Euronext (Europe)
7. London Stock Exchange (LSE) (United Kingdom)
8. Shenzhen Stock Exchange (SZSE) (China)
9. Toronto Stock Exchange (TSX) (Canada)
10. Bombay Stock Exchange (BSE) (India)

NEW YORK STOCK EXCHANGE (NYSE)

The New York Stock Exchange (NYSE) is one of the world's most iconic and influential financial institutions on Wall Street in New York City. Established in 1817, it has become the largest stock exchange by market capitalization and plays a critical role in global finance and the economy.

Historical Background

The NYSE traces its roots to the Buttonwood Agreement in 1792 when twenty-four stockbrokers gathered under a buttonwood tree to create a system for trading securities. Over the years, this informal arrangement evolved into a formal exchange. The NYSE

was officially formed in 1817, initially known as the New York Stock & Exchange Board. It adopted the name New York Stock Exchange in 1867, reflecting its status as a central marketplace for securities trading.

Structure and Operations

The NYSE operates as an auction market, where buyers and sellers trade securities through a system of floor brokers and market makers. Unlike electronic exchanges, the NYSE utilizes a physical trading floor, which facilitates face-to-face transactions. This structure enables brokers to negotiate prices and execute trades in real-time.

- **Floor trading:** The trading floor is home to numerous specialized professionals, including floor traders, who facilitate transactions and maintain liquidity in the market. The bustling environment of the NYSE, characterized by open outcry trading and the iconic ringing of the opening and closing bells, symbolizes the vibrancy of the financial markets.
- **Market makers:** Market makers facilitate trading by providing liquidity. They quote buy-and-sell security prices and are obligated to maintain an orderly market, ensuring that trades can be executed promptly.
- **Listed companies:** The NYSE is home to many of the world's largest and most well-known corporations, including General Motors, General Electric, and Coca-Cola. To be listed on the NYSE, companies must meet stringent financial performance, governance, and market capitalization requirements.

Indices and Benchmarking

The NYSE is associated with several key stock market indices, the most notable being the Dow Jones Industrial Average (DJIA) and the NYSE Composite Index.

- **Dow Jones Industrial Average:** This index includes thirty large publicly traded companies and serves as a barometer of the overall performance of the U.S. stock market. As of 2024, the thirty stocks that make up the Dow Jones Industrial Average are Amazon.com Inc., American Express Co., Amgen Inc., Apple Inc., Boeing Co., Caterpillar Inc., Cisco Systems Inc., Chevron Corp., Goldman Sachs Group Inc., Home Depot Inc., Honeywell International Inc., International Business Machines Corp., Nvidia Corporation, Johnson & Johnson, Coca-Cola Co., JPMorgan Chase & Co., McDonald's Corp., 3M Co., Merck & Co. Inc., Microsoft Corp., Nike Inc., Procter & Gamble Co., Travelers Companies Inc., United Health Group Inc., Salesforce Inc., Verizon Communications Inc., Visa Inc., Walmart Inc., Walt Disney Co., and Sherwin-Williams Company.
- **NYSE Composite Index:** This index tracks all common stocks listed on the NYSE, providing a broader view of market trends and performance.

Impact on Global Finance

The NYSE plays a vital role in the global financial system. It acts as a platform for companies to raise capital by issuing stocks, enabling them to grow and expand their operations. The exchange attracts investors worldwide, offering opportunities for portfolio diversification and investment in some of the most prominent companies.

Additionally, the NYSE is critical in setting market trends and influencing economic policy. Its movements are closely monitored by investors, analysts, and policymakers alike, making it a crucial indicator of financial health and investor sentiment.

Technological Advancements

The NYSE has recently embraced technological advancements to enhance its trading capabilities. Integrating electronic trading systems alongside traditional floor trading has improved efficiency and accessibility. The NYSE's commitment to innovation ensures it remains competitive in an ever-evolving financial landscape.

The New York Stock Exchange is not merely a marketplace but a cornerstone of the global financial system. Its rich history, robust structure, and ongoing evolution reflect the dynamic nature of capital markets. As the largest stock exchange in the world, the NYSE continues to facilitate economic growth, empower investors, and shape the future of finance on a global scale. Its role as a leading venue for securities trading cements its status as a symbol of financial opportunity and resilience.

NATIONAL ASSOCIATION OF SECURITIES DEALERS AUTOMATED QUOTATIONS (NASDAQ)

The National Association of Securities Dealers Automated Quotations (Nasdaq) is a major American stock exchange and a key player in global financial markets. Established in 1971, Nasdaq was the world's first electronic stock market, revolutionizing how securities are traded and paving the way for the future of trading technology.

Historical Background

Nasdaq was created to provide a transparent and efficient electronic trading platform for over-the-counter (OTC) securities. The initiative stemmed from the need to modernize the trading process, primarily conducted through phone calls and paper-based systems. By introducing an automated system for quoting prices and executing trades, Nasdaq established a new standard for market speed and efficiency.

Structure and Operations

Unlike traditional exchanges such as the New York Stock Exchange (NYSE), which operates on a physical trading floor, Nasdaq is a fully electronic exchange. This allows for faster trade execution and greater accessibility for investors.

- **Electronic trading system:** Nasdaq's electronic trading platform connects buyers and sellers through a sophisticated network, utilizing advanced algorithms to match orders in real time. This technology enables rapid transactions and reduces the need for human intervention.
- **Market makers:** Nasdaq relies on a system of market makers—firms that facilitate trading by providing liquidity. Market makers continuously quote buy and sell prices for securities and are obligated to maintain fair and orderly markets. This system allows for efficient price discovery and helps ensure that trades can be executed quickly.
- **Listed companies:** Nasdaq is home to many of the world's leading technology and growth-oriented companies, including giants like Apple, Amazon, and Microsoft. The exchange has specific listing requirements, focusing on innovative companies with substantial market capitalizations.

Indices and Benchmarking

Nasdaq is associated with several important stock market indices, the most prominent being the Nasdaq Composite Index and the Nasdaq-100 Index.

- **Nasdaq Composite Index:** This index includes all common stocks listed on the Nasdaq exchange, providing a comprehensive view of the exchange's performance. It is particularly known for its heavy weighting in technology stocks, making it a key indicator of tech sector trends.

- **Nasdaq-100 Index:** This index comprises the 100 largest nonfinancial companies listed on Nasdaq, serving as a benchmark for investors focused on growth-oriented, innovative firms. Investors and fund managers widely use it to gauge the performance of leading companies in various industries.

Impact on Global Finance

Nasdaq has played a significant role in shaping the landscape of modern finance. It has become synonymous with technological innovation and growth, attracting investors interested in emerging companies and sectors. Its electronic trading model has influenced other exchanges worldwide, driving technology adoption in trading practices.

Moreover, Nasdaq's emphasis on high-growth companies has helped facilitate the rise of the tech sector, contributing to economic development and job creation. It serves as a platform for initial public offerings (IPOs) for many innovative companies, providing them with the capital needed to expand and innovate.

Technological Advancements

As a pioneer in electronic trading, Nasdaq continues to invest in technological advancements to enhance its trading systems and provide better services to its participants. Innovations such as algorithmic trading, high-frequency trading, and data analytics have solidified Nasdaq's reputation as a leader in the financial technology space. Its commitment to continuous improvement ensures it remains competitive in an ever-evolving market environment.

The National Association of Securities Dealers Automated Quotations (Nasdaq) stands as a testament to the transformative power of technology in financial markets. Its unique electronic trading model and focus on growth-oriented companies have redefined how securities are traded, making it a cornerstone of the global financial system. As one of the world's largest and most influential stock exchanges, Nasdaq continues to drive innovation, connect investors with opportunities, and shape the future of finance in an increasingly interconnected and dynamic economy. Its legacy as a leader in electronic trading and commitment to fostering innovation ensures its position as a vital player in the global market landscape.

SHANGHAI STOCK EXCHANGE (SSE)

The Shanghai Stock Exchange (SSE) is one of the largest and most significant stock exchanges in Asia and the world. Established in 1990, it plays a crucial role in China's capital markets and is a critical platform for raising capital, trading securities, and facilitating investment in the Chinese economy.

Historical Background

The SSE was founded on 26 November 1990 as part of China's economic reforms to modernize the country's financial system and attract foreign investment. Following decades of centralized economic planning, its establishment marked a significant shift towards a market-oriented economy. The SSE quickly gained prominence as a key financial institution in China, reflecting the rapid growth and development of the country's economy.

Structure and Operations

The SSE operates as a centralized marketplace for the buying and selling of securities, including stocks, bonds, exchange-traded funds (ETFs), and other financial instruments. The exchange is regulated by the China Securities Regulatory Commission (CSRC), which oversees its operations and enforces market rules to ensure transparency and fairness.

- **Listing requirements:** To be listed on the SSE, companies must meet stringent criteria related to financial performance, governance, and market capitalization. This rigorous process ensures that only financially sound and reputable companies can access public capital.

- **Market segments:** The SSE features several market segments, including the Main Board, the SSE Science and Technology Innovation Board (STAR Market), and the SSE Bond Market. The STAR Market, launched in 2019, is designed to support innovative and high-tech companies and offers a more flexible listing process than the Main Board.
- **Trading mechanism:** The SSE employs an electronic trading system, allowing investors to trade securities in real time. The trading hours are typically from 9.30 a.m. to 3 p.m. (local time), with a break for lunch. The exchange operates under a price-limit system to prevent excessive volatility, allowing stocks to rise or fall by a specified percentage daily.

Indices and Benchmarking

The SSE is associated with several key stock market indices that provide insights into market performance:

- **SSE Composite Index:** This index tracks all stocks listed on the SSE's Main Board and serves as a primary indicator of the Chinese stock market's overall performance.
- **SSE 50 Index:** Composed of the fifty most extensive and most liquid stocks listed on the SSE, this index provides a benchmark for investors looking to gauge the performance of major blue-chip companies in China.
- **SSE STAR 50 Index:** This index includes the top fifty stocks listed on the STAR Market, reflecting the performance of innovative companies in emerging sectors.

Impact on Global Finance

The SSE plays a vital role in the global financial landscape. China's premier stock exchange attracts domestic and international investors, facilitating capital flows into the country. The SSE is a crucial platform for companies looking to raise funds for expansion, innovation, and development, contributing significantly to the growth of the Chinese economy.

In recent years, the SSE has also sought to enhance its global presence by welcoming foreign investments and participating in international financial markets. This openness has been crucial in positioning China as a significant player in the worldwide economy.

Technological Advancements

The SSE is committed to leveraging technology to improve trading efficiency and market transparency. The exchange has implemented advanced trading systems and data analytics tools to support investors and market participants. Continuous investment in technology ensures that the SSE remains competitive and capable of handling the complexities of modern trading.

The Shanghai Stock Exchange is a pillar of China's financial system, embodying the country's rapid economic development and commitment to market reform. With its rigorous listing standards, diverse market segments, and influential indices, the SSE is critical in facilitating investment and capital formation in China. As one of the world's largest and most significant stock exchanges, it continues to shape the dynamics of global finance, making it an essential destination for investors seeking opportunities in the growing Chinese market. The SSE's ongoing commitment to innovation and transparency positions it as a key player in the evolving landscape of international finance, solidifying its status as a vital hub for investment and economic growth.

EUROPEAN NEW EXCHANGE TECHNOLOGY (EURONEXT)

Euronext is a pan-European stock exchange that is an essential financial hub for trading equities, derivatives, exchange-traded funds (ETFs), and other securities. Established in 2000, Euronext has rapidly evolved into one of Europe's largest stock exchanges, integrating several national exchanges and providing a unified platform for trading across multiple countries.

Historical Background

Euronext was formed by merging the Amsterdam Stock Exchange, the Brussels Stock Exchange, and the Paris Bourse. This consolidation was driven by the need for a more competitive and efficient trading environment in the face of globalization and technological advancements. The establishment of Euronext marked a significant step towards creating a single European market for financial securities. Over the years, Euronext has expanded its footprint, acquiring additional exchanges, including the Lisbon Stock Exchange and the Irish Stock Exchange. In 2014, Euronext became independent after being spun off from the Intercontinental Exchange, further solidifying its position as a leading European exchange.

Structure and Operations

Euronext operates multiple market segments, each designed to cater to different types of securities and investor needs:

- **Cash market:** This segment allows the trading of equities and ETFs, providing a platform for companies to raise capital through initial public offerings (IPOs) and for investors to buy and sell shares. Euronext's cash market is characterized by high liquidity and transparency.
- **Derivatives market:** Euronext offers a robust derivatives market for trading options and futures contracts. This segment is essential for investors seeking to hedge risks or speculate on price movements of underlying assets.
- **Euronext Growth:** Aimed at small- and medium-sized enterprises (SMEs), Euronext Growth provides a flexible listing framework that supports the growth of innovative

companies. It offers a simplified regulatory process, making it easier for SMEs to access capital markets.

- **Euronext access:** This entry-level market is designed for startups and smaller companies looking to raise capital. It provides an accessible platform for companies at various stages of development.

Indices and Benchmarking

Euronext is associated with several important stock market indices, which serve as benchmarks for the performance of the exchange:

- **Euronext 100 Index:** This index tracks the performance of the 100 most extensive and most liquid stocks listed on Euronext, representing a diverse range of sectors and industries.
- **Euronext All-Share Index:** This comprehensive index encompasses all stocks listed on Euronext, providing a broad view of market trends and performance.
- **Euronext Tech 40:** This index focuses on the forty leading technology companies listed on Euronext, highlighting the growing significance of the tech sector in the European market.

Impact on European Finance

Euronext is pivotal in the European financial landscape, serving as a critical platform for capital formation and investment. It facilitates access to funding for companies across Europe, enabling them to grow and innovate. The exchange attracts diverse investors, including institutional investors, retail investors, and multinational corporations, fostering a dynamic investment ecosystem. Euronext's emphasis on transparency, regulatory compliance, and market integrity has bolstered investor confidence. The exchange's commitment to maintaining high standards contributes to the overall stability of the European financial system.

Technological Advancements

Euronext is at the forefront of technological innovation in trading. The exchange utilizes advanced electronic trading systems that enhance efficiency, speed, and accuracy in executing trades. Its embracing of technology ensures that Euronext remains competitive in an evolving market landscape. Introducing new trading platforms and integrating data analytics and artificial intelligence have further enhanced the trading experience for market participants. Euronext continues to invest in technology to improve market accessibility and transparency, ensuring that it meets the needs of a diverse investor base.

Euronext is a cornerstone of European finance, embodying the principles of innovation, collaboration, and market integration. By unifying multiple national exchanges into a single platform, Euronext has created a dynamic marketplace that fosters investment, drives economic growth, and enhances access to capital for businesses across Europe. Its diverse market segments, influential indices, and commitment to technological advancement position Euronext as a vital player in the global financial landscape. As Europe continues to evolve amid economic challenges and opportunities, Euronext remains a key hub for investment and financial activity, reflecting the resilience and ambition of the European capital markets.

HONG KONG STOCK EXCHANGE (HKEX)

The Hong Kong Stock Exchange (HKEX) is one of the largest and most significant stock exchanges in Asia and globally. Established in 1891, HKEX has played a crucial role in developing Hong Kong as a major financial center and a gateway for international investors looking to access the Chinese market.

Historical Background

HKEX traces its roots back to the establishment of the Hong Kong Stockbrokers Association, which was formed in 1891. The exchange grew in prominence through the twentieth century, becoming an essential venue for trading equities and bonds in the region. In 1986, the Hong Kong Stock Exchange merged with the Hong Kong Futures Exchange to form a more integrated financial marketplace. In 2000, it underwent a significant transformation by demutualizing, allowing for a corporate structure that enabled public ownership. The exchange further solidified its status as a global financial hub by successfully attracting many initial public offerings (IPOs) from mainland Chinese companies, making it an essential platform for accessing the Chinese economy.

Structure and Operations

HKEX operates a modern and sophisticated trading platform, allowing for the seamless buying and selling of a wide range of securities, including stocks, bonds, ETFs, and derivatives. The exchange features several key components:

- **Main Board:** This segment lists large established companies with significant market capitalizations. To qualify for listing, companies must meet stringent financial performance, governance, and transparency requirements.
- **Growth enterprise market (GEM):** The 1999 GEM was designed for smaller growth-oriented companies. It provides a platform for emerging businesses that might not yet meet the criteria for the Main Board, enabling them to raise capital and develop their operations.
- **Derivatives market:** HKEX also operates a robust derivatives market, offering various products, including futures and options contracts. This segment enables investors to hedge risks and speculate on price movements of underlying assets.

- **Bond market:** The exchange facilitates the trading of government and corporate bonds, contributing to the development of a comprehensive fixed-income market.

Indices and Benchmarking

HKEX is associated with several important stock market indices that serve as benchmarks for performance:

- **Hang Seng Index:** This is the most prominent index in Hong Kong. It tracks the performance of the largest and most liquid companies listed on the exchange and serves as a barometer for the overall health of the Hong Kong stock market.
- **Hang Seng China Enterprises Index (HSCEI):** This index focuses on Chinese companies listed in Hong Kong and reflects H-shares' performance (shares of Chinese companies incorporated in mainland China but traded in Hong Kong).
- **Hang Seng Composite Index:** This comprehensive index includes all stocks listed on the Main Board and GEM, providing a broad view of market trends and performance.

Impact on Global Finance

HKEX is a vital bridge between East and West, facilitating capital flows and investment opportunities in Hong Kong and mainland China. It has become a key platform for companies seeking to access international capital markets, particularly Chinese firms seeking to raise global investors' funds. The exchange's reputation for transparency and regulatory oversight has attracted substantial foreign investment, reinforcing its position as a significant financial center. Furthermore, HKEX has significantly supported the Belt and Road Initiative, promoting investment and cooperation between China and other countries. This strategic positioning enhances Hong Kong's critical global trade and finance node status.

Technological Advancements

HKEX is committed to leveraging technology to enhance trading efficiency and market accessibility. The exchange has implemented advanced electronic trading systems and data analytics tools to streamline operations and provide better services to its participants. Initiatives such as introducing a new trading platform and enhancing its market infrastructure have positioned HKEX as a regional financial technology leader. Additionally, HKEX has been actively exploring integrating blockchain technology and other innovations to improve settlement processes and increase transparency in trading activities.

The Hong Kong Stock Exchange is a cornerstone of Asia's financial landscape, exemplifying the dynamic interplay of global finance and local enterprise. With its rich history, diverse market offerings, and commitment to innovation, HKEX continues to attract investors and companies from around the world, fostering economic growth and development in the region. As a major hub for capital formation and investment, HKEX plays a critical role in connecting global markets, enhancing the flow of capital, and shaping the future of finance in Asia and beyond. Its ongoing evolution reflects the resilience and adaptability of Hong Kong's financial ecosystem in an increasingly interconnected world.

TOKYO STOCK EXCHANGE (TSE)

The Tokyo Stock Exchange (TSE) is Japan's premier stock exchange and one of the world's largest and most influential financial markets. Established in 1878, it is a critical hub for capital formation, investment, and securities trading in Asia and globally.

Historical Background

The TSE was founded during the Meiji era as Japan sought to modernize its economy and integrate into the global financial system. The exchange began operations in a modest building but grew important as Japan's economy expanded. Over the decades, the TSE has undergone several transformations, adapting to changes in the financial landscape and the needs of market participants.

During World War II, the TSE was temporarily closed in 1943 and later reorganized under new regulations. It reopened in 1949, marking a fresh start for the exchange in the postwar economic environment. The TSE has since become a leading international financial center that is pivotal in Japan's economic development.

Structure and Operations

The TSE operates as a centralized marketplace for the buying and selling of various securities, including stocks, bonds, and derivatives. It features a structured trading environment to ensure transparency, efficiency, and fair competition among market participants.

- **Market segments:** The TSE comprises several market segments, including:
    - **First Section:** This segment lists large established companies with significant market capitalizations. These companies are typically leaders in their respective industries.
    - **Second Section:** The Second Section is designed for medium-sized companies, providing a platform to raise capital and grow.
    - **JASDAQ:** This is a market for emerging and smaller companies, similar to the Nasdaq in the United States. It caters to growth-oriented businesses seeking access to public capital.
    - **TOKYO PRO Market:** A specialized market for professional investors that allows for listing various financial instruments, including equity and debt.
- **Trading mechanism:** The TSE employs an electronic trading system that enables real-time securities trading. The trading

hours typically run from 9 a.m. to 3 p.m. (local time), with a lunch break, allowing for efficient order execution and price discovery.

Indices and Benchmarking

The TSE is associated with several key stock market indices that serve as benchmarks for market performance:

- **Nikkei 225:** Japan's most famous stock market index, comprising 225 of the largest and most liquid companies listed on the TSE. It is a critical indicator of the Japanese stock market's performance and investor sentiment.
- **TOPIX (Tokyo Stock Price Index):** This index tracks all the companies listed in the First Section of the TSE, providing a broader perspective on the market's overall performance. TOPIX is market capitalization-weighted, reflecting the relative size of companies.

Impact on Global Finance

The TSE plays a vital role in the global financial landscape, serving as a gateway for international investors looking to access the Japanese market. It facilitates capital flows and investment opportunities, making it an essential platform for domestic and foreign companies seeking to raise funds. The exchange has been instrumental in Japan's economic development, supporting the growth of major corporations and contributing to the country's position as a leading economic power. The TSE's reputation for regulatory rigor and transparency has attracted significant foreign investment, reinforcing its status as a key player in the global economy.

Technological Advancements

The TSE has continually embraced technological innovation to enhance trading efficiency and market accessibility. Its electronic trading system has undergone several upgrades, incorporating advanced features that improve the speed and accuracy of transactions. The TSE has also explored integrating blockchain technology and other innovations to streamline operations and enhance transparency. The exchange actively promotes financial literacy and technological adaptation among market participants, ensuring it remains competitive in an increasingly digital marketplace.

The Tokyo Stock Exchange is a cornerstone of Japan's financial system, embodying the principles of transparency, efficiency, and innovation. With its rich history, diverse market segments, and influential indices, the TSE is critical in facilitating investment, supporting economic growth, and connecting global markets. As one of the world's largest and most significant stock exchanges, the TSE not only reflects the health of the Japanese economy but also shapes the dynamics of global finance, ensuring its position as a vital hub for capital formation and investment in the Asia-Pacific region. Its ongoing commitment to technological advancement and market integrity positions the TSE as a leader in the evolving landscape of international finance.

SHENZHEN STOCK EXCHANGE (SZSE)

The Shenzhen Stock Exchange (SZSE) is one of mainland China's two major stock exchanges, alongside the Shanghai Stock Exchange (SSE). Established in 1990, SZSE has rapidly grown to become a significant player in the global financial landscape, providing a platform for trading diverse securities, including stocks, bonds, exchange-traded funds (ETFs), and derivatives.

Historical Background

The SZSE was founded in 1990 during economic reform and opening in China, aimed at modernizing the country's financial markets. Its establishment was part of the government's efforts to promote capital formation and attract foreign investment. Initially operating as a small market, the SZSE has undergone significant development over the years, reflecting the rapid growth of China's economy and the increasing importance of its capital markets. In the early years, the SZSE focused primarily on trading with state-owned enterprises. However, it quickly evolved to include a broader range of companies, mainly as China's private sector flourished. Today, the exchange is a crucial venue for large state-owned enterprises and innovative technology startups.

Structure and Operations

The SZSE operates as a centralized marketplace for the buying and selling of securities, facilitating efficient trading and investment. The exchange is regulated by the China Securities Regulatory Commission (CSRC), which oversees its operations and enforces market rules to ensure transparency and fairness.

- **Market segments:** The SZSE features several market segments, including:
    - **Main Board:** This segment lists large established companies that meet stringent listing requirements. These companies are typically leaders in their respective industries.
    - **SME Board (Small and Medium Enterprises Board):** Launched in 2004, the SME Board is designed to support small- and medium-sized enterprises seeking access to capital. It provides a platform for innovative companies that may not yet meet the criteria for the Main Board.
    - **ChiNext:** Established in 2009, ChiNext is a board aimed at high-growth and innovative companies like the Nasdaq in the United States. It offers a more flexible listing process, encouraging investment in technology and emerging sectors.
- **Trading mechanism:** The SZSE employs an electronic trading system that enables real-time securities trading. The trading

hours typically run from 9.30 a.m. to 3 p.m. (local time), with a break for lunch. The exchange uses a price-limit system, allowing stocks to rise or fall by a specified percentage daily to prevent excessive volatility.

Indices and Benchmarking

The SZSE is associated with several key stock market indices that serve as benchmarks for performance:

- **SZSE Composite Index:** This index tracks all stocks listed on the SZSE's Main Board, providing a comprehensive view of the overall market performance.
- **ChiNext Index:** This index focuses on the performance of stocks listed on the ChiNext board, highlighting the growth and innovation of emerging companies.
- **SZSE 100 Index:** Composed of the 100 largest and most liquid stocks on the SZSE, this index serves as a benchmark for investors looking to gauge the performance of major market firms.

Impact on Global Finance

The SZSE plays a vital role in the global financial landscape, serving as a crucial platform for capital formation and investment in China. It has become an essential venue for domestic and foreign investors seeking exposure to the rapidly growing Chinese economy. The exchange has facilitated significant capital inflows into China, enabling companies to raise funds for expansion and innovation. Its focus on high-growth industries, particularly in technology and biotech, has made it a key driver of economic development in these sectors.

Technological Advancements

The SZSE is committed to leveraging technology to enhance trading efficiency and market accessibility. The exchange has implemented advanced trading systems and data analytics tools to improve operational efficiency and provide better services to market participants.

Furthermore, the SZSE promotes financial literacy and investor education, ensuring market participants are well-informed about trading practices and investment opportunities.

The Shenzhen Stock Exchange is a dynamic and vital component of China's financial system, exemplifying the country's rapid economic growth and commitment to market reform. With its diverse market segments, influential indices, and ongoing technological advancements, the SZSE continues attracting investors and companies worldwide, fostering economic development and innovation. As a critical player in the global financial arena, the SZSE reflects the health of the Chinese economy and shapes the future of investment and capital formation in the Asia-Pacific region. Its evolution and adaptability position the SZSE as a leading hub for capital markets in an increasingly interconnected world.

LONDON STOCK EXCHANGE (LSE)

The London Stock Exchange (LSE) is one of the world's oldest and most prestigious stock exchanges, with a rich history dating back to the late seventeenth century. As a key player in the global financial markets, the LSE is a central hub for capital formation, trading, and investment across various asset classes, including equities, bonds, derivatives, and exchange-traded funds (ETFs).

Historical Background

The origins of the LSE can be traced back to 1698 when stockbrokers began meeting in coffee-houses in London to trade shares of companies. The first official stock exchange was established in 1801, formalizing the trading process and providing a regulated marketplace for investors. Over the years, the LSE has evolved significantly, adapting to the changing dynamics of the financial landscape. The exchange played a pivotal role during the Industrial Revolution, facilitating the growth of major companies and industries in Britain. In the twentieth century, the LSE continued to expand its influence, embracing technological advancements and globalization to remain competitive. In 2000, the LSE merged with the Italian stock exchange, Borsa Italiana, further solidifying its position as a leading European exchange. In recent years, the LSE has also focused on enhancing its international presence by attracting foreign listings and investments.

Structure and Operations

The LSE operates as a centralized marketplace for buying and selling securities, providing a transparent and efficient trading environment. It is regulated by the UK's Financial Conduct Authority (FCA), ensuring strict rules and standards compliance.

- **Market segments:** The LSE comprises several key market segments, including:
  - **Main market:** This segment lists established companies that meet stringent requirements related to market capitalization, financial performance, and governance. It includes well-known blue-chip companies and serves as a platform for IPOs.
  - **Alternative investment market (AIM)**: Launched in 1995, AIM is a submarket designed for smaller high-growth companies. It offers a more flexible regulatory environment, making it easier for SMEs to access capital.
  - **Borsa Italiana:** Following the merger with Borsa Italiana, the LSE expanded its offerings to include a variety of financial instruments traded on the Italian market.

- **Trading mechanism:** The LSE utilizes an electronic trading system that facilitates real-time securities trading. It employs a combination of order-driven and quote-driven trading, allowing market participants to execute trades efficiently. Trading hours typically run from 8 a.m. to 4.30 p.m. (local time), with pre- and postmarket trading sessions available.

Indices and Benchmarking

The LSE is associated with several key stock market indices that serve as benchmarks for market performance:

- **FTSE 100 Index:** This index tracks the 100 largest companies listed on the LSE, serving as a primary indicator of the performance of the UK stock market. Investors use it to gauge market trends and economic health.
- **FTSE 250 Index:** This index includes the following 250 largest companies on the LSE, providing insights into the performance of medium-sized firms in the UK.
- **FTSE All-Share Index:** This comprehensive index encompasses all eligible companies listed on the LSE, offering a broad view of the UK equity market.

Impact on Global Finance

The LSE plays a vital role in the global financial system, serving as a major center for capital formation and investment. It attracts companies from around the world seeking to raise funds through public listings, making it an essential platform for international investors. The exchange is particularly significant for sectors such as finance, technology, and natural resources, with many multinational corporations choosing to list on the LSE to access a diverse pool of investors. Its reputation for regulatory integrity and transparency has reinforced investor confidence, making it a preferred destination for capital.

Technological Advancements

The LSE has embraced technological innovations to enhance trading efficiency and market accessibility. The exchange has invested in advanced trading systems and platforms to improve execution speed and reduce transaction costs. Initiatives such as introducing the LSE's Millennium Exchange, which utilizes cutting-edge technology for order matching, demonstrate its commitment to remaining at the forefront of financial technology. Additionally, the LSE actively promotes initiatives related to fintech and digital assets, recognizing the evolving landscape of finance and the importance of innovation in maintaining competitiveness.

The London Stock Exchange stands as a pillar of the global financial system, embodying the principles of transparency, efficiency, and innovation. With its rich history, diverse market segments, and influential indices, the LSE continues to play a crucial role in facilitating investment, supporting economic growth, and connecting global markets. As one of the world's largest and most prestigious stock exchanges, the LSE not only reflects the health of the UK economy but also shapes the dynamics of international finance, ensuring its position as a vital hub for capital formation and investment in an increasingly interconnected global economy. Its ongoing commitment to technological advancement and market integrity positions the LSE as a leader in the evolving landscape of financial markets.

TORONTO STOCK EXCHANGE (TSX)

The Toronto Stock Exchange (TSX) is Canada's largest stock exchange and one of the largest in the world by market capitalization. Founded in 1861, the TSX plays a critical role in the Canadian economy, providing a platform for companies to raise capital and investors to trade diverse financial instruments.

Historical Background

The TSX was established in 1861 as a response to the growing need for a regulated market to trade securities in Canada. Originally known as the Toronto Stock & Mining Exchange, it focused primarily on trading mining stocks, reflecting the importance of the resource sector in Canada's economic development. Over the years, the TSX has evolved significantly, expanding its listings to include various sectors such as technology, healthcare, finance, and consumer goods. The exchange became fully electronic in 1997 with the introduction of the TSX Trading System, which enhanced trading efficiency and accessibility. In 2000, the TSX merged with the Montreal Exchange, further consolidating its position as the premier stock exchange in Canada.

Structure and Operations

The TSX operates as a centralized marketplace for buying and selling securities, facilitating efficient trading and investment. It is regulated by the Ontario Securities Commission (OSC), which ensures compliance with strict rules and standards to protect investors.

- **Market segments:** The TSX features several key market segments:
  - o **Main market:** This segment lists established companies that meet stringent requirements related to market capitalization, financial performance, and governance. The Main Market is home to many of Canada's largest and most well-known companies, including banks, energy firms, and telecommunications companies.
  - o **TSX Venture Exchange (TSXV):** Established in 1999, the TSXV caters to smaller and emerging companies seeking access to capital. It offers a more flexible regulatory environment, allowing startups and high-growth firms to raise funds and expand their operations.

- **Trading mechanism:** The TSX employs an electronic trading system, allowing for real-time securities trading. The trading hours typically run from 9.30 a.m. to 4 p.m. (Eastern Time), with premarket and after-hours trading sessions available. The exchange uses an order-driven market model, where buy-and-sell orders are matched based on price and time priority.

Indices and Benchmarking

The TSX is associated with several key stock market indices that serve as benchmarks for performance:

- **S&P/TSX Composite Index:** This is the primary benchmark index for the Canadian stock market, tracking the performance of the largest and most liquid companies listed on the TSX. It includes diverse sectors and is widely used by investors to gauge market trends.
- **S&P/TSX 60 Index:** This index includes sixty of the largest companies listed on the TSX. It provides a more focused view of the market's performance and is often used by institutional investors as a benchmark.
- **S&P/TSX Venture Composite Index:** This index tracks the performance of companies listed on the TSXV, reflecting the health of the venture capital market and the growth potential of emerging businesses.

Impact on Global Finance

The TSX plays a vital role in the global financial system, serving as a critical platform for capital formation and investment in Canada. It attracts domestic and international investors, facilitating capital flows and providing opportunities for investment across various sectors. As a major exchange, the TSX is particularly significant in the natural resources, finance, and technology sectors. Canada's rich resources and solid financial institutions make the TSX an essential venue for investors seeking exposure to these industries.

Technological Advancements

The TSX is committed to leveraging technology to enhance trading efficiency and market accessibility. The exchange continually invests in its trading infrastructure, incorporating advanced trading systems and data analytics tools to improve operational efficiency and support market participants. Initiatives such as implementing the TMX Quantum XA trading platform have modernized the exchange's trading capabilities, ensuring rapid execution and reduced investor transaction costs.

The Toronto Stock Exchange is a cornerstone of Canada's financial landscape, embodying the principles of transparency, innovation, and market integrity. With its rich history, diverse market segments, and influential indices, the TSX facilitates investment, supports economic growth, and connects global markets. As one of the world's largest and most important stock exchanges, the TSX reflects the health of the Canadian economy and plays a vital role in shaping the dynamics of international finance. Its ongoing commitment to technological advancement and regulatory excellence positions the TSX as a leader in the evolving landscape of capital markets, ensuring its place as a premier destination for investment in North America and beyond.

BOMBAY STOCK EXCHANGE (BSE)

The Bombay Stock Exchange (BSE) is one of the oldest and most prominent stock exchanges in Asia and the first stock exchange in India. Established in 1875, the BSE has played a pivotal role in developing the Indian capital market and has become a significant platform for trading securities in the country.

Historical Background

The BSE was founded as the Native Share & Stockbrokers' Association in 1875, initially operating under a banyan tree in Bombay (now Mumbai). It served as a meeting place for stockbrokers who traded stocks relatively informally. The BSE received recognition from the government in 1957 and was subsequently granted permanent recognition under the Securities Contracts (Regulation) Act, 1956. Over the years, the BSE has undergone significant changes, transitioning from an open outcry system to a fully electronic trading platform. In 1995, the BSE introduced the BSE Online Trading System (BOLT), revolutionizing trading practices and increasing efficiency and transparency.

Structure and Operations

The BSE operates as a centralized marketplace for the buying and selling of a wide range of securities, including equities, debt instruments, derivatives, and mutual funds. It is regulated by the Securities and Exchange Board of India (SEBI), which oversees its operations and enforces compliance with market regulations.

- **Market segments:** The BSE comprises several key market segments:
    - **Equity market:** This segment lists thousands of companies, including large-cap, mid-cap, and small-cap stocks. It serves as a platform for companies to raise capital through initial public offerings (IPOs) and for investors to trade shares.
    - **Debt market:** The BSE facilitates trading in various debt instruments, including corporate bonds, government securities, and other fixed-income products.
    - **Derivatives market:** The BSE offers a robust derivatives market where investors can trade futures and options contracts, providing tools for hedging and speculation.
    - **Mutual funds:** The BSE provides a platform for trading mutual fund units, allowing investors to access various investment options.
- **Trading mechanism:** The BSE employs a fully electronic trading system, enabling real-time securities trading. The

trading hours typically run from 9.15 a.m. to 3.30 p.m. (Indian Standard Time), with premarket and after-hours trading sessions available. The exchange uses an order-driven model, where buy-and-sell orders are matched based on price and time priority.

Indices and Benchmarking

The BSE is associated with several important stock market indices that serve as benchmarks for market performance:

- **S&P BSE SENSEX:** This is the BSE's flagship index, comprising thirty of the largest and most actively traded stocks on the exchange. The SENSEX is widely regarded as a key indicator of the Indian stock market's overall performance and investor sentiment.
- **S&P BSE 500:** This index tracks the performance of 500 companies listed on the BSE, providing a broader view of market trends and performance across various sectors.
- **S&P BSE Mid-Cap and Small-Cap Indices:** These indices focus on the performance of mid-cap and small-cap companies, reflecting the growth potential of emerging businesses in India.

Impact on Global Finance

The BSE plays a vital role in the Indian financial system and has significant implications for the global market. As one of the leading stock exchanges in Asia, the BSE attracts domestic and foreign investors, facilitating capital inflows and investments across various sectors. The exchange is particularly significant for finance, information technology, consumer goods, and pharmaceuticals. Its reputation for regulatory integrity and transparency has helped foster investor confidence, making it a preferred destination for capital.

Technological Advancements

The BSE is committed to leveraging technology to enhance trading efficiency and market accessibility. The exchange continually invests in its trading infrastructure, incorporating advanced trading systems and data analytics tools to improve operational efficiency and support market participants. The BSE has also explored integrating blockchain technology and other innovations to enhance the trading process and improve transaction transparency in recent years.

The Bombay Stock Exchange is a cornerstone of India's financial landscape, embodying the principles of transparency, efficiency, and market integrity. With its rich history, diverse market segments, and influential indices, the BSE continues to facilitate investment, support economic growth, and connect global markets. As one of the world's oldest and most important stock exchanges, the BSE reflects the health of the Indian economy and plays a vital role in shaping the dynamics of international finance. Its ongoing commitment to technological advancement and regulatory excellence positions the BSE as a leader in the evolving landscape of capital markets, ensuring its place as a premier destination for investment in Asia and beyond.

In concluding this chapter, we have explored the fundamental role of stock market exchanges in the global financial system, highlighting their significance as platforms for facilitating the buying and selling of securities. This chapter has provided a comprehensive overview of various exchanges, including their structures, operations, and the diverse instruments they offer, underscoring their critical function in capital formation and investment.

We began by examining the historical development of stock exchanges, tracing their evolution from informal trading practices to organized markets that uphold stringent regulatory standards. This historical context emphasizes how stock exchanges have adapted to changes in the economic landscape, technological advancements, and the growing complexities of global finance. Understanding this evolution is crucial for recognizing the current dynamics of financial markets.

Next, we delved into the operational mechanisms of stock exchanges, focusing on key components such as market makers, trading systems, and the various market segments that cater to different types of securities. This knowledge is vital for investors and traders alike, as it equips them with the insights needed to navigate the complexities of trading environments effectively.

Additionally, we highlighted the role of major stock exchanges, such as the New York Stock Exchange, Nasdaq, London Stock Exchange, and others, showcasing their unique characteristics and contributions to the global economy. Each exchange operates under its regulatory framework, reflecting the economic, cultural, and legal environments of its respective regions. This diversity underscores the interconnectedness of global financial markets and the importance of international investing.

Furthermore, we explored the various indices associated with stock exchanges, which serve as vital benchmarks for measuring market performance. Understanding these indices is essential for evaluating investment strategies and assessing the overall health of the stock market.

The chapter also addressed the impact of technological advancements on stock exchanges, illustrating how electronic trading systems and digital innovations have transformed the trading landscape. These advancements enhance trading efficiency and improve accessibility for a wider range of investors, thereby democratizing participation in the financial markets.

This chapter has established a solid foundation for understanding the vital role of stock market exchanges in the financial ecosystem. As you move forward in your investment journey, this knowledge will be critical in making informed decisions, navigating market dynamics, and capitalizing on investment opportunities. The stock market exchange is more than just a venue for trading; it is a cornerstone of economic activity that facilitates growth, innovation, and the flow of capital in an increasingly interconnected world. Embracing this understanding will empower you to engage confidently with the complexities of investing and trading in the stock market.

Chapter 3

UNDERSTANDING THE BASICS OF STOCK MARKET

'Understanding the Basics of the Stock Market' serves as an introductory primer to the dynamic world of the stock market. It explores the fundamental concepts underlying the market's operation, providing readers with a solid foundation to build their understanding of investing and trading.

The chapter explores the various stocks available in the market, ranging from standard to preferred. Readers gain insights into the rights and privileges associated with each type, empowering them to make informed investment decisions that align with their financial goals and risk tolerance.

'Understanding the Determinants of Stock Prices' delves into the intricate mechanisms that govern how stock prices are set. This comprehensive exploration clarifies the roles of supply-and-demand dynamics, market sentiments, and fundamental factors that drive stock market valuations. By mastering these basic principles, investors can adeptly navigate market volatility, discern trends, and capitalize on strategic investment prospects.

'Exploring Market Indices and Benchmarks' explains the critical role of market indices and benchmarks in assessing overall market performance and specific sector trends. This exploration gives readers insights into prominent indices like the S&P 500, Dow Jones Industrial Average, and Nasdaq Composite. By understanding these benchmarks, investors can effectively track market movements, benchmark their investment returns, and strategically position their portfolios based on market trends and performance indicators.

This chapter presents readers with a comprehensive overview of the stock market's fundamental principles. Starting with an introduction to the market itself, the chapter explores various types of stocks, mechanisms for determining prices, and the significance of market indices. This foundational knowledge equips readers with the essential understanding needed to begin their journey into investing and trading confidently.

THE STOCK MARKET

The stock market, often called the epitome of capitalism, symbolizes economic dynamism and opportunity. It's a bustling marketplace where investors and traders come together to buy and sell ownership stakes in publicly traded companies. Yet beyond its bustling activity lies a world of complexity and intricacy that can be daunting to the unskilled.

At its core, the stock market represents the intersection of business and investment. It provides companies with a platform to raise capital for growth and expansion while offering investors the opportunity to participate in the success of these enterprises. By buying and selling stocks, individuals and institutions play a pivotal role in allocating capital, driving innovation, and fostering economic growth.

The stock market operates on the principles of supply and demand. The value of a company's stock is determined by myriad factors, including its financial performance, industry outlook, macroeconomic conditions, and investor sentiments. This dynamic interplay of forces gives rise to fluctuations in stock prices, creating opportunities for profit and risks for those who engage in trading and investing.

Understanding the stock market requires familiarity with its key participants, from individual investors and institutional traders to market makers and regulators. Each plays a distinct role in shaping market dynamics and ensuring its integrity and efficiency. Moreover, grasping the fundamental concepts of stock ownership, market indices, and trading mechanics is essential for confidently navigating this complex ecosystem.

While the stock market offers the potential for significant returns, it also entails inherent risks. Volatility, uncertainty, and unforeseen events can lead to rapid fluctuations in stock prices, sometimes with profound consequences. Thus, prudent risk management and disciplined investment strategies are paramount for safeguarding capital and achieving long-term financial goals.

Despite its challenges, the stock market remains a cornerstone of wealth creation and prosperity for millions worldwide. Whether you're a seasoned investor or a novice trader, embarking on your journey into the stock market opens doors to a world of opportunity and possibility. With diligence, education, and sound judgement, you can harness the power of the stock market to build wealth, secure your financial future, and participate in the growth of the global economy. We'll delve deeper into the intricacies of the stock market, exploring its various facets and equipping you with the knowledge and tools to navigate its complexities successfully.

TYPES OF STOCKS

Stocks, also known as equities, represent ownership shares in a company. While all stocks confer ownership rights, there are different types of stocks, each with its own characteristics and privileges. Understanding the various types of stocks is essential for investors as it influences their investment decisions and risk exposure. Here are some of the most common types of stocks:

COMMON STOCKS

Common stocks represent ownership shares in a corporation, entitling shareholders to a portion of the company's profits and assets. They are the most prevalent publicly traded stock issued and widely sold on stock exchanges. Here are the key features and characteristics of common stocks:

- **Ownership rights:** Common stockholders are company owners and have a claim on their assets and earnings. They have the right to vote on corporate matters, including the election of the board of directors, approval of significant corporate actions such as mergers or acquisitions, and changes to the company's charter or bylaws. Each ordinary share typically carries one vote, although some companies may have dual-class share structures that give certain shareholders multiple votes per share.
- **Dividend payments:** Common stockholders may receive dividends, which represent a portion of the company's profits distributed to shareholders. However, dividends are not guaranteed, and companies have discretion over whether to pay dividends and the amount distributed. Companies that pay dividends typically do so every quarter, although some may pay semi-annually or annually. The company's board of directors determines the dividend amount and is subject to factors such as financial performance, capital allocation priorities, and growth prospects.
- **Capital appreciation:** Common stocks offer the potential for capital appreciation, allowing shareholders to profit from the company's stock price increases over time. When the company's earnings and prospects improve, demand for its stock may increase, driving up its market price. Conversely, everyday stock prices can also decline due to factors such as poor financial performance, industry downturns, or negative news about the company. Stock prices fluctuate in response

to changes in supply and demand, investor sentiment, and macroeconomic conditions.

- **Risk and volatility:** Investing in common stocks carries inherent risks, including the risk of loss of principal. Stock prices can fluctuate daily in response to market dynamics and company-specific factors. Common stockholders are considered residual claimants, meaning they have the lowest priority in the event of liquidation or bankruptcy. If a company is bankrupt or liquidated, common stockholders receive assets only after bondholders, preferred stockholders, and other creditors have been paid.
- **Voting Rights:** Common stockholders have the right to vote on critical corporate decisions, including the election of the board of directors and approval of significant corporate actions. The voting power of ordinary shareholders is proportional to their ownership stake in the company. Shareholders typically receive one vote per share owned, although some companies may have dual-class share structures granting certain shareholders multiple ballots.
- **Market liquidity:** Common stocks are traded on public stock exchanges, providing investors with liquidity and the ability to buy and sell shares quickly. A stock's liquidity refers to the ease with which it can be purchased or sold without significantly impacting its price. Stocks of larger, more widely traded companies tend to have higher liquidity compared to smaller, less-liquid stocks. Liquidity is influenced by trading volume, market capitalization, and investor interest in the company's stock.
- **Growth potential:** Common stocks of growth-oriented companies offer investors the potential for long-term capital appreciation. These companies typically reinvest a significant portion of their earnings into the business to fuel growth and expansion. Growth stocks are characterized by above-average revenue and earnings growth rates, driven by technological innovation, market expansion, or competitive advantages

in their respective industries. Investing in growth stocks entails higher risk than more established companies, as their valuations may be based on future earnings expectations rather than current profitability. However, successful investments in growth stocks can yield substantial returns for investors over time.

Common stocks represent ownership shares in a corporation, allowing investors to participate in the company's growth and success. While they carry inherent risks, common stocks also provide the potential for capital appreciation, dividend income, and voting rights in corporate governance matters. By understanding common stocks' key features and characteristics, investors can make informed decisions to build diversified portfolios aligned with their investment objectives and risk tolerance.

PREFERRED STOCKS

Preferred stocks are a type of hybrid security that combines features of both stocks and bonds. They represent ownership in a corporation, similar to common stocks, but offer specific preferences and privileges not available to common stockholders. Here are the key features and characteristics of preferred stocks:

- **Fixed dividends:** Preferred stockholders are entitled to receive fixed dividends at regular intervals, typically quarterly or semi-annually. Unlike ordinary stock dividends, which may vary or be omitted at the discretion of the company's board of directors, preferred dividends are contractual obligations. Preferred dividends are usually a fixed percentage of the stock's par or face value. For example, a preferred stock with a par value of $100 and a dividend rate of 5% would pay an annual dividend of $5 per share.

- **Priority in dividend payments:** In the event of dividend distributions, preferred stockholders have priority over common stockholders in receiving dividends. Companies must first fulfill their obligations to preferred shareholders before paying dividends to common shareholders. However, preferred dividends are typically noncumulative, meaning that if a company skips or reduces dividend payments, it is not obligated to make up for missed dividends in the future. As a result, preferred stockholders bear the risk of dividend suspension or reduction. However, it's important to note that while many preferred dividends are noncumulative, meaning missed payments aren't required to be made up later, there are also types of cumulative preferred stock where unpaid dividends accumulate and must be paid before any ordinary stock dividends can be issued.
- **Preference in liquidation:** In the event of liquidation or bankruptcy, preferred stockholders have priority over common stockholders in receiving assets from the company's remaining assets. Preferred stockholders are entitled to receive the par value of their shares plus any accrued but unpaid dividends before common stockholders receive any distribution. However, preferred stockholders rank below bondholders and other creditors in the hierarchy of claimants to the company's assets. As a result, preferred stocks are often considered to have a higher level of safety than common stocks but lower priority than bonds.
- **Lack of voting rights:** Unlike common stockholders, preferred stockholders generally do not have voting rights in corporate governance matters. They do not participate in the election of the board of directors or other corporate decisions that require shareholder approval. While preferred stockholders may have some limited voting rights in certain circumstances, such as voting on matters that directly affect their rights as preferred shareholders, these rights are typically minimal compared to those of common stockholders.

- **Callable and convertible features:** Some preferred stocks may have callable or convertible features that provide additional flexibility to the issuer and potential benefits to the investor. Callable preferred stocks give the issuer the right to redeem or call back the shares at a predetermined price after a specified date. This allows the issuer to refinance the preferred stock if interest rates decline or if it wants to replace it with a new issue offering lower dividends. Convertible preferred stocks allow holders to convert their preferred shares into a specified number of common shares at a predetermined conversion ratio. This feature provides the potential for capital appreciation if the expected stock price increases while still providing the stability of preferred dividends.
- **Fixed par value:** Preferred stocks typically have a fixed or face value, the initial price at which the company issues the shares. The par value represents the nominal value of the preferred stock and is used to calculate dividend payments and liquidation preferences. While the market price of the preferred stocks may fluctuate based on factors such as interest rates, credit quality, and investor demand, the par value remains constant throughout the life of the stock.
- **Yield characteristics:** Preferred stocks are often valued based on their dividend yield relative to prevailing interest rates and credit risk. Because preferred dividends are fixed, the yield is calculated by dividing the annual dividend by the stock's current market price. Preferred stocks typically offer higher dividend yields than common stocks but lower yields than bonds of similar credit quality and maturity. They are favored by income-oriented investors seeking higher yields than those available from fixed-income securities.

Preferred stocks offer investors a unique combination of fixed dividends, priority in dividend payments and liquidation, and potential capital appreciation through callable and convertible features. While they lack voting rights and may carry lower growth potential than common stocks, preferred stocks provide income-oriented investors with stable and predictable cash flows and a degree of downside protection in volatile markets. By understanding the key features and characteristics of preferred stocks, investors can evaluate their suitability for their investment objectives and risk tolerance.

GROWTH STOCKS

Growth stocks are shares of companies expected to grow above average compared to other companies in the market or industry. These companies typically exhibit substantial revenue and earnings growth potential driven by technological innovation, market expansion, or competitive advantages in their respective industries. Here are the key features and characteristics of growth stocks:

- **Revenue and earnings growth**: Growth stocks are characterized by above-average revenue and earnings growth rates relative to the broader market or industry peers. These companies often operate in high-growth sectors such as technology, healthcare, biotechnology, and consumer discretionary. Growth is typically driven by product innovation, market expansion, increased market share, or disruptive technologies that create new business opportunities and revenue streams.
- **High price-to-earnings (P/E) ratio:** Growth stocks often trade at higher price-to-earnings (P/E) ratios than the overall market or value stocks. The P/E ratio measures the price investors are willing to pay per dollar of earnings generated by the company. Investors are willing to pay a premium for growth stocks based on expectations of future earnings growth and potential capital appreciation. As a result, growth stocks may appear expensive relative to their current earnings but may justify their valuation based on future growth prospects.

- **Limited or no dividends:** Many growth companies reinvest significant earnings into the business to fuel growth and expansion rather than paying dividends to shareholders. As a result, growth stocks typically offer investors limited or no dividend income. While dividends are a source of passive income for investors, growth companies prioritize reinvesting profits into research and development, marketing, acquisitions, and other initiatives to drive future growth.
- **Volatility and risk:** Investing in growth stocks entails higher volatility and risk than investing in established companies or value stocks. Due to their higher valuation multiples and growth expectations, growth stocks are more sensitive to changes in investor sentiment, market conditions, and macroeconomic factors. Growth stocks may experience sharp price fluctuations, both on the upside and downside, in response to quarterly earnings reports, product announcements, regulatory developments, or changes in industry trends.
- **Competitive advantage:** Successful growth companies often possess competitive advantages or moats that enable them to sustain their growth trajectory and outperform competitors over the long term. These competitive advantages may include proprietary technology, strong brand recognition, network effects, economies of scale, or superior distribution channels. Companies with durable competitive advantages are better positioned to defend their market share, expand into new markets, and generate sustainable revenue and earnings growth over time.
- **Long-term investment horizon:** Investing in growth stocks requires a long-term perspective and patience, as it may take time for the company to realize its growth potential and for investors to realize a return on their investment. While growth stocks may experience periods of underperformance or volatility in the short term, investors who maintain a long-term investment horizon may be rewarded with substantial

capital appreciation if the company successfully executes its growth strategy.

- **Growth strategies:** Growth companies employ various strategies to drive revenue and earnings growth, including product innovation, market penetration, geographic expansion, strategic acquisitions, and partnerships. These companies prioritize investments in research and development of products or services that address unmet customer needs or disrupt existing markets. They also focus on building brand awareness, customer loyalty, and market share to sustain their competitive advantage and drive long-term growth.

Growth stocks offer investors the opportunity to participate in the potential growth and success of high-growth companies. While they carry higher volatility and risk than more conservative investments, growth stocks provide the potential for above-average returns over the long term. By understanding the key features and characteristics of growth stocks, investors can evaluate their suitability for their investment objectives and risk tolerance and incorporate them into a diversified investment portfolio.

VALUE STOCKS

Value stocks are shares of companies that are considered undervalued relative to their intrinsic worth or financial metrics such as earnings, book value, or cash flow. These companies often trade at a lower price than their fundamentals, making them potentially attractive investments for value-oriented investors. Here are the key features and characteristics of value stocks:

- **Low price-to-earnings (P/E) ratio:** Value stocks trade low price-to-earnings (P/E) ratios compared to the overall market or growth stocks. The P/E ratio measures the price investors are willing to pay per dollar of earnings generated by the company. Value investors are attracted to stocks with low P/E ratios because they believe these companies are undervalued relative to their earnings potential. A low P/E ratio may indicate that the stock is trading at a discount to its intrinsic value or historical valuation levels.

- **High dividend yields:** Many value stocks offer high dividend yields relative to their stock price. These companies prioritize returning profits to shareholders through dividends, making them attractive income-generating investments for dividend-oriented investors. Value stocks with high dividend yields provide investors with a reliable and steady income stream, which can help offset potential losses during market downturns and provide downside protection.
- **Fundamental metrics:** Value investors analyze fundamental metrics such as price-to-earnings (P/E) ratio, price-to-book (P/B) ratio, price-to-sales (P/S) ratio, and dividend yield to identify undervalued stocks. A low P/E ratio relative to historical averages, industry peers, or the overall market may indicate that the stock is trading at a discount to its intrinsic value. Similarly, a low P/B ratio suggests the stock is trading below its book value. At the same time, a high dividend yield may signal that the stock is undervalued relative to its dividend-paying capacity.
- **Margin of safety:** Value investors seek a margin of safety when investing in undervalued stocks. The safety margin refers to the difference between the stock's intrinsic value and market price, providing a cushion against potential downside risk. By purchasing stocks trading below their intrinsic value, value investors aim to minimize the risk of capital loss while maximizing the potential for capital appreciation when the market corrects, and the stock's price converges toward its intrinsic worth.
- **Contrarian investing:** Value investing is often characterized by contrarianism, as value investors are willing to go against the prevailing market sentiment and invest in stocks out of

favor or overlooked by other investors. Contrarian investors believe that market inefficiencies and irrational behavior create opportunities to buy undervalued stocks at discounted prices, allowing them to profit from subsequent market corrections or revaluations.

- **Cyclical and turnaround opportunities:** Value stocks may include companies that operate in cyclical industries or are experiencing temporary setbacks or challenges. These companies may be trading at depressed valuations due to economic downturns, industry downturns, or company-specific issues. Value investors identify turnaround opportunities by thoroughly analyzing the company's underlying business prospects, financial health, competitive position, and management's ability to execute a successful turnaround strategy.
- **Long-term investment horizon:** Value investing requires a long-term perspective and patience, as it may take time for the market to recognize and reflect the intrinsic value of undervalued stocks. Value investors focus on the company's underlying fundamentals and are willing to hold their investments for an extended period to realize their full potential.

Value stocks offer investors the opportunity to purchase shares of companies trading at a discount to their intrinsic value. While they may carry higher risk and volatility than more conservative investments, value stocks provide the potential for long-term capital appreciation and income generation. By understanding value stocks' key features and characteristics, investors can identify undervalued opportunities, build a diversified investment portfolio, and achieve their financial goals.

INCOME STOCKS

Income stocks, or dividend stocks, are companies that consistently pay dividends to shareholders. These companies typically have stable cash flows, strong balance sheets, and a history of returning profits to investors in the form of dividends. Income stocks are favored by investors seeking regular income streams and are often considered defensive investments during market downturns. Here are the key features and characteristics of income stocks:

- **Dividend payments:** Income stocks pay regular dividends to shareholders, providing them a reliable and steady income stream. Dividends are typically distributed quarterly, although some companies may pay them semi-annually or annually. Dividend payments are funded from the company's profits and represent a portion of its earnings that are returned to shareholders as cash distributions. Companies with a consistent track record of dividend payments are often viewed favorably by income-oriented investors.
- **Dividend yield:** The dividend yield measures a stock's dividend income relative to its price. It is calculated by dividing the annual dividend per share by the stock's current market price and expressing the result as a percentage. Income stocks typically offer higher dividend yields than the overall market or growth stocks. The dividend yield reflects the company's dividend-paying capacity and is an essential metric for income-oriented investors evaluating dividend stocks.
- **Dividend growth:** Some income stocks have a history of increasing their dividend payments over time, a trend known as dividend growth. Companies that consistently raise their dividends demonstrate financial stability, strong cash flow generation, and shareholder-friendly management practices. Dividend growth stocks are favored by income investors seeking to preserve their purchasing power against inflation

and generate a growing stream of passive income over the long term.

- **Defensive characteristics:** Income stocks are often considered defensive investments due to their stable cash flows, consistent dividend payments, and lower volatility than growth stocks. During periods of market uncertainty or economic downturns, income stocks may provide investors with a degree of downside protection. Companies that pay dividends tend to be more mature, established, and less cyclical than growth-oriented companies. They operate in sectors such as utilities, healthcare, consumer staples, and telecommunications, which provide essential goods and services that remain in demand regardless of economic conditions.
- **Capital preservation:** Income stocks prioritize the preservation of capital and the generation of steady income for investors. While they may offer lower capital appreciation potential compared to growth stocks, income stocks provide a reliable source of passive income that can supplement other sources of retirement income, such as pensions or Social Security. Investors in income stocks value the stability and predictability of dividend payments, which can help offset market volatility and provide a cushion against capital losses during market downturns.
- **Yield considerations:** Income investors assess dividend stocks based on their dividend yield relative to prevailing interest rates, inflation, and other investment opportunities. A higher dividend yield may attract income-oriented investors seeking income-generating investments that offer competitive yields compared to fixed-income securities. However, investors should also consider the sustainability of dividend payments, the company's financial health, and its ability to maintain or grow dividends over the long-term when evaluating income stocks.

- **Reinvestment opportunities:** Income stocks allow investors to reinvest dividends into additional company shares, known as dividend reinvestment plans (DRIPs). Reinvesting dividends allows investors to compound their investment returns over time and accelerate wealth accumulation through compounding. DRIPs enable investors to purchase additional shares at discounted prices or with minimal fees, making them a cost-effective way to reinvest dividends and increase ownership in income-generating assets.

Income stocks allow investors to generate regular income through dividend payments while preserving capital and reducing portfolio volatility. With their stable cash flows, consistent dividends, and defensive characteristics, income stocks play a valuable role in a diversified investment portfolio, providing investors with a reliable source of passive income and long-term wealth accumulation. By understanding the key features and characteristics of income stocks, investors can identify high-quality dividend-paying companies, build a portfolio of income-generating assets, and achieve their financial goals.

CYCLICAL STOCKS

Cyclical stocks are shares of companies whose performance is closely tied to the economic cycle. These companies operate in industries that experience fluctuations in demand and profitability in response to changes in economic conditions, such as expansions and contractions in gross domestic product (GDP), interest rates, consumer spending, and business investment. Here are the key features and characteristics of cyclical stocks:

- **Sensitivity to Economic Conditions:** Cyclical stocks are susceptible to economic conditions and business cycle changes. They operate in industries that experience above-average growth during economic expansions and contractions during economic downturns. Industries traditionally associated with cyclical stocks include consumer discretionary (e.g. automobiles, travel and leisure, and retail); industrials (e.g. manufacturing, construction, and transportation); technology (e.g. semiconductors and electronics); and materials (e.g. chemicals, metals, and mining).

- **Revenue and earnings volatility:** Cyclical companies typically experience volatility in revenue and earnings due to changes in demand for their products or services throughout the economic cycle. During economic expansions, cyclical companies benefit from increased consumer and business spending, leading to higher sales, profits, and stock prices. Conversely, demand for their products or services may decline during economic contractions, leading to lower sales, profits, and stock prices.
- **Capital-intensive operations:** Many cyclical industries are capital-intensive, requiring significant investments in plant, equipment, and inventory to support production and operations. Cyclical companies may have high fixed costs and operating leverage, meaning that sales volume changes can disproportionately impact profitability and financial performance.
- **Correlation with market indices:** Cyclical stocks correlate highly with broader market indices, such as the S&P 500 or Dow Jones Industrial Average. During economic expansions, cyclical stocks often outperform the broader market as investors anticipate more robust earnings growth and economic activity. Conversely, cyclical stocks may underperform the broader market during economic downturns as investors anticipate weaker earnings and economic contractions.
- **Timing and duration of economic cycles:** Timing the performance of cyclical stocks requires an understanding of the phases of the economic cycle, including expansion,

peak, contraction, and trough. Investors may adjust their exposure to cyclical stocks based on their expectations of changes in economic conditions, interest rates, inflation, and government policies that impact business activity and consumer spending.

- **Sector rotation and investment strategies:** Sector rotation refers to the shifting of investment capital between different sectors of the economy based on changes in economic conditions and market trends. Investors may adopt sector rotation strategies to overweight or underweight cyclical sectors of the economy depending on their outlook for the economic cycle and the relative valuation of cyclical stocks compared to defensive or growth-oriented sectors.
- **Risks and considerations:** Investing in cyclical stocks carries inherent risks, including exposure to economic downturns, industry-specific challenges, and changes in consumer preferences or technological advancements. Cyclical companies may face challenges such as excess capacity, pricing pressure, competition, regulatory changes, and supply-chain disruptions that impact their financial performance and stock prices.

Cyclical stocks allow investors to capitalize on economic conditions and business cycle changes. While they may offer the potential for above-average returns during economic expansions, cyclical stocks also carry higher volatility and risk than defensive or growth-oriented stocks. By understanding cyclical stocks' key features and characteristics, investors can assess their suitability for their investment objectives and risk tolerance and incorporate them into a diversified investment portfolio.

DEFENSIVE STOCKS

Defensive stocks are shares of companies that provide essential goods and services that remain in demand regardless of economic conditions. These companies operate in sectors that tend to be less cyclical and more resilient during economic downturns, often characterized by stable revenues, consistent earnings, and reliable dividends. Here are the key features and characteristics of defensive stocks:

- **Stable demand:** Defensive stocks operate in industries that provide products or services that are necessities rather than luxuries. These industries include utilities, healthcare, consumer staples, and telecommunications. Demand for the products or services offered by defensive companies tends to be stable or relatively resilient to changes in economic conditions, as they are essential for everyday life and consumption.
- **Noncyclical revenue:** Defensive companies generate revenue from products or services that are needed regardless of economic conditions. For example, utilities provide electricity, water, and gas to households and businesses, while healthcare companies offer medical treatments and pharmaceuticals. The noncyclical nature of their revenue stream makes defensive stocks less susceptible to economic downturns than cyclical stocks, which may experience fluctuations in demand and profitability throughout the economic cycle.
- **Defensive characteristics:** Defensive stocks exhibit defensive characteristics that help mitigate downside risk and stabilize investment portfolios during market downturns. These characteristics may include low price elasticity of demand, high barriers to entry, inelastic pricing, steady cash flows, strong brand recognition, and customer loyalty.
- **Recession-resistant:** Defensive stocks are often considered recession-resistant or countercyclical, meaning they perform

relatively well during economic downturns or periods of market volatility. Investors gravitate towards defensive stocks during times of uncertainty or market turmoil to preserve capital, generate income, and reduce portfolio volatility.

- **Dividend yield:** Many defensive stocks offer attractive dividend yields relative to their stock price. These companies prioritize returning profits to shareholders through dividends, making them attractive income-generating investments for dividend-oriented investors. The reliable and steady dividends of defensive stocks provide investors a source of passive income and cushion against market volatility and capital loss.
- **Defensive sectors:** Defensive stocks are typically found in sectors such as utilities, healthcare, consumer staples, and telecommunications, which provide products and services that are necessities for daily living and consumption.
- **Performance during market downturns:** Due to their stable revenue streams and defensive characteristics, defensive stocks outperform the broader market during market downturns or recessions. Investors view defensive stocks as safe havens or defensive assets that provide stability and downside protection to investment portfolios during periods of economic uncertainty or market volatility.

Defensive stocks allow investors to preserve capital, generate income, and reduce portfolio volatility during economic downturns or market volatility. While they may offer lower growth potential than cyclical or growth-oriented stocks, defensive stocks provide stability and resilience to investment portfolios, making them suitable for risk-averse investors seeking downside protection and income generation. By understanding the key features and characteristics of defensive stocks, investors can assess their suitability for their investment objectives and risk tolerance and incorporate them into a diversified investment portfolio.

PENNY STOCKS

Penny stocks are shares of small speculative companies that trade at low prices, often below a certain threshold, such as $5 per share. Companies typically issue these stocks with small market capitalizations and limited operating histories, and they are traded on over-the-counter (OTC) markets or smaller exchanges rather than significant stock exchanges like the New York Stock Exchange (NYSE) or Nasdaq. Here are the key features and characteristics of penny stocks:

- **Low market capitalization:** Penny stocks are issued by companies with small market capitalizations, typically ranging from a few million to a few hundred million dollars. These companies are often in the early stages of development, with limited revenue, earnings, and market presence. Due to their small size, penny stocks may lack the financial stability, resources, and institutional investor interest typically associated with larger more established companies.
- **Speculative nature:** Penny stocks are highly speculative investments that carry significant risk and volatility. Compared to stocks listed on major exchanges, they are often subject to wide price fluctuations, low liquidity, and limited regulatory oversight. Due to their speculative nature, penny stocks are favored by speculative traders, day traders, and individual investors seeking high-risk, high-reward opportunities.
- **Lack of information and transparency:** Companies issuing penny stocks may have limited operating histories, incomplete financial disclosures, and opaque business models, making it difficult for investors to conduct thorough due diligence and assess investment risks. Many penny stocks trade on the OTC markets, where regulatory requirements for financial reporting and transparency are less stringent than major

exchanges, resulting in a lack of information and investor protection.

- **High volatility:** Penny stocks are known for their high volatility, with prices often experiencing sharp and sudden movements in response to news, rumors, or speculative trading activity. The low liquidity of penny stocks, combined with their small market capitalizations and limited investor interest, can exacerbate price volatility and increase the risk of market manipulation and price manipulation schemes.
- **Lack of institutional interest:** Institutional investors, such as mutual funds, pension funds, and hedge funds, typically avoid penny stocks due to their small size, lack of liquidity, and speculative nature. The absence of institutional interest in penny stocks can further contribute to their low liquidity, limited market depth, and susceptibility to price manipulation.
- **Regulatory risks:** Penny stocks are subject to regulatory risks, including potential violations of securities laws, fraudulent practices, and pump-and-dump schemes. The Securities and Exchange Commission (SEC) and the Financial Industry Regulatory Authority (FINRA) have warned investors about the risks associated with penny stocks, including fraud, manipulation, and loss of investment capital.
- **Limited investment suitability:** Due to their high risk and speculative nature, penny stocks may not be suitable for all investors. They are typically considered speculative investments and should only represent a small portion of an investor's overall portfolio. Those considering investing in penny stocks should conduct thorough research, assess their risk tolerance, and be prepared to accept the possibility of losing their entire investment.

Penny stocks are highly speculative investments that carry significant risk and volatility. While they may offer the potential for substantial returns, they are also subject to wide price fluctuations, low liquidity, and limited regulatory oversight. Investors should exercise caution when investing in penny stocks and be prepared to conduct thorough due diligence, manage risk effectively, and diversify their investment portfolios accordingly.

HOW STOCK PRICES ARE DETERMINED

Stock prices are determined by the interaction of supply-and-demand forces in the financial markets. The stock cost represents the value investors are willing to pay for a share of ownership in a company at a given time. Several factors influence the supply-and-demand dynamics that ultimately determine stock prices. Here are the key factors that contribute to the determination of stock prices:

Supply and demand: Stock prices are primarily driven by supply and demand. Prices tend to rise when there is strong demand for a stock, and limited supply is available for sale. Conversely, prices tend to fall due to weak demand and excess supply. Demand for a stock is influenced by factors such as investor sentiment, expectations of future earnings growth, company performance, industry trends, macroeconomic conditions, interest rates, and geopolitical events. The supply of a stock is influenced by factors such as corporate actions (e.g. stock issuances and share buybacks), insider selling, institutional trading activity, and market liquidity.

Earnings and revenue growth: A company's financial performance, including its earnings growth and revenue growth, significantly impacts its stock price. Investors value companies with strong and growing earnings and revenue streams more highly than those with stagnant or declining financial metrics. Positive-earnings surprises or better-than-expected revenue growth can lead to upward revisions in earnings estimates and increased demand for the company's stock, driving up its price.

Fundamental analysis: Fundamental analysis involves evaluating a company's financial statements, business model, industry dynamics, competitive position, management team, and growth prospects to determine its intrinsic value and assess whether its stock is undervalued or overvalued. Analysts and investors use various financial metrics and valuation methods, such as price-to-earnings (P/E) ratio, price-to-book (P/B) ratio, price-to-sales (P/S) ratio, dividend yield, discounted cash flow (DCF) analysis, and comparable company analysis (CCA), to estimate a company's fair value and make investment decisions.

Technical analysis: Technical analysis involves analyzing historical price and volume data, as well as chart patterns and technical indicators, to identify trends, patterns, and trading opportunities in the stock market. Technical analysts believe that past price movements and market psychology can provide insights into future price movements, allowing them to identify support and resistance levels, trend reversals, and entry and exit points for trades. Common technical indicators used in stock price analysis include moving averages, relative strength index (RSI), stochastic oscillators, moving average convergence divergence (MACD), and Bollinger Bands.

Market sentiment and investor psychology: Market sentiment and investor psychology significantly drive stock prices in the short-term. Investor sentiment reflects market participants' collective mood, emotions, and attitudes towards a particular stock, sector, or market. Positive sentiment can lead to bullish behavior, increased buying activity, and upward price momentum, while negative sentiment can result in bearish behavior, selling pressure, and downward price trends. News events, economic data releases, corporate earnings announcements, analyst recommendations, geopolitical developments, and central bank policies influence market sentiment.

Market efficiency and information: Stock prices reflect all available information and expectations about a company's prospects, including publicly available information, private information, and market rumors. The efficient market hypothesis (EMH) posits that stock prices reflect all known information and are, therefore, impossible to outperform consistently through fundamental or technical analysis. However, the degree of market efficiency varies; and markets may be more or less efficient depending on market liquidity, information availability, investor behavior, and regulatory oversight.

Trading activity and liquidity: Stock prices are influenced by trading activity and liquidity in the financial markets. Higher trading volumes and liquidity tend to result in narrower bid-ask spreads and greater price efficiency. In comparison, lower trading volumes and liquidity may lead to wider bid-ask spreads and increased price volatility. Liquidity refers to the ease with which a stock can be bought or sold in the market without significantly impacting its price. Stocks with higher liquidity are more attractive to investors because they offer greater flexibility and lower transaction costs.

Stock market prices are determined by the interaction of supply-and-demand forces in the financial markets. They are driven by earnings and revenue growth, fundamental analysis, technical analysis, market sentiment, investor psychology, market efficiency, information availability, trading activity, and liquidity. While stock prices may fluctuate in the short-term due to market dynamics and investor sentiment, over the long-term, they tend to reflect the underlying fundamentals and intrinsic value of the companies they represent.

MARKET INDICES AND BENCHMARKS

Market indices and benchmarks are measures used to track the performance of a group of stocks or securities representing a specific segment of the financial markets. These indices serve as barometers of market performance, providing investors with insights into the overall direction and trends of the stock market or specific sectors or asset classes. Here are the key features and characteristics of market indices and benchmarks:

Definition and composition: A market index is a mathematical representation of the performance of a group of stocks or securities, often referred to as constituents or components. Indices are constructed using various methodologies, such as market capitalization weighting, price weighting, equal weighting, or fundamental weighting. The composition of a market index depends on its objective and focus. Broad market indices, such as the S&P 500, represent a diverse cross-section of the overall stock market, while sector-specific indices, such as the Nasdaq Biotechnology Index, track the performance of companies within a particular industry or sector. Indices may include stocks listed on a specific exchange (e.g. NYSE and Nasdaq); stocks of companies within a certain market capitalization range (e.g. large-cap, mid-cap, and small-cap); or stocks from a particular region or country (e.g. U.S. stocks, European stocks, and emerging markets).

Calculation methodology: Market indices are calculated using various methodologies, depending on their construction and objectives. The most common methods include price-weighted, market capitalization-weighted, equal-weighted, and fundamental-weighted indices. Price-weighted indices, such as the Dow Jones Industrial Average (DJIA), calculate the index value by summing the prices of all constituent stocks and dividing by a divisor. Market capitalization-weighted indices, such as the S&P 500, assign weights to constituent stocks based on their market capitalizations, with larger companies carrying greater influence on the index value.

Representation of performance: Market indices serve as benchmarks for evaluating the performance of investment portfolios, mutual funds, exchange-traded funds (ETFs), and other investment products. Investors use indices to assess whether their investments outperform or underperform relative to the broader market or specific sectors.

Indices provide a reference point for comparing investment returns, tracking market trends, identifying investment opportunities, and making informed investment decisions.

Diversification and risk management: Market indices offer investors exposure to diversified portfolios of stocks or securities, reducing idiosyncratic risk and enhancing portfolio diversification. By investing in index funds or ETFs that track market indices, investors can gain broad exposure to the stock market or specific sectors at a relatively low cost. Indices help investors manage risk by spreading their investments across multiple stocks, industries, and asset classes, reducing the impact of individual stock performance on overall portfolio returns. **Benchmarking and performance measurement:** Market indices serve as benchmarks for evaluating the performance of investment managers, portfolio strategies, and investment products. Fund managers aim to outperform their respective benchmarks by generating returns that exceed the index return net of fees. Benchmarking allows investors to assess the effectiveness of active management strategies and evaluate whether investment managers are adding value through stock selection, sector allocation, or market timing.

Popular market indices: Numerous market indices cover various segments of the global financial markets. Some of the most widely followed and recognized indices include the following:

- S&P 500 tracks the performance of 500 large-cap U.S. stocks representing approximately 80% of the total U.S. equity market capitalization
- Dow Jones Industrial Average (DJIA) consists of thirty blue-chip U.S. stocks across various sectors, representing a diverse cross-section of the U.S. economy.
- Nasdaq Composite Index measures the performance of over 2,500 stocks listed on the Nasdaq stock market, including technology, biotechnology, and internet companies.
- FTSE 100 tracks the performance of the 100 largest companies listed on the London Stock Exchange by market capitalization.
- Nikkei 225 represents the performance of 225 blue-chip stocks listed on the Tokyo Stock Exchange, reflecting the performance of the Japanese stock market.

Index investing and passive Management: Index investing involves replicating the performance of a market index by investing in index funds or ETFs that track the index. Index funds and ETFs offer low-cost, diversified investment options that provide exposure to broad market indices or specific sectors. Passive management strategies aim to match the index's performance rather than outperform it. Passive investors seek to capture market returns by holding a diversified portfolio of securities that mirrors the index's composition.

Stock market indices and benchmarks are essential for tracking market performance, evaluating investment portfolios, and benchmarking investment strategies. By providing a reference point for market performance, indices help investors monitor trends, assess relative performance, and make informed investment decisions. Whether used for benchmarking, diversification, risk management, or passive investing, market indices play a crucial role in the functioning of the global financial markets.

'Understanding the Basics' has comprehensively introduced the stock market's foundational elements. By exploring the fundamental concepts of stock market operations, types of stocks, stock price determination, and market indices and benchmarks, this chapter equips readers with essential knowledge for navigating the financial markets.

We began with an overview of the stock market, demystifying its role as a dynamic platform where company ownership is bought and sold. Understanding the different types of stocks—common and preferred—helps clarify how investors can align their choices with their financial goals and risk tolerance.

The exploration of stock price determination illuminated the forces of supply and demand, market sentiment, and the impact of fundamental factors. By grasping these dynamics, readers can better anticipate market movements and make informed investment decisions.

Furthermore, examining market indices and benchmarks provided insights into how overall market performance is measured and how specific sectors are tracked. Familiarity with prominent indexes like the S&P 500, Dow Jones Industrial Average, and Nasdaq Composite offers a valuable perspective on market trends and performance.

This chapter lays a solid foundation for understanding the stock market's basic principles. With these core concepts, readers are well-prepared to delve deeper into more advanced topics and develop a strategic approach to investing and trading. The knowledge gained here is critical for making informed decisions and embarking on a successful journey in the stock market.

Chapter 4

GETTING STARTED

'Getting Started' is your gateway to confidently navigating the foundational steps of investing. This chapter is designed to equip you with the essential tools and knowledge needed to begin investing effectively. First, we delve into setting investment goals, the crucial starting point for any successful investment strategy. Clear, well-defined goals will guide your investment decisions, whether saving for retirement, making a significant purchase, or simply growing your wealth. Setting realistic and achievable goals ensures that your investment plan aligns with your financial aspirations and risk tolerance.

Next, we explore the pivotal role of choosing a brokerage account, an essential step in gaining access to the stock market. The choice of brokerage can significantly impact your trading experience, fees, and the tools available. We'll discuss the different types of brokerage accounts—from full-service brokers to online platforms—and help you determine which best suits your needs and investing style. The following section covers how to buy and sell Stocks, providing a step-by-step guide to executing trades. Understanding the mechanics of buying and selling, from selecting stocks to placing orders, is a fundamental aspect of building and managing your investment portfolio. We'll walk you through the various order types and strategies to help you make informed decisions in the stock market.

Finally, we introduce the fundamentals of risk management, a critical aspect of safeguarding your investments. Effective risk management techniques will help you navigate market volatility and protect your assets. We'll discuss strategies for diversifying your portfolio, setting stop-loss orders, and assessing your risk tolerance to ensure that you are prepared for the uncertainties of investing. By the end of this chapter, you will have a solid understanding of how to set investment goals, choose the correct brokerage account, buy and sell stocks effectively, and manage risk. This comprehensive foundation will empower you to take your first steps in the stock market with clarity and confidence.

SETTING INVESTMENT GOALS

Setting clear and achievable investment goals is a crucial first step in developing a successful strategy. Investment goals are your financial plan's foundation, guiding investment decisions and providing a roadmap for achieving your desired outcomes. Whether your objectives are short-term or long-term, setting specific, measurable, achievable, relevant, and time-bound (SMART) investment goals is essential for clarity, focus, and accountability. Here's a detailed description of setting investment goals:

Specific: Specificity is critical when setting investment goals. Clearly define what you want to accomplish with your investments. Ask yourself: What do I want to achieve with my investments? Do I want to grow my wealth, generate passive income, or preserve capital? What are my financial needs, priorities, and aspirations? You can tailor your investment strategy to match your unique financial circumstances and preferences by articulating specific investment objectives.

Measurable: Your investment goals should be measurable, allowing you to track progress and evaluate performance over time.

Establish quantifiable metrics or milestones to assess whether you are on track to achieve your goals. For example, set a target rate of return or investment performance benchmark. Specify a desired portfolio value, income level, or net worth. Determine the amount of money you aim to save or invest within a specific timeframe. Measurable goals provide clarity and accountability, enabling you to make informed decisions and adjustments to stay on course.

Achievable: Ensure your investment goals are realistic and attainable given your financial resources, risk tolerance, time horizon, and market conditions. Set goals that stretch your capabilities but are within reach with diligent effort and prudent planning. Consider factors such as your income level, savings capacity, investment knowledge, and market expectations when assessing the achievability of your goals. Breaking down larger goals into smaller actionable steps can make them more manageable and achievable over time.

Relevant: Your investment goals should reflect your financial plan, lifestyle preferences, and life stage. Align your investment objectives with broader financial goals, such as retirement planning, education funding, homeownership, or wealth accumulation. Consider the impact of external factors, economic trends, and personal circumstances on the relevance and feasibility of your investment goals. Prioritize meaningful and impactful goals in the context of your financial well-being and future aspirations.

Time-bound: Time-bound goals have a defined timeline or deadline for achievement, providing a sense of urgency and focus. Establish specific time frames or target dates for reaching each investment goal. For example, set short-term goals (e.g., one year) for building an emergency fund or saving for a vacation. Define medium-term goals (e.g. three to five years) for purchasing a home or funding a child's education. Determine long-term goals (e.g. 10+ years) for retirement planning or wealth accumulation. Time-bound goals create a sense of accountability and enable you to allocate resources, plan investments, and monitor progress effectively.

By following the SMART criteria in investment goals, you can clarify your financial objectives, stay focused on your priorities, and increase your likelihood of investment success. Regularly review and update your goals as your circumstances change and market conditions evolve, and celebrate milestones as you progress towards achieving your financial aspirations.

CHOOSING A BROKERAGE ACCOUNT

The brokerage industry is a dynamic and evolving sector that plays a crucial role in financial markets. With a vast and continually changing landscape, the number of brokerage firms worldwide can be challenging to quantify accurately due to market dynamics, mergers and acquisitions, and the emergence of new players. To better understand this sector, brokerage firms can be categorized into several distinct types, each offering unique services and catering to different investors.

1. **Full-Service Brokers**

Full-service brokers provide comprehensive services designed to meet their clients' diverse needs. These firms offer personalized investment advice, financial planning, and account management services. They cater to investors seeking professional guidance and are willing to pay higher fees for individualized attention. Full-service brokers often have extensive research capabilities, access to exclusive investment opportunities, and dedicated financial advisors. Examples of full-service brokers are Morgan Stanley, known for its wealth management and investment services. Morgan Stanley offers a broad spectrum of financial products and personalized advice. Merrill Lynch is a division of Bank of America. Merrill Lynch provides various financial services, including brokerage, financial planning, and investment management.

2. Discount Brokers

Discount brokers focus on providing lower-cost trading services with fewer added features. They typically charge lower trading fees and commissions, making them attractive to cost-conscious investors who prefer to manage their investments independently. Discount brokers usually offer online platforms where investors can execute trades without needing personal financial advice or support. Examples of discount brokers are Charles Schwab—a major player in the discount brokerage space offering low trading fees, a robust trading platform, and various investment options—and E*TRADE. Known for its user-friendly online platform, E*TRADE provides low-cost trading and investment tools for self-directed investors.

3. Online Brokers

Online brokers operate primarily through digital platforms, enabling investors to trade securities with minimal direct interaction. These firms often provide a range of tools and resources for self-directed trading, including real-time data, advanced charting, and research reports. Online brokers have revolutionized trading by making it more accessible and affordable for individual investors. Examples of online brokers are Robinhood—a well-known online broker that offers commission-free trades and a streamlined mobile app, catering to a new generation of investors—and Interactive Brokers, a global online brokerage firm offering a comprehensive trading platform with low fees and access to a wide range of financial instruments.

4. Robo-Advisors

Robo-advisors are automated platforms that use algorithms to provide investment management services based on user preferences and risk tolerance. These services are designed to be cost-effective and accessible, with automated portfolio rebalancing and investment recommendations. Robo advisors appeal to investors seeking a hands-off approach to managing their investments. Examples of robo-advisors are Betterment, a leading robo-advisor that offers automated portfolio management and financial planning with low fees, and Wealthfront, which provides automated investment management and financial planning services, focusing on low-cost, diversified portfolios.

5. **International Brokers**

International brokers cater to investors who seek to trade across multiple countries and global markets. These firms often provide access to international stock exchanges and financial products, enabling investors to diversify their portfolios globally. International brokers are essential for those looking to capitalize on opportunities beyond their domestic markets. Examples of international brokers are Saxo Bank, a Danish investment bank offering a global trading platform with access to various international markets and asset classes, and IG Group, a UK-based firm providing trading services across multiple asset classes and markets worldwide. A Danish investment bank that offers access to over 71,000 financial instruments through its online trading platform.

Estimates and Industry Landscape

1. **United States:** The United States has many brokerage firms, with hundreds operating in various market segments. Prominent names include Fidelity, TD Ameritrade, and Vanguard, each offering distinct services and platforms to cater to different investor needs.
2. **Internationally:** The number of brokerage firms globally is likely in the thousands, considering the numerous financial hubs such as London, Hong Kong, Tokyo, and other major cities. Each region may have its own set of brokers, varying in size, services, and market focus. While the exact number

of brokerage firms worldwide is complex due to the industry's ever-changing nature, the brokerage landscape is evident because it is diverse and caters to a wide range of investor preferences and trading needs.

HOW TO BUY AND SELL STOCKS

A Guide to Buying Stocks

1. Find a Broker That You Like

Choosing the right brokerage firm is a critical first step in your investing journey. Look for a broker that aligns with your investment goals, trading style, and needs. Consider fees, platform usability, customer support, and available tools. Whether you prefer a full-service broker for personalized advice or a discount broker for low-cost trades, selecting a broker that suits your preferences will set the foundation for your investing experience. We have chosen five friendly and easy-to-use brokerage firms for your reference, not recommendation:

- Robinhood is known for its user-friendly mobile app and commission-free trading. It provides a straightforward platform for buying and selling stocks, ETFs, and cryptocurrencies without charging trading fees. Robinhood is particularly popular among new investors due to its easy-to-use interface and educational resources.
- Webull offers a robust trading platform with zero-commission trades on stocks, ETFs, and options. It features advanced charting tools, technical indicators, and real-time market data, making it suitable for beginner and experienced traders. Webull's desktop and mobile apps are well-regarded for their usability and range of features.

- Morgan Stanley and E*TRADE provide various services, from basic trading to comprehensive financial planning. E*TRADE, now part of Morgan Stanley, is known for its intuitive trading platforms, diverse investment options, and extensive research tools. It offers commission-free trading for stocks and ETFs, and its educational resources help investors make informed decisions.
- Charles Schwab and TD Ameritrade (now merged) are prominent brokerage firms known for their comprehensive services. Both offer commission-free trading for stocks and ETFs, robust research tools, educational content, and customer support. Charles Schwab is recognized for its low fees and broad range of investment options, while TD Ameritrade is known for its advanced trading platforms and tools.
- Interactive Brokers is a leading brokerage firm known for its advanced trading platform and global market access. It offers competitive pricing, low commissions, and extensive research tools suitable for active traders and investors. Interactive Brokers supports various asset classes, including stocks, options, futures, and forex, making it a versatile choice for experienced traders.

2. Pick Your Stocks

Once you have a brokerage account, the next step is to select the stocks you want to invest in. Research potential stocks by analyzing company fundamentals, industry trends, and market conditions. To reduce risk, consider diversifying your investments by choosing stocks from different sectors or industries. Use your broker's tools and resources to evaluate and compare various stocks.

3. Decide How Many Shares to Buy

Determine the number of shares you want to purchase based on your budget, investment strategy, and stock price. Consider how the number of shares fits your portfolio and risk management strategy. Ensure that your investment aligns with your financial goals and that you're not overcommitting to any stock.

4. Choose Your Order Type

Decide on the type of order you want to place to buy stocks. Standard order types include:

- **Market order:** You buy the stock at the current market price.
- **Limit order:** You set a maximum price you're willing to pay and execute the trade only if the stock reaches that price.
- **Stop order:** It triggers a market order once the stock hits a specified price. Choose the order type based on your trading strategy and how quickly you want the transaction completed.

5. Learn the Lingo

Understanding the terminology used in stock trading is essential for making informed decisions. Familiarize yourself with key terms such as:

- **Ticker symbol:** A unique identifier for a stock.
- **Dividend:** A portion of a company's earnings distributed to shareholders.
- **P/E ratio:** The price-to-earnings ratio is a valuation measure. Grasping these concepts will help you navigate the stock market more effectively and communicate with your broker or financial advisor.

6. Start Buying Stocks

With everything in place, you can begin purchasing stocks. Execute your chosen order through your brokerage account and monitor the performance of your investments. Stay informed about market conditions and news related to your stocks to adjust as needed. Investing in stocks is an ongoing process, so continuously review your portfolio and investment strategy to align with your financial objectives.

Steps to Selling Stocks

Selling stocks can be straightforward, but following the steps is essential to ensure you make informed decisions and execute your trades correctly.

1. **Review your investment goals.** Evaluate your investment objectives before selling. Consider whether selling aligns with your financial goals and whether it is the right time to sell based on your strategy.
2. **Assess your current holdings.** Review your stocks and analyze their performance. Consider factors such as price appreciation, dividends received, and overall portfolio balance.
3. **Log into your brokerage account.** Access your account using your credentials. Ensure you have a stable internet connection to avoid interruptions during selling.
4. **Locate the stock you want to sell.** Navigate to your portfolio section and find the stock you wish to sell. Ensure you have all the necessary details, such as the number of shares you own and the current market price.
5. **Decide on the number of shares to sell.** Determine how many shares you want to sell. Depending on your strategy and needs, you can sell all or a portion of your holdings.
6. **Choose your order type.** Select the type of order you want to place:

- **Market order**: This order sells your shares at the current market price. It is executed immediately but may not guarantee a specific price.
- **Limit order:** This order allows you to set a specific price for selling your shares. The order will only execute if the stock reaches that price, providing more control over the selling price.
- **Stop order:** This order becomes a market order once the stock reaches a specified stop price. It can help limit losses.

7. **Review transaction fees.** Know any commissions or fees for selling stocks. Different brokers have varying fee structures, which can affect your overall profit from the sale.
8. **Confirm and place your order.** Review all the details of your order, including the number of shares, order type, and any associated fees. Once you're satisfied, confirm and place the order.
9. **Monitor the sale.** After placing the order, monitor its status. If you place a market order, it should execute almost immediately. Check back for limit or stop orders to see if your order has been filled.
10. **Keep records.** After the sale, update your records. For tax purposes, keep track of the sale price, number of shares sold, and any capital gains or losses.
11. **Evaluate the outcome.** Reflect on the sale and evaluate how it aligns with your investment strategy. Consider what you can do differently in the future based on this experience.

Selling stocks requires careful consideration and a clear understanding of your investment goals. By following these steps, you can ensure a smooth transaction and make informed decisions that align with your financial objectives. Always stay informed about market conditions and investment portfolios to optimize your trading strategies.

Fees and commissions: Evaluate the brokerage firms' fee structure and commission rates. Standard fees include trading commissions, account maintenance, inactivity, wire transfers, and mutual fund transaction fees. Compare fee schedules and waivers offered by various brokerage platforms to identify the most cost-effective option for your investment needs. Look for brokers that offer competitive pricing and transparent fee disclosure to avoid hidden costs and unexpected charges.

Trading platforms and tools: Assess the quality and functionality of the brokerage's trading platform, including its user interface, ease of use, order execution speed, and availability of advanced trading tools and features. Look for brokerage platforms that offer intuitive trading interfaces, real-time market data, customizable charts and graphs, research reports, screening tools, technical analysis indicators, and mobile trading apps for seamless access to your account from anywhere.

Investment offerings: Consider the range of investment products and asset classes available through the brokerage account. Determine whether the brokerage offers access to stocks, bonds, options, ETFs, mutual funds, forex, futures, and other investment instruments. Assess the diversity and depth of investment offerings, including the availability of commission-free ETFs, no-load mutual funds, fixed-income securities, international stocks, and alternative investments, to ensure that the brokerage can meet your investment preferences and objectives.

Account minimums and requirements: Determine whether the brokerage imposes account minimums or requirements for opening and maintaining a brokerage account. Some brokers may require a minimum initial deposit to open an account, while others may waive minimums for certain account types or promotions. When evaluating account minimums and requirements, consider your budget, investment capital, and liquidity needs to ensure they align with your financial situation and investment goals.

Customer service and support: Evaluate the quality and responsiveness of the brokerage's customer service and support.

Look for brokers that offer multiple communication channels, including phone support, email support, live chat, and in-person assistance at branch locations. Assess the availability of educational resources, tutorials, webinars, and customer support materials to help you navigate the platform, troubleshoot issues, and enhance your investing knowledge and skills.

Security and regulation: When choosing a brokerage account, prioritize security and regulatory compliance. Ensure that the brokerage is registered with relevant regulatory authorities, such as the Securities and Exchange Commission (SEC) or Financial Industry Regulatory Authority (FINRA), and adheres to industry best practices and standards. Verify that the brokerage employs robust security measures, such as encryption, multifactor authentication, account protection, and insurance coverage (e.g. Securities Investor Protection Corporation [SIPC] coverage) to safeguard your assets and personal information against cyber threats and fraud.

Reputation and reviews: Research the brokerage firm's reputation and track record by reading customer reviews, testimonials, and independent ratings from reputable sources. Look for brokers with positive reviews; high client satisfaction ratings; and a strong reputation for reliability, transparency, and integrity. Consider factors such as the broker's history, longevity in the industry, regulatory compliance record, financial stability, and any past disciplinary actions or legal disputes when assessing its reputation and credibility.

By carefully evaluating factors such as types of brokerage firms, fees and commissions, trading platforms and tools, investment offerings, account minimums, and requirements, customer service and support, security and regulation, and reputation and reviews, you can make an informed decision when choosing a brokerage account that aligns with your investment needs, preferences, and objectives. Take the time to compare different brokerage options, weigh their pros and cons, and select the broker that best meets your criteria and expectations. Remember that your choice of brokerage can significantly impact your investing experience and success, so choose wisely and start investing confidently.

When buying stocks or selling stocks, an investor must understand the following terms to execute their orders successfully:

Margin Account

A margin account is a type of brokerage account that allows an individual to borrow money from the brokerage firm to buy securities. This means an individual can buy securities by putting up only a percentage of the purchase price, with the remainder being borrowed from the brokerage firm. This can allow an individual to increase their buying power and potentially generate greater profits, but it also increases the risk, as the individual can create more significant losses. The main features of a margin account include:

- **Increased buying power:** With a margin account, an individual can buy securities by putting up only a percentage of the purchase price. This allows them to increase their buying power and generate greater profits.
- **Interest charges:** The borrowed funds carry interest charges, typically based on the prevailing market interest rates.
- **Margin calls:** If the value of the securities in the margin account falls below a certain level, the brokerage firm may issue a margin call, which requires the individual to deposit additional funds or sell securities to bring the account back into compliance with the firm's maintenance margin requirement.
- **Higher risk:** A margin account carries higher risk as the individual can generate more significant losses if the value of the securities in the account falls. A margin account is unsuitable for all investors, and it's essential to understand the risks before opening a margin account. It's important to have a well-defined strategy and a plan for risk management and to regularly monitor the account to ensure it stays within the safe zone. It's also essential to consult a financial professional before opening a margin account.

Cash Accounts

A cash account is an investment account requiring the account holder to have sufficient funds to cover the purchase of securities. The account holder must pay for securities in full before the trade is executed. The account holder can also only sell securities they already own, and they can't borrow money from the broker to purchase securities, unlike a margin account. Cash accounts are also known as regular or non margin accounts, as they do not allow for borrowing against securities held in the account. They are considered the safest type of investment account as the account holder cannot lose more money than what is in the account. Cash accounts are typically used by conservative investors who want to minimize risk and are not interested in using leverage to boost their returns. They are also commonly used by individual investors new to the stock market and want to gain experience before moving on to more advanced investment strategies. One of the main advantages of a cash account is that it eliminates the risk of margin calls and the potential for unlimited losses. This can be beneficial for people who want to avoid the risk of losing more money than they have invested. However, it's important to note that cash accounts also have some drawbacks. They can limit the potential returns generated because they do not allow the account holder to borrow money to invest.

Brokerage Account Balance

A brokerage account balance is the total amount of money in a brokerage account, including cash, stocks, bonds, and other securities. The balance can change daily as the securities' value fluctuates and the account holder makes trades, deposits, or withdrawals. The brokerage account balance is important because it represents the money an investor has available to trade and invest. It is also used to determine if an investor has sufficient funds to meet the requirements of a trade, such as the margin requirement for a margin account. Investors can check their brokerage account balance by logging into their account online or contacting their brokerage firm directly. Brokerage firms also typically provide account holders with regular statements showing the account balance and any recent trades, deposits, or withdrawals. It's important to note that the value of a brokerage account can go up or down depending on the performance of the securities held within the account and the market conditions. Additionally, brokerage accounts can have different types of accounts, such as cash, margin, and retirement accounts, which may have different balance requirements and restrictions. It's essential to understand the terms of your brokerage account and consult with a financial advisor if you have any questions.

Buying Power

Buying power refers to the money an individual has to purchase securities in a brokerage account. This amount can change depending on the type of account and any borrowing or margin in use. In a cash account, buying power is the amount of cash an individual has to purchase securities. This amount is equal to the account's cash balance. In a margin account, buying power is the amount of cash and securities an individual has available to purchase securities, plus the amount that can be borrowed from the brokerage firm. The exact amount of buying power will depend on the brokerage firm's margin requirement and the individual's maintenance margin. For example, if an individual has $10,000 in a cash account, their buying power is $10,000. If an individual has $10,000 in a margin account with a margin requirement of 50%, their buying power would be $20,000 ($10,000 cash balance + $10,000 that can be borrowed). It's important to note that buying power is not the same as the amount of money an individual has available to invest. Individuals should only invest money they can afford to lose and be aware of the risks associated with investing with borrowed money. It's also important to regularly monitor the account and ensure it stays within the safe zone defined by the brokerage firm.

Trade Volume

Trade volume refers to the number of shares or contracts of a security bought and sold in a specific period, usually a day. It measures how much activity occurs in a stock or other security. High trade volume can indicate that a stock or security is widespread and actively bought and sold by traders and investors. Low trade volume can suggest that a stock or security is not as popular and needs to be actively bought and sold. Trade volume can be used as an indicator of market sentiment. High trade volume indicates investors are bullish or optimistic about a stock or security, while low trade volume indicates that investors are bearish or pessimistic. Additionally, high trade volume can suggest a stock is volatile, meaning its price will likely fluctuate. Trade volume can be used as a tool for technical analysis, as high trade volume can indicate that a stock or security is reaching a new high or low and can be used to confirm or refute trends and patterns. It's important to note that high trade volume does not always indicate that a stock or security is a good investment, and it's essential to do your research and consider the company's fundamentals before making an investment decision.

Account Volume

Account volume refers to the total number of shares or contracts of a security bought and sold by a specific account, such as a brokerage account or a trading account, over a particular period, usually a day. Account volume is critical to track because it can indicate how active an account is and how much buying and selling takes place. High account volume can suggest that an account is making many trades and potentially taking on more risk, while low account volume can indicate that an account is less active and less risky. Account volume does not always suggest that an account is making profitable trades, and it's essential to monitor the account's performance over time and compare it to a benchmark such as the S&P 500. It's also necessary to monitor the account's risk level and ensure it's aligned with its risk tolerance and investment goals. Account volume can help track how active you are as a trader and whether you are sticking to your plan. If your account volume is high, but you are consistently losing money, it may be a sign that you need to adjust your strategy or the types of securities you buy and sell. In contrast, if your account volume is low but you are consistently making money, it may be a sign that you are too conservative and could benefit from being more active.

Stock Quantity

Stock quantity refers to the number of shares of a stock that an investor or trader buys or sells in a trade. It measures the trade size in terms of the number of shares. When an investor or trader places an order to buy or sell stocks, they specify the number of shares they want to trade. The quantity of shares purchased or sold can significantly impact the overall cost of a trade and the potential profit or loss. For example, if an investor buys 100 shares of a stock at $50 per share, the total cost of the trade is $5,000. If the investor instead buys 1,000 shares at the same price, the total cost of the trade would be $50,000. Stock quantity can also be used to define the position size of a trade, which refers to the amount of money an investor is willing to put at risk in a single trade. The position size is determined by the quantity of shares bought or sold multiplied by the stock price. It's important to note that the stock quantity bought or sold should align with the risk management strategy and investment goals and should be, at most, the available buying power or cash in the account.

Stock Symbol

A stock symbol, also known as a ticker symbol, is a unique identifier assigned to publicly traded stocks on a stock exchange. It is a short combination of letters representing a specific company or security listed on an exchange. The symbol identifies the stock and allows traders and investors to track its price and trading volume. For example, the stock symbol for Apple Inc. is AAPL on the Nasdaq and TSLA for Tesla Inc. Each stock exchange, such as the New York Stock Exchange (NYSE) and Nasdaq, has stock symbols for listed companies. The symbol is usually composed of one to four letters and is unique to that company on that particular exchange. Stock symbols are used to track the performance of a specific stock or security on financial websites and news outlets. They are also used in stock trading platforms, such as online brokers, to identify the stock when placing a buy or sell order. The stock symbols are unique to a specific exchange and should not be confused with the company's name or stock exchange. When looking for a particular company's stock symbol, make sure to check the correct exchange it is traded on.

Market Order

A market order is a type of order that is placed in the stock market to buy or sell a stock at the current market price. It is an instruction to a broker to execute a trade immediately at the best available price. When an investor places a market order to buy, the broker will execute the trade at the best available ask price, which is the lowest price at which a seller is willing to sell the stock. When an investor places a market order to sell, the broker will execute the trade at the best available bid price, which is the highest price at which a buyer is willing to buy the stock. Market orders are often used by investors who want to quickly enter or exit a position in a stock, as they are usually swiftly executed. However, the price at which the trade is executed may differ from the price specified in the order, especially during high volatility periods. The market orders are not guaranteed to be filled at the desired price, and the execution price may be influenced by market conditions such as volatility and liquidity.

Open Order

An open order is a type of order that is placed in the stock market but has yet to be executed. An order to buy or sell a stock at a specific price or better remains in effect until it is filled or cancelled. There are two types of open orders: limit orders and market orders. A limit order is buying or selling a stock at a specific price or better.

For example, a buy limit order would be placed at a particular price or lower, and a sell limit order would be placed at a specific price or higher. Limit orders ensure that the trade is executed at a particular price or better, but they may not be filled if the stock price never reaches the specified price. A market order is an order to buy or sell a stock at the current market price. Market orders are usually executed quickly, but the price at which the trade is executed may differ from the price specified in the order, especially during high volatility periods. It's important to note that open orders can be impacted by market conditions, such as volatility and liquidity, and may not be filled at the desired price or time.

Market on Close

Market on close (MOC) is a market order placed in the stock market to buy or sell a stock at the market's closing price at the end of the trading day. It is an instruction to a broker to execute a trade at the last available price at the market close. When an investor places an MOC order, the exchange holds the order until the close of the market and is then executed at the last traded price for that security. This type of order is used by investors who want to enter or exit a position based on the closing price of a stock rather than the current market price. MOC orders are executed at the same price as the last trade of the day and can be used as a way to ensure that the trade is executed at the price that reflects the overall market sentiment for that day; it can also be used in case the investor doesn't want to be exposed to the intraday volatility. It's important to note that MOC orders are subject to the same risks as any other market order, such as the possibility of not being executed at the desired price. If the market is closed due to an event, such as a holiday or a technical issue, the order will not be executed.

Limit Order

A limit order is a type of order that is placed in the stock market to buy or sell a stock at a specific price or better. It is an instruction to a broker to execute a trade at a particular price or at a better price if it becomes available. When an investor places a limited order to buy, the order is filled at the specified price or lower. If the specified price is higher than the current market price, the order will be held by the exchange until the stock price reaches the specified price or lower; at that point, the order will be executed. When an investor places a limit order to sell, the order is filled at the specified price or higher. If the specified price is lower than the current market price, the order will be held by the exchange until the stock price reaches the specified price or higher; at that point, the order will be executed. Limit orders can ensure that a trade is executed at a specific price or better and are often used by investors who want to enter or exit a position at a particular price point. They can also limit potential losses by setting a stop-loss order at a specific price. The limit orders are not guaranteed to be filled, as the specified price may not be reached, or the order may be filled at a different price due to market conditions such as volatility and liquidity.

Stop-on-Quote Order

A stop-on-quote order is a type of order that is placed in the stock market to buy or sell a stock at a specific price or worse. It is a combination of a stop order and a limit order. This type of order is triggered when the stock price reaches a specified level, known as the stop price, and then it becomes a limit order. When an investor places a stop-on-quote order to buy, the exchange holds the order until the stock price reaches the stop price. Once the stock price reaches the stop price, the order is triggered and converted into a limit order to buy at the price or better. When an investor places a stop-on-quote order to sell, the exchange holds the order until the stock price reaches the stop price. Once the stock price reaches the stop price, the order is triggered and converted into a limit order to sell at the limit price or better. Stop-on-quote orders are helpful for investors who want to limit their losses on a position. For example, an investor can place a stop-on-quote order to sell at a specific price; if the stock price falls below that price, the order will be triggered, and the investor's position will be sold, limiting their potential losses. The stop-on-quote orders are not guaranteed to be filled, as the specified price may not be reached, or the order may be filled at a different price due to market conditions such as volatility and liquidity.

Stop-Limit-on-Quote Order

A stop-limit-on-quote order is placed in the stock market to buy or sell a stock at a specific price or better once a specified trigger price is reached. It is a combination of a stop order and a limit order. This type of order gives the investor more control over their trade execution. When an investor places a stop limit on a quote order to buy, the exchange holds the order until the stock price reaches the stop price. Once the stock price reaches the stop price, the order is triggered and converted into a limit order to buy at the price or better. The limit order will only be filled if the stock price trades at or below the limit price. When an investor places a stop-limit-on-a-quote order to sell, the exchange holds the order until the stock price reaches the stop price. Once the stock price reaches the stop price, the order is triggered and converted into a limit order to sell at the limit price or better. The limit order will only be filled if the stock price trades at or above the limit price. Stop-limits-on-quote orders are helpful for investors who want to limit their losses on a position but also want to have more control over the price at which their trade is executed. For example, an investor can place a stop-limit-on-a-quote order to sell at a specific stop price and limit price; if the stock price falls below the stop price, the order will be triggered, and the investor's position will be sold only if the stock price is at or above the limit price, limiting their potential losses. The stop-limit-on-quote orders are not guaranteed to be filled, as the specified price may not be reached, or the order may be filled at a different price due to market conditions such as volatility and liquidity.

Trailing Stop $

A trailing stop $ is a type of stop-loss order placed in the stock market to sell a stock when it falls below a specific price. This type of order is used to lock in profits on a stock that has been rising in value while providing some downside protection. When an investor places a trailing stop $ order, they set a dollar amount (for example, $5) below the current market price at which they would like to sell the stock. The stop price rises as the stock price rises, maintaining a $5 trailing stop behind the current market price. If the stock price falls by $5 or more, the trailing stop order will be triggered, and the stock will be sold at the next available market price. For example, if an investor buys a stock at $50 and places a $5 trailing stop, the initial stop price will be $45. If the stock price rises to $55, the stop price will also rise to $50. If the stock price falls to $52, the stop price will remain at $50, so the order will not be triggered. But if the stock price falls to $49, the order will be triggered, and the stock will be sold at the next available market price. Trailing stop $ orders can be helpful for investors who want to lock in profits on a stock that has been rising in value but still want to keep a close eye on the stock's price movements and protect their investment in case of a significant price drop. However, the trailing stops may not be executed at the desired price if market conditions change rapidly, and the order can be filled at a price different from the one specified by the trailing stop due to market conditions such as volatility and liquidity.

Trailing Stop %

A trailing stop % is a type of stop-loss order placed in the stock market to sell a stock when it falls below a certain percentage of its highest value. This type of order is used to lock in profits on a stock rising in value while providing some downside protection. When an investor places a trailing stop % order, they set a percentage (for example, 5%) below the highest value they would like to sell the stock. As the stock price rises, the stop price also rises, maintaining a 5% trailing stop behind the highest value of the stock. If the stock price falls by more than 5% from its highest value, the trailing stop order will be triggered, and the stock will be sold at the next available market price. For example, if an investor buys a stock at $50 and places a 5% trailing stop, the initial stop price will be $47.50. If the stock price rises to $55, the stop price will also rise to $52.25. If the stock price falls to $52, the stop price will remain at $52.25, so the order will not be triggered. But if the stock price falls to $49, the order will be triggered, and the stock will be sold at the next available market price. Trailing stop % orders can be helpful for investors who want to lock in profits on a stock that has been rising in value but still want to keep a close eye on the stock's price movements and protect their investment in case of a significant price drop. However, it's important to note that trailing stops may not be executed at the desired price if market conditions change rapidly. The order can be filled at a price different from the one specified by the trailing stop due to market conditions such as volatility and liquidity. Additionally, monitoring the trailing stop regularly and adjusting it if necessary is essential.

Ask Price

The asking price, also known as the offer price, is the price at which a seller is willing to sell a security or a financial instrument. It is the lowest price that a seller is willing to accept for the security or instrument. The asking price is typically higher than the bid price, the highest price a buyer is willing to pay for the security or instrument. The difference between the bid and ask prices is known as the bid-ask spread. The asking price is often quoted alongside the bid price and the last traded price in stock market quotes and financial news. The asking price may not be the price at which a stock is sold, as market conditions such as volatility and liquidity may affect the final price of the trade. The asking price is a crucial element of the stock market, as it helps determine the price of a security and the level of demand for that security. When the asking price is high, it indicates less demand for the stock and vice versa. For example, if the asking price of a stock is $50 and the bid price is $49, the seller is willing to sell the stock at

$50, and the buyer is willing to buy the stock at $49. The stock can be sold at $50 or any price between $49 and $50.

Bid Price

The bid price, also known as the bid, is the highest price a buyer is willing to pay for a security or a financial instrument. It is the price a buyer will pay to purchase a security or instrument. The bid price is typically lower than the asking price, which is the price at which a seller is willing to sell the security or instrument. The difference between the bid and ask prices is known as the bid-ask spread. The bid price is often quoted alongside the asking price and the last traded price in stock market quotes and financial news. It is important to note that the bid price may not be the price at which a stock is bought, as market conditions such as volatility and liquidity may affect the final price of the trade. Bid prices are crucial elements of the stock market, as they help determine the price of a security and the level of demand for that security. When the bid price is high, it indicates more demand for the stock and vice versa. For example, if the bid price of a stock is $50 and the asking price is $51, the buyer is willing to pay $50 to buy the stock, and the seller is willing to sell the stock at $51. The stock can be purchased at $50 or between $50 and $51.

Good for Day

Good for the day (GFD) is an order type that allows traders to buy or sell a stock on the same day, and if the order is not filled, it will be cancelled at the end of the trading day. This is the default order type for most online trading platforms and is commonly used for day trading, which involves buying and selling securities within the same day. GFD orders are helpful for day traders because they ensure that the trader's positions will be closed by the end of the trading day, regardless of whether the order is filled. This can help traders to manage their risk and avoid overnight exposure to market movements. However, GFD orders may not be executed at the desired price if market conditions change rapidly and the order can be filled

extended period. However, GTC orders may not be executed at the desired price if market conditions change rapidly, and the order can be filled at a different price than the one specified by the GTC due to market conditions such as volatility and liquidity.

Immediate or Cancel

Immediate or cancel (IOC) is an order type that allows traders to buy or sell a stock at a specific price, and the order must be filled immediately, or it will be cancelled. This order type is less common than the good-for-day (GFD) order, which is usually the default option for online trading platforms and the most frequently used for day trading, which involves buying and selling securities within the same trading day. IOC orders are helpful for traders who want to buy or sell stock quickly and at a specific price. This order type is typically used when a trader wants to take advantage of a sudden price movement or when the trader wants to exit a position quickly. When an IOC order is placed, the trader's brokerage will try to fill the order immediately at the specified price or better. If the order cannot be filled immediately, it will be cancelled. If the trader wants to buy a stock at $50 and the current bid price is $49.50, the order will be filled at $49.50. It will be cancelled if the order cannot be filled at $49.50. IOC orders may not be executed at the desired price if market conditions change rapidly, and the order can be filled at a different price than the one specified by the IOC due to market conditions such as volatility and liquidity.

Extended-Hours Day

Extended-hours trading refers to buying and selling securities outside the regular stock market hours, typically the premarket session (before the market opens) and the after-hours session (after the market closes). During extended hours of trading, the prices of securities can be more volatile, and there can be less liquidity, which means that it may be harder to buy or sell a stock at a specific price or in a particular quantity. Additionally, there may be less information about the companies whose stocks are being traded, as there is no regulatory requirement for companies to release information outside regular market hours. It is essential to understand that not all stocks are available for trading during extended hours, and some brokerage firms may have different rules and restrictions around extended-hours trading. Therefore, checking with your brokerage firm for their specific policies and procedures before engaging in extended-hours trading is essential.

Extended Hours Immediate or Cancel

Extended hours immediate or cancel (IOC) is an order type that allows traders to buy or sell stock during extended hours trading at a specific price, and the order must be filled immediately, or it will be cancelled. This type is similar to the regular market hours' IOC order, allowing traders to buy or sell stock quickly and at a specific price. However, during extended hours of trading, prices of securities can be more volatile, and there may be less liquidity, which makes it harder to buy or sell a stock at a specific price or in a specific quantity. Additionally, there may be less information about the companies whose stocks are being traded, as there is no regulatory requirement for companies to release information outside regular market hours. When an extended hours IOC order is placed, the trader's brokerage will try to fill the order immediately at the specified price or better. If the order cannot be filled immediately, it will be cancelled.

FUNDAMENTALS OF RISK MANAGEMENT

Risk management is a fundamental aspect of successful investing, aiming to identify, assess, mitigate, and monitor investment risks to protect capital and achieve long-term financial objectives. Understanding the fundamentals of risk management is essential for investors to navigate the complexities of the financial markets, preserve wealth, and make informed investment decisions. Here's a detailed description of the fundamental principles and strategies of risk management:

Identifying investment risks: The first step in risk management is identifying potential risks affecting your investment portfolio. Investment risks can arise from various sources, including:

- Market risk is fluctuations in stock prices, interest rates, currency exchange rates, and commodity prices that impact the overall value of investment assets.
- Credit risk is the risk of default or credit deterioration by bond issuers or counterparties, which can lead to potential losses on fixed-income investments.
- Liquidity risk is the risk of being unable to buy or sell assets at desired prices due to insufficient market depth, which can result in increased transaction costs or price volatility.
- Inflation risk is the risk that inflation erodes the purchasing power of investment returns over time, reducing the actual value of investment income and principal.
- Operational risk is the risk of losses from internal errors, system failures, fraud, legal disputes, or regulatory compliance failures within investment firms or financial institutions.

By identifying and understanding different types of investment risks, investors can assess their exposure, evaluate potential impacts on their portfolios, and implement risk mitigation strategies accordingly.

Assessing risk tolerance and appetite: Risk tolerance refers to an investor's willingness and ability to accept fluctuations in investment returns and tolerate potential losses in pursuit of higher long-term returns. Risk appetite refers to an investor's preference for assuming certain risks based on their investment objectives, time horizon, and financial circumstances. Assessing risk tolerance and appetite involves understanding your investment goals, time horizon, financial situation, income needs, liquidity requirements, and emotional capacity to withstand market volatility and uncertainty. Investors with higher risk tolerance may allocate more of their portfolio to equities, growth-oriented assets, and alternative investments. In comparison, those with lower risk tolerance may favor more conservative investments, such as bonds, cash, and defensive stocks.

Implementing Risk Mitigation Strategies

Once investment risks have been identified and assessed, investors can implement risk mitigation strategies to minimize potential losses and protect their capital. Standard risk mitigation strategies include:

- Diversification spreads investment capital across different asset classes, sectors, industries, and geographic regions to reduce concentration risk and enhance portfolio resilience.
- Asset allocation is the strategic allocation of investment capital across asset classes (e.g., stocks, bonds, cash, and real estate) based on risk-return objectives, investment horizons, and market conditions.
- Position sizing is the control of the size of individual investments within a portfolio to limit exposure to specific risks and manage portfolio volatility.
- Hedging uses derivative instruments, such as options, futures, and swaps, to protect against adverse price movements, hedge against specific risks, or generate additional income.
- Risk-adjusted return analysis evaluates investment opportunities based on their risk-adjusted return potential, considering both expected returns and associated risks to optimize portfolio performance.

By incorporating risk mitigation strategies into their investment approach, investors can improve portfolio diversification, reduce downside risk, and enhance the risk-return profile of their investment portfolios.

Monitoring and Reviewing Risks

Risk management is an ongoing process that requires regular monitoring and review of investment risks, market conditions, and portfolio performance. Investors should continually assess changes in risk factors, market dynamics, and economic trends that may impact their investment objectives and adjust their risk management strategies accordingly. Conduct periodic portfolio reviews, performance evaluations, and stress tests to identify emerging risks, rebalance asset allocations, and make necessary adjustments to maintain alignment with investment goals and risk tolerance levels. Stay informed about macroeconomic indicators, geopolitical events, regulatory developments, and industry trends that may affect investment markets and adjust portfolio positioning accordingly to mitigate downside risks and capitalize on opportunities.

Mastering the fundamentals of risk management is essential for investors to navigate the uncertainties of the financial markets, protect capital, and achieve long-term investment success. By identifying, assessing, mitigating, and monitoring investment risks, investors can make informed decisions, build resilient portfolios, and confidently pursue their financial objectives. Whether a novice investor or a seasoned trader, incorporating risk management principles into your investment strategy is critical for managing volatility, preserving wealth, and achieving sustainable growth over time.

This chapter has provided a comprehensive roadmap for initiating your investment journey. By exploring 'Setting Investment Goals', you've learned the importance of defining clear objectives that align with your financial aspirations. These goals will be the cornerstone of your investment strategy, guiding your decisions and helping you stay focused on your long-term vision.

We then navigated the 'Choosing a Brokerage Account' process, emphasizing the significance of selecting a platform that matches your investment style and needs. Whether you opt for a full-service broker, a discount platform, or an online trading account, the right brokerage is essential for efficient trading and effective portfolio management.

The next crucial step is understanding 'How to Buy and Sell Stocks'. We've broken down the process of executing trades, from selecting stocks to placing various orders. Mastering these fundamentals ensures you can make informed trading decisions and confidently manage your investments.

Lastly, we covered the 'Fundamentals of Risk Management', an indispensable element of successful investing. By learning how to diversify your portfolio, set appropriate stop-loss levels, and assess your risk tolerance, you are better equipped to navigate market fluctuations and protect your investments.

It has laid the groundwork for a structured and strategic approach to investing. With clear goals, the proper brokerage account, a solid understanding of stock transactions, and effective risk management techniques, you are now prepared to take informed and deliberate steps in the stock market. As you move forward, these principles will help you build a resilient investment strategy and work towards achieving your financial objectives.

Chapter 5

FUNDAMENTAL ANALYSIS

Fundamental analysis is a cornerstone of investment research, focusing on the intrinsic value of a company and its underlying financial performance to assess investment opportunities. In this chapter, we will explore the principles of fundamental analysis, including the evaluation of financial statements, assessment of company performance, and interpretation of economic indicators. Whether you're a beginner seeking to understand the fundamentals of company analysis or an experienced investor looking to refine your analytical skills, this chapter will provide valuable insights and practical techniques to make informed investment decisions based on fundamental analysis.

'Introduction to Fundamental Analysis' explains fundamental analysis as an investment approach that involves examining the underlying fundamentals of a company to determine its intrinsic value and assess its investment potential. Unlike technical analysis, which focuses on price patterns and market sentiment, fundamental analysis seeks to understand the economic, industry, and company-specific factors that drive a company's financial performance and prospects. By analyzing key financial metrics, evaluating business fundamentals, and assessing qualitative factors, fundamental analysts aim to identify undervalued or overvalued stocks and make investment decisions based on the underlying fundamentals of the companies.

'Evaluating Financial Statements', including the income statement, balance sheet, and cash flow statement, provides a comprehensive view of a company's financial health, operating performance, and cash flow dynamics. Fundamental analysts analyze financial statements to assess profitability, liquidity, solvency, and operational efficiency; identify trends and patterns; and compare company performance with industry peers and benchmarks. Analysts can gain insights into a company's financial strength, stability, and growth potential by scrutinizing revenue growth, profit margins, asset quality, debt levels, and cash flow generation.

'Assessing Company Performance' involves evaluating various quantitative and qualitative factors that impact a company's competitive position, market share, growth prospects, and long-term sustainability. Fundamental analysts examine industry dynamics, competitive advantages, business models, management quality, product innovation, customer relationships, and regulatory environment to assess a company's intrinsic value and investment attractiveness. By conducting thorough due diligence and industry research, analysts can identify companies with strong fundamentals, sustainable competitive advantages, and attractive growth opportunities.

'Understanding Economic Indicators' covers key metrics and data points that provide insights into the health and direction of the broader economy, industry sectors, and financial markets. Fundamental analysts monitor economic indicators, such as GDP growth, inflation rate, unemployment rate, consumer spending, interest rates, and business sentiment, to gauge economic trends, identify potential risks and opportunities, and adjust investment strategies accordingly. Analysts can anticipate market trends, assess investment risks, and make informed decisions based on macroeconomic fundamentals by understanding the relationship between economic indicators and financial markets.

INTRODUCTION TO FUNDAMENTAL ANALYSIS

Fundamental analysis is a cornerstone of investment research. It focuses on a company's intrinsic value and financial performance to assess investment opportunities. Unlike technical analysis, which relies on price patterns and market sentiment, fundamental analysis delves into the economic, industry, and company-specific factors that drive a company's financial health and prospects.

Critical concepts of fundamental analysis include the following:

- **Intrinsic value:** At the core of fundamental analysis is the concept of intrinsic value, which represents the true worth of a company's stock based on its underlying fundamentals. Intrinsic value is determined by analyzing earnings, cash flow, assets, growth potential, competitive position, and industry dynamics. Fundamental analysts seek to identify companies whose intrinsic value exceeds their current market price, indicating potential undervaluation and investment opportunities.
- **Financial statements:** Financial statements, including the income statement, balance sheet, and cash flow statement, are primary sources of information for fundamental analysis. These statements provide insights into a company's revenue, expenses, assets, liabilities, and cash flows over a specific period. Fundamental analysts analyze financial statements to assess profitability, liquidity, solvency, and operational efficiency; identify trends; and compare company performance with industry benchmarks and competitors.
- **Key financial metrics:** Fundamental analysis involves evaluating a range of financial metrics to gauge a company's financial health and performance. Key metrics include:
    - **Earnings per share (EPS):** Net income divided by the number of outstanding shares, indicating profitability on a per-share basis.

    - **Price-to-earnings (P/E) ratio:** The ratio of a company's stock price to its earnings per share, reflecting investors' expectations of future earnings growth.
    - **Price-to-book (P/B) ratio:** The ratio of a company's stock price to its book value per share, indicating the value investors pay for each asset dollar.
    - **Return on equity (ROE):** Net income divided by shareholders' equity, measuring a company's ability to generate profits from shareholders' investments.
    - **Debt-to-equity (D/E) ratio:** The ratio of a company's total debt to its shareholders' equity, assessing its financial leverage and solvency.
- **Industry and competitive Analysis:** Fundamental analysts conduct industry and competitive analysis to assess a company's competitive position, market share, growth prospects, and long-term sustainability. They evaluate industry dynamics, market trends, competitive landscape, regulatory environment, technological innovation, and barriers to entry to identify companies with competitive advantages and strong growth potential.
- **Qualitative factors:** Besides quantitative analysis, fundamental analysis incorporates qualitative factors such as management quality, corporate governance, business model, brand reputation, customer relationships, and innovation capabilities. Fundamental analysts assess management's strategic vision, execution capabilities, integrity, and alignment with shareholders' interests to evaluate a company's long-term prospects and sustainability.
- **Economic and market trends:** Fundamental analysis considers macroeconomic factors, market trends, and geopolitical events that may impact a company's business operations, industry dynamics, and financial performance. Analysts monitor economic indicators, such as GDP growth, inflation rate, interest rates, consumer spending, and business

sentiment, to assess the economy's overall health and anticipate potential risks and opportunities for investment.

The fundamental analysis provides investors with a systematic approach to evaluating investment opportunities based on the underlying fundamentals of companies and economies. By analyzing financial statements, assessing vital financial metrics, conducting industry and competitive analysis, considering qualitative factors, and monitoring economic trends, fundamental analysts seek to identify undervalued or overvalued stocks and make informed investment decisions based on the intrinsic value of the companies. Whether you're a value investor seeking bargains or a growth investor focusing on high-growth companies, fundamental analysis is essential for identifying quality investments and building a successful investment portfolio.

EVALUATING FINANCIAL STATEMENTS

Financial statements are comprehensive reports that provide insights into a company's financial performance, position, and cash flow activities over a specific period. Analyzing financial statements is a critical component of fundamental analysis, enabling investors to assess a company's profitability, liquidity, solvency, efficiency, and overall economic health. Here's a detailed description of key components and techniques for evaluating financial statements:

- **Income statement analysis:** The income statement, or the profit-and-loss statement, summarizes a company's revenues, expenses, and net income over a specified period, typically quarterly or annually. Fundamental analysts analyze the income statement to assess a company's profitability, revenue growth, expense management, and operating efficiency.

Key metrics evaluated from the income statement include:

- Revenue: Total sales or revenue from its core business operations.
- Cost of goods sold (COGS): Direct costs associated with producing goods or services, including raw materials, labor, and manufacturing expenses.
- Gross profit: Revenue minus COGS, representing the profit margin before deducting operating expenses.
- Operating expenses: Costs incurred in running the business's day-to-day operations, such as salaries, rent, utilities, and marketing expenses.
- Operating income: Gross profit minus operating expenses, indicating the profitability of core business operations.
- Net income: Total profit after deducting all expenses, taxes, and interest, reflecting the bottom-line profitability of the company.

- **Balance sheet analysis:** The balance sheet provides a snapshot of a company's financial position at a specific time, detailing its assets, liabilities, and shareholders' equity. Fundamental analysts analyze the balance sheet to assess a company's liquidity, solvency, leverage, and asset quality.

Key metrics evaluated from the balance sheet include:

a) **Assets:** Resources owned or controlled by the company, including cash, accounts receivable, inventory, property, plant, and equipment.
b) **Liabilities:** Obligations owed by the company to creditors, suppliers, and lenders, such as accounts payable, loans, bonds, and accrued expenses.

c) **Shareholders' equity:** The residual value of assets after deducting liabilities, representing shareholders' ownership in the company.
d) **Liquidity ratios:** Measures of a company's ability to meet short-term financial obligations, such as the current ratio (current assets divided by current liabilities) and the quick ratio (liquid assets divided by current liabilities).
e) **Solvency ratios:** Measures of a company's ability to meet long-term financial obligations and withstand financial distress, such as the debt-to-equity ratio (total debt divided by shareholders' equity) and interest coverage ratio (earnings before interest and taxes divided by interest expense).

- **Cash flow statement analysis:** The cash flow statement provides a detailed account of a company's cash inflows and outflows from operating, investing, and financing activities during a specific period. Fundamental analysts analyze the cash flow statement to assess a company's cash flow generation, liquidity, capital expenditures, debt repayment capacity, and dividend sustainability.

Key metrics evaluated from the cash flow statement include:

- o **Operating cash flow:** Cash generated or used by the company's core business operations, excluding noncash expenses and working capital changes.
- o **Investing cash flow:** Cash used for investing activities, such as capital expenditures, acquisitions, and investments in securities.
- o **Financing cash flow:** Cash used for financing activities, such as debt issuance, equity issuance, dividend payments, and share repurchases.
- o **Free cash flow:** Operating cash flow minus capital expenditures, representing the cash available for debt

repayment, dividend distribution, share buybacks, or reinvestment in the business.

- **Ratio analysis:** Ratio analysis involves calculating and interpreting financial ratios derived from the financial statements to assess various aspects of a company's financial performance, position, and efficiency. Fundamental analysts use ratios to compare a company's performance with industry peers, historical trends, and benchmarks; identify trends; and pinpoint areas of strength or weakness. Standard financial ratios analyzed include profitability ratios (e.g. return on equity and gross margin), liquidity ratios (e.g. current ratio and quick ratio), solvency ratios (e.g. debt-to-equity ratio and interest coverage ratio), efficiency ratios (e.g. inventory turnover and accounts receivable turnover), and valuation ratios (e.g. price-to-earnings ratio and price-to-book ratio).
- **Trend analysis and comparative analysis:** Fundamental analysts perform trend analysis and comparative analysis to evaluate changes in financial performance over time and compare a company's performance against industry peers, competitors, and benchmarks. Trend analysis involves examining historical financial data to identify patterns, trends, and anomalies in key financial metrics and assess the direction and magnitude of changes over multiple periods. Comparative analysis involves comparing a company's financial ratios, operating metrics, and performance indicators with similar companies within the same industry or sector to assess relative strengths and weaknesses, competitive positioning, and valuation metrics.

By conducting a thorough analysis of financial statements, including the income statement, balance sheet, and cash flow statement, and applying techniques such as ratio analysis, trend analysis, and comparative analysis, fundamental analysts can gain valuable insights into a company's financial performance, position, and prospects. Evaluating financial statements provides investors with the information needed to make reliable investment decisions, identify quality investment opportunities, and build diversified portfolios based on sound fundamental analysis principles.

ASSESSING COMPANY PERFORMANCE

Assessing company performance is a crucial aspect of fundamental analysis, enabling investors to evaluate a company's financial health, operational efficiency, competitive position, and growth prospects. By analyzing key performance indicators and qualitative factors, investors can gain insights into a company's ability to generate profits, sustain growth, and create shareholder value over time. Here's a detailed description of key factors and techniques for assessing company performance:

- **Revenue growth:** Revenue growth is a fundamental measure of a company's top-line performance, reflecting its ability to increase sales and expand its customer base. Fundamental analysts assess revenue growth trends, including historical growth rates, quarterly fluctuations, and forecasted growth projections, to gauge the company's market share, competitive position, and growth potential. Factors influencing revenue growth include product innovation, market demand, pricing strategies, customer retention, and expansion into new markets or product lines.
- **Profitability:** Profitability metrics measure a company's ability to generate profits from its core business operations and efficiently utilize its resources to maximize shareholder returns.

Key profitability ratios analyzed by fundamental analysts include:

- **Gross profit margin:** Gross profit divided by revenue, indicating the percentage of revenue retained after deducting the cost of goods sold (COGS).
- **Operating profit margin:** Operating income divided by revenue, measuring the efficiency of operating expenses relative to revenue.
- **Net profit margin:** Net income divided by revenue, representing the percentage of revenue converted into net profit after deducting all costs. Analysts evaluate profitability ratios to assess the company's pricing power, cost management, efficiency, and competitive advantage compared to industry peers and benchmarks.
- **Return on investment (ROI):** Return on investment (ROI) measures the return generated from investing capital in the company's operations, assets, or projects relative to the initial investment.

Key ROI metrics analyzed by fundamental analysts include:

- **Return on equity (ROE):** Net income divided by shareholders' equity, indicating the return generated on shareholders' investments.
- **Return on assets (ROA):** Net income divided by total assets, measuring asset utilization efficiency in generating profits.
- **Return on invested capital (ROIC):** Operating income divided by invested capital, assessing the return generated on all invested capital, including equity and debt. High ROI ratios indicate effective capital allocation, operational efficiency, and shareholder value creation.
- **Cash flow generation:** Cash flow generation is a critical measure of a company's ability to generate cash from its business operations, manage working capital, fund investments, and meet financial obligations. Fundamental

analysts assess cash flow metrics, such as operating cash flow, free cash flow, and cash conversion cycle, to evaluate liquidity, solvency, and financial flexibility. Positive cash flow indicates healthy cash generation, while negative cash flow may signal liquidity constraints, economic distress, or aggressive growth strategies requiring external financing.

- **Balance sheet strength:** The balance sheet provides insights into a company's financial position, including its asset base, debt levels, and capital structure. Fundamental analysts assess balance sheet strength by analyzing liquidity, solvency, leverage, and asset quality metrics, such as:
    - **Current ratio:** Current assets divided by current liabilities, measuring the company's ability to meet short-term financial obligations.
    - **Debt-to-equity ratio:** Total debt divided by shareholders' equity, indicating the proportion of financing provided by debt versus equity.
    - **Interest coverage ratio**: Earnings before interest and taxes (EBIT) divided by interest expense, assessing the company's ability to cover interest payments with operating profits.
    - **Asset turnover ratio:** Revenue divided by total assets, measuring asset utilization efficiency in generating revenue.

A strong balance sheet with manageable debt levels, ample liquidity, and solid asset quality provides a foundation for sustainable growth and resilience against economic downturns.

- **Growth prospects and competitive position:** Assessing a company's growth prospects and position involves analyzing industry dynamics, market trends, competitive landscape, product differentiation, and strategic initiatives. Fundamental analysts evaluate factors such as market share, customer loyalty, brand reputation, technological innovation, regulatory environment, and barriers to entry to assess the company's ability to maintain or enhance its competitive advantage and capture market opportunities. Companies with strong competitive positions, innovative product offerings, and sustainable growth prospects are better positioned to create long-term shareholder value.

Assessing company performance involves analyzing vital financial metrics, profitability indicators, cash flow generation, balance sheet strength, growth prospects, and competitive positioning to evaluate a company's financial health, operational efficiency, and value-creation potential. By conducting thorough analysis and applying qualitative judgment, fundamental analysts can identify quality companies with solid fundamentals, sustainable competitive advantages, and attractive investment opportunities. Assessing company performance is critical in fundamental analysis, enabling investors to make informed investment decisions and build successful portfolios based on sound financial analysis principles.

UNDERSTANDING ECONOMIC INDICATORS

Economic indicators are key metrics and data points that provide insights into the health, direction, and performance of the broader economy, industry sectors, and financial markets. Fundamental analysts and investors closely monitor economic indicators to assess macroeconomic trends, anticipate changes in market conditions, and make informed investment decisions.

Types of Economic Indicators

Economic indicators are classified into three main categories based on their timing, relevance, and impact on economic activity:

- **Leading indicators:** Leading indicators precede changes in economic activity and provide early signals of future economic trends. Examples include stock market indices, consumer confidence surveys, business sentiment surveys, and building permits.

- **Lagging indicators:** Lagging indicators follow changes in economic activity and confirm prevailing trends. Examples include unemployment, inflation, corporate earnings, GDP growth, and interest rates.
- **Coincident indicators:** Coincident indicators move with economic activity changes and reflect the current economy. Examples include industrial production, retail sales, personal income, and manufacturing activity.

Key Economic Indicators

- **Gross domestic product (GDP):** GDP measures the total value of goods and services produced within a country's borders over a specific period. It is considered the most comprehensive measure of economic output and growth.
- **Unemployment rate:** The unemployment rate measures the percentage of the labor force that is unemployed and actively seeking employment. It reflects labor market conditions, job creation, and economic health.
- **Consumer price index (CPI):** CPI measures changes in the prices of a basket of consumer goods and services over time and verifies inflationary pressures on consumer purchasing power.
- **Producer price index (PPI):** PPI measures changes in the prices producers receive for goods and services sold at the wholesale level. It provides insights into inflationary pressures in the production process.
- **Interest rates:** Central banks use interest rates to control monetary policy, stimulate economic growth, and manage inflation. Changes in interest rates influence borrowing costs, consumer spending, investment decisions, and currency exchange rates.

- **Retail sales:** Retail sales measure retailers' total sales of goods and services to consumers and provide insights into consumer spending patterns, confidence levels, and overall economic activity.
- **Industrial production:** Industrial production measures the output of manufacturing, mining, and utilities and serves as a leading indicator of economic activity and business investment.
- **Housing market indicators:** Housing market indicators, such as housing starts, building permits, home sales, and home prices, provide insights into the health of the real estate market, construction activity, and consumer sentiment.

Significance of Economic Indicators

Economic indicators are critical in guiding monetary policy decisions, fiscal policy initiatives, business planning, investment strategies, and risk management practices. They provide valuable insights into the overall health and direction of the economy, helping policymakers, businesses, investors, and consumers anticipate changes in economic conditions and adjust their actions accordingly. Economic indicators influence financial markets, asset prices, interest rates, currency exchange rates, and investor sentiment, driving market volatility and investment returns. By analyzing economic indicators, investors can identify trends, assess risks, identify investment opportunities, and allocate capital strategically across asset classes, sectors, and regions.

Interpreting Economic Indicators

Interpreting economic indicators involves analyzing trends, comparing data points with historical averages and consensus forecasts, and understanding the underlying drivers and implications for the economy and financial markets. Fundamental analysts use economic indicators to develop macroeconomic forecasts, assess business cycle phases, identify potential risks and opportunities, and adjust investment strategies based on changing market conditions. Investors should consider economic indicators' reliability, accuracy, timeliness, relevance, and potential impact on specific sectors, industries, and asset classes when making investment decisions. Understanding economic indicators is essential for investors to navigate the financial markets' complexities, anticipate economic conditions changes, and make informed investment decisions. By monitoring vital economic indicators, assessing their significance, and interpreting their implications for the economy and financial markets, investors can gain valuable insights into macroeconomic trends, identify investment opportunities, and manage investment risks effectively. Whether you're a long-term investor, trader, or economist, a solid understanding of economic indicators is critical for building successful investment strategies and achieving financial goals in dynamic and evolving market environments. Fundamental analysis has provided a comprehensive toolkit for evaluating investment opportunities by thoroughly examining company performance and economic conditions. By delving into the core principles of fundamental analysis, this chapter has equipped you with the essential skills to make informed investment decisions based on a company's intrinsic value and broader economic context.

We began with an introduction to fundamental analysis, establishing it as a crucial method for assessing a stock's underlying value by examining its financial health, operational performance, and market position. This analytical approach helps investors identify undervalued stocks and avoid overvalued ones.

The chapter then explored the intricacies of evaluating financial statements. You learned how to gauge a company's profitability, liquidity, and overall economic stability by dissecting balance sheets, income statements, and cash flow statements. Understanding these documents is pivotal in assessing a company's value and making well-informed investment choices.

Assessing company performance was the next focus. We examined key financial metrics and ratios, such as earnings per share (EPS), price-to-earnings (P/E) ratio, and return on equity (ROE). These indicators provide insights into a company's operational efficiency, growth potential, and investment attractiveness.

Finally, we discussed the role of economic indicators in fundamental analysis. Understanding macroeconomic factors such as GDP growth, inflation rates, and unemployment levels helps contextualize a company's performance within the broader economic environment. This knowledge is vital for anticipating market trends and making strategic investment decisions.

This chapter has laid a solid foundation in fundamental analysis, empowering you to evaluate companies comprehensively and strategically. By mastering the analysis of financial statements, assessing company performance, and understanding economic indicators, you are well-positioned to make informed investment decisions and identify opportunities that align with your financial goals.

Chapter 6

TECHNICAL ANALYSIS

Technical analysis is a powerful tool traders and investors use to analyze historical price data, identify patterns, trends, and trading signals, and make informed decisions about buying and selling financial assets. In this chapter, we will introduce technical analysis, analyze chart patterns and trends, explore the use of technical indicators and oscillators, and discuss developing technical analysis trading strategies based on technical analysis principles. Whether you're a beginner seeking to understand the basics of technical analysis or an experienced trader looking to refine your technical analysis skills, this chapter will equip you with the knowledge and techniques to navigate the financial markets confidently.

Introduction to Technical Analysis

Technical analysis is a methodology for evaluating financial markets and forecasting future price movements based on historical price data, trading volume, and market psychology. Unlike fundamental analysis, which focuses on analyzing the intrinsic value of assets, technical analysis relies primarily on price action and market trends to make trading decisions. Analysts study charts, patterns, and technical indicators to identify trends, support and resistance levels, and trading signals.

Technical indicators and oscillators are essential analytical tools in trading and investing. These mathematical calculations are applied to historical price and volume data to generate actionable trading signals, enabling investors to make informed decisions based on market behavior. Technical indicators encompass various metrics that help traders identify trends, assess market conditions, and predict price movements.

Developing Technical Analysis Trading Strategies

Developing technical analysis trading strategies involves combining technical analysis tools, chart patterns, and trading signals to create a systematic approach to trading financial markets. Traders use technical analysis to identify entry and exit points, set stop-loss orders, manage risk, and optimize trade execution based on their trading objectives, risk tolerance, and market conditions. Successful trading strategies incorporate sound risk management principles, clear trading rules, disciplined execution, and continuous evaluation and refinement based on performance metrics and feedback.

Technical analysis is a valuable tool for traders and investors to analyze financial markets, identify trading opportunities, and make informed decisions based on price action, chart patterns, and technical indicators. By understanding the principles of technical analysis, including the analysis of chart patterns and trends, the use of technical indicators and oscillators, and the development of trading strategies, traders can gain a competitive edge in the financial markets and achieve their trading objectives with greater precision and confidence. Whether you're a short-term trader, swing trader, or long-term investor, mastering the principles of technical analysis can enhance your trading skills and improve your ability to navigate the dynamic and ever-changing landscape of the financial markets.

INTRODUCTION TO TECHNICAL ANALYSIS

Technical analysis is a methodology traders and investors use to analyze financial markets and forecast future price movements based on historical price data, trading volume, and market psychology. Unlike fundamental analysis, which focuses on analyzing the intrinsic value of assets, technical analysis relies primarily on the study of price action and market trends to make trading decisions. Here's a detailed description of key concepts and principles of technical analysis:

Price-action analysis: Price-action analysis is at the core of technical analysis, focusing on studying past price movements and patterns to predict price movements. Technical analysts believe price action reflects all available information and market sentiment, making it the primary indicator of market dynamics. By analyzing price patterns, trends, support and resistance levels, and chart formations, technical analysts aim to identify trading opportunities and forecast future price movements.

Assumptions of technical analysis: Technical analysis is based on several key assumptions, including:

- **Market efficiency:** Technical analysts believe that market prices reflect all available information and that price movements are not entirely random.
- **Price trends:** Technical analysts assume that prices tend to move in trends upwards (bullish), downwards (bearish), or sideways (range-bound).
- **History repeats itself:** Technical analysts believe that price patterns and trends tend to repeat over time due to recurring investor behavior and market psychology.

Tools and techniques: Technical analysts use various tools and techniques to analyze price data and identify trading opportunities, including:

- Price charts, such as line, bar, and candlestick charts, visually represent price movements over time.
- Chart patterns, such as trendlines, support and resistance levels, head-and-shoulders patterns, and continuation patterns, help identify potential trend reversals and trading opportunities.
- Technical indicators, such as moving averages, oscillators (e.g. RSI and MACD), and volume indicators help quantify price momentum, trend strength, and market sentiment.
- Volume analysis examines trading volume patterns to confirm price trends, identify accumulation or distribution phases, and assess the strength of price movements.

Behavioral finance and market psychology: Technical analysis incorporates principles of behavioral finance and market psychology to understand investor behavior and market dynamics. Technical analysts study investor sentiment, market cycles, and psychological biases, such as fear, greed, and herd behavior, to anticipate changes in market direction and identify contrarian trading opportunities. Understanding market psychology helps technical analysts interpret price patterns, chart formations, and trading signals within prevailing market sentiment and investor behavior.

Limitations of technical analysis: While technical analysis is a valuable tool for short-term trading and identifying trends, it has limitations, including:

- **Subjectivity:** Technical analysis involves interpreting price data and chart patterns, which can be subjective and prone to individual biases.
- **Lagging indicators:** Many technical indicators are based on historical price data and may lag behind actual market movements, leading to delayed signals.
- **Market noise:** Financial markets can be noisy and unpredictable, and it is challenging to distinguish between genuine trading signals and random price fluctuations.

- **External factors**: Technical analysis may not fully account for external factors, such as macroeconomic events, geopolitical developments, or unexpected news events, influencing market behavior.

Technical analysis is a valuable tool for traders and investors to analyze financial markets; identify trading opportunities; and make informed decisions based on price action, chart patterns, and technical indicators. By understanding the principles of technical analysis, including price action analysis, key assumptions, tools and techniques, market psychology, and limitations, traders can develop effective trading strategies and enhance their ability to navigate the dynamic and ever-changing landscape of financial markets.

CHART PATTERNS AND TRENDS

Chart patterns and trends are fundamental concepts in technical analysis, which traders and investors use to identify potential trading opportunities, forecast price movements, and make informed decisions in financial markets. By analyzing historical price data and observing recurring patterns and trends, technical analysts aim to gain insights into market dynamics, investor sentiment, and potential price direction.

Trend analysis refers to the general direction in which prices move over time. Trends can be classified into three main categories:

- **Uptrend:** A series of higher highs and higher lows, indicating bullish momentum and investor optimism.
- **Downtrend:** A series of lower highs and lower lows, indicating bearish momentum and investor pessimism.
- **Sideways (or range-bound):** Prices move within a horizontal trading range with no clear direction or trend.

Trend analysis helps traders and investors identify the prevailing market direction, assess the trend's strength, and make trading decisions based on the trend's momentum.

Chart patterns are formations or configurations of price movements on a price chart that indicate potential trend reversals or continuation patterns. Common chart patterns include:

- **Head and shoulders**: Characterized by three peaks, with the middle peak (head) higher than the other two (shoulders), signaling a potential trend reversal from bullish to bearish.
- **Double top and double bottom:** Patterns formed by two consecutive peaks (double top) or troughs (double bottom), indicating potential trend reversals.
- **Flags and pennants:** Consolidation patterns that form after a firm price movement, signaling a temporary pause before continuing the prevailing trend.
- **Triangles (ascending, descending, symmetrical):** Patterns characterized by converging trendlines, indicating tightening price ranges and potential breakout opportunities. Traders use chart patterns to identify critical support and resistance levels, anticipate trend reversals or breakouts, and determine entry and exit points for trades.

Trendlines are diagonal lines drawn on a price chart to connect successive highs or lows, providing visual representations of trend direction and support/resistance levels. Upward-sloping trendlines connect consecutive higher lows in an uptrend, serving as dynamic support levels. Downward-sloping trendlines connect consecutive lower highs in a downtrend, acting as dynamic resistance levels. Traders use trendlines to identify trend reversals, confirm trend continuations, and set stop-loss orders or profit targets.

Importance of Chart Patterns and Trends

Chart patterns and trends are essential for technical analysts to assess market sentiment, identify trading opportunities, and manage risk. Recognizing chart patterns and trends allows traders to anticipate price movements, validate trading signals, and adjust trading strategies accordingly. Chart patterns and trends provide valuable insights into market psychology, investor behavior, and supply-and-demand dynamics, helping traders make informed decisions in fast-paced and volatile market environments. By combining chart patterns and trend analysis with other technical indicators and risk management techniques, traders can develop robust trading strategies and achieve consistent profitability in financial markets.

Limitations of Chart Patterns and Trends

While chart patterns and trends can provide valuable insights into market dynamics, they are not foolproof indicators and may sometimes produce false signals. Market conditions, news events, and unexpected developments can influence price movements and invalidate chart patterns or trend signals. Traders should exercise caution and use additional confirmation tools and risk management strategies to validate trading signals and minimize potential losses. Chart patterns and trends are essential components of technical analysis that traders and investors use to analyze market behavior, identify trading opportunities, and make informed decisions in financial markets. By understanding the significance of chart patterns and trend analysis and their role in technical analysis, traders can enhance their ability to navigate market trends, anticipate price movements, and achieve their trading objectives with greater precision and confidence.

TECHNICAL INDICATORS AND OSCILLATORS

Technical indicators and oscillators are quantitative tools traders and investors use in technical analysis to analyze historical price data, identify trends, measure market momentum, and generate trading signals. These indicators help traders make informed decisions about buying and selling financial assets by objectively measuring market conditions and potential price movements. Here's a detailed description of vital technical indicators and oscillators commonly used in technical analysis:

- **Moving averages:** These are trend-following indicators that smooth out price data by calculating the average price of a security over a specified period.
- **Simple moving average (SMA):** The SMA calculates the average price of a security over a specified number of periods (e.g. 20-day, 50-day, 200-day) and plots the result as a line on a price chart.
- **Exponential moving average (EMA):** The EMA gives more weight to recent price data, making it more responsive to short-term price changes than the SMA. Moving averages help traders identify trend direction, gauge trend strength, and generate trading signals such as moving average crossovers (e.g. golden cross and death cross).
- **Relative strength index (RSI):** It is a momentum oscillator that measures the speed and change of price movements to assess overbought or oversold conditions in the market. The RSI oscillates between 0 and 100 and is calculated based on the ratio of average gains to average losses over a specified period (usually fourteen periods). RSI values above 70 indicate overbought conditions, suggesting that the security may be due for a pullback or reversal, while RSI values below 30 indicate oversold conditions, signaling a potential buying opportunity.

- **Moving average convergence divergence (MACD):** It is a trend-following momentum indicator that measures the relationship between two moving averages. The MACD consists of three components: the MACD line (the difference between the 12-day and 26-day exponential moving averages), the signal line (a 9-day exponential moving average of the MACD line), and the MACD histogram (the difference between the MACD line and the signal line). MACD crossovers and divergences are used to generate buy-and-sell signals, with bullish signals occurring when the MACD line crosses above the signal line (bullish crossover) and bearish signals occurring when the MACD line crosses below the signal line (bearish crossover).
- **Stochastic oscillator:** It is a momentum oscillator that compares a security's closing price to its price range over a specified period to determine overbought or oversold conditions. The stochastic oscillator consists of two lines (%K and %D) oscillating between 0 and 100. The %K line represents the current price relative to the price range, while the %D line is a moving average of the %K line. Stochastic readings above 80 indicate overbought conditions, suggesting that the security may be due for a pullback, while readings below 20 indicate oversold conditions, signaling a potential buying opportunity.
- **Bollinger Bands:** These are volatility bands plotted above and below a moving average to indicate potential overbought or oversold conditions and volatility expansion or contraction. Bollinger Bands consist of three lines: the middle band (a simple moving average), the upper band (the middle band plus two standard deviations), and the lower band (the middle band minus two standard deviations). Bollinger Bands help traders identify price extremes, volatility patterns, and potential reversal points, with price often reverting to the mean (middle band) after reaching the upper or lower band.

- **Volume indicators:** These measure trading volume and its relationship to price movements to assess market participation and confirm price trends. Common volume indicators include on-balance volume (OBV), Chaikin money flow (CMF), and volume-weighted average price (VWAP). Volume analysis helps traders confirm the validity of price movements, identify trend reversals or continuations, and assess market sentiment and liquidity conditions.

These are just a few examples of the technical indicators and oscillators available to traders and investors in technical analysis. By combining multiple indicators, analyzing price patterns, and considering factors such as market fundamentals and risk management principles, traders can develop robust trading strategies and make informed decisions in dynamic and ever-changing financial markets.

DEVELOPING TECHNICAL ANALYSIS TRADING STRATEGIES

Developing technical analysis trading strategies is critical to successful trading, enabling traders to navigate financial markets effectively, capitalize on opportunities, and manage risk. A trading strategy outlines a systematic approach to entering and exiting trades based on predefined rules, criteria, and indicators. Whether you're a novice trader or an experienced investor, developing a well-defined trading strategy is essential for achieving consistent profitability and long-term success in the markets. Here's a detailed description of the key components and steps involved in developing trading strategies:

Define your trading objectives. Before developing a trading strategy, it's essential to define your trading objectives, including your financial goals, risk tolerance, time horizon, and preferred trading style (e.g. day trading, swing trading, and position trading). Clarifying your objectives helps you align your trading strategy with your personal preferences, resources, and constraints, ensuring your approach is realistic and achievable.

Select a trading methodology. Traders have various trading methodologies and approaches available, including technical analysis, fundamental analysis, quantitative analysis, and sentiment analysis. Choose a trading methodology that aligns with your skills, knowledge, and preferences. For example, technical analysis may be suitable if you prefer analyzing price charts and patterns. Fundamental analysis may be more appropriate if you're interested in analyzing company fundamentals and macroeconomic trends.

Identify entry and exit signals. Define straightforward entry and exit signals based on your chosen trading methodology, indicators, and criteria. Entry signals indicate when to enter a trade, while exit signals determine when to exit a trade to capture profits or limit losses. Standard entry signals include moving-average crossovers, breakouts from chart patterns, and oversold/overbought conditions signaled by oscillators like RSI or stochastic. Exit signals may consist of profit targets based on support/resistance levels, trailing stop-loss orders, or reversal signals generated by indicators.

Manage risk. Implement robust risk management strategies to protect your capital and minimize potential losses. Risk management involves determining position size, setting stop-loss orders, and establishing risk-reward ratios for each trade. Calculate position size based on your risk tolerance and the size of your trading account. Many traders limit their risk per trade to a certain percentage of their account balance (e.g. 1–2%). Use stop-loss orders to exit losing trades before losses escalate beyond a predetermined threshold. Traders often place stop-loss orders below support levels for long trades and above resistance levels for short trades.

Perform backtesting and optimization. Backtesting involves testing your trading strategy on historical price data to assess its performance and profitability over time. Use a trading simulator or backtesting software to evaluate your strategy's performance in past market conditions. Based on backtesting results, optimize your trading strategy by adjusting parameters, indicators, and rules. Fine-tune your plan to improve its risk-adjusted returns, win rate, and other performance metrics.

Conduct paper trading and real-time testing. Once you've backtested and optimized your trading strategy, trade or demo it in real-time market conditions to validate its effectiveness and gain practical experience. Paper trading allows you to practice executing trades without risking real money, helping you refine your strategy and gain confidence in your ability to execute trades effectively.

Continuously monitor and evaluate. Monitor the performance of your trading strategy in real-time and evaluate its effectiveness over time. Keep detailed records of your trades, including entry and exit points, trade outcomes, and performance metrics. Review your trading results regularly and adjust your strategy based on changing market conditions, trade feedback, and evolving market dynamics.

Adapt and continuously learn. Financial markets are dynamic, requiring traders to adapt and develop their trading strategies continuously. Stay informed about market developments, economic events, and industry trends to adjust your strategy accordingly. Invest in continuous learning to improve your trading skills, stay abreast of new trading techniques and technologies, and refine your approach over time.

Developing trading strategies involves defining objectives, selecting a methodology, identifying entry and exit signals, implementing risk management, performing backtesting and optimization, conducting paper trading, and continuously monitoring and evaluating. By following these steps and adhering to your trading plan with discipline and patience, you can develop effective trading strategies that align with your goals, preferences, and risk tolerance, increasing your chances of success in the dynamic and competitive world of financial markets. Technical analysis has comprehensively explored the methodologies used to interpret and predict market movements by examining historical price data and trading volumes. We've journeyed through the fundamental technical analysis concepts, including chart patterns and trends that indicate future price movements. The chapter has delved into the tools and techniques of technical indicators and oscillators, which offer insights into market momentum, volatility, and potential reversal points.

Furthermore, we have discussed the critical aspect of developing effective trading strategies grounded in technical analysis principles. By integrating chart patterns, technical indicators, and a solid understanding of market trends, investors and traders can craft strategies that align with their investment goals and risk tolerance.

In conclusion, technical analysis provides a valuable framework for understanding market behavior and making informed trading decisions. Whether you are a novice trader or an experienced investor, mastering technical analysis equips you with the tools to navigate the complexities of the stock market with greater confidence and precision. By applying these techniques, you can better identify opportunities, manage risk, and enhance your overall trading strategy, paving the way for more informed and potentially successful investment endeavors.

Chapter 7

TRADING STRATEGIES

In this chapter, we explore various approaches to trading, from long-term investing to short-term trading techniques. Whether you're a seasoned investor looking to build wealth over the long-term or an active trader seeking to capitalize on short-term market opportunities, this chapter will provide valuable insights into different trading strategies and their fundamental principles. We'll cover topics such as value investing, growth investing, momentum trading, day trading, and scalping, helping you understand the pros and cons of each approach and how to implement them effectively in your trading journey.

'Long-Term Investing vs. Short-Term Trading' examines the fundamental differences between long-term investing and short-term trading. Long-term investing focuses on building wealth over an extended period, typically years or decades, through strategically allocating capital into undervalued assets with solid growth potential. On the other hand, short-term trading involves taking advantage of short-term price fluctuations and market inefficiencies to generate profits over shorter time frames, ranging from minutes to days.

'Value Investing' explores the principles of a strategy popularized by legendary investor Benjamin Graham and his disciple Warren Buffett. Value investing involves identifying undervalued stocks trading below their intrinsic value and holding them long-term, allowing the market to recognize their true worth.

Next, 'Growth Investing' delves into a strategy focused on investing in companies with high growth potential and robust earnings-growth prospects. Growth investors seek companies with innovative products, expanding market opportunities, and substantial competitive advantages, aiming to capitalize on their future growth prospects and outperform the market over time.

'Momentum Trading' is a short-term trading strategy based on the premise that assets that have performed well in the past will continue to perform well shortly. Momentum traders seek to capitalize on the upward momentum of stocks or other assets by buying securities with strong price trends and selling those with weak ones.

Finally, 'Day Trading and Scalping' explores the high-octane world of day trading and scalping, where traders execute multiple trades within a single day, even minutes or seconds. Day traders aim to profit from intraday price movements, leveraging technical analysis tools, chart patterns, and market momentum to identify short-term trading opportunities and capitalize on small price fluctuations.

Throughout this chapter, we'll provide practical insights, tips, and strategies to help you navigate the complexities of different trading approaches and find the ones that best suit your goals, risk tolerance, and trading style. Whether you aim to build long-term wealth through patient investing or seek to generate short-term profits through active trading, mastering these trading strategies will equip you with the knowledge and skills needed to succeed in the dynamic and ever-changing world of financial markets.

LONG-TERM INVESTING VS. SHORT-TERM TRADING STRATEGY

Long-term investing and short-term trading are two distinct approaches to participating in financial markets, each with objectives, strategies, and time horizons. Understanding the differences between these two approaches is essential for investors and traders to align their goals, risk tolerance, and investment strategies with their preferred time frames.

Long-Term Investing

Long-term investing is a strategy focused on building wealth over an extended period, typically years or decades, through strategically allocating capital into assets such as stocks, bonds, mutual funds, and real estate. Long-term investing primarily aims to generate capital appreciation and income over time, allowing investors to achieve their financial goals, such as retirement planning, education funding, or wealth accumulation. Long-term investors take a buy-and-hold approach, investing in fundamentally sound companies or assets with solid growth potential, durable competitive advantages, and attractive valuations relative to their intrinsic value. Fundamental principles of long-term investing include diversification, patience, discipline, and the compounding effect of reinvested dividends and capital appreciation over time. Long-term investors often focus on fundamental analysis, analyzing company financials, business models, industry trends, and economic fundamentals to identify quality investments with long-term growth prospects. Long-term investment strategies include value, growth, dividend, and passive index investing through vehicles such as exchange-traded funds (ETFs) or index funds.

Short-Term Trading

Short-term, active, or speculative trading involves buying and selling financial assets within relatively short time frames, ranging from minutes to days or weeks. The primary objective of short-term trading is to capitalize on short-term price movements, market inefficiencies, and momentum trends to generate quick profits, often without focusing on the underlying fundamentals of the traded assets. Short-term traders employ various trading strategies, techniques, and tools, such as technical analysis, chart patterns, trading indicators, and algorithmic trading algorithms, to identify short-term trading opportunities and execute trades precisely and quickly. Short-term trading carries higher risk and volatility levels than long-term investing, as traders are exposed to market fluctuations, news events, and intraday price movements that can result in significant gains or losses within a short period. Common short-term trading strategies include day trading, swing trading, momentum trading, scalping, and arbitrage, each with a risk-reward profile, time horizon, and trading style. Short-term traders often focus on technical analysis, analyzing price charts, trading volumes, and market patterns to identify short-term trends, support and resistance levels, and trading signals.

Long-term investing and short-term trading represent two distinct approaches to participating in financial markets, each suited to different goals, time frames, and risk tolerances. While long-term investing focuses on wealth accumulation and capital appreciation over a period, short-term trading aims to profit from immediate price movements and market inefficiencies. By understanding the differences between these two approaches and aligning them with your investment objectives and trading preferences, you can develop effective strategies to achieve your financial goals and navigate the dynamic and ever-changing landscape of financial markets.

VALUE INVESTING STRATEGY

Value investing is an investment strategy identifying undervalued stocks or assets trading below their intrinsic value. Benjamin Graham popularized and refined it with Warren Buffett, both legendary value investors. The core principle of value investing is to buy assets priced below their intrinsic value, hold them for the long-term, and sell them when their market price reflects their true worth. Intrinsic value refers to the true cost of an asset based on its fundamental characteristics, such as earnings potential, cash flow generation, growth prospects, and asset value (e.g. book value). Value investors believe market prices often deviate from intrinsic value due to market inefficiencies, investor sentiment, and short-term market fluctuations, creating opportunities to buy undervalued assets.

- **Margin of safety:** The margin of safety is a critical concept in value investing. It represents the difference between an asset's intrinsic value and its market price. Value investors seek to invest in assets with a significant margin of safety, ensuring that even if their estimates of intrinsic value are slightly off or market conditions change, there is still a cushion of safety to protect against losses.
- **Fundamental analysis:** Value investing relies heavily on fundamental analysis to assess the financial health, performance, and valuation of companies or assets. Key metrics used in fundamental analysis include the price-to-earnings (P/E) ratio, the price-to-book (P/B) ratio, the earnings growth rate, the dividend yield, the return on equity (ROE), and the debt levels. Value investors look for companies with solid fundamentals, stable earnings, competitive advantages (e.g. moat), low debt, and attractive valuations relative to their peers or historical averages.
- **Contrarian approach:** Value investing often takes a contrarian approach, meaning it is willing to go against the market consensus and invest in assets out of favor or experiencing temporary setbacks. Contrarian investing can lead to opportunities to buy undervalued assets when market sentiment is negative, providing potential for significant upside when the market eventually recognizes its actual value.
- **Long-term horizon:** Value investing is typically a long-term strategy. Investors aim to hold undervalued assets until their market price converges with their intrinsic value. The long-term horizon allows value investors to benefit from the compounding effect of reinvested dividends, earnings growth, and capital appreciation over time.

Value Investing Strategies

There are different strategies within value investing:

- **Deep value investing**: It focuses on highly undervalued or distressed assets trading at deep discounts to their intrinsic value, often due to temporary setbacks or market pessimism.
- **Growth at a reasonable price (GARP):** This strategy combines value investing and growth investing elements, seeking companies with strong growth potential but trading at reasonable valuations.
- **Special situations investing:** It involves investing in companies undergoing special situations, such as spin-offs, restructurings, mergers, or acquisitions, where market mispricing may occur.

Risks and Challenges

While value investing has proven to be a successful strategy over the long-term, it has risks and challenges:

- **Value traps:** Some stocks may appear cheap based on traditional value metrics but may continue to decline or underperform due to fundamental issues or industry headwinds.
- **Market timing:** Timing the market and accurately identifying undervalued opportunities can be challenging, requiring patience, discipline, and thorough research.

Value investing is a time-tested investment strategy that involves identifying undervalued assets, assessing their intrinsic value, and investing with a margin of safety. By focusing on fundamental analysis, adopting a contrarian approach, and maintaining a long-term perspective, value investors seek to achieve superior risk-adjusted returns and build wealth over time. While value investing requires patience, diligence, and a deep understanding of financial markets, it can be a rewarding strategy for investors who prioritize long-term growth and capital preservation.

GROWTH INVESTING STRATEGIES

Growth investing is an investment strategy focusing on identifying and investing in companies with solid growth potential, robust earnings growth rates, and expanding market opportunities. Unlike value investing, which seeks undervalued assets, growth investing prioritizes companies expected to grow their revenues, profits, and market share at an above-average rate compared to their peers or the overall market. Growth investors are willing to pay a premium for these companies' stocks based on their anticipated growth prospects.

- **Focus on growth potential:** Growth investors prioritize companies with solid growth potential in sales, earnings, cash flow, and market expansion. They look for companies operating in growing industries or sectors with innovative products, services, or technologies that have the potential to disrupt markets and gain significant market share.
- **Earnings growth rate:** One of the primary metrics investors focus on is the earnings growth rate, which measures the percentage increase in a company's earnings over a specific period. Companies with consistently high earnings growth rates attract growth investors as they can generate profits and create value for shareholders.
- **Market leadership and competitive advantages:** Growth investors seek companies that demonstrate market leadership, substantial competitive advantages, and barriers to entry that protect their market position. Competitive advantages may include proprietary technology, strong brand recognition, economies of scale, patents or intellectual property, customer loyalty, or regulatory advantages.

- **Total addressable market (TAM) and expansion:** Growth investors assess a company's total addressable market (TAM), representing the market demand or revenue opportunity for its products or services. Companies with significant room for market expansion, global growth prospects, or opportunities to penetrate new markets are attractive to growth investors.
- **Investment in research and development (R&D):** Growth-oriented companies often invest heavily in research and development (R&D) to innovate, develop new products, improve existing offerings, and stay ahead of competitors. Growth investors value companies that allocate resources to R&D, which can drive future growth, competitive differentiation, and market leadership.
- **Valuation metrics:** While growth investors prioritize future growth prospects, they also consider valuation metrics to assess whether a stock is reasonably priced relative to its growth potential. Standard valuation metrics for growth stocks include the price-to-earnings (P/E) ratio, price-to-sales (P/S) ratio, price-to-earnings growth (PEG) ratio, and other measures of relative valuation.
- **Risks and challenges**: Growth investing carries certain risks and challenges, including high valuations. Growth stocks often trade at higher valuations relative to their earnings or book value, leading to potential price volatility and corrections if growth expectations are unmet.
- **Market sentiment:** Growth stocks can be sensitive to changes in investor sentiment, macroeconomic conditions, industry trends, or regulatory developments that impact growth expectations.
- **Volatility:** Growth stocks may experience higher volatility than value stocks, as market sentiment, news events, or sector rotation may influence prices.
- **Growth at a reasonable price (GARP):** It combines elements of value investing and growth investing, seeking companies

with strong growth potential but trading at reasonable valuations.

- **Top-down and bottom-up analysis:** Growth investors may use top-down analysis to identify promising industries or sectors for growth opportunities and then conduct bottom-up analysis to select individual stocks within those sectors.

Growth investing is a dynamic strategy focused on identifying companies with strong growth potential, market leadership, competitive advantages, and expanding market opportunities. Growth investors prioritize future growth prospects over current valuations and are willing to pay a premium for stocks of companies expected to deliver above-average earnings and revenue growth rates. While growth investing can offer opportunities for capital appreciation and wealth creation, it also carries risks related to valuation, market sentiment, and volatility, requiring investors to conduct thorough research, diversify their portfolios, and maintain a long-term perspective.

MOMENTUM TRADING STRATEGIES

Momentum trading is a strategy used by investors and traders to capitalize on the continuation of existing market trends. It relies on the premise that assets that have performed well in the past will likely continue performing well shortly. Momentum refers to the speed or strength of price movements in financial markets. In momentum trading, investors identify assets exhibiting strong upward or downward price movements and aim to profit from these trends.

Price Trends

Momentum traders believe that assets with solid price trends, whether upwards (bullish momentum) or downwards (bearish momentum), will likely continue moving in the same direction for a certain period. Momentum trading is based on the idea that markets may not always be fully efficient. This leads to delayed reactions to new information and creates opportunities for traders to exploit price momentum. RSI is a momentum oscillator that measures the speed and change of price movements. It indicates overbought or oversold conditions. Traders use RSI to identify potential entry or exit points. Traders often use moving-average indicators, such as the 50-day or 200-day moving average, to assess the direction and strength of price trends.

- **Breakout trading:** Momentum traders look for breakouts, where prices move above resistance levels (for bullish momentum) or below support levels (for bearish momentum), signaling potential trend continuations. Momentum traders adopt trend-following strategies, entering positions in the direction of prevailing trends and exiting when trends show signs of reversal. Traders analyze chart patterns, such as flags, triangles, and head-and-shoulders patterns, to identify momentum-driven price movements and potential trade opportunities.
- **Momentum trading risk management:** Momentum traders use stop-loss orders to limit potential losses by automatically selling positions if prices move against their expectations. Proper position sizing and risk management techniques help traders control the amount of capital at risk in each trade, considering factors like volatility and market conditions.
- **Time horizon:** Momentum trading typically has a short-term time horizon, with trades lasting from hours to days. Traders aim to capture rapid price movements during solid trends. Momentum traders actively monitor their positions, market news, and technical indicators to make timely decisions and capitalize on momentum shifts.
- **Volatility considerations:** High volatility can amplify momentum-driven price movements, presenting opportunities for significant gains and increasing risk and potential losses. Traders use volatility indicators, such as the

average true range (ATR) or Bollinger Bands, to assess market volatility and adjust their trading strategies accordingly.

- **Behavioral biases:** The herd mentality can influence momentum trading, where traders follow the crowd or chase hot trends. This leads to exaggerated price movements and potential reversals, and some momentum traders may succumb to overtrading, making excessive trades based on short-term price fluctuations rather than sound analysis.
- **Market conditions:** Momentum trading thrives in trending markets with strong and sustained price movements, providing clear signals for entry and exit points. Choppy or range-bound markets with limited price trends can challenge momentum traders, as false breakouts and whipsaws may occur more frequently.
- **Backtesting and analysis:** Momentum traders often conduct backtesting and historical analysis to evaluate the performance of momentum strategies under different market conditions and time frames. They seek to make data-driven decisions and improve the effectiveness of their momentum trading strategies by using quantitative analysis, statistical models, and technical indicators.
- **Psychological factors:** Successful momentum traders exhibit discipline, patience, and emotional control. They avoid impulsive trades and stick to their predefined trading rules. Traders assess risk tolerance and align their trading strategies with risk-reward preferences, understanding that momentum trading can involve higher volatility and rapid price changes.
- **Regulatory considerations:** Margin trading, often used by momentum traders to amplify returns, requires careful consideration of margin requirements, leverage ratios, and margin calls. Traders must comply with regulatory guidelines, trading rules, and disclosure requirements, especially when engaging in leveraged or derivative trading strategies.

Momentum trading involves identifying and capitalizing on solid price trends, utilizing technical analysis tools, managing risk through stop-loss orders and position sizing, adapting to market conditions, and staying disciplined amid market volatility and behavioral biases. Traders should conduct a thorough analysis, continuously monitor market dynamics, and refine their strategies to navigate the challenges and opportunities momentum presents.

DAY TRADING AND SCALPING STRATEGY

Day trading involves buying and selling financial instruments within the same day, with all positions closed before the market closes. Day traders aim to profit from short-term price movements and capitalize on intraday volatility.

- **Time horizon:** Day traders operate with a short-term time horizon, focusing on capturing price fluctuations within the trading day. Positions are typically held for minutes to hours, but all trades are closed by the end of the day.
- **Market accessibility:** Day trading is commonly conducted in highly liquid markets, such as stocks, currencies (forex), futures contracts, and options. These markets offer ample trading opportunities and tight bid-ask spreads.
- **Trading techniques:** Day traders employ various trading techniques, including technical analysis, chart patterns, price-action analysis, momentum indicators, and volume analysis. They use these tools to identify entry and exit points based on short-term market movements.
- **Risk management:** Effective risk management is crucial in day trading due to the rapid pace of trading and the potential for significant price fluctuations. Day traders use stop-loss orders, position sizing, and risk-reward ratios to manage risk and protect capital.
- **Regulatory considerations:** In some jurisdictions, day trading is subject to specific regulations, such as pattern day

trading rules in the United States. These regulations may impose requirements on minimum equity, trading frequency, and margin accounts for day traders.

Scalping

The definition is a high-frequency trading strategy focused on profiting from small price movements by executing many trades within short time frames, often seconds to minutes.

- **Objective:** Scalpers aim to capture small price increments, known as ticks or pips, by rapidly entering and exiting trades. They seek to generate quick profits from multiple small trades throughout the trading day.
- **Execution speed:** Scalping requires fast execution speeds and advanced trading platforms to capitalize on fleeting price opportunities. Scalpers rely on direct market access (DMA) and low-latency connections to execute trades swiftly.
- **Market focus:** Scalpers often target liquid markets with tight bid-ask spreads, such as forex currency pairs, major stock indices, and highly traded stocks. These markets provide ample liquidity and price efficiency for scalping strategies.
- **Risk management:** Effective risk management is essential in scalping due to the high volume of trades and rapid market movements. Scalpers use tight stop-loss orders, position sizing, and strict discipline to manage risk and preserve capital.
- **Technology and automation:** Scalpers may utilize algorithmic trading strategies, automated trading systems (bots), and intelligent order routing to execute trades quickly and efficiently. Due to its fast-paced nature, technology plays a crucial role in scalping.
- **Regulatory considerations:** Scalping activities are subject to regulatory oversight; and traders must comply with market rules, order execution requirements, and fair trading

practices. Some jurisdictions may have specific regulations related to high-frequency trading and scalping strategies.

Key Differences

- **Time horizon:** Day trading typically involves holding positions for minutes to hours within the same trading day, while scalping focuses on ultra-short time frames of seconds to minutes.
- **Profit targets:** Day traders aim for more significant price moves and may hold positions longer to capture intraday trends. However, scalpers target small price increments for quick profits and execute numerous daily trades.
- **Trading frequency:** Scalpers execute a high volume of trades, often in quick succession, compared to day traders, who may have fewer but more strategic trades.
- **Risk-reward ratio:** Day traders often seek higher risk-reward ratios, aiming for larger profits relative to their risk exposure. However, scalpers target smaller but more frequent gains with tighter risk management.
- **Psychological demands:** Scalping is psychologically demanding compared to day trading, as it requires intense focus, rapid decision-making, and the ability to handle stress and market fluctuations.
- **Technology requirements:** Scalping relies heavily on technology, high-speed internet connections, low-latency trading platforms, and advanced-order execution tools to compete effectively in fast-paced markets.

Both day trading and scalping are active trading strategies that require skill, discipline, risk management, and market knowledge. Before choosing between these strategies, traders should consider their trading style, risk tolerance, and market conditions carefully. This thoughtful consideration is crucial in ensuring that the chosen strategy aligns with their financial goals and market conditions, leading to more successful trading outcomes.

'Trading Strategy' has provided an in-depth analysis of various approaches to investing and trading, each tailored to different objectives, time horizons, and risk tolerances. We have explored the dichotomy between long-term and short-term trading, understanding how each approach aligns with varying investor and market conditions profiles. It has illuminated the principles behind value investing, focusing on identifying undervalued stocks based on intrinsic value and growth investing, which seeks out companies poised for significant expansion and potentially high returns. Momentum trading has been dissected as a strategy that capitalizes on existing market trends and price movements. In contrast, day trading and scalping have been examined for their high-frequency, short-term strategies to capture small price fluctuations for quick gains.

By analyzing these diverse trading strategies, we have gained insight into how various methods can be applied to align with specific financial goals and market conditions. Each strategy presents unique opportunities and challenges, and understanding their nuances enables investors to tailor their approach according to their individual needs and objectives. This chapter underscores the importance of selecting a trading strategy that matches your investment philosophy, risk tolerance, and market outlook. Whether you choose to invest for the long-term, trade based on value, pursue growth, or engage in high-frequency trading, having a well-defined strategy and a clear understanding of its principles is crucial for navigating the complexities of the stock market. Armed with this knowledge, you are better positioned to make informed decisions, optimize your investment approach, and achieve your financial goals more effectively.

Chapter 8

RISK MANAGEMENT AND PSYCHOLOGY

This pivotal chapter delves into the critical aspects of risk management and psychology—two pillars fundamental to success in trading and investing. We will explore the intricacies of managing risk effectively, maintaining emotional control and discipline, understanding the psychology of market cycles, and overcoming common trading pitfalls.

First and foremost, 'Managing Risk in Trading and Investing' is a cornerstone of sound financial practices. Here, we delve into the various risk management techniques and strategies investors and traders employ to protect their capital and minimize potential losses. From setting stop-loss orders and using position sizing techniques to diversifying portfolios and hedging against market risks, we equip you with the tools and knowledge needed to navigate the inherent risks of financial markets.

Emotional control and discipline are pivotal to consistent success in trading and investing. In this section, we explore the psychological aspects of decision-making, the impact of emotions such as fear and greed on investment decisions, and practical techniques for maintaining discipline during volatile market conditions. By mastering emotional control, you'll be better equipped to make rational, well-thought-out decisions that align with your investment goals.

Understanding the 'Psychology of Market Cycles' is crucial for investors and traders to navigate the cyclical nature of financial markets. We delve into the different phases of market cycles, from expansion and peak to contraction and trough, and discuss how investor sentiment and behavior evolve. By gaining insights into market psychology, you'll be better prepared to anticipate market trends and adjust your strategies accordingly.

'Overcoming Common Trading Pitfalls' is a comprehensive exploration of traders' mistakes and challenges. From overtrading and chasing hot trends to neglecting risk management and succumbing to cognitive biases, we highlight common pitfalls and provide practical tips and strategies for avoiding these pitfalls. By learning from the mistakes of others and adopting a disciplined approach, you can enhance your trading and investing outcomes.

MANAGING RISK IN TRADING AND INVESTING

Managing risk is fundamental to successful trading and investing, essential for preserving capital and achieving long-term profitability.

Risk Assessment

Identification: The first step in managing risk is identifying the various types of risk associated with trading and investing. These may include market, credit, liquidity, geopolitical, and operational risks.

Quantification: Once risks are identified, traders and investors quantify them by assessing the potential impact and likelihood of each risk event occurring. This helps prioritize risks and allocate resources accordingly.

Diversification:

Asset allocation: Diversification involves spreading investments across different asset classes, sectors, and geographic regions. This strategy aims to reduce portfolio volatility and minimize the impact of adverse events affecting a single asset or market segment.

Portfolio rebalancing: Regularly rebalancing a diversified portfolio ensures that risk exposure remains aligned with investment objectives and risk tolerance. It involves selling overperforming assets and buying underperforming ones to maintain desired asset allocations.

Position Sizing

Risk per trade: Traders determine the maximum amount of capital they are willing to risk on each trade, often expressed as a percentage of their trading account balance or as a dollar amount.

Position size calculation: Position sizing calculations consider entry price, stop-loss level, and target price to determine the appropriate position size that limits potential losses to a predefined percentage of capital.

Stop-Loss Orders

A stop-loss order is a risk management tool that automatically executes a trade to exit a position when the market price reaches a predetermined level, limiting potential losses. Standard stop-loss orders include fixed percentage, volatility-based, and chart pattern stops, each tailored to the trader's risk tolerance and market conditions.

Risk-Reward Ratio

The risk-reward ratio measures the potential reward of a trade relative to the risk taken. It helps traders assess whether a trade offers a favorable risk-reward profile before entering the position.

Optimal Ratio: Traders often aim for a risk-reward ratio of at least 1:2 or higher, meaning the potential reward is at least twice the potential risk. This ensures that winning trades can offset losses from losing trades over time.

Use of Leverage

Leverage ratio: Leverage amplifies both gains and losses in trading. Traders should use leverage cautiously and consider its impact on risk exposure and margin requirements.

Margin management: Proper margin management involves monitoring leverage ratios, maintaining sufficient margin levels, and avoiding overleveraging positions that could lead to margin calls and forced liquidations.

Risk Monitoring and Review

Regular assessment: Traders and investors should monitor their risk exposure, assess the effectiveness of risk management strategies, and adjust based on changing market conditions.

Post-trade analysis: Conducting post-trade analysis helps evaluate the success of risk management decisions, identify areas for improvement, and refine trading strategies over time.

Adaptation to Market Conditions

Dynamic risk management: Risk management strategies should be adaptable to different market environments, such as high volatility, low liquidity, or changing economic conditions. Flexibility in risk management allows traders to adjust their approach as market conditions evolve. By implementing effective risk management practices, traders and investors can mitigate potential losses, protect capital, and create a more resilient and sustainable investment approach. Combining risk management with sound investment strategies and disciplined execution forms the foundation for long-term success in trading and investing.

EMOTION CONTROL AND DISCIPLINE

Emotion control and discipline are critical aspects of successful trading and investing. Emotions can lead to impulsive decisions, cloud judgement, and poor outcomes.

Understanding Emotional Influences

Fear and greed: Emotions like fear and greed can significantly impact trading decisions. Fear of loss may lead to hesitation or avoidance of necessary risk, while greed can drive traders to take excessive risks for potential gains. Overconfidence can arise after a series of successful trades, leading traders to underestimate risks and overestimate their abilities. This can result in reckless trading behavior and losses.

Regret aversion: Traders may be influenced by regret aversion, in which they avoid taking necessary actions or admitting mistakes to avoid feeling regret.

Developing Emotional Awareness

Self-reflection: Traders should regularly self-reflect to identify their emotional triggers, biases, and behavior patterns. This self-awareness helps them recognize and manage their emotions effectively.

Journaling: Keeping a trading journal allows traders to track their emotions, decisions, and outcomes. Analyzing past trades helps traders understand emotional influences and improve decision-making processes.

Establishing Trading Rules

Predefined rules: Establishing predefined trading rules, including entry and exit criteria, risk management parameters, and position sizing guidelines, reduces reliance on emotions during trading decisions.

Trading plan: A comprehensive trading plan outlines strategies, goals, risk tolerance, and contingency plans. Following a well-defined plan promotes discipline and reduces emotional decision-making.

Implementing Risk Management Strategies

Stop-loss orders: Stop-loss orders help limit potential losses and remove emotional biases from trade management. Traders should adhere to stop-loss levels without hesitation or second-guessing.

Position sizing: Proper position sizing based on risk-reward ratios and account size prevents overexposure and emotional attachment to individual trades.

Portfolio diversification: Diversifying across asset classes and sectors reduces concentration risk and minimizes the impact of individual trade outcomes on overall portfolio performance.

Practicing Patience and Discipline

Avoiding impulse trading: Traders should avoid making impulsive trades based on emotions or short-term market fluctuations. Patience allows for thorough analysis and better decision-making.

Sticking to plan: Discipline involves sticking to the trading plan, even during challenging market conditions or periods of emotional stress. Consistency in execution leads to more reliable results over time.

Seeking External Support

Mentorship and education: Seeking guidance from experienced mentors or educational resources helps develop emotional resilience and effective trading strategies.

Professional help: In extreme cases of emotional distress or trading addiction, seeking professional help from therapists or counselors trained in behavioral finance can be beneficial.

Continuous Improvement

Learning from mistakes: Embracing failures as learning opportunities and adapting strategies based on past experiences fosters continuous improvement and emotional growth.

Adapting to market changes: Markets evolve, and traders must adjust their strategies and emotional control techniques to adapt to changing conditions and dynamics.

PSYCHOLOGY OF MARKET CYCLES

The psychology of market cycles delves into how investor sentiment and behavior drive market movements through distinct phases. Understanding these cycles can help traders and investors anticipate market trends, make informed decisions, and adjust strategies accordingly.

Expansion Phase

- **Euphoria and optimism:** In the early stages of an expansion phase, optimism and euphoria prevail among investors. Positive economic indicators, strong corporate earnings, and bullish market sentiment fuel buying activity.
- **Risk appetite:** Risk appetite increases as investors chase higher returns, increasing asset prices across various markets and sectors.
- **FOMO (fear of missing out):** The fear of missing out on potential gains drives investor behavior, increasing speculation and heightened market activity.
- **Investor psychology:** Investors exhibit confidence, overlook risks, and may become overconfident in their ability to predict market movements.

Peak Phase

- **Exuberance and overvaluation:** Exuberance and overvaluation become prevalent as markets peak. Asset prices may become disconnected from the underlying fundamentals, leading to inflated valuations.
- **Herding behavior:** Herding behavior intensifies as investors follow the crowd and ignore contrarian signals. The fear of missing out on further gains drives more investors to enter the market.
- **Speculative bubbles:** Speculative bubbles may form in certain asset classes or sectors, characterized by rapid price appreciation fueled by speculative buying.
- **Psychological traps:** Investors may fall into psychological traps such as anchoring bias (fixating on past prices), confirmation bias (seeking information that confirms existing beliefs), and recency bias (placing undue importance on recent events).

Contraction Phase (Bear Market)

Pessimism and fear: As markets enter a contraction phase, pessimism and fear grip investors. Negative economic news, geopolitical uncertainties, or corporate failures contribute to a decline in market sentiment.

Risk aversion: As risk aversion increases, investors tend to sell assets and move to safer investments or cash equivalents.

Capitulation: Capitulation occurs when investors, overwhelmed by losses and pessimism, sell their holdings in a panic, often at significantly reduced prices.

Psychological impact: Fear, panic, and loss aversion dominate investor psychology, driving market downturns and amplifying selling pressure.

Trough Phase

- **Despondency and disinterest:** The trough phase is characterized by pessimism, disinterest, and a lack of confidence in the market's recovery. Investor sentiment hits rock bottom.
- **Value opportunities:** Contrarian investors start seeing value opportunities as asset prices reach attractive relative to fundamentals.
- **Market reversal signals:** Market stabilization, improving economic indicators, or policy interventions may signal a potential market reversal.
- **Psychological resilience:** Successful investors maintain psychological resilience, avoid emotional decision-making, and focus on long-term investment objectives.

Recovery and Expansion Phase (Bull Market)

- **Hope and optimism:** The recovery phase brings renewed hope and optimism as markets rebound. Positive economic data, corporate earnings growth, or stimulus measures contribute to investor confidence.
- **Early adopters:** Early adopters and contrarian investors enter the market, recognizing the potential for growth and recovery.
- **Gradual shift in sentiment:** Market sentiment gradually shifts from pessimism to optimism, driving a sustained upward trend in asset prices.
- **Psychological rebalancing:** Investors regain confidence, but lessons from the previous cycle's volatility and risks influence more cautious decision-making and risk management practices.

OVERCOMING COMMON TRADING PITFALLS

Overcoming common trading pitfalls is essential for traders to achieve consistent success and avoid costly mistakes.

Overtrading

- **Description:** Overtrading occurs when traders execute too many trades, often based on impulsive decisions or a desire to be constantly active in the market.
- **Impact**: Overtrading can lead to higher transaction costs, increased exposure to market volatility, and reduced focus on quality trades.
- **Solution:** Develop a disciplined trading plan with precise entry and exit criteria. Set daily or weekly trade limits and avoid trading excessively during low market volatility or uncertainty.

Chasing Hot Trends

- **Description:** Chasing hot trends involves buying assets that have already experienced significant price increases, driven by market hype or momentum.
- **Impact:** Chasing hot trends can result in buying at inflated prices, overlooking fundamental analysis, and exposing traders to potential reversals or corrections.
- **Solution:** Focus on value investing principles and conduct thorough research before entering trades. Avoid FOMO (Fear of missing out) and prioritize long-term investment objectives over short-term market trends.

Neglecting Risk Management

- **Description:** Neglecting risk management involves failing to implement proper risk mitigation strategies, such as stop-loss orders, position sizing, and portfolio diversification.

- **Impact:** Without adequate risk management, traders expose themselves to larger-than-expected losses, margin calls, and portfolio volatility.
- **Solution:** Prioritize risk management in every trade. Use stop-loss orders to limit losses, practice proper position sizing based on risk-reward ratios, and diversify across asset classes to reduce portfolio risk.

Emotional Trading

- **Description**: Emotional trading occurs when traders make decisions based on fear, greed, or other emotions rather than rational analysis and strategy.
- **Impact:** Emotional trading can lead to impulsive decisions, inconsistent performance, and deviations from trading plans.
- **Solution:** Develop emotional awareness and control through mindfulness techniques, journalling, and regular self-assessment. Stick to predefined trading rules and avoid making decisions based on temporary emotions or market noise.

Lacking Patience

- **Description:** Impatience in trading manifests as a desire for quick profits or immediate results, leading traders to enter and exit trades hastily.
- **Impact:** Lack of patience can result in missed opportunities, premature exits, and increased trading costs.
- **Solution:** Cultivate patience by focusing on long-term goals, practicing disciplined trading, and avoiding impulsive decisions. Let trades act according to the predefined plan without succumbing to short-term market fluctuations.

Overleveraging

- **Description:** Overleveraging involves excessive leverage or margin in trades, amplifying gains and losses.
- **Impact:** If trades move against expectations, overleveraging can lead to margin calls, forced liquidations, and substantial losses.
- **Solution:** Use leverage judiciously and within manageable limits. Avoid risking more than a small percentage of your account balance on any single trade and maintain sufficient margin levels to withstand market fluctuations.

Having confirmation bias

- **Description:** Confirmation bias occurs when traders seek information that confirms their beliefs or biases, leading to selective interpretation of data.
- **Impact:** Confirmation bias can result in overlooking contradictory information, neglecting thorough analysis, and making biased trading decisions.
- **Solution:** Stay objective by considering diverse viewpoints, challenging assumptions, and conducting comprehensive research. Avoid cherry-picking information that supports preconceived notions and remain open to alternative perspectives.

'Risk Management and Psychology' have delved into the critical aspects of managing risk and maintaining psychological resilience in trading and investing. Effective risk management is essential for safeguarding capital and ensuring long-term success in the financial markets. We have examined strategies for assessing and mitigating risk, including diversification, position sizing, and stopping-loss orders to protect against significant losses.

Equally important is the psychological component of trading and investing. This chapter has explored the role of emotional control and discipline, emphasizing the need to manage emotions and avoid impulsive decisions that derail investment strategies. We've discussed how understanding the psychology of market cycles can help investors recognize patterns and trends and maintain a balanced perspective during periods of market volatility.

By addressing common trading pitfalls, such as overtrading, chasing losses, and succumbing to herd mentality, we have highlighted the importance of developing a disciplined approach to trading and investing. This involves setting clear goals, adhering to well-defined strategies, and remaining adaptable to changing market conditions.

This chapter underscores that successful investing and trading are not solely about understanding market mechanics and strategies but also about mastering oneself. Effective risk management and psychological resilience are foundational to navigating the complexities of the stock market. By integrating robust risk management practices with emotional discipline and self-awareness, you can enhance your decision-making process, reduce the impact of psychological biases, and achieve more consistent and rewarding outcomes in your investment endeavors.

Chapter 9

ADVANCED TOPICS IN TRADING AND INVESTING

This chapter delves into the sophisticated realm of advanced trading and investing strategies. It is designed for those ready to elevate their understanding beyond the basics and explore the intricate mechanisms that drive professional trading and investment decisions. As you embark on this advanced exploration, you will encounter a range of complex instruments and techniques that can significantly enhance your trading arsenal.

'Options Trading Strategies' marks the beginning of our advanced journey. Options are versatile financial instruments that provide the right but not the obligation to buy or sell an asset at a predetermined price within a specific timeframe. We will explore various strategies, such as covered calls, protective puts, straddles, and spreads. Understanding these strategies will enable you to hedge risk, speculate on price movements, and enhance your overall investment strategy with precision. Following options, we will discuss 'How to Buy and Sell Stock Options', a crucial skill for implementing your options strategies effectively. This section will guide you through trading options, from selecting the proper contracts to executing trades on various platforms. Mastering these processes will ensure you can navigate the options market with confidence and efficiency.

Next, we focus on 'Futures and Derivatives'—financial instruments that derive value from underlying assets like commodities, currencies, or indices. Futures contracts oblige the buyer to purchase and the seller to sell an asset at a future date for a predetermined price. On the other hand, derivatives include a broader range of contracts, such as swaps and options. Understanding these instruments will equip you with the knowledge to manage risk, speculate on market movements, and leverage opportunities in various asset classes.

In our exploration of 'Leveraged Trading and Margin Accounts', we will examine how traders use borrowed funds to increase their exposure to financial markets. Leverage amplifies potential gains and losses, making it a powerful but risky tool. We will cover how margin accounts work, the implications of leverage on your trading strategy, and strategies for managing the risks associated with high leverage.

'Algorithmic Trading' is another advanced topic we will cover. This approach involves using computer algorithms to automate trading decisions based on predefined criteria. Algorithmic trading can process vast amounts of data at high speeds, enabling traders to execute trades precisely and efficiently. We will explore the basics of developing trading algorithms, their applications, and the benefits they offer in modern trading environments.

'High-Frequency Trading (HFT)' represents the cutting edge of trading technology. It involves executing many orders at extremely high speeds, leveraging sophisticated algorithms and high-speed data feeds. This section will delve into the mechanics of HFT, its impact on the markets, and the controversies surrounding its practices.

Finally, we will examine the role of 'Artificial Intelligence (AI)' in trading and investing. AI technologies, including machine learning and neural networks, are revolutionizing how data is analyzed and decisions are made. We will explore how AI can be used for predictive analytics, pattern recognition, and trading strategies, providing you with insights into the future of trading technology.

It offers a deep dive into advanced trading and investing topics that can enhance your strategic approach to the markets. Whether you are interested in leveraging complex instruments, automating trades, or harnessing the power of AI, this chapter provides the knowledge and tools to take your trading and investing skills to the next level.

OPTIONS TRADING STRATEGIES

A stock option is a contract that gives the holder the right, but not the obligation, to buy or sell shares of a particular stock at a specific price (strike price) on or before a certain date (expiration date). Stock options are often used as compensation for company employees and can be traded on various stock option exchanges. Traders and investors can use different stock options trading strategies with unique risks and potential rewards.

- **Covered Call**

A covered call is a popular options trading strategy that allows investors to generate additional income from stocks they own. The investor holds shares of a stock, which is known as an extended position. The investor sells (or 'writes') call options on that stock. In return for trading these options, the investor receives a premium, which can provide income or help reduce the stock's overall cost. For a covered call strategy to succeed, selecting a stock that is expected to remain relatively stable or increase in value in the short-term is essential.

Outcomes of the Strategy

If the stock price rises above the strike price of the call options, the options will be exercised. This means the investor must sell their shares at the strike price. While they may miss out on potential gains above that price, they still benefit from the premium received.

If the stock price stays below the strike price, the options will expire worthless. The investor keeps their shares and retains the premium as income.

If the stock price falls, the investor still owns the shares even if the stock price declines. The premium received from selling the call options can help offset some losses from the decrease in stock value. It's essential to understand that while covered calls can generate income, they can also limit the potential upside of the investment. If the stock price rises significantly, the investor must sell at the agreed strike price, missing out on higher profits. Covered calls are best used as a strategy for generating income or reducing the costs of stock ownership rather than for achieving significant capital gains.

- **Protective Put**

A protective put is an options trading strategy that helps investors safeguard their stock investments. The investor owns shares of a stock, creating an extended position. The investor purchases put options for that same stock. A put option gives the investor the right to sell their shares at a specified price, known as the strike price. The put option acts like insurance against a decline in the stock's value. It helps limit potential losses if the stock price falls.

Outcomes of the Strategy

The investor can exercise the option if the stock price falls below the put option's strike price. This allows them to sell their shares at a higher strike price, minimizing loss. If the stock price remains above the strike price, the put option will expire worthless. In this case, the investor keeps their shares but loses the premium paid for the put option.

This strategy benefits investors who are optimistic about a stock's long-term potential but want to protect themselves from significant short-term declines. The protective put strategy incurs costs in the form of the premium paid for the put option. This premium is a trade-off for the downside protection it provides. If the stock price rises significantly, the potential gains may be limited since the investor has already committed to selling at the put option's strike price.

It's essential to understand that a protective put is a form of hedging designed to reduce risk. It should complement, not replace, a well-diversified investment portfolio. A protective put strategy allows investors to limit their losses while still participating in potential gains, making it a valuable tool for managing risk in their investment strategy.

- **Bull Call Spread**

A bull call spread is an options trading strategy in which an investor buys a call option at a lower strike price (the long call) and sells a call option at a higher strike price (the short call). This strategy aims to profit from a moderate stock price rise. When the stock price rises above the short call's strike price, the options will be exercised, and the investor will have to sell their shares at the higher strike price. However, since the investor also bought a call option at the lower strike price, they can repurchase the shares at a lower price, resulting in a profit. The bull call spread strategy is used when an investor is bullish on a stock but wants to limit their potential loss. The premium received from selling the short call will offset the cost of buying the long call, which can help limit the potential loss if the stock price does not rise as expected. It's important to note that the bull call spread strategy has a limited potential profit because the maximum gain is the difference between the strike prices of the two options minus the net premium paid. Additionally, the strategy will be profitable only if the stock price rises above the short call's strike price and remains above that price level.

- **Bear Put Spread**

A bull call spread is an options trading strategy used by investors who expect a moderate increase in a stock's price. The investor purchases a call option at a lower strike price, known as the long call. At the same time, the investor sells a call option at a higher strike price, called the short call.

Objective: This strategy aims to profit from a modest stock price rise.

How it works: Both options may be exercised if the stock price rises above the short call's strike price. The investor will sell shares at the higher strike price of the short call. Because the investor bought the long call at a lower strike price, they can acquire the shares at that lower price, allowing them to profit from the difference.

Limiting losses: The bull call spread is designed to limit potential losses. The premium received from selling the short call helps offset the cost of buying the long call. This means the investor's risk is reduced if the stock price doesn't rise as expected.

Potential profit and limitations: The maximum profit from a bull call spread is limited to the difference between the two strike prices minus the net premium paid for the options. For the strategy to be profitable, the stock price must rise above the short call's strike price and remain above that level. A bull call spread is a strategic way to benefit from a moderate increase in stock prices while managing risk. By combining the purchase of a lower-strike call option with the sale of a higher-strike call option, investors can potentially profit while limiting their losses.

- **Iron Condor**

An iron condor is an options trading strategy that simultaneously holds a bull call spread and a bear put spread. The investor sells a call option at a higher strike price.

- **Buy-a-call option:** They also buy a call option at an even higher strike price.
- **Sell-a-put option:** The investor sells a put option at a lower strike price.
- **Buy-a-put option:** Finally, they buy a put option at an even lower strike price.

The iron condor aims to profit from a stock expected to remain relatively stable, moving only slightly in either direction.

Income generation: By selling the options, the investor receives a net premium, which can serve as income or help offset some of the trade's costs.

Profit Range: The iron condor can be profitable if the stock price stays within a specific range defined by the strike prices of the options.

Potential profit and loss: The maximum profit is the net premium from selling the options. The maximum loss occurs if the stock price moves beyond the defined range. It is calculated as the difference between the strike prices minus the net premium received.

The iron condor is a limited-risk, limited-reward strategy. It is unsuitable for stocks expected to make significant moves in either direction. Executing an iron condor can be complex, so investors must understand options trading before attempting this strategy. The iron condor strategy allows investors to profit from a stable stock price by selling and buying calls and putting options within a specific range. While it offers limited risk and reward, it requires careful execution and a solid understanding of options.

- **Call Spread**

A call spread is an options trading strategy that involves two steps: buying a call option at a lower strike price and selling a call option at a higher strike price, both with the same expiration date. The difference between these two strike prices is called the spread. This strategy is often called a bull call spread because it is used when an investor is optimistic about the underlying asset and expects its price to rise. Suppose an investor buys a call option with a strike price of $50 and sells a call option with a strike price of $55, both expiring in three months. The stock is currently trading at $50. If the stock price rises to $55, the investor can exercise the bought-call option and sell the stock at $55, making a profit of $5 per share. If the stock price rises to $60, the investor still profits $5 per share, but their maximum gain is capped at $5 because the sold-call option limits their profits to $55. If the stock price falls, The investor will not profit but won't incur any losses beyond the premium paid for the options.

Advantages of a Call Spread

- **Limited risk:** This strategy allows investors to limit potential losses while benefiting from upward price movement.
- **Reduced cost:** Selling the higher strike-call option offsets some of the cost of buying the lower strike call, making it more affordable.

A call spread is a strategy bullish investors use to capitalize on expected price increases while managing risk. It offers limited profit potential but protects against significant losses, making it a popular choice for those looking to trade options with a positive market outlook.

- **Married Put**

A married put is an options trading strategy where an investor buys a put option for a stock they own. This approach is often called a protective put because it offers downside protection for the stock. For example, an investor purchases 100 shares of a stock currently trading at $50 and simultaneously buys a put option with a strike price of $45. The put option expires in three months and costs $2 per share. The put option gives the investor the right to sell their shares at the strike price of $45, regardless of how low the market price falls. This limits their potential losses. If the stock price drops to $45, the investor can exercise the put option and sell the shares at $45, preventing more significant losses. In this case, their loss would be limited to $5 per share (the difference between the purchase price of $50 and the sale price of $45) plus the $2 premium paid for the put option. If the stock price falls to $40, the investor can still sell the shares at $45, resulting in a profit of $5 per share after accounting for the premium. If the stock price rises above $50, the investor will not realize any gains from the put option. However, they will not incur any losses beyond the premium paid for the option.

A married put strategy allows investors to protect their stock investments from significant declines while still benefiting from potential price increases. This strategy allows investors to limit their losses and manage risk effectively, making it a valuable tool for those looking to safeguard their portfolios.

- **Collars**

A collar is an options trading strategy that combines buying a put option and selling a call option, both with the same expiration date. The premium received from selling the call option is typically used to cover the cost of the put option. This strategy is also known as a risk reversal or fence because it helps limit potential losses and gains on the underlying asset.

For example, an investor owns 100 shares of a stock currently trading at $50. They buy a put option with a strike price of $45 and sell a call option with a strike price of $55, both expiring in three months. By selling the call option, the investor receives a premium of $1 per share, which helps offset the cost of purchasing the put option. If the stock price drops to $45, the investor can exercise the put option and sell their shares at $45, minimizing their loss to $5 per share (the difference between the purchase price of $50 and the strike price of $45). If the stock price rises to $55, the investor can sell their shares at the call option's strike price of $55, realizing a profit of $5 per share after accounting for the premium. If the stock price exceeds $55 or falls below $45, the investor will not make any additional profit, but they also won't incur further losses beyond the premium paid for the options. The collar strategy allows investors to protect their stock investments from significant declines while still capping potential gains. This strategy will enable investors to effectively manage risk, safeguarding their portfolios while navigating market fluctuations.

- **Straddle**

A straddle is an options trading strategy where an investor buys both a call option and a put option with the same strike price and expiration date. This strategy is proper when the investor expects significant price movement in the underlying asset but is still determining the direction of that movement. For example, an investor buys a call option and a put option with a strike price of $50 that expires in three months. The stock is currently trading at $50. If the stock price rises to $55, the investor can exercise the call option, selling the stock at $55. This results in a profit of $5 per share. If the stock price falls to $45, the investor can exercise the put option, selling the stock at $50, which will result in a profit of $5 per share.

Profit from both directions: The essential advantage of a straddle is that it allows investors to profit from both upward and downward price movements of the stock. The straddle strategy can be expensive because the investor pays premiums for both the call and put options. Additionally, there may be other fees associated with the strategy. It's important to note that a straddle is a high-risk, high-reward strategy. The stock must move significantly in either direction for the investor to cover the costs of the options and make a profit. This strategy best suits experienced investors with a solid understanding of the underlying asset and the options market. A straddle is an effective way to capitalize on significant price movements in either direction while managing risk. However, investors must approach this strategy cautiously and properly due to the costs and inherent risks.

- **Strangle**

Strangle, much like a straddle, is an options trading strategy. However, the strike prices for the call and put options differ. In a strangle, the investor buys a call option with a higher strike price and a put option with a lower strike price, both set to expire on the same date. For example, an investor purchases a call option with a strike price of $55 and a put option with a strike price of $45. Both options expire in three months, while the stock trades at $50.

If the stock price rises to $55, the investor can exercise the call option and sell the stock at $55, resulting in a profit of $5 per share. If the stock price falls to $45, the investor can exercise the put option and sell the stock at $45, making a profit of $5 per share. One advantage of a strangle compared to a straddle is the lower cost. The investor only pays a premium for each option, making the overall investment less expensive. However, the potential profit is also lower. The stock price must move significantly to make a profit, exceeding the difference between the two strike prices. Like the straddle, a strangle is a high-risk, high-reward strategy. Before using this strategy, investors need to understand the underlying asset and the options market. A strangle allows investors to profit from significant price movements in either direction while keeping costs lower than a straddle. However, investors must approach this strategy with caution and expertise due to the risks and the need for the stock price to move beyond a particular range.

- **Horizontal Calendar Spread**

A horizontal calendar spread is an options trading strategy that involves buying and selling options contracts with the same strike price but different expiration dates. This strategy is designed to take advantage of the differing time values of these options, notably when an investor anticipates a change in the underlying asset's volatility.

An investor buys a call option that expires in three months and sells a call option that expires in six months, both with a strike price of $50. The stock is currently trading at $50. The investor pays a higher premium for the shorter-term option (the one expiring in three months) and receives a premium for the longer-term option (the one expiring in six months). If the stock price reaches $55 by the expiration date of the shorter-term option, the investor can exercise that call option and sell the stock at $55, realizing a profit. If the stock price does not rise to $55, the investor won't make a profit, but they also won't incur any losses beyond the premium paid for the options.

Uses of calendar spreads: Investors who expect changes in volatility can use calendar spreads to capitalize on those expectations. Investors uncertain about the stock's price movement can use calendar spreads to reduce overall portfolio risk. A calendar spread allows investors to benefit from differences in time value between options with the same strike price but different expiration dates. This strategy can be effective for speculation and hedging, making it a versatile tool for managing risk and taking advantage of market conditions.

- **Diagonal Spread**

A diagonal spread, also known as a diagonal option spread, is an options trading strategy that involves buying and selling options contracts with different strike prices and expiration dates. This strategy aims to capitalize on the options' differences in time value and implied volatility. An investor might buy a call option with a strike price of $50 that expires in three months and simultaneously sell a call option with a strike price of $55 that expires in six months. The investor hopes the stock price will rise and reach the higher strike price of $55 before the shorter-term option expires. The diagonal spread allows the investor to benefit from the time decay of the sold (short) option while also positioning for potential price increases in the underlying asset. The strategy takes advantage of the options' different time values and implied volatilities. The success of this strategy depends on several factors, including the underlying asset's price movement. The specific strike prices and expiration dates are chosen. This strategy can also be used to manage risk in a portfolio. However, diagonal spreads are more complex and require a solid understanding of the underlying asset and options market. They are generally not recommended for inexperienced investors. A diagonal spread is an advanced options trading strategy that allows investors to benefit from varying strike prices and expiration dates. This strategy can offer speculation and risk management opportunities by leveraging time decay and potential price movements. Still, implementing options trading requires more profound knowledge to execute successfully.

- **Butterfly Spread**

A butterfly spread is a neutral options trading strategy that aims to profit from minimal price movement in the underlying asset. This strategy involves buying and selling options contracts with different strike prices, all having the same expiration date. The basic setup includes buying the lowest strike price, selling two options at a middle strike price and buying at the highest strike price. All options in this strategy share the same expiration date. For instance, an investor could buy a call option with a strike price of $50, sell two call options with a strike price of $55, and buy another call option with a strike price of $60. The investor hopes the stock price will remain close to the middle strike price of $55 at expiration. The butterfly spread can be profitable if the stock price is around the middle strike price at expiration, as this creates a situation where the sold options expire worthless, and the bought options can generate gains. This strategy can be employed for both speculation—betting on minimal price movement and hedging—protecting against volatility. While a butterfly spread can be an effective strategy, it is more complex and requires a solid understanding of the underlying asset and options trading. Therefore, it may not be suitable for less experienced investors. A butterfly spread is a neutral options strategy that allows investors to profit from minor to no movement in the stock price. By combining different options at varying strike prices, this strategy aims to capitalize on market stability, but it requires careful execution and knowledge of options to be successful.

- **Iron Butterfly**

An iron butterfly is an options trading strategy that builds on the traditional butterfly spread by incorporating both a short put option and a short call option. This strategy combines elements of a bear spread and a bull spread and is designed to profit from a neutral outlook on the underlying asset. The iron butterfly consists of buying a put option at the lowest strike price, selling a put option and a call option at the middle strike price and buying a call option at the highest strike price. All options share the same expiration date. For instance, an investor could buy a put option with a strike price of $45, sell a put option with a strike price of $50, sell a call option with a strike price of $50, and buy a call option with a strike price of $55. The investor aims for the stock price to remain around the middle strike price of $50 at expiration. The strategy is most profitable if the stock price stays near the middle strike price at expiration, allowing the sold options to expire worthless. In contrast, the bought options can potentially generate gains.

Uses: The iron butterfly can be used for both speculation—betting on minimal price movement and hedging—protecting against volatility. This more advanced strategy requires a solid understanding of the underlying asset, the options market, and the associated risks. Therefore, it may not be suitable for less experienced investors. An iron butterfly is an advanced options trading strategy that profits from a stable stock price. Using a combination of put and call options at different strike prices, this strategy aims to benefit from minimal price movement. Still, it requires careful execution and knowledge of the options market to be effective.

- **Condor Spread**

A condor spread is an options trading strategy like a butterfly spread with more comprehensive strike price ranges. It is designed to profit from a neutral, moderately bullish, or bearish outlook on the underlying asset.

Structure of the condor spread: The basic setup includes buying a call or put option at the lowest strike price, selling a call or put option at the next higher strike price, selling another call or put option at an even higher strike price, and buying a call or put option at the highest strike price. All options have the same expiration date. For instance, an investor could buy a put option with a strike price of $40, sell a put option with a strike price of $45, sell another put option with a strike price of $50, and buy a put option with a strike price of $55. The investor aims for the stock price to remain between the two middle strike prices of $45 and $50 at expiration. The condor spread is most profitable if the stock price stays within the range of the two middle strike prices. This allows the sold options to expire worthless while the bought options provide limited protection. This strategy can be employed for both speculation—betting on stable price movement and hedging—protecting against volatility. The condor spread is more advanced and requires a solid understanding of the underlying asset, the options market, and the associated risks. As such, it may not be suitable for less experienced investors. A condor spread is an advanced options strategy that profits from limited price movement in the underlying asset. Investors can benefit from a stable market while managing risk by using a series of calls or put options at varying strike prices. However, it requires careful execution and a firm grasp of options trading.

- **Combo**

A combo, or combination, is an options trading strategy that merges two or more different options strategies to achieve a specific investment goal. This approach is typically used when an investor anticipates significant price movement in the underlying asset but still determines that movement's direction. For example, an investor might combine a straddle and a strangle to profit from upward and downward price movements. Alternatively, they could use a bull call spread and a bear put spread to take advantage of a moderately bullish outlook. Combo strategies are more complex and require a solid understanding of the underlying asset, the options market, and the associated risks. Therefore, they are generally not recommended for less experienced investors. Combos can be employed for both speculation—betting on price movement and hedging—protecting against volatility. The profitability of a combo strategy depends on the specific combination of strategies used, the actual price movement, and the underlying asset's volatility. A combo strategy allows investors to tailor their approach by combining different options strategies to capitalize on potential price changes. While it offers flexibility and the opportunity for profit, it requires careful execution and a firm grasp of options trading concepts.

- **Custom Options**

A custom options trading strategy is a personalized approach to options trading that aligns with an individual investor's specific investment goals, risk tolerance, and market outlook. This strategy can be crafted by combining various options or using a unique approach not commonly found in the market. Custom options strategies can serve multiple purposes, including hedging, protecting against potential losses and speculation, betting on price movements, generating income, and creating revenue from options premiums.

Targeting market conditions: These strategies can also be tailored to respond to specific market conditions, such as high volatility, low volatility, and a particular market trend or outlook. Developing a custom options strategy requires a solid understanding of the underlying asset, the options market, and the associated risks. Investors must clearly define their investment goals and risk tolerance to create an effective strategy. For less experienced investors, working with a professional advisor or expert is advisable to develop a custom strategy that meets your specific needs and objectives. A custom options trading strategy is a flexible and personalized approach that allows investors to tailor their options trading to fit their goals and market conditions. While these strategies can provide significant benefits, they require careful planning and a good understanding of the options market, making professional guidance beneficial for those new to trading.

The advantages of stock options trading are:

1. Leverage

One significant advantage of stock options trading is the potential for substantial gains through leverage. Leverage empowers investors to control a more extensive stock for a relatively small investment, amplifying potential gains. An investor must pay the total price when purchasing stock. For instance, if a stock is priced at $100 per share, the investor must invest $100 to buy one share. In contrast, when purchasing an option, the investor only pays a fraction of the stock's price, known as the option premium. For example, if an investor buys a call option with a strike price of $100 and a premium of $2, they only pay $2 to control that share of stock. This leverage enables investors to maintain control over a significant amount of stock with a smaller investment, enhancing their profit potential. It's essential to recognize that while leverage can amplify gains, it also increases the risk of loss. If the stock price does not move as anticipated, the investor could lose the entire premium paid for the option. This loss can be more substantial than if the investor bought the stock outright. Stock options trading offers the advantage of leverage, allowing investors to control more prominent positions with less capital. While this can enhance profit potential, knowing the associated risks is crucial, as leverage can lead to significant losses.

2. Flexibility

One significant advantage of stock options trading is its flexibility. This flexibility allows investors to adapt their strategies to various market conditions, whether the market is rising, falling, or remaining stable. If investors anticipate a stock will increase, they can buy a call option. This option grants them the right to purchase the stock at a predetermined price (strike price) on or before a specified date (expiration date). If the stock price rises, the investor can exercise the option of buying the stock at the lower strike price and potentially realizing a profit. Conversely, if an investor believes that a stock will decrease in price, they can purchase a put option. This gives them the right to sell the stock at the strike price. If the stock price falls, they can exercise the option and sell at a higher strike price, potentially making a profit. Options trading also enables strategies for stocks expected to remain stable. For example, an investor can employ a straddle by selling a call option and buying a put option at the same strike price. This strategy profits when the stock price stays relatively stable but incurs losses if the price moves significantly in either direction.

Trading can be a source of income. Investors can sell options, such as covered calls or cash-secured puts, which provide a steady income stream during stable market conditions. Stock options trading offers remarkable flexibility, allowing investors to capitalize on various market scenarios. Whether seeking to profit from price movements or generate income, options provide diverse strategies for effectively adapting to changing market conditions.

3. Risk Management

Another advantage of stock options trading is risk management. Options trading can be used as risk management, allowing investors to limit their potential losses or lock in profits. For example, an investor who owns a stock and is concerned about a possible price decline can use options to protect their position. They can buy a put option at a strike price below the current stock price. If the stock price does decline, the investor can exercise their put option and sell the stock at the higher strike price, limiting their potential loss. Options trading can also be used to take profits on a stock that has risen in price. An investor who owns a stock and is concerned about a potential price decline can use options to lock in profits. They can sell a call option at a strike price above the current stock price. If the stock price does decline, the investor can keep the stock and the premium received from selling the call option, locking in their profit. Additionally, options trading allows investors to take advantage of a stock expected to remain relatively stable. For example, an investor can sell a call option and buy a put option at the same strike price, a straddle. This strategy profits if the stock price remains relatively stable but loses if the stock price moves too much in either direction. Overall, options trading can be used to manage risk and limit potential losses or lock in profits, which is a powerful tool for investors.

4. Income Generation

Another advantage of stock options trading is income generation. Options trading can be used to generate income by selling options, such as covered calls or cash-secured puts. A covered call is a strategy where an investor sells call options on a stock they own. The investor receives a premium for selling the call option, which is income. If the stock price rises, the investor may have to sell their stock at the strike price, but they will already receive the premium as income. If the stock price falls, the investor can keep the stock and the premium, generating income without selling the stock. A cash-secured put is a strategy where investors sell options on a stock they don't own. The investor receives a premium for selling the put option, which is income. If the stock price falls, the investor may have to buy the stock at the strike price, but they will already receive the premium as income. If the stock price rises, the investor can keep the premium, generating income without buying the stock. Both of these strategies provide an investor with a steady income stream in relatively stable market conditions, making options trading an attractive way to generate income. Additionally, options trading can generate income through other strategies such as iron condors, calendar spread, etc. Overall, options trading offers great flexibility and allows investors to generate income in various market conditions, making it a powerful tool for income generation.

The disadvantages of stock options trading are:

1. Complexity

One of the disadvantages of stock options trading is its complexity. Options trading can be challenging to understand, especially for new investors. It involves several different terms and concepts, such as strike price, expiration date, call options, put options, and pricing models, that can take time to grasp. Additionally, the strategies involved in options trading can be complex, making it hard for new investors to navigate. Options trading also involves a greater risk than other forms of investment. The potential for large profits is matched by the potential for significant losses, which can be daunting for new investors. For example, if an investor buys a call option at a strike price higher than the current stock price and the stock price never reaches the strike price, the investor will lose the entire premium paid for the option. Similarly, if an investor buys a put option at a strike price lower than the current stock price and the stock price never falls below the strike price, the investor will lose the entire premium paid for the option. Moreover, successful options trading requires a high degree of knowledge and research. Understanding the underlying stock, the market conditions, and the volatility is essential before entering an options trade. Investors must be familiar with the different strategies and the concepts of implied volatility—Greeks delta, theta, gamma, etc. Overall, while options trading can be a powerful tool for investors, it also involves a greater degree of complexity and risk, which can be difficult for new investors to navigate.

2. Risk of Loss

One of the primary disadvantages of stock options trading is the risk of loss. This form of investment is inherently high risk, and investors can incur significant losses if their decisions do not pay off. A critical risk is that options can expire worthless if the underlying stock price does not reach the strike price before the expiration date. For instance, if an investor buys a call option with a strike price of $50 and the stock never reaches that price before expiration, the option becomes worthless and loses the entire premium paid for the option. Similarly, if an investor purchases a put option at a strike price of $50 and the stock price does not fall below that level, the option will also expire worthless, resulting in a complete loss of the premium. Options trading can lead to substantial losses if the stock price moves against the option holder. For example, if an investor buys a call option with a strike price of $50 and the stock price drops to $40, they lose the premium and the difference between the strike price and the stock price. In the case of a put option, if the stock price rises to $60, the investor again faces losses that include the premium paid plus the difference between the strike price and the current stock price. The options market is characterized by high volatility, meaning options prices can change rapidly due to fluctuations in the underlying stock price, market conditions, and other factors. This volatility adds another layer of risk, making options trading even more unpredictable. Due to the high level of risk and the potential for significant losses, options trading may only be suitable for some investors, particularly those less experienced or with a low-risk tolerance. Stock options trading carries substantial disadvantages, particularly the risk of loss. With the potential for options to expire worthless and the ability for investors to incur significant losses, this high-risk investment strategy requires careful consideration and a strong understanding of the market dynamics involved.

3. Timing

One significant disadvantage of stock options trading is the critical importance of timing. Successful options trading heavily relies on making timely decisions regarding when to buy or sell options. Options come with an expiration date, meaning they will become worthless if not exercised or sold before this date. Investors must be vigilant about these expiration dates and promptly act. The timing of buying or selling options can significantly influence the success of a trade. For example, investors can profit if they purchase a call option at a strike price of $50 and the stock price rises to $60 before expiration. However, if the investor had bought the option at a higher strike price or waited until after the stock price had increased, their profit could be diminished, or they might even incur a loss. The volatility and implied volatility of the underlying stock are also crucial factors that impact the success of options trades. Options values are significantly affected by changes in market volatility, so traders need to be aware of current market conditions. Overall, options trading requires a strong understanding of the timing of the underlying asset, market conditions, and volatility. Investors must proactively monitor their options and make quick decisions to maximize their potential returns. Timing is critical in stock options trading, affecting everything from expiration to profitability. Investors must be highly aware of expiration dates and market conditions to make informed decisions, as even slight miscalculations can lead to losses or missed opportunities.

4. Limited Profit Potential

One notable disadvantage of stock options trading is the limited profit potential. While options can yield significant returns in certain situations, the profit opportunities are generally more restricted than other investment methods. When an investor buys a call option, the maximum profit is capped at the difference between the strike price and the underlying stock price at expiration, plus any premium received. For a put option, the maximum profit is the difference between the strike price and the underlying stock price minus the premium paid at expiration. This means that profit potential is constrained by the difference between the strike price and the stock price, which can be relatively small. Options come with an expiration date. If the underlying stock price does not reach the strike price before this date, the options will expire worthless, resulting in a total loss of the premium paid. The profit potential becomes even more limited due to the multiple legs involved in these trades when employing complex strategies like the iron condor, butterfly, or calendar spread. Each component can affect overall profitability, often capping returns. While options trading can offer substantial returns under certain conditions, the profit potential is typically lower than that of other investment forms. Investors should know the limited profit potential associated with stock options trading. Understanding these limitations is crucial for managing expectations and preparing for the possibility of modest returns.

HOW TO BUY AND SELL STOCKS OPTIONS

Buying Stock Options

1. **Educate yourself.** Familiarize yourself with options trading concepts, including terms like strike price, expiration date, and premiums, and the differences between call and put options.
2. **Choose a brokerage account.** Open a brokerage account that supports options trading. Ensure that the platform offers the necessary tools and educational resources. Based on your investment experience and risk profile, you may need to apply for options trading approval.
3. **Research underlying stocks.** Identify the stocks on which you want to trade options. Analyses their performance, market trends, and relevant news to make informed decisions.
4. **Determine your strategy.** Based on your market outlook, decide on an options trading strategy. Common strategies include buying calls, buying puts, or implementing spreads and straddles.
5. **Select the option.** Select a specific option contract, determine the strike price you want to target, and select the expiration date that aligns with your trading strategy.

6. **Review the premium.** Check the premium of the option (its cost) and understand how this affects your potential profit and loss.
7. **Place the order.** Log into your brokerage account and place your order. Choose between a market order (executed immediately at current prices) or a limit order (executed at your specified price).
8. **Monitor your position.** After purchasing, keep track of the underlying stock's performance and market conditions. Be prepared to make decisions based on changes in the market.

Selling Stock Options

1. **Decide to sell.** Determine when to sell your option position. This could be when the option is profitable or you need to limit losses.
2. **Review current market conditions.** Assess the current market environment, including the stock's price movement, volatility, and any news affecting the option's value.
3. **Place the sell order.** Log into your brokerage account and place a sell order for your option. Like buying, you can choose a market or limit order, depending on your strategy and current market conditions.
4. **Confirm the transaction.** Ensure the transaction is executed as planned after placing the order. Check your account to verify the sale and update your portfolio.
5. **Evaluate the outcome.** After selling the option, review the trade results. Analyze what worked well and any lessons learned for future trading.

By following these steps for buying and selling stock options, you can effectively manage your options trading activities. Understanding the entire process—from research and strategy development to execution and evaluation—will help you make informed decisions and enhance your trading success.

TYPES OF OPTIONS

There are two primary types of options: Call Option and Put Option

Call Option

A call option is a financial contract that gives the holder the right, but not the obligation, to purchase a stock at a specified price, known as the strike price, on or before a specified expiration date. The holder of a call option is betting that the underlying stock's price will increase above the strike price, allowing them to purchase the stock at a lower price and sell it at a higher price for a profit. To use a call option, the holder must first buy the option. If the price of the underlying stock increases above the strike price before the expiration date, the holder can choose to exercise the option, purchasing the stock at the strike price and selling it at the higher market price. If the underlying stock's price does not increase above the strike price, the holder can let the option expire worthless. Call options can be useful for hedging or speculative purposes, allowing the holder to benefit from stock price movements without actually owning the stock.

Put Option

A put option is a financial contract that gives the holder the right, but not the obligation, to sell a stock at a specified price, known as the strike price, on or before a specified expiration date. The holder of a put option is betting that the underlying stock's price will decrease below the strike price, allowing them to sell the stock at a higher price and purchase it back at a lower price for a profit. To use a put option, the holder must first purchase the option. Suppose the underlying stock's price decreases below the strike price before expiration. In that case, the holder can choose to exercise the option of selling the stock at the higher strike price and repurchasing it at a lower market price. If the underlying stock's price does not decrease below the strike price, the holder can let the option expire worthless. Put options can be a valuable tool for hedging or speculative purposes, allowing the holder to benefit from stock price movements without owning the stock. However, it is essential to clearly understand options trading, as options can also result in significant losses if the stock price does not move in the expected direction.

In addition to the primary call and put options, there are several other types of options and variations that investors can utilize:

- **American options:** American options are a type of options contract that can be exercised before or on the expiration date. This flexibility allows investors to take advantage of favorable price movements in the underlying asset at any point during the option's life. For example, suppose an investor holds a call option, and the stock price rises significantly before expiration. In that case, they can exercise the option to purchase the stock at the strike price, maximizing their potential profit. This feature makes American options particularly attractive for traders who want the ability to respond quickly to market conditions.
- **European options:** European options are a type of options contract that can only be exercised on the expiration date, not before. This means that investors must wait until the specified expiration date to exercise their rights to buy or sell the underlying asset. While this limitation can restrict flexibility compared to American options, European options often have simpler pricing models and can be more straightforward for specific trading strategies. Investors typically use European options when they have a clear outlook on the underlying asset's price movement and are willing to wait until expiration to realize their gains or losses.
- **Bermudian options:** Bermudian options are a type of options contract that can be exercised on specific dates before and on the expiration date itself. This feature provides

more flexibility than European options, which can only be exercised at expiration, but less flexibility than American options, which can be exercised at any time. Investors may use Bermudian options to take advantage of favorable market conditions at predetermined intervals, making them suitable for strategies anticipating specific price movements within a set time frame.

- **Exotic options:** Exotic options are a category of options that feature complex structures and unique conditions, setting them apart from standard options. Some common types include Asian options. The payoff for these options is based on the average price of the underlying asset over a specified period rather than the price at expiration, which can help reduce the impact of volatility. Barrier options activate or deactivate when the cost of the underlying asset reaches a predetermined barrier level. They can be either knock-in options (activated upon reaching the barrier) or knock-out options (rendered worthless if the barrier is breached). Also known as binary options, digital options provide a fixed payout if the underlying asset meets certain conditions. Depending on whether the conditions are met, they typically result in either a predetermined profit or no payoff at all. Exotic options are often used to hedge or capitalize on unique market conditions, but they may be more complex and riskier.
- **Employee stock options (ESOs):** Employee stock options (ESOs) are options a company grants its employees the right to purchase company shares at a predetermined price, known as the strike price. ESOs are typically part of an employee's compensation package designed to incentivize employees to contribute to the company's success. Employees can exercise these options after a specified vesting period, allowing them to benefit from any company stock price increase. If the stock price rises above the strike price, employees can purchase shares at the lower strike price, potentially realizing significant financial gains. ESOs help align the interests of

employees with those of shareholders, fostering a sense of ownership in the company.

- **Incentive stock options (ISOs):** Incentive stock options (ISOs) are employee stock options that qualify for special tax treatment under the U.S. Internal Revenue Code. Unlike nonqualified stock options, employees who exercise ISOs do not incur an immediate tax liability. Instead, the difference between the exercise price and the stock's fair market value is reported as alternative minimum tax (AMT) income. If specific holding period requirements are met upon selling the shares, the profits may qualify for lower long-term capital gains tax rates. ISOs are typically granted to key employees as an incentive to increase company performance and align their interests with shareholders. However, ISOs have specific limitations, such as the maximum value of options that can be granted to an employee each year.
- **Nonqualified stock options (NQSOs)**: Nonqualified Stock options (NQSOs) are stock options that do not qualify for special tax treatment under the U.S. Internal Revenue Code. Unlike incentive stock options (ISOs), NQSOs can be granted to a broader range of recipients, including employees and non-employees. When an employee exercises an NQSO, the difference between the exercise price and the stock's fair market value is considered taxable income in the year of exercise, leading to immediate tax liability. Any profit from selling the stock after exercising the option may be subject to capital gains tax. NQSOs are commonly used by companies to provide compensation and incentives, but they come with different tax implications compared to ISOs.
- **Cash-settled options:** Cash-settled options are a type of options contract settled in cash rather than through the physical delivery of the underlying asset. When the option is exercised or expires, the difference between the strike price and the underlying asset's market price is paid out in cash to the holder. This type of settlement is commonly used

for options on indices or certain commodities where the underlying asset may not be easily deliverable. Cash-settled options provide a straightforward way for investors to realize gains or losses without the complications of transferring the actual asset, making them an efficient choice for many trading strategies.

Options trading is a complex investment activity; and it is essential to understand the mechanics of options trading, including the concepts of strike price, expiration date, and volatility, before getting into it. As options trading is also subject to leverage, it can be a high-risk investment, and traders should be aware of its associated risks.

When buying or selling stock option call/put, an investor must understand the following terminologies to execute their trades successfully:

Option Quantity

The quantity of options contracts in an options trading strategy refers to the number of contracts an investor buys or sells. The number of contracts can significantly impact an options strategy's potential profitability and risk. In general, the more options contracts an investor buys or sells, the greater the potential profitability and risk of the strategy. When buying options contracts, the more contracts an investor buys, the more they pay in premium, which increases the potential loss if the option expires worthless. On the other hand, when selling options contracts, the more contracts an investor sells, the more they receive in premium, which increases the potential loss if the option is exercised. It is crucial to remember that the number of options contracts should be determined based on the investor's investment goals, risk tolerance, market outlook, and the specific characteristics of the underlying asset and the options market. It is advisable to consult a financial advisor or expert before determining the quantity of options contracts for a strategy.

Option Strike Price

The strike price, also known as the exercise price, is the price at which the underlying asset can be bought or sold when an option is exercised. The strike price is one of the critical components of an options contract, and it plays a significant role in determining the potential profitability and risk of an options trading strategy. When buying call options, the strike price is the price at which the investor has the right to buy the underlying asset. The higher the strike price, the cheaper the option, but the more the underlying asset price needs to rise for the option to become profitable. When buying put options, the strike price is the price at which the investor has the right to sell the underlying asset. The lower the strike price, the cheaper the option, but the more the underlying asset price needs to fall for the option to become profitable. When selling options contracts, the choice of strike price will depend on the investor's outlook on the underlying asset and the market. Typically, a strike price closer to the underlying asset's current market price will generate a higher premium and risk. It is important to note that the strike price should be determined based on the investor's investment goals, risk tolerance, market outlook, and the specific characteristics of the underlying asset and the options market.

Option Expiration Date

The expiration date is when an options contract becomes invalid, and the right to buy or sell the underlying asset at the specified strike price is no longer valid. The expiration date is one of the critical components of an options contract, and it plays a significant role in determining the potential profitability and risk of an options trading strategy. Options contracts can have different expiration dates; the expiration date chosen will depend on the investor's investment goals, risk tolerance, and market outlook. Shorter-term option contracts have less time for the underlying asset price to move in the desired direction, which means that the potential profit is lower, but the risk is also lower. Longer-term option contracts have more time for the underlying asset price to move in the desired direction, which means that the potential profit is higher, but the risk is also higher. When buying options contracts, it's common for investors to choose expiration dates that align with their investment horizon. For example, an investor looking for a quick profit might choose a shorter-term option, while an investor looking for a longer-term investment might choose a longer-term option. When selling options contracts, the expiration date selected will depend on the investor's outlook on the underlying asset and the market. Typically, an expiration date that is later in the future will generate a higher premium and risk.

Option Bid Price

The bid price is the highest price a buyer is willing to pay for an asset, such as a stock, bond, commodity, or currency. The bid price determines the value of an investment in the marketplace and is one of the critical components of an options contract. In the context of options trading, the bid price is the price at which an option seller is willing to sell their option to a buyer. The bid price is determined by supply and demand in the market. It can fluctuate based on market conditions, such as changes in interest rates, economic conditions, and the underlying asset's price. When buying options contracts, the bid price is essential, as it will determine the price at which the option can be purchased. Investors should compare the bid price to the asking price, which is the lowest price a seller is willing to accept for the option, to determine whether the price is reasonable. When selling options contracts, the bid price is also an essential factor to consider, as it will determine the price at which the option can be sold. Investors should compare the bid price to the asking price to determine whether the option's price is reasonable and an excellent time to sell the option.

Option Ask Price

The asking price, or the offer price, is the lowest price a seller is willing to accept for an asset, such as a stock, bond, commodity, or currency. The asking price determines the value of an investment in the marketplace and is one of the critical components of an options contract. In the context of options trading, the ask price is the price at which an option buyer is willing to buy an option from a seller. The asking price is determined by supply and demand in the market. It can fluctuate based on market conditions, such as changes in interest rates, economic conditions, and the underlying asset's price. When buying options contracts, the asking price is an essential factor to consider, as it will determine the price at which the option can be purchased. Investors should compare the asking price to the bid price, the highest price a buyer is willing to pay for the option, to determine whether the price is reasonable. When selling options contracts, the asking price is also an essential factor to consider, as it will determine the price at which the option can be sold. Investors should compare the asking price to the bid price to determine whether the option's price is reasonable and an excellent time to sell the option.

Option Bid Size

Bid size refers to the number of shares or contracts offered at the bid price. In the context of options trading, the bid size represents the number of options contracts a buyer is willing to purchase at the bid price. The bid size is an essential factor to consider when buying or selling options contracts because it can indicate the level of interest in the options contract. A large bid size may suggest that there is strong demand for the options contract, while a small bid size may indicate that there is limited interest. When buying options contracts, investors should look at the bid size to determine whether enough contracts are being offered to meet their needs. A small bid size may indicate that purchasing the desired number of contracts at the bid price will be challenging. When selling options contracts, investors should also look at the bid size to determine whether there is enough demand for the contracts they sell. A small bid size may indicate that selling the desired number of contracts at the bid price will be challenging. Bid size can fluctuate rapidly in response to market conditions, so investors should monitor it closely and make their trading decisions accordingly.

Option Ask Size

Ask size refers to the number of shares or contracts offered for sale at the ask price. In the context of options trading, the ask size represents the number of options contracts a seller is willing to sell at the ask price. The ask size is an essential factor to consider when buying or selling options contracts because it can indicate the supply level of the options contract. An enormous ask size may indicate many contracts being offered for sale, while a small ask size may indicate a limited supply. When buying options contracts, investors should look at the ask size to determine whether enough contracts are being offered for sale to meet their needs. A small ask size may indicate that purchasing the desired number of contracts at the asking price will be difficult. When selling options contracts, investors should also look at the ask size to determine whether there is enough supply of contracts to meet the demand. A small ask size may indicate that selling the desired number of contracts at the asking price will be difficult. The ask size can fluctuate rapidly in response to market conditions, so investors should monitor it closely and make their trading decisions accordingly.

Option Leg

An option leg refers to a single side of an options trade, either the purchase or sale of a call or put option. An options trade can have one or more legs, depending on the complexity of the strategy. For example, a simple options trade, such as buying a call option, would have one leg. In contrast, a more complex strategy, such as a butterfly spread, would have four legs: the purchase of one call option at a lower strike price, the sale of two call options at a middle strike price, and the purchase of one call option at a higher strike price. A multi-legged options trade is a strategy that involves the simultaneous buying or selling of two or more options contracts. These trades can create various strategies, such as spreads, straddles, strangles, and combinations, which can be used for speculation and hedging.

FUTURES AND DERIVATIVES

Futures and derivatives are financial instruments commonly used in the investment and trading sectors. Futures are standardized financial contracts that obligate the buyer to purchase (in the case of a long position) or the seller to sell (in the case of a short position) a specific asset (commodity, currency, stock index, etc.) at a predetermined price (the futures price) on a specified future date (the expiration date). Futures contracts are standardized in quantity, quality, expiration date, and delivery terms, facilitating trading on organized exchanges. Futures contracts typically require a fraction of the total contract value as margin, allowing traders to control a more prominent position with a smaller initial investment. Daily settlement of gains and losses occurs by marking futures contracts to market prices and minimizing counterparty risk. Futures contracts have a fixed expiration date, after which they settle through either physical delivery of the underlying asset or cash settlement.

Futures are commonly used for hedging against price fluctuations in the underlying asset. For example, producers and consumers of commodities may use futures to hedge against adverse price movements. Traders and investors engage in futures trading to speculate on price movements, aiming to profit from buying low and selling high (long position) or selling high and buying low (short position). Arbitrageurs exploit price discrepancies between futures and underlying assets or different futures contracts to make risk-free profits.

Steps to Buying and Selling Futures

Investing in futures contracts can be an effective way to hedge against risks or speculate on price movements.

Buying Futures

1. **Master futures contracts.** Empower yourself with futures contracts, including terms like contract size, expiration dates, and margin requirements. Understand the underlying asset, whether a commodity, currency, or financial instrument, to feel confident and in control.
2. **Choose a brokerage account.** Open a brokerage account that offers futures trading. Select a broker that provides a trading platform equipped with the tools and resources for futures trading. You may need to complete an application process to demonstrate your understanding of futures and associated risks. This step ensures you are well-guided and secure in your trading journey.
3. **Research the market.** Conduct thorough research on the specific futures market you wish to trade. Analyze factors influencing price movements, including supply and demand dynamics, economic indicators, and geopolitical events.
4. **Develop a trading strategy.** Create a strategy based on your market analysis and risk tolerance. Decide whether you want to go long (buy) on a futures contract to capitalize on rising prices or short (sell) to benefit from falling prices.
5. **Select the futures contract.** Choose the specific futures contract you want to buy. Consider the contract size, expiration date, and underlying asset. Ensure that the contract aligns with your trading strategy and market outlook.
6. **Place the order.** Log into your brokerage account and place your order to buy the futures contract. You can typically choose between a market order (executed immediately at the current market price) or a limit order (executed at your specified price).
7. **Monitor your position.** After purchasing the futures contract, closely monitor your position. Keep an eye on market conditions and any factors that may impact the underlying asset's price.

Selling Futures

1. **Determine when to sell.** Based on your trading strategy and market conditions, decide when to sell your futures contract. This could be when you reach your profit target or if market conditions change and you need to cut losses.
2. **Review current market conditions.** Analyze the current market environment, including price trends, volatility, and any news that may affect your future position. Staying informed will help you make timely decisions.
3. **Place the sell order.** Log into your brokerage account and place your order to sell the futures contract. Like buying, you can choose between a market or limit orders.
4. **Confirm the transaction.** After placing the order, confirm that the transaction has been executed as planned. Check your account to verify the sale and update your trading records.
5. **Evaluate the outcome.** Review the trade results after selling the futures contract. Analyze what worked well and didn't, and use this information to refine your approach for future trading.

By following these steps, you can effectively navigate buying and selling futures contracts. Understanding the intricacies of the futures market, having a well-defined strategy, and continuously monitoring market conditions are essential for success in futures trading.

Derivatives are financial contracts derived from the value of an underlying asset, index, interest rate, or other variable. They can be traded on exchanges or over the counter (OTC), including options, swaps, forwards, and futures contracts. Derivatives derive value from underlying assets or variables, such as stocks, commodities, interest rates, currencies, cryptocurrencies, or market indices. Like futures, derivatives often provide leverage, allowing traders to control a more prominent position with a smaller initial investment. Derivatives are commonly used for risk management, including hedging against price fluctuations, interest rate changes, or currency fluctuations.

Derivatives offer flexibility regarding contract customization, allowing parties to tailor contracts to specific risk profiles or investment objectives.

Steps for Trading Derivatives

Trading derivatives can be a powerful way to manage risk, speculate on price movements, and leverage investments.

1. **Understand derivatives.** Familiarize yourself with the concept of derivatives, including different types such as options, futures, forwards, and swaps. Understand how these instruments work, their underlying assets, and the specific risks associated with each type.
2. **Choose a brokerage account.** Open a brokerage account for trading derivatives. Ensure the broker offers a user-friendly trading platform with access to the necessary tools, research resources, and educational materials. You may need to complete an application demonstrating your understanding of derivatives and associated risks.
3. **Research and analysis.** Conduct thorough research on the underlying assets associated with the derivatives you plan to trade. Analyze market trends, economic indicators, and any news events that could impact prices. Utilize technical and fundamental analysis to inform your trading decisions.
4. **Develop a trading strategy.** Create a trading strategy that aligns with your investment goals, risk tolerance, and market outlook. Decide on specific techniques, such as hedging against risks, speculating on price movements, or using spreads to limit exposure.
5. **Select the derivative contract.** Choose the specific derivative contract you want to trade. For options, this includes selecting the strike price and expiration date; for futures, this involves determining the contract size and expiration month.

6. **Determine position size.** Assess how much capital you will allocate to the trade and determine the position size accordingly. Be mindful of margin requirements and ensure your position aligns with your risk management strategy.
7. **Place the order.** Log into your brokerage account and place your order to trade the derivative contract. You can select a market order for immediate execution at the current price or a limit order to set a specific entry point.
8. **Monitor your position.** After entering the trade, actively monitor your position and the underlying asset's performance. Stay informed about market developments, price movements, and relevant news that could impact your derivatives trade.
9. **Manage risk.** Implement risk management strategies, such as setting stop-loss orders to limit potential losses. Adjust your position size or hedge your exposure if market conditions change.
10. **Decide when to exit.** Based on your trading strategy, determine when to close your position. This could involve taking profits when the market moves in your favor or cutting losses if the trade goes against you.
11. **Close the position.** Log into your brokerage account and place an order to close your derivative position. Ensure the order type (market or limit) aligns with your exit strategy.
12. **Evaluate the trade.** Review the trade to assess its performance after closing the position. Analyze what worked well and identify areas for improvement. Use this information to refine your future trading strategies.

By following these steps, you can effectively navigate the process of trading derivatives. A solid understanding of derivative instruments, a well-defined trading strategy, and proactive risk management are essential for success in the derivatives market.

Options give the holder the right (but not the obligation) to buy (call option) or sell (put option) an underlying asset at a specified price (strike price) on or before the expiration date. Swaps are agreements between parties to exchange cash flows based on specified terms, such as interest rates, currencies, or other variables. Forwards are contracts between two parties to buy or sell an asset at a specified price on a future date, with terms customized to the parties' requirements. As discussed earlier, futures contracts are standardized derivatives traded on organized exchanges, obligating the buyer or seller to transact at a predetermined price and date. Derivatives are crucial in managing and mitigating various financial risks, including price, interest rate, currency, and credit risks. Traders and investors use derivatives for speculative purposes, aiming to profit from anticipated price movements or market trends. Derivatives can diversify investment portfolios and gain exposure to asset classes or markets that may not be accessible through direct investment.

LEVERAGED TRADING AND MARGIN ACCOUNTS

Leveraged trading and margin accounts are standard features in financial markets that allow investors to amplify their exposure to assets and potentially increase their returns. However, they also entail increased risk and require a good understanding of how it works. Leveraged trading involves using borrowed funds or margins to increase the size of a trading position beyond what would be possible with only the investor's capital. It allows traders to control more prominent positions with a smaller initial investment. Investors must deposit a percentage of the total position's value as a margin to engage in leveraged trading. The rest of the position's value is borrowed from the broker. The leverage ratio determines how much exposure a trader can have compared to their margin deposit. For example, a leverage ratio of 10:1 means that for every $1 of margin, the trader can control a $10 position.

If the value of the leveraged position declines significantly, the broker may issue a margin call, requiring the trader to deposit additional funds to maintain the position or risk liquidation. Leveraged trading can magnify profits when the market moves in the trader's favor; traders can access more prominent positions with a smaller amount of capital, allowing for greater diversification or exposure to multiple assets. Leverage amplifies both profits and losses. A slight adverse price movement can lead to significant losses or even wipe out the entire margin deposit. Margin calls can occur if the market moves against the trader, requiring additional funds and potentially leading to forced liquidation.

Margin accounts accrue interest on borrowed funds, increasing the cost of trading. Traders should consider the interest rates and costs associated with margin borrowing. A margin call occurs when the account's equity falls below the maintenance margin level. The broker may require the trader to deposit additional funds or close out positions to restore the required margin level. Margin accounts enable investors to engage in leveraged trading, amplifying their market exposure. Margin accounts allow traders to sell securities short, betting on price declines and potentially profiting from falling markets. Margin is often required for options and futures trading to cover potential losses and ensure contract fulfilment. Margin accounts amplify gains and losses, and traders should know the increased risk of significant losses. Borrowed funds in a margin account accrue interest, which can reduce overall returns. Margin calls can occur during volatile market conditions or if positions move against the trader, requiring prompt action to avoid forced liquidation.

ALGORITHMIC TRADING AND HIGH-FREQUENCY TRADING

Algorithmic trading and high-frequency trading (HFT) are sophisticated strategies used in financial markets, leveraging technology and automation to execute trades at high speeds. Algorithmic trading, or algo trading or automated trading, involves using computer algorithms to execute trades based on predefined rules, strategies, and parameters. These algorithms analyze market data, price movements, and other factors to make trading decisions without human intervention. Algorithms can execute trades much faster than human traders, taking advantage of market opportunities and reacting to millisecond price changes. Algo trading removes emotional bias from trading decisions, relying on data-driven analysis and predetermined rules. Algorithmic strategies can be scaled across multiple assets, markets, and time frames, allowing for efficient portfolio management and diversification. Before deployment, algorithms are often backtested using historical data to assess their performance and optimize parameters.

These algorithms optimize trade execution by minimizing market impact, slippage, and transaction costs. They also identify and capitalize on market trends, buying during uptrends and selling during downtrends. Arbitrage algorithms exploit price discrepancies between related assets or markets to generate risk-free profits. These algorithms use mathematical models and statistical analysis to identify trading opportunities based on complex patterns and indicators.

Market makers and liquidity providers use algo trading to provide liquidity to markets, improving trading efficiency and reducing spreads. Institutional investors and hedge funds use algorithms to execute large orders efficiently without significantly impacting market prices. Algo trading can incorporate risk management strategies, such as stop-loss orders and position sizing, to mitigate potential losses.

High-frequency trading is a subset of algorithmic trading that focuses on executing many trades at extremely high speeds, often in microseconds or milliseconds. HFT strategies capitalize on small price inefficiencies and exploit market microstructure patterns. HFT relies on cutting-edge technology, low-latency infrastructure, and direct market access (DMA) to execute trades at lightning speed. HFT firms often co-locate their servers near exchange servers to minimize latency and gain a speed advantage. HFT firms act as market makers, providing market liquidity and profiting from bid-ask spreads. HFT strategies use statistical models, algorithms, and real-time data analysis to identify short-term trading opportunities based on price discrepancies and market inefficiencies.

HFT firms continuously quote bids and ask prices, profiting from the spread of buy-and-sell prices. These strategies exploit statistical anomalies and correlations in asset prices to generate profits. HFT algorithms predict market direction based on order flow data and execute trades accordingly. Critics argue that HFT can contribute to market volatility, especially during periods of high uncertainty. Some concerns center around fairness, transparency, and potential market manipulation in HFT. HFT has faced regulatory scrutiny regarding market structure, co-location practices, and possible systemic risks.

UTILIZING ARTIFICIAL INTELLIGENCE (AI)

Artificial intelligence (AI) has revolutionized the stock market, offering transformative capabilities that enhance trading strategies, investment decisions, and market analysis. AI's integration into financial markets has introduced a range of advanced techniques and tools that leverage data, algorithms, and computational power to provide deeper insights and more accurate predictions.

Critical Applications of AI in the Stock Market

1. **Algorithmic trading:** AI-driven algorithmic trading uses sophisticated algorithms to execute trades at high speeds and frequencies. These algorithms analyze market data, historical trends, and real-time information to automatically identify trading opportunities and manage orders. This approach minimizes human error, reduces transaction costs, and precisely capitalizes on market inefficiencies.
2. **Predictive analytics:** AI models utilize machine learning techniques to predict stock price movements and market trends. AI can accurately forecast potential market movements by analyzing historical and real-time data, including financial statements, news articles, and social media sentiment. These predictions help investors make informed decisions and optimize their portfolios.

3. **Sentiment analysis:** AI-powered sentiment analysis tools analyze social media, news feeds, and other textual data to gauge market sentiment and investor emotions. AI can provide insights into market sentiment shifts by assessing the tone and context of financial news and public opinion, helping traders anticipate market reactions and adjust their strategies accordingly.
4. **Risk management:** AI enhances risk management by accurately evaluating and quantifying financial risks. Machine learning algorithms can identify potential risks, assess market volatility, and simulate various scenarios. This enables investors to develop more effective risk mitigation strategies and protect their portfolios from adverse market conditions.
5. **Portfolio optimization:** AI tools assist in optimizing investment portfolios by analyzing asset correlations, market trends, and individual stock performance. AI algorithms can suggest optimal asset allocations, rebalancing strategies, and diversification options based on investor goals and risk tolerance. This leads to more efficient portfolio management and improved investment outcomes.
6. **Fraud detection:** AI is crucial in detecting and preventing financial fraud. Advanced machine learning algorithms can identify unusual trading patterns, detect anomalies, and flag potentially fraudulent activities in real time. This helps maintain market integrity and protects investors from fraudulent schemes.
7. **Personalized investment advice:** AI-driven robo-advisors provide personalized investment recommendations based on individual investor profiles, including financial goals, risk tolerance, and investment preferences. These automated advisors use AI to continuously analyze market conditions and adjust investment strategies to align with clients' objectives.

Benefits of AI

- **Speed and efficiency**: AI systems can process and analyze vast amounts of data rapidly, executing trades and generating insights much faster than human capabilities.
- **Data-driven insights:** AI leverages large datasets and advanced algorithms to uncover patterns and trends that may not be apparent through traditional analysis.
- **Reduced human bias:** AI eliminates emotional and cognitive biases, leading to more objective and data-driven decision-making.
- **Enhanced accuracy:** AI models improve prediction accuracy and risk assessment by incorporating various variables and data sources.

Challenges and Considerations:

- **Data quality:** AI models' effectiveness depends on the data's quality and accuracy. Inaccurate or incomplete data can lead to misleading results.
- **Algorithmic risk:** Over-reliance on AI algorithms can lead to unintended consequences if flawed algorithms fail to account for unforeseen market events.
- **Regulatory compliance:** AI in trading and investment must adhere to regulatory guidelines to ensure fair and transparent market practices.

AI has become a powerful tool in the stock market, offering innovative solutions that enhance trading efficiency, investment strategies, and risk management. By harnessing the power of AI, investors and traders can gain a competitive edge, make more informed decisions, and navigate the complexities of financial markets with greater precision. As AI technology continues to evolve, its role in shaping the future of investing and trading will likely become even more profound, offering new opportunities and challenges for market participants.

This chapter has traversed the intricate landscape of advanced trading and investing, equipping you with insights into some of the most sophisticated strategies and tools in the financial markets. From mastering options trading strategies to understanding the complexities of futures and derivatives, we have explored how these instruments can be leveraged to manage risk, speculate on price movements, and enhance your investment strategy.

We delved into the process of buying and selling stock options, emphasizing the importance of strategic execution and platform navigation. This foundational knowledge is crucial for implementing effective options strategies and achieving desired outcomes in your trading endeavors.

Examining leveraged trading and margin accounts taught you how borrowed capital can amplify potential returns and risks. The power of leverage offers significant opportunities but requires careful risk management to avoid substantial losses. This understanding is vital for those looking to incorporate leverage into their trading strategies.

In exploring 'Algorithmic Trading and High-Frequency Trading [HFT]', we showcased the transformative impact of technology on modern markets. Leveraging algorithms and high-speed trading systems and executing trades with unparalleled precision and efficiency can give you a competitive edge. However, it is essential to recognize the complexities and potential market impacts associated with these advanced trading methods.

Finally, we ventured into artificial intelligence (AI), uncovering how AI technologies revolutionize trading and investing. From predictive analytics to pattern recognition, AI is reshaping the landscape of financial markets, offering innovative tools and strategies for enhancing decision-making and strategy development.

This chapter has provided a comprehensive overview of advanced topics in trading and investing, highlighting the diverse tools and strategies available to experienced investors and traders. As you integrate these advanced concepts into your approach, combine them with fundamental knowledge and rigorous risk management practices. The dynamic nature of financial markets demands continuous learning and adaptation, making this chapter a critical step in mastering the art and science of sophisticated trading and investing strategies.

Chapter 10

GLOBAL MARKETS AND INTERNATIONAL INVESTING

Understanding and navigating global markets is essential for investors seeking diversification, growth, and risk management in the ever-evolving landscape of investment opportunities. This chapter in Mastering the Stock Market delves into the intricacies of international investing, providing an overview of global markets, currency risk, investing in emerging markets, and strategies for global diversification. In summary, let's explore each component.

Global markets encompass various geographic regions, economies, and financial instruments, offering investors diverse opportunities beyond domestic markets. Understanding international markets involves analyzing geopolitical factors, economic indicators, regulatory frameworks, market structures, and cultural nuances that influence investment dynamics. International markets provide exposure to different sectors, industries, currencies, and asset classes, allowing investors to capitalize on growth trends, technological advancements, and demographic shifts worldwide.

Currency risk, also known as foreign exchange (FX) risk, arises from fluctuations in exchange rates between currencies, impacting the value of international investments denominated in foreign currencies. Exchange rate movements can affect investment returns, portfolio diversification, purchasing power, and corporate earnings of multinational companies operating in global markets. Investors should employ hedging strategies, currency overlays, and diversification across currencies to mitigate currency risk and optimize risk-adjusted returns in international portfolios.

Emerging markets represent economies with rapid growth potential, increasing industrialization, urbanization, technological innovation, and demographic dividends. Investing in emerging markets offers opportunities for high returns, diversification benefits, exposure to dynamic industries, and access to untapped consumer markets. However, emerging markets also pose political instability, regulatory uncertainties, currency volatility, liquidity constraints, and governance issues, requiring thorough due diligence and risk assessment.

Global diversification is a cornerstone of modern portfolio theory. It emphasizes the benefits of spreading investments across different countries, regions, and asset classes to reduce risk and enhance returns. Diversification strategies may include allocating capital to developed markets, emerging markets, frontier markets, alternative investments, tangible assets, and non-correlated assets to achieve optimal risk-adjusted returns. Investors can utilize exchange-traded funds (ETFs), mutual funds, global indices, multi-asset portfolios, and asset allocation models to implement global diversification strategies tailored to their risk tolerance, investment objectives, and time horizon.

OVERVIEW OF INTERNATIONAL MARKETS

The overview of international markets provides investors with a comprehensive understanding of the various geographic regions, economies, financial instruments, and investment opportunities available beyond domestic markets.

Geographic Regions

Geographic regions play a crucial role in international markets, representing distinct economic, political, and cultural landscapes that influence investment opportunities and risk profiles. **Developed economies** encompass North America (United States and Canada), Western Europe (United Kingdom, Germany, and France), Japan, Australia, and other advanced economies. These regions typically have well-established financial markets, regulatory frameworks, infrastructure, technological capabilities, and diversified industries. Investors often perceive developed economies as stable, mature, and relatively low-risk, offering opportunities for steady income, dividend-paying stocks, blue-chip companies, and investment-grade bonds.

Emerging markets include regions such as Asia (China, India, and South Korea); Latin America (Brazil and Mexico); Eastern Europe (Russia and Poland); Africa (South Africa and Nigeria); and the Middle East (Saudi Arabia and UAE). These regions exhibit rapid economic growth, industrialization, urbanization, demographic dividends, and increasing consumer demand. Investors are attracted to emerging markets for their high growth potential, expanding middle class, rising consumption, infrastructure development, and technological advancements. However, emerging markets also pose currency volatility, political instability, regulatory uncertainties, governance issues, and liquidity constraints.

Frontier markets represent less developed or developing economies with smaller capital markets, limited liquidity, and higher risk profiles than emerging markets. These regions include countries in Africa (Kenya and Ghana), the Middle East (Qatar and Kuwait), Asia (Vietnam and Bangladesh), and Eastern Europe (Ukraine and Serbia). Frontier markets expose investors to early-stage growth opportunities, untapped markets, niche industries, and entrepreneurial ventures. However, they also entail higher risks, including political risks, liquidity risks, market inefficiencies, and limited investor protections.

Global financial centers are hubs for international finance, capital markets, banking, asset management, and corporate headquarters. Major financial centers include New York (Wall Street), London (City of London), Tokyo, Hong Kong, Singapore, Zurich, Frankfurt, and Dubai. These centers facilitate cross-border investments, capital flows, mergers and acquisitions, foreign exchange trading, and investment banking activities. Global financial centers attract institutional investors, multinational corporations, financial institutions, and high-net-worth individuals seeking access to international capital markets, liquidity, expertise, and financial services. Regional economic blocs, such as the European Union (EU), North American Free Trade Agreement (NAFTA), Association of Southeast Asian Nations (ASEAN), and Mercosur, promote economic integration, trade liberalization, and cooperation among member countries. These blocs create opportunities for cross-border trade, investment, market access, regulatory harmonization, and financial partnerships. Investors consider regional economic blocs when assessing market trends, regulatory changes, trade agreements, and investment opportunities across member countries.

ECONOMIC INDICATORS AS RELATES TO INTERNATIONAL MARKET

Economic indicators are essential metrics that provide insights into the overall health, performance, and trends of economies influencing the international market. GDP measures the total value of goods and services produced within a country's borders. International investors monitor GDP growth rates to gauge economic expansion or contraction, which impacts investment decisions and market sentiment. The inflation rate measures the rate of change in the general price level of goods and services. Inflation affects international markets' purchasing power, interest rates, investment returns, and currency values.

The unemployment rate reflects labor market conditions and job creation. High unemployment rates may signal economic weakness, impacting global consumer spending, business investment, and market confidence. Central banks set interest rates, influencing borrowing costs, investment returns, and currency valuations. Changes in interest rates affect bond yields, mortgage rates, capital flows, and financial market volatility internationally.

The trade balance measures the difference between exports and imports of goods and services. A country's trade balance impacts its currency strength, current account balance, and international trade dynamics. Exchange rates reflect the value of one currency relative to another. Currency exchange rates affect trade competitiveness, export/import volumes, capital flows, and investment returns for international investors.

The Consumer Confidence Index measures consumer sentiment, spending intentions, and economic optimism. Consumer confidence influences retail sales, consumer behavior, business revenues, and market demand internationally. Business Confidence Index assesses business sentiment, investment intentions, and industry outlook. High business confidence supports global corporate investment, economic growth, and market expansion.

Global economic indicators include GDP growth, international trade volumes, commodity prices, and geopolitical risks. These indicators assess global economic trends, market interconnections, and investment opportunities across countries and regions. Financial market indicators include stock market indices, bond yields, credit spreads, and volatility indices. These indicators reflect investor sentiment, market liquidity, risk appetite, and asset valuations in international financial markets. Understanding and analyzing economic indicators help international investors make informed decisions, assess risk, identify opportunities, and navigate market trends in a globalized economy.

INTERNATIONAL MARKET STRUCTURES

Market structures in the international market refer to the organization and framework that facilitate trading, investment, and capital flows across borders. Stock exchanges are platforms where investors buy and sell securities such as stocks and bonds. International stock exchanges, such as the New York Stock Exchange (NYSE), Nasdaq, London Stock Exchange (LSE), Tokyo Stock Exchange (TSE), and Shanghai Stock Exchange (SSE), provide liquidity and price discovery for global equities and securities.

Bond markets facilitate issuing and trading fixed-income securities such as government, corporate, and municipal bonds. International bond markets offer opportunities for sovereign debt, corporate financing, and capital raising through bond issuances in multiple currencies. Currency markets, also known as foreign exchange (FX) markets, enable the buying and selling of currencies. They determine exchange rates, currency values, and cross-border transactions, influencing international trade, investment flows, and currency risk management.

Commodity markets trade physical goods such as agricultural products, energy commodities (oil and natural gas), metals (gold and silver), and soft commodities (coffee and cotton). International commodity markets provide price discovery, hedging mechanisms, and investment opportunities for commodities traded globally. Derivatives markets include futures contracts, options, swaps, and other financial instruments derived from underlying assets such as stocks, bonds, currencies, and commodities.

International derivatives markets offer risk management tools, speculation opportunities, and hedging strategies for investors and businesses operating in global markets.

Alternative investment platforms include private equity, venture capital, hedge funds, real estate investment trusts (REITs), and infrastructure funds. International alternative investment platforms provide sophisticated investors access to nontraditional assets, diversification benefits, and higher-risk/higher-return opportunities.

Multi-asset portfolios combine different asset classes, including stocks, bonds, commodities, real estate, and alternative investments. International multi-asset portfolios optimize risk-adjusted returns, asset allocation strategies, and diversification across global markets.

Regulatory frameworks govern market operations, investor protections, disclosure requirements, and market integrity in international financial markets. Global regulatory bodies, such as the Securities and Exchange Commission (SEC), Financial Conduct Authority (FCA), European Securities and Markets Authority (ESMA), and International Organization of Securities Commissions (IOSCO), establish standards and regulations for cross-border investments and market activities.

INTERNATIONAL FINANCIAL INSTRUMENTS

Financial instruments in the international market refer to various tradable assets and contracts that investors use to manage risk, invest capital, and generate returns across global markets. Stocks represent ownership in a company and provide shareholders with voting rights and dividends. International stocks are traded on global exchanges, exposing investors to companies from different countries, sectors, and industries. Bonds are debt instruments governments, corporations, or municipalities issued to raise capital. International bonds allow investors to lend money to entities outside their home country and earn fixed interest payments (coupon) until maturity.

Foreign exchange instruments include currencies, currency pairs, spot contracts, forwards, options, and futures. FX markets facilitate currency trading, exchange rate hedging, international trade settlements, and speculation on currency movements. Commodities are physical goods such as agricultural products (wheat and corn), energy commodities (crude oil and natural gas), metals (gold and silver), and soft commodities (coffee and cotton). International commodity markets offer futures contracts, options, and spot trading for hedging, speculation, and investment in global commodity prices.

Derivatives are financial contracts derived from underlying assets such as stocks, bonds, currencies, commodities, or indices. International derivatives markets include futures contracts, options, swaps, and forwards for risk management, speculation, leverage, and arbitrage. ETFs are investment funds that track indices, sectors, or asset classes and trade on stock exchanges. International ETFs provide exposure to global markets, regions, industries, and investment themes through diversified portfolios of stocks, bonds, or commodities.

International mutual funds pool money from investors to invest in a diversified portfolio of securities managed by professional fund managers. International mutual funds invest in global equities, bonds, or a mix of assets to achieve diversification and investment objectives across international markets. REITs own, operate, or finance income-generating real estate properties. International REITs invest in commercial, residential, or industrial properties in different countries, exposing investors to global real estate markets. Hedge funds are alternative investment vehicles that employ various strategies (long/short, arbitrage, macro, and event-driven) to generate absolute returns. International hedge funds target global opportunities, leverage, and specialized techniques to manage risk and enhance portfolio performance. Private equity and venture capital funds invest in private companies, startups, or distressed assets to provide capital, expertise, and strategic support. International private equity and venture capital firms focus on cross-border investments, growth opportunities, and value creation in global markets.

INTERNATIONAL INVESTMENT OPPORTUNITIES

Investment opportunities in the international market refer to various avenues and assets available to investors seeking to allocate capital outside their domestic borders. Investing in global equities provides exposure to publicly traded companies from different countries, sectors, and industries. International stocks offer diversification benefits, growth potential, dividend income, and opportunities to capitalize on worldwide sector-specific trends and economic cycles. Global bonds are debt securities issued by governments, corporations, or municipalities outside the investor's home country. Investing in international bonds offers fixed income, currency diversification, yield enhancement, and access to sovereign debt, corporate bonds, and emerging market bonds.

Forex trading involves buying and selling currencies in the foreign exchange market. Currency trading provides opportunities for speculation, hedging currency risk, capitalizing on exchange rate movements, and conducting international trade transactions. Investing in commodities involves trading physical goods such as agricultural products, energy commodities, metals, and soft commodities. Commodity investments offer diversification, inflation protection, hedging against commodity price fluctuations, and exposure to global supply-demand dynamics.

International real estate investments include commercial properties, residential properties, REITs, and development projects. Real estate investing offers rental income, capital appreciation, portfolio diversification, and exposure to global property markets and economic cycles. Investing in emerging markets involves allocating capital to economies with high growth potential, expanding consumer markets, and rapid industrialization. Emerging markets offer opportunities in sectors like technology, healthcare, consumer goods, infrastructure, and financial services but pose currency volatility risks and political instability.

Exchange-traded funds (ETFs) and mutual funds offer diversified portfolios of international stocks, bonds, commodities, and sectors. Global ETFs and mutual funds provide easy access to international markets, professional management, liquidity, and risk-adjusted returns for investors seeking broad exposure. Alternative investments include hedge funds, private equity, venture capital, commodities futures, and structured products. Alternative investments offer non-correlated returns, risk mitigation, capital preservation, and specialized strategies for sophisticated international investors.

Investing in infrastructure projects, energy assets, and renewable energy sources provides exposure to global infrastructure development, energy transition, and sustainability initiatives. Infrastructure investments offer stable cash flows, long-term returns, inflation protection, transportation, utilities, and renewable energy opportunities. Investing in global dividend-paying stocks provides income, capital appreciation, and exposure to companies with solid fundamentals and sustainable dividend policies. Dividend stocks offer a source of passive income, diversification across regions and sectors, and participation in global economic growth.

RISKS AND CHALLENGES IN INTERNATIONAL MARKETS

Investing in the international market presents various risks and challenges that investors must consider when allocating capital across borders. Currency risk, also known as exchange rate risk, arises from fluctuations in currency values relative to the investor's home currency. Exchange rate movements can impact investment returns, asset valuations, and international trade competitiveness.

Political instability, geopolitical tensions, government policies, and regulatory changes in foreign countries can affect investment decisions and business operations. Political and regulatory risks include changes in taxation, trade policies, legal frameworks, and government stability. Economic risks stem from macroeconomic factors such as GDP growth, inflation, interest rates, unemployment, and fiscal deficits. Financial risks include market volatility, credit risks, liquidity constraints, systemic risks, and financial market disruptions. Each country has unique risks related to economic conditions, political stability, legal systems, infrastructure, cultural differences, and market transparency. Country-specific risks impact investment opportunities, market access, and risk-adjusted returns in international markets. Investing in emerging markets entails currency volatility, liquidity risks, political instability, regulatory uncertainties, and governance challenges. Emerging markets may offer high growth potential but pose higher risks than developed economies.

International market risks include price volatility, market corrections, liquidity shocks, and unexpected events, which refer to the various challenges and uncertainties that investors face when engaging in foreign markets. International markets can experience significant fluctuations in asset prices due to factors like economic data releases, geopolitical tensions, and changes in investor sentiment. This volatility can impact the value of investments. Global markets are susceptible to corrections, where asset prices adjust downwards after a period of rapid appreciation. These corrections can be triggered by economic indicators, shifts in monetary policy, or external shocks. Liquidity risk arises when there is a sudden decrease in the availability of capital or market participants. This can make it difficult for investors to buy or sell assets without significantly impacting prices, particularly in less liquid markets. Events such as natural disasters, political upheaval, or regulatory environment changes can unexpectedly disrupt markets. These unforeseen circumstances can lead to rapid changes in asset values and investor behavior.

Liquidity risks refer to the ease of buying or selling assets without significantly affecting prices. International markets may experience liquidity challenges, especially in less liquid assets, smaller markets, or during periods of market stress. Operational risks include technology failures, cyber threats, fraud, compliance failures, supply-chain disruptions, and operational errors. International investments require robust operational processes, risk management frameworks, and due diligence to mitigate operational risks.

Cultural differences, social unrest, labor disputes, environmental concerns, and ethical considerations can impact business operations and investor perceptions. Understanding cultural nuances, social dynamics, and stakeholder expectations is crucial for successfully navigating international markets. While diversification can reduce portfolio risks, overdiversification or concentration in certain regions, sectors, or asset classes may lead to unintended risks. Balancing diversification with concentration risks requires strategic asset allocation, risk assessment, and portfolio rebalancing.

Managing risks and challenges in the international market requires comprehensive risk analysis, due diligence, diversification strategies, risk mitigation techniques, and active portfolio management. Investors should assess risk-return profiles, conduct thorough research, monitor market developments, and stay informed about global economic trends and geopolitical events. International investing involves risks and challenges such as currency risk, geopolitical risk, regulatory risk, financial volatility, liquidity constraints, cultural differences, legal considerations, and market uncertainties. Investors conduct thorough risk assessments, due diligence, and portfolio analysis to manage risks effectively and optimize risk-adjusted returns in international portfolios.

GLOBALIZATION AND INTERCONNECTEDNESS

Globalization and interconnectedness are fundamental concepts that define the dynamics of the international market. Globalization refers to the increasing integration and interdependence of worldwide economies, industries, markets, cultures, and societies. It is driven by technological advancements, trade liberalization, capital flows, communication networks, transportation infrastructure, and multinational corporations. Interconnectedness represents the interconnected nature of global markets, financial systems, supply chains, and information networks. It reflects the seamless flow of goods, services, capital, information, and ideas across borders, regions, and continents. Globalization has led to market integration, where financial markets, stock exchanges, commodity markets, and currency markets operate globally, facilitating cross-border investments, trading, and capital flows. Market integration enhances liquidity, price discovery, market efficiency, and access to diverse investment opportunities for investors worldwide.

Globalization fosters international trade and investment by reducing trade barriers, tariffs, quotas, and regulatory hurdles through trade agreements, free trade zones, and economic blocs. It promotes specialization, comparative advantage, economies of scale, and market access for businesses seeking global expansion and market penetration.

Multinational corporations play a pivotal role in globalization by operating across multiple countries; establishing global supply chains; and accessing international markets for production, sales, and distribution. They leverage global resources, talent pools, technology transfer, and innovation ecosystems to drive global growth, competitiveness, and market share. Globalization facilitates the free flow of capital, investments, and financial products across borders, enabling portfolio diversification, risk management, and access to global investment opportunities. Financial flows include foreign direct investment (FDI), portfolio investments, remittances, foreign exchange transactions, and international banking services.

Technological advancements, digitalization, internet connectivity, and communication networks have accelerated globalization by enabling real-time information sharing, online transactions, e-commerce, and virtual collaborations. They connect businesses, investors, consumers, and markets globally, driving innovation, productivity, and competitiveness. Global supply chains encompass sourcing, manufacturing, logistics, distribution, and delivery networks that span multiple countries and continents. Supply-chain globalization optimizes production efficiencies, cost savings, product quality, market responsiveness, and access to diverse markets.

Globalization fosters cultural exchange, diversity, multiculturalism, and cross-cultural interactions through travel, tourism, education, media, arts, and entertainment. It promotes cultural understanding, tolerance, global citizenship, and appreciation of diverse perspectives and values. While globalization offers numerous benefits, such as economic growth, innovation, job creation, and market expansion, it poses challenges like income inequality, environmental impact, social disruptions, and geopolitical tensions. Managing globalization requires effective governance, regulatory frameworks, sustainability initiatives, inclusive growth strategies, and international cooperation.

CURRENCY RISK AND EXCHANGE RATES

Currency risk, also known as exchange rate risk, is the risk that changes in exchange rates between currencies can negatively impact the value of investments denominated in foreign currencies. Currency risk arises from holding investments, assets, or liabilities denominated in a foreign currency. Investors, businesses, and financial institutions face currency risk when their domestic currency weakens relative to the foreign currency in which their investments are held. There is a risk that exchange rate fluctuations will impact the value of financial transactions involving foreign currencies, such as imports, exports, and cross-border payments. The risk multinational corporations face when converting financial statements from foreign subsidiaries into the reporting currency leads to fluctuations in reported earnings. The risk is that exchange rate changes affect companies' competitiveness in international markets, impacting sales, profits, and market share.

Economic indicators, central bank policies, interest rate differentials, inflation rates, GDP growth, trade balances, and political stability influence exchange rate movements. Market perceptions, investor sentiment, risk appetite, geopolitical events, and global economic trends can lead to currency fluctuations. Currency speculation, market interventions by central banks, currency pegs, and government policies can impact exchange rates. Currency fluctuations can enhance or erode investment returns for foreign investors depending on whether the domestic currency strengthens or weakens against the foreign currency. Hedging strategies such as forward contracts, options, and currency swaps can mitigate currency risk but may incur costs and impact overall portfolio performance. Currency risk affects the competitiveness of exporters, importers, multinational corporations, and tourism industries by influencing prices, costs, revenues, and profit margins.

Exchange rates represent the value of one currency relative to another in the foreign exchange market. Exchange rates are quoted as currency pairs (e.g. USD/EUR or GBP/JPY) and can be expressed as spot rates (current market rates) or forward rates (future delivery rates). Higher interest rates in a country attract foreign capital, strengthening the currency. Lower interest rates can lead to currency depreciation. Countries with lower inflation rates typically have stronger currencies as purchasing power remains stable. Strong economic fundamentals, robust GDP growth, low unemployment rates, and trade surpluses can support a currency's value. Political stability, sound governance, rule of law, and institutional strength enhance investor confidence and currency stability. Market perceptions, risk aversion, geopolitical tensions, and global economic trends influence investor currency demand.

Floating Exchange Rates

Exchange rates are determined by supply-and-demand market forces without government intervention. Governments or central banks peg their currency's value to another currency, a basket of currencies, or a commodity like gold. Exchange rates fluctuate within a range, but central banks intervene to stabilize or influence currency values. Exchange rates affect the competitiveness of exports and imports, trade balances, trade flows, and terms of trade between countries. Exchange rates influence capital flows, foreign direct investment (FDI), portfolio investments, and capital allocation decisions by investors. Exchange rate movements impact financial markets, asset prices, interest rates, bond yields, equity valuations, and currency-linked derivatives.

Hedging strategies such as forward contracts, options, currency swaps, and futures can help mitigate exchange rate risk for businesses, investors, and financial institutions. A diversified portfolio of assets denominated in different currencies can reduce overall currency risk exposure. Continuous monitoring of exchange rate movements, economic indicators, geopolitical developments, and central bank policies is essential for managing currency risk effectively. Understanding currency risk and exchange rates is crucial for investors, businesses, governments, and central banks operating in the global economy. Managing currency risk requires a comprehensive understanding of market dynamics, risk assessment, hedging strategies, and proactive risk management practices to navigate currency fluctuations and protect against potential losses.

INVESTING IN EMERGING MARKETS

Investing in emerging markets refers to allocating funds to economies in the early stages of development but with promising growth prospects. Emerging markets often exhibit faster economic growth rates compared to developed economies. This growth is fueled by a young and growing population, increasing urbanization, rising consumer demand, and technological advancements. These economies typically have the potential to leapfrog stages of development and offer lucrative investment opportunities. Many emerging markets are rich in natural resources like minerals, energy sources, and agricultural products. Investments in sectors related to these resources can benefit from global demand, commodity price cycles, and infrastructure development. Emerging markets often have a demographic advantage, with a large proportion of the population being working age. This demographic dividend can drive consumption, innovation, entrepreneurship, and productivity growth. Investments in sectors catering to the needs and preferences of this demographic, such as technology, healthcare, education, and consumer goods, can be desirable.

Urbanization and Infrastructure Development

Rapid urbanization in emerging markets increases demand for infrastructure development in areas like transportation, energy, telecommunications, and real estate. Investments in infrastructure projects offer long-term returns, contribute to economic growth, create jobs, and support urban development. Rising incomes and a growing middle class in emerging markets boost consumer spending on goods and services. This trend creates investment opportunities for retail, e-commerce, healthcare, entertainment, and hospitality. Companies catering to the rising consumer demand often experience strong growth trajectories. Emerging markets embrace technological innovations, digitalization, and internet penetration. Investments in information technology, e-commerce, fintech, and telecommunications capitalize on these trends. Technological advancements drive efficiency, connectivity, and market penetration in emerging economies.

Strategies for Investing in Emerging Markets

Investing in emerging markets can offer significant growth potential and unique risks and challenges. Here are several strategies to consider when investing in these markets:

1. **Diversify geographically.** Spread investments across multiple emerging markets rather than concentrating on a single country. This reduces exposure to country-specific risks, such as political instability or economic downturns.
2. **Diversify sectors.** Invest in various sectors (e.g. technology, healthcare, consumer goods) within emerging markets to balance risk and capture growth across different industries.
3. **Focus on long-term growth.** Emerging markets may experience higher volatility, so adopting a long-term investment horizon can help mitigate short-term fluctuations. Look for countries with strong economic fundamentals, favorable demographics, and increasing consumer demand.

4. **Invest in local companies.** Consider investing in local companies poised for growth. These firms often better understand the local market dynamics and consumer behavior, which can lead to better performance than foreign companies.
5. **Use exchange-traded funds (ETFs).** ETFs focused on emerging markets can provide exposure to a diverse range of stocks or bonds within these regions. They offer liquidity, lower fees, and easy access to a broad portfolio of emerging market assets without needing to pick individual stocks.
6. **Evaluate economic indicators.** Monitor vital economic indicators such as GDP growth, inflation rates, currency stability, and political stability. Understanding the economic environment can help you make informed investment decisions.
7. **Be aware of currency risk.** Currency fluctuations can significantly impact returns in emerging markets. Consider strategies such as hedging to protect against adverse currency movements or focus on companies with natural currency hedges.
8. **Research and understand local regulations.** Each emerging market has rules and regulations that can affect investment opportunities. Stay informed about changes in laws, taxation, and foreign investment policies that could impact your investments.
9. **Consider active management.** Given the complexities and risks associated with emerging markets, an actively managed fund or portfolio may provide a better approach. Experienced fund managers can navigate these markets more effectively than individual investors.
10. **Invest in infrastructure and real assets.** Emerging markets often require significant infrastructure investments, such as transportation, energy, and telecommunications. Investing in infrastructure projects or tangible assets can provide stable returns while contributing to economic growth.

11. **Stay informed and adaptive.** Keep abreast of global economic trends, political developments, and changes in market sentiment. Adapting your investment strategy based on new information is crucial in the dynamic landscape of emerging markets. Investing in emerging markets can offer substantial growth opportunities, but it requires careful consideration of risks and an informed strategy. By diversifying investments, focusing on long-term growth, and staying updated on economic and regulatory changes, investors can effectively navigate these markets and enhance their potential for success.

Risks and Challenges in Emerging Markets

Political instability, policy changes, regulatory frameworks, corruption, governance issues, and legal uncertainties can affect investment environments and business operations in emerging markets. Investors need to assess political and regulatory risks before making investment decisions and consider country-specific factors that impact market stability. Emerging markets can experience economic volatility due to currency fluctuations, inflationary pressures, fiscal deficits, external debt, trade imbalances, and global economic cycles. Economic volatility affects market sentiment, investment flows, asset valuations, and financial stability in emerging market economies. Currency risk arises from exposure to foreign exchange fluctuations and exchange rate movements. Currency depreciation can impact the returns on investments denominated in foreign currencies. Exchange rate risks affect cross-border transactions, international trade, capital flows, and foreign currency exposures in investment portfolios. Liquidity constraints, low trading volumes, bid-ask spreads, and market inefficiencies can hinder investment liquidity and price discovery in emerging market securities. Transparency issues related to financial reporting, disclosure standards, accounting practices, corporate governance, and insider trading regulations can undermine investor confidence. Geopolitical tensions, global events, trade disputes, diplomatic relations, security concerns, and natural disasters can impact emerging economies and financial markets. External factors such as commodity prices, interest rate changes, capital flows, global demand trends, and technological disruptions influence market conditions in emerging markets. Operational risks include infrastructure challenges, supply-chain disruptions, regulatory compliance, cybersecurity threats, fraud, data privacy, and business continuity risks. Execution risks include investment implementation, asset allocation decisions, trade timing, portfolio rebalancing, and performance monitoring in emerging market investments.

GLOBAL DIVERSIFICATION STRATEGIES

Global diversification strategies involve spreading investment capital across different geographic regions, asset classes, sectors, currencies, and instruments to reduce risk and enhance portfolio performance. Investors can allocate funds to North America, Europe, Asia-Pacific, Latin America, Africa, and the Middle East based on economic outlook, market conditions, growth potential, and risk profiles. Regional diversification helps mitigate country-specific risks, currency fluctuations, geopolitical events, regulatory changes, and market volatility.

Within each region, investors can further diversify by allocating capital to specific countries based on factors like GDP growth, political stability, regulatory environment, inflation rates, interest rates, and market liquidity. Country exposure diversifies risks related to economic cycles, sovereign risks, policy decisions, social developments, and market sentiment.

Balancing exposure between emerging markets and developed markets offers diversification benefits. Emerging markets provide growth opportunities, while developed markets offer stability, liquidity, and established infrastructure. Emerging markets diversify portfolios with higher growth potential but have higher volatility and risk factors than developed markets.

Asset Class Diversification

Investing in stocks across different sectors, industries, and market capitalizations diversifies equity exposure. Allocation to domestic and international equities provides geographic diversification. Equity diversification balances growth-oriented stocks, value stocks, dividend-paying stocks, and defensive stocks based on market conditions and investment objectives. Diversifying fixed-income investments include government bonds, corporate bonds, municipal bonds, high-yield bonds, investment-grade bonds, inflation-linked bonds, and emerging market bonds. Fixed income diversification considers interest rate sensitivity, credit risks, currency risks, maturity profiles, and yield curves across bond portfolios. Allocating alternative investments like real estate, commodities, infrastructure, private equity, hedge funds, venture capital, and structured products provides diversification beyond traditional asset classes. In diversified portfolios, alternative investments offer non-correlated returns, inflation hedging, downside protection, and diversification benefits.

Sector and Industry Diversification

Diversifying across cyclical sectors (e.g. technology, consumer discretionary, and energy) and defensive sectors (e.g. healthcare, consumer staples, and utilities) balances exposure to economic cycles and market trends. Cyclical sectors benefit from economic expansions, while defensive sectors provide stability during economic downturns. Sector diversification includes exposure to global industries such as technology, healthcare, financials, consumer goods, industrials, energy, utilities, telecommunications, and materials. Industry diversification captures growth themes, market trends, innovation, disruption, and competitive advantages across diverse sectors.

Currency Diversification

Managing currency exposure involves diversifying currency holdings across major currencies like the U.S. dollar (USD), euro (EUR), Japanese yen (JPY), British pound (GBP), Swiss franc (CHF), Australian dollar (AUD), Canadian dollar (CAD), and emerging market currencies. Currency diversification hedges against exchange rate risks, currency devaluations, inflation differentials, geopolitical events, and monetary policy shifts.

Investment Instrument Diversification

They combine passive investment strategies (e.g. index funds, exchange-traded funds [ETFs], and active management [e.g. mutual funds and actively managed portfolios]) to diversify investment approaches. Passive strategies offer low-cost diversification, while active strategies provide opportunities for alpha generation and tactical asset allocation. Diversifying between direct investments (e.g. stocks, bonds, and real estate properties) and indirect investments (e.g. investment funds, managed accounts, and structured products) optimizes portfolio diversification. Indirect investments offer access to diversified portfolios managed by investment professionals and provide liquidity, risk management, and diversification benefits.

Benefits of Global Diversification Strategies

Global diversification reduces portfolio risk by spreading exposure across multiple regions, asset classes, sectors, currencies, and investment instruments. Diversification helps minimize volatility, downside risk, correlation, concentration risk, and single-event impacts on investment portfolios. Diversified portfolios can enhance returns by capturing opportunities in different markets, sectors, and asset classes that outperform over time. Global diversification optimizes risk-adjusted returns, reduces idiosyncratic risks, and improves portfolio efficiency and performance consistency. Global diversification enables investors to capitalize on growth opportunities, market trends, sector rotations, and asset allocation shifts across diverse markets and regions. Opportunities in emerging markets, developed markets, cyclical sectors, defensive sectors, and thematic investments contribute to portfolio growth potential. Diversified portfolios provide liquidity, accessibility, and investment options across global markets, asset classes, and investment vehicles. Access to diversified assets enhances investment flexibility, portfolio rebalancing, tactical adjustments, and capital allocation based on market conditions and investment objectives.

Challenges and Considerations

Currency fluctuations can impact returns and portfolio valuations in globally diversified portfolios. Hedging strategies, currency overlays, and risk management techniques mitigate currency risks. Investors must monitor exchange rate movements, economic indicators, central bank policies, geopolitical events, and trade developments affecting currency markets. Correlations between global markets, asset classes, and sectors can vary based on market conditions, economic cycles, geopolitical factors, and investor sentiment. Understanding correlations helps optimize portfolio diversification, asset allocation, risk assessment, and portfolio rebalancing strategies. Regulatory environments, tax policies, withholding taxes, capital gains taxes, and investment restrictions differ across countries and jurisdictions. When diversifying globally, investors need to consider regulatory compliance, tax implications, legal requirements, and reporting obligations. Market liquidity, trading volumes, bid-ask spreads, market hours, and accessibility vary across global markets, exchanges, and investment instruments. Investors should assess liquidity risks, execution capabilities, trading costs, and market transparency in diverse markets and asset classes.

This chapter has taken us through the expansive and multifaceted world of global markets and international investing. As we explored the nuances of international markets, you gained a deeper understanding of how different regions and countries contribute to the global economic landscape. This overview is essential for appreciating the diverse opportunities and challenges of investing beyond domestic borders.

We delved into the complexities of currency risk and exchange rates, emphasizing how fluctuations in currency values can impact international investments. Understanding these dynamics is crucial for managing exposure and optimizing returns in a global portfolio. By mastering currency risk, you can better navigate the intricacies of international finance and protect your investments from adverse currency movements.

It also provided insights into investing in emerging markets, highlighting the potential for significant growth and the associated risks in these dynamic regions. Emerging markets offer unique opportunities for investors willing to embrace their volatility and complexity. With a well-informed approach, you can tap into the high growth potential of these markets while managing the inherent risks.

Finally, we discussed global diversification strategies, underscoring the importance of spreading investments across various geographic regions to enhance portfolio resilience. By diversifying internationally, you can mitigate risk and capitalize on opportunities across different economic environments. This strategy is decisive for achieving long-term financial goals and ensuring a balanced investment approach. This chapter has equipped you with the knowledge and tools to navigate the global investment landscape. You can create a robust and well-rounded investment portfolio by integrating international market insights, managing currency risk, exploring emerging markets, and employing global diversification strategies. As you venture into global markets, remember to stay informed, adapt to changing conditions, and continuously refine your approach to align with your investment objectives and risk tolerance.

Chapter 11

PUTTING IT ALL TOGETHER

This chapter is a complete guide to synthesizing the key concepts, strategies, and tools discussed throughout this journey into a cohesive framework for building, managing, and optimizing your investment portfolio. 'Putting It All Together' is not just about theory; it's a practical guide to help you navigate the complexities of the financial markets and achieve your long-term investment goals.

In 'Building and Managing a Successful Portfolio', the cornerstone of successful investing lies in constructing a well-diversified portfolio that balances risk and return according to your financial goals and risk tolerance. This section will delve into asset allocation strategies, portfolio construction techniques, and risk management principles to help you build a robust investment portfolio. From understanding the role of different asset classes to implementing diversification strategies, this chapter provides actionable insights to guide investment decisions.

In 'Reviewing and Adjusting Your Investment Strategy', investing is a dynamic process that requires regular review and adjustments. This section focuses on monitoring your portfolio's performance, evaluating your investment strategy, and making necessary adjustments to align with your financial objectives. We'll discuss the significance of periodic portfolio rebalancing, tax considerations, cost management, and staying disciplined during market fluctuations.

In 'Resources for Ongoing Learning and Improvement', continuous learning is vital for navigating the ever-evolving landscape of finance and investing. This chapter provides a curated list of resources and tools to support your ongoing education and skill development as an investor. Whether you're interested in fundamental analysis, technical analysis, portfolio management, or specific investment strategies, these resources offer valuable insights and educational materials to enhance your investment acumen. This chapter aims to empower you with the knowledge, skills, and resources needed to successfully navigate the complexities of investing. By putting together the pieces of the investment puzzle and adopting a disciplined approach, you can build a resilient portfolio, manage risks effectively, and work towards achieving your financial aspirations. Building and managing a successful investment portfolio requires a strategic approach that aligns with your financial goals, risk tolerance, and time horizon.

BUILDING AND MANAGING A SUCCESSFUL PORTFOLIO

Begin by defining your investment objectives, whether they are long-term wealth accumulation, retirement planning, education funding, or other specific financial goals.

Risk tolerance refers to your capacity and inclination to endure market volatility and potential losses within your investment portfolio. It's crucial to consider as it directly impacts your asset allocation decisions and overall investment strategy. Your capacity to bear risk depends on your financial situation, investment horizon, income stability, and liquidity needs. For instance, if you have a stable income, a longer investment horizon, and sufficient emergency funds, you may be more likely to take on more risk in your investments. Your emotional comfort with risk reflects your psychological tolerance for market fluctuations and investment losses. Some investors are more comfortable with market volatility and can withstand short-term fluctuations without feeling the need to make impulsive decisions. Others may be more risk-averse and prefer investments with lower volatility, even if it means potentially lower returns. Your risk tolerance directly influences your asset allocation decisions. A higher risk tolerance may lead to a more aggressive asset allocation with a higher proportion of equities, which have the potential for higher returns and volatility. On the other hand, a lower risk tolerance may result in a more conservative allocation, with a more significant portion allocated to fixed-income securities or cash equivalents for stability and capital preservation. Risk tolerance guides your overall investment strategy, including selecting specific investments, diversification levels, and risk management techniques. For instance, a risk-tolerant investor may focus on a growth-oriented strategy, such as investing in emerging markets or technology stocks. In contrast, a risk-averse investor may prioritize capital preservation and income generation through dividend-paying stocks or bonds. It's essential to regularly assess your risk tolerance, especially during significant life changes or market shifts. Reassessing your risk tolerance allows you to make informed adjustments to your investment portfolio, ensuring that it remains aligned with your financial goals and comfort level with risk. Finding the right balance between risk and return is critical to optimizing investment outcomes. While higher-risk investments offer the potential for greater returns, they also come with increased volatility and the possibility of more significant losses. Understanding your risk tolerance helps you strike a balance that aligns with your financial objectives and emotional resilience.

Diversification spreads your investment capital across different asset classes, such as stocks, bonds, cash equivalents, and alternative investments (e.g. real estate and commodities). By diversifying, you reduce the risk of significant losses from a single investment or asset class, as different assets may react differently to market conditions. For example, during a stock market downturn, bonds or cash equivalents may provide stability and offset losses in equity investments, thereby reducing overall portfolio volatility. Asset class selection involves determining the appropriate mix of asset classes based on your risk profile, investment goals, time horizon, and financial situation. Your asset allocation should align with your risk tolerance, with higher-risk assets potentially offering higher returns and greater volatility. For instance, a younger investor with a longer investment horizon and higher risk tolerance may allocate more of their portfolio to equities for growth potential. Equities have historically offered higher returns over the long-term but have higher volatility than fixed-income securities like bonds. Your asset allocation strategy aims to strike a balance between risk and return. Higher-risk assets like stocks or alternative investments may offer the potential for greater returns but also carry higher volatility and risk of losses. On the other hand, lower-risk assets such as bonds or cash equivalents provide stability but may offer lower returns. Your risk tolerance, financial goals, and time horizon are crucial in determining the optimal asset allocation mix that aligns with your investment objectives. Regularly review and rebalance your asset allocation to maintain the desired risk-return profile of your portfolio. Market fluctuations or changes in your financial situation may necessitate adjustments to your asset allocation. Rebalancing involves selling overperforming assets and reallocating funds to underperforming or underweighted asset classes to maintain the target allocation. Rebalancing ensures that your portfolio remains aligned with your risk tolerance, investment goals, and changing market conditions, helping you manage risk and optimize returns over time.

Portfolio construction involves selecting and combining various investments to achieve financial objectives while managing risk effectively. When considering individual stocks for your portfolio, conducting thorough research and analysis is essential. Focus on identifying quality companies with solid fundamentals, including robust financials, competitive advantages (such as unique products or services), and a history of sustainable growth. Key factors to consider in stock selection include revenue and earnings growth, profitability margins, debt levels, industry trends, management quality, and shareholder-friendly practices (e.g. dividends and share buybacks). Utilize fundamental analysis techniques, such as financial statement analysis, ratio analysis, and valuation models, to assess the intrinsic value of potential investments. Consider qualitative factors like industry positioning, brand reputation, regulatory environment, and competitive landscape when evaluating stocks for inclusion in your portfolio. When incorporating bonds into your portfolio, consider several factors to match your risk-return preferences. Start by evaluating the credit quality of bond issuers and assessing their ability to repay debt obligations. Higher credit ratings indicate lower default risk but may offer lower yields, while lower-rated bonds carry higher yields but higher default risk. Evaluate bond maturity periods to align with your investment horizon and liquidity needs. Short-term bonds offer lower interest rate risk but lower yields, while long-term bonds may provide higher yields but are more sensitive to interest rate fluctuations. Other considerations include bond yields, coupon rates, duration (interest-rate sensitivity), and the prevailing interest rate environment. To manage risk and optimize returns, a diversified bond portfolio may include government, corporate, municipal, and international bonds. Alternative investments offer diversification benefits and potential returns beyond traditional asset classes like stocks and bonds. To enhance portfolio diversification and potential returns, consider exploring opportunities in alternative investments such as real estate, commodities, private equity, and hedge funds. Real estate investments can include direct property ownership, trusts (REITs), or crowdfunding platforms. Commodities like gold, silver, oil, and agricultural products provide exposure to different economic sectors and inflation protection. Private equity investments involve investing in private companies or venture capital funds. They offer the potential for high returns but with longer investment horizons and illiquidity considerations. Hedge funds employ strategies such as long-short equity, arbitrage, and macroeconomic investing to generate less correlated returns with traditional markets.

Risk management strategies safeguard your investment portfolio against potential losses and volatility. Diversification is a fundamental risk management strategy that spreads your investment capital across different asset classes, industries, and geographic regions. By diversifying, you reduce the impact of adverse events on any single investment or sector. Avoid overconcentration in any particular investment or sector, as this can increase your portfolio's vulnerability to market fluctuations and sector-specific risks. A well-diversified portfolio can help mitigate risk and enhance overall portfolio resilience. Regularly review and rebalance your portfolio to maintain the desired asset allocation. Asset allocation refers to the distribution of your investments across various asset classes (e.g. stocks, bonds, and cash equivalents) based on your risk tolerance and investment objectives. Rebalancing involves adjusting your portfolio's asset allocation by selling overperforming assets and reallocating funds to underperforming or underweighted asset classes. This helps control risk, ensures your portfolio stays aligned with your goals, and prevents overexposure to any asset class. Consider using derivatives, such as options or futures contracts, for risk management. Derivatives allow investors to hedge against market downturns, volatility, or specific risks associated with their investment portfolios. Options can be used to protect against downside risk by purchasing put options or generating income through covered call writing. Futures contracts enable investors to hedge against price fluctuations in commodities, currencies, or market indices. While derivatives can be practical risk management tools, they also carry risks, such as counterparty and leverage. Understanding the mechanics of derivatives and their potential impact on your portfolio is essential before incorporating them into your risk management strategy.

Monitoring and reviewing your investment portfolio are essential to ensure it remains aligned with your financial goals and risk tolerance. Regularly monitor the performance of your portfolio by tracking key metrics such as investment returns, volatility, and overall portfolio health. Compare your portfolio's performance to relevant benchmarks, such as market indices or peer portfolios, to gauge its relative performance. Evaluate investment returns over different periods (e.g. monthly, quarterly, and annually) to assess performance consistency and identify trends. Analyze volatility metrics, such as standard deviation or beta, to understand the level of risk associated with your portfolio. Assess the overall health of your portfolio by considering factors like diversification, asset allocation, and the performance of individual investments relative to their respective benchmarks. Conduct periodic portfolio reviews to evaluate its alignment with your investment goals, risk tolerance, and changing market conditions. A comprehensive review typically includes an assessment of your financial situation, investment objectives, time horizon, and any significant life changes that may impact your investment strategy. Reassess your investment goals and risk tolerance to ensure they remain consistent with your current financial circumstances and future aspirations. When reviewing your portfolio, consider your capacity to bear risk, investment time horizon, liquidity needs, and income requirements. Evaluate market conditions, economic trends, and geopolitical factors influencing investment opportunities and risks. Adjust your investment strategy to capitalize on emerging opportunities or mitigate potential threats. Make informed decisions about portfolio adjustments, such as rebalancing asset allocations, reallocating funds to underperforming sectors or asset classes, and pruning or replacing underperforming investments. Seek professional advice or conduct thorough research before implementing significant portfolio changes.

Managing your investment's tax efficiency is an important consideration that can significantly impact your after-tax returns. Take advantage of tax-advantaged accounts like 401(k)s, individual retirement accounts (IRAs), or other retirement accounts offered by your country's tax laws. These accounts provide tax benefits that can help maximize portfolio growth over time. Contributions to traditional 401(k)s and IRAs are typically tax-deductible, allowing you to reduce your taxable income in the year of contribution in the United States. Additionally, earnings within these accounts grow tax-deferred until withdrawal, potentially compounding your returns more effectively. On the other hand, Roth 401(k)s and Roth IRAs offer tax-free withdrawals in retirement, as contributions are made with after-tax dollars. These accounts can be beneficial if you anticipate being in a higher tax bracket during retirement or prefer tax-free withdrawals. Tax-loss harvesting is a strategy to offset capital gains with capital losses in taxable investment accounts. By selling investments that have experienced losses, you can realize these losses for tax purposes and use them to offset taxable gains or up to a specific limit of ordinary income. Tax-loss harvesting helps reduce your tax liabilities and can improve your after-tax returns. It's essential to adhere to tax regulations and avoid violating the 'wash-sale rule', which prohibits repurchasing a substantially identical security within 30 days before or after the sale for tax-loss harvesting purposes. This strategy can be beneficial in volatile markets or during market downturns, as it allows you to optimize your tax position while maintaining your investment strategy.

Seeking professional advice from a financial advisor or investment professional can provide valuable insights and guidance tailored to your specific financial situation and goals. A financial advisor can offer personalized advice based on your unique financial circumstances, risk tolerance, investment goals, and time horizon. They can help you develop a customized investment plan that aligns with your objectives and addresses your financial concerns. By understanding your needs and preferences, a financial advisor can recommend suitable investment strategies, asset allocation, and portfolio diversification that align with your long-term financial goals. Working with a financial advisor allows you to create a tailored investment plan to help you achieve your specific financial objectives. They can assist you in setting realistic and achievable investment goals, whether saving for retirement, funding education, or building wealth over time. An advisor can help you navigate complex investment decisions, such as choosing the right mix of asset classes, selecting appropriate investment vehicles, and implementing tax-efficient strategies to maximize returns and minimize risks. Financial advisors have access to expertise, market research, and resources that can provide valuable insights into investment opportunities and market trends. They can help you make informed decisions based on comprehensive analysis and data-driven recommendations. Advisors can also guide financial planning topics beyond investments, including retirement planning, estate planning, tax optimization, insurance coverage, and wealth preservation strategies. Beyond initial consultations and plan creation, financial advisors provide ongoing monitoring and support to help you stay on track toward your financial goals. They can regularly review your portfolio, assess performance, and make necessary adjustments based on changing market conditions or life events. Having a trusted advisor by your side can provide peace of mind and confidence in your financial decisions, as you know that you have a professional guiding you through the complexities of investing and financial planning.

REVIEWING AND ADJUSTING YOUR INVESTMENT STRATEGY

Reviewing and adjusting your investment strategy is crucial to successful portfolio management, ensuring that your investments remain aligned with your financial goals, risk tolerance, and market conditions. Regular portfolio reviews are critical to effective investment management, ensuring that your investments align with your financial goals and risk tolerance. Conducting periodic assessments of your investment portfolio is crucial to evaluate its performance, risk exposure, and alignment with your financial objectives. Depending on factors such as your investment horizon and prevailing market conditions, aim to review your portfolio quarterly, semi-annually, or annually. During these reviews, it's essential to assess key metrics that provide insights into your portfolio's health and performance. This includes analyzing investment returns, volatility levels, asset allocation percentages, sector exposures, and the overall level of diversification within your portfolio. Comparing your portfolio's performance to relevant benchmarks or peer portfolios can also help you gauge its relative performance within the market. Regularly conducting these comprehensive reviews can identify areas of strength and weakness within your portfolio, make informed decisions regarding asset allocation adjustments or investment reallocations, and ensure that your investment strategy remains aligned with your long-term financial goals and risk tolerance.

It's crucial to regularly reassess your investment goals and risk tolerance to ensure they align with your financial circumstances and objectives. Consider any life changes impacting your investment strategy, such as career advancements, family responsibilities, or retirement planning. Evaluate your risk tolerance by assessing your ability to handle risk, comfort level with market fluctuations, and investment time horizon. Adjust your asset allocation and risk exposure accordingly to reflect changes in your risk profile and investment objectives.

Monitoring market conditions is crucial for informed investment decisions. Stay updated on market trends, economic indicators, geopolitical events, and industry developments that can affect your investments. Watch changes in interest rates, inflation rates, corporate earnings, and global economic factors impacting investment opportunities and risks. Adjust your investment strategy accordingly. For instance, during economic expansions, you might increase exposure to growth-oriented assets, while in market downturns, prioritize capital preservation and defensive strategy. When adjusting your investment strategy, it's crucial to do so based on a comprehensive analysis of your portfolio review, investment goals, risk tolerance, and market outlook. Consider rebalancing your asset allocation by selling assets that have performed well and reallocating funds to those underperforming or underweight based on your targets. Implement tax-efficient strategies such as tax-loss harvesting to offset gains with losses, which can reduce tax liabilities and improve after-tax returns. Additionally, explore opportunities in alternative investments or asset classes to enhance diversification and potential returns while effectively managing risk. It's advisable to seek guidance from a financial advisor or investment professional for personalized advice and expert insights. They can offer objective analysis, recommend suitable investment strategies, and assist you in navigating complex investment decisions with confidence.

RESOURCES FOR ONGOING LEARNING AND IMPROVEMENT

Resources for ongoing learning and improvement in investing are vital for staying informed, making informed decisions, and enhancing one's financial acumen. Financial publications and websites are invaluable sources of information about economic news, market trends, and investment insights.

Wall Street Journal

Known for its in-depth coverage of business news, economics, and financial markets, the *Wall Street Journal* (*WSJ*) provides comprehensive analysis and reporting on global economic events, corporate developments, and investment trends. Subscribers gain access to articles, opinion pieces, and market data that can aid in making informed investment decisions.

Financial Times

The Financial Times (FT) is renowned for its global coverage of financial news, economic analysis, and geopolitical events. It offers insights into market trends, industry perspectives, and investment strategies, making it a valuable resource for investors seeking a broader understanding of the global economy and financial markets.

Bloomberg

Bloomberg is a leading provider of financial news, market data, and analytics. Its platform offers real-time updates on stock prices, bond yields, currency rates, and commodities, allowing investors to track market movements and make data-driven decisions. Bloomberg also features in-depth research reports, interviews with industry experts, and economic indicators contributing to informed investing.

Bloomberg Terminal

Bloomberg Terminal is a widely used platform by financial professionals. It offers various financial data, news, analytics, and trading tools. It provides real-time market updates, economic indicators, earnings reports, and company profiles. Investors can use Bloomberg Terminal for equity research, fixed-income analysis, portfolio management, and algorithmic trading strategies.

CNBC

CNBC is a prominent financial news network that covers a wide range of topics, including stock market updates, business headlines, investment insights, and more. Its programming includes interviews with market analysts, CEOs, and policymakers, offering viewers diverse perspectives on market dynamics and investment opportunities.

Investopedia

Investopedia is a comprehensive online resource for financial education. It offers articles, tutorials, and guides on various investment topics and explains economic concepts, investment strategies, and market terminology, making it a valuable learning platform for novice and experienced investors.

Seeking Alpha

Seeking Alpha is a unique platform where investors can access stock analysis, investment ideas, and market commentary from a community of contributors and experts. It features articles, research reports, and investment insights across various industries, fostering a collaborative environment that helps investors stay updated on company news, earnings reports, and market trends.

MarketWatch

MarketWatch provides real-time news, analysis, and insights on financial markets, stocks, bonds, and economic indicators. Its tools for tracking stock prices, creating watchlists, and accessing market data ensure that investors are always up to date, making it an invaluable resource for those seeking real-time market information and analysis.

Morningstar

Morningstar is a comprehensive platform that provides access to various financial data, investment research, and portfolio analysis tools. Investors can use Morningstar to evaluate mutual funds, ETFs, and individual stocks, analyze performance metrics, and assess risk factors. The platform also offers fund ratings, investment recommendations, and portfolio management features.

Yahoo Finance

Yahoo Finance is a comprehensive financial news and data platform providing a wide range of information for investors and finance enthusiasts. It offers real-time stock quotes, financial news, portfolio management tools, and data on various asset classes, including stocks, bonds, cryptocurrencies, and commodities. Users can access historical economic data, company profiles, and performance charts, track market trends, and receive personalized news updates. Yahoo Finance's feature of expert analysis and opinions serves as a guiding light, making it a valuable resource for novice and experienced investors seeking to make informed decisions.

Google Finance

Google Finance is an online financial news and data platform developed by Google. It provides users with real-time stock market data, financial news, and comprehensive company information. The platform offers interactive charts, historical performance data, and market analysis, allowing users to track stock prices, monitor market trends, and access financial news updates. Google Finance also integrates with Google's search and news services, offering personalized financial insights and tools to help investors and finance enthusiasts stay informed and make educated investment decisions.

Twitter (X)

Stock traders can leverage Twitter (now known as X) as a valuable source of real-time information and insights in several ways. Traders can follow financial analysts, economists, and experienced traders who share market insights, analysis, and trading strategies. Twitter provides instant access to breaking news and market updates. Traders can track news outlets, financial institutions, and reporters for the latest information affecting stock prices. Traders can participate in or observe conversations around market trends and stock performance, gaining different perspectives and ideas. Analyzing tweets about specific stocks or market conditions can help traders gauge public sentiment and market psychology, which can be crucial for making informed trading decisions. Traders can use relevant hashtags (e.g. #stocks, #investing, and #trading) to find and follow discussions about specific stocks or broader market themes. Many financial professionals share research reports, charts, and analyses on Twitter, allowing traders to access valuable resources quickly. Traders can set up alerts for specific keywords or accounts to receive updates on price changes, earnings reports, or other critical events affecting their investments. Twitter (X) is a dynamic platform for stock traders to access timely information, engage with industry experts, and monitor market sentiment. By effectively utilizing this social media tool, traders can enhance their trading strategies and stay informed in a fast-paced financial landscape.

Reddit

Reddit has emerged as a significant platform for investors, providing a unique community-driven resource for sharing information, insights, and opinions on various investment topics. Subreddits such as r/stocks, r/investing, and r/wallstreetbets serve as forums where users discuss stock market trends, trading strategies, and specific companies. Users often share personal experiences, analysis, and research, fostering a collaborative environment for learning and debating. While Reddit offers valuable insights and can highlight emerging investment opportunities, investors need to approach the information critically. The platform's open nature means that content can vary in reliability, and users should verify claims with independent research before making financial decisions. Overall, Reddit can be a powerful tool for connecting with other investors and staying informed about market movements, but it should complement, rather than replace, traditional research methods

Educational Materials from Investment Firms and Institutions

Many investment firms, brokerage platforms, and financial institutions offer a wealth of educational materials to help investors enhance their knowledge. These resources include webinars, white papers, research reports, and online courses covering various investment topics such as portfolio management, asset allocation, risk assessment, and investment strategies. Take advantage of these educational materials to deepen your understanding of investment concepts, learn about market trends and best practices, and stay updated on industry developments.

Books by Renowned Investors and Experts

Explore books authored by renowned investors and financial experts to gain insights into investment strategies, market principles, and economic concepts. For example, *The Intelligent Investor* by Benjamin Graham is a timeless classic that emphasizes value investing and risk management principles. *A Random Walk Down Wall Street* by Burton Malkiel explores efficient market theory and investment strategies for individual investors. *Common Stocks and Uncommon*

Profits by Philip Fisher focuses on identifying quality growth stocks and understanding company fundamentals.

Recommended Titles

Besides the books above, consider exploring other recommended titles based on your areas of interest and investment goals. Some additional books that are highly regarded in the investment community include *One Up on Wall Street* by Peter Lynch, *Security Analysis* by Benjamin Graham and David Dodd, *The Little Book That Still Beats the Market* by Joel Greenblatt, and *The Warren Buffett Way* by Robert G. Hagstrom.

Online Courses and Certification Programs

Enroll in online courses and certification programs from reputable institutions and organizations. Platforms like Coursera, edX, and Khan Academy provide investment principles, financial analysis, risk management, and portfolio construction courses. Pursuing certifications such as the Chartered Financial Analyst (CFA) designation or Certified Financial Planner (CFP) certification can also enhance your credibility and expertise in investment management. Financial analysis tools and software are essential for conducting thorough research, analyzing market data, and evaluating investment opportunities.

Thomson Reuters Eikon

Thomson Reuters Eikon is an influential financial analysis tool professionals use to access real-time market data, news, and research insights. It offers a customizable interface, advanced charting capabilities, and data visualization tools for analyzing market trends, conducting technical analysis, and identifying investment opportunities. Eikon provides economic data, company fundamentals, and sector analysis for informed decision-making.

Stock Screening Tools

Financial analysis tools often include stock screening features that allow investors to filter stocks based on specific criteria such as market capitalization, industry sector, valuation metrics, and performance indicators. These tools help identify potential investment opportunities that align with your investment strategy and criteria.

Portfolio Analysis Features

Many financial analysis tools offer portfolio analysis features that enable investors to assess portfolio performance, track asset allocation, and measure risk exposure. These features include risk-adjusted return metrics, portfolio optimization tools, and scenario analysis capabilities for evaluating portfolio diversification and asset allocation strategies. Professional organizations and associations in the finance and investing sector offer valuable resources and opportunities for professionals to enhance their skills, knowledge, and networking.

CFA Institute

The CFA Institute is a globally recognized organization with the Chartered Financial Analyst (CFA) designation, considered the gold standard in investment analysis and portfolio management. Joining the CFA Institute provides access to a vast network of finance professionals, educational resources, and career development opportunities. Members benefit from continuing education programs, research publications, and industry conferences that contribute to their expertise in finance and investing.

Financial Planning Association (FPA)

The Financial Planning Association is a leading financial planner and advisor organization, offering resources and support to enhance their practice and serve clients effectively. FPA members gain access to professional development programs, networking events, and educational resources focused on financial planning, investment strategies, and wealth management. The association also advocates for the profession and promotes ethical standards among its members.

National Association of Personal Financial Advisors (NAPFA)

NAPFA is a community of fee-only financial advisors committed to providing fiduciary services and acting in the best interests of their clients. Joining NAPFA provides advisors access to educational opportunities, peer networking forums, and practice management resources. Members benefit from sharing best practices, staying updated on industry trends, and upholding high standards of professionalism and ethics.

Investment Management Consultants Association (IMCA)

IMCA is a professional association for investment consultants, wealth managers, and financial advisors. It offers certifications such as the Certified Investment Management Analyst (CIMA) designation. IMCA members gain access to advanced education, research publications, and networking events focused on investment management, asset allocation, and financial planning strategies.

Society of Financial Service Professionals (SFSP)

SFSP is an organization that brings together financial service professionals from various disciplines, including financial planning, insurance, estate planning, and retirement planning. Members of SFSP benefit from professional development programs, industry conferences, and networking opportunities that support their career growth and expertise in financial services.

Online courses and certifications enhance investment management knowledge, skills, and credibility.

Platforms and Course Offerings

Platforms like Coursera, edX, and Khan Academy offer a diverse range of courses on investment principles, financial modeling, risk management, and other relevant topics. Top institutions and industry experts often develop these courses, ensuring high-quality content and practical insights. Coursera features courses from universities like Yale, Wharton, and Stanford, covering subjects such as portfolio management, behavioral finance, and financial markets analysis. edX offers courses from institutions like Harvard, MIT, and Columbia, focusing on investment strategies, asset pricing, and financial risk management. Khan Academy provides free courses on finance and economics, making it accessible to a wide audience interested in learning about investment concepts.

Certifications and Designations

Pursuing certifications such as the Chartered Financial Analyst (CFA) designation or Certified Financial Planner (CFP) certification can significantly enhance your credibility and expertise in investment management. The CFA designation is globally recognized and demonstrates proficiency in investment analysis, portfolio management, and ethical standards. It involves rigorous exams and requirements, making it a prestigious credential for finance professionals. The CFP certification focuses on financial planning and advisory services, covering retirement, tax strategies, estate planning, and risk management. It signifies expertise in holistic financial planning and adherence to ethical standards.

Benefits of Online Learning

- **Flexibility:** Online courses allow learners to study at their own pace and schedule, making it convenient for working professionals or those with busy schedules. **Accessibility**: Online platforms offer a wide range of courses, ensuring access to diverse content and specialized topics that may not be available locally.
- **Interactivity:** Many online courses feature interactive elements such as quizzes, case studies, and discussion

forums, fostering engagement and a deeper understanding of concepts.

- **Cost-Effectiveness:** Online courses are often more affordable than traditional classroom-based programs, making them accessible to a broader audience.

Seeking guidance from experienced financial advisors, mentors, or industry professionals can immensely benefit individuals looking to enhance their financial knowledge and skills.

Personalized Advice and Mentorship

Financial advisors and mentors can offer advice tailored to your financial goals, risk tolerance, and investment preferences. They can help you develop a comprehensive financial plan, identify investment opportunities, and navigate complex financial decisions. Through mentorship, you can gain insights into industry best practices, investment strategies, and risk management techniques from seasoned professionals with hands-on experience.

Expert Insights and Experience

Experienced financial advisors and mentors bring a wealth of knowledge and experience. They can provide valuable insights into market trends, economic conditions, and investment opportunities, helping you make informed decisions and optimize your investment portfolio. By tapping into their expertise, you can learn about asset classes, investment vehicles, and wealth management strategies aligning with your financial objectives.

Continuous Learning and Improvement

Building a network of knowledgeable individuals, including financial advisors and mentors, creates constant learning and improvement opportunities. Through ongoing discussions and mentorship sessions, you can stay updated on industry developments, investment trends, and regulatory changes. Engaging with seasoned professionals allows you to ask questions, seek clarification on complex financial concepts, and gain practical insights that contribute to your professional growth and development.

Networking and Opportunities

Financial advisors and mentors can facilitate networking opportunities and connect you with industry peers, potential clients, or investment opportunities. They may introduce you to relevant events, conferences, or networking groups where you can expand your professional network and explore new possibilities. Leveraging their network and connections can open doors to collaboration, partnership opportunities, and career advancement within the financial services industry.

Ethical and Professional Guidance

Working with reputable financial advisors and mentors ensures you receive ethical and professional guidance. They adhere to industry standards, regulatory requirements, and ethical codes of conduct, prioritizing your best interests and financial well-being.

In conclusion, this chapter has described the intricate process of building and managing a successful investment portfolio, emphasizing the importance of continuous learning and adaptation in the ever-evolving financial landscape. The key takeaways from this chapter are:

- **Holistic portfolio management:** Building a successful portfolio requires a holistic approach considering asset allocation, risk management, and investment strategies tailored to individual goals and risk tolerance. Diversification across asset classes, sectors, and geographies is fundamental to mitigating risk and enhancing long-term returns.
- **Review and adjustment:** Regularly reviewing your portfolio's performance, asset allocation, and risk exposure is essential

for aligning with your investment objectives. Adjustments should be made based on changes in market conditions, economic outlook, and personal circumstances to optimize portfolio performance and manage risk effectively.

- **Continuous learning and improvement:** The journey of investment management is a constant learning process. Online courses, certifications, and networking with industry professionals and mentors can enhance your knowledge, skills, and decision-making capabilities. Staying informed about market trends, economic indicators, and emerging investment opportunities is crucial in making informed investment decisions.
- **Risk management and adaptation:** Effective risk management involves diversifying, rebalancing asset allocation, and considering tax-efficient strategies. Being adaptable to changing market conditions, geopolitical events, and economic shifts is crucial for navigating uncertainties and capitalizing on investment opportunities.
- **Professional guidance:** Seeking advice from experienced financial advisors, mentors, or industry professionals can provide valuable insights, personalized guidance, and adherence to ethical standards. Collaborating with professionals ensures alignment with regulatory requirements, ethical standards, and best practices in investment management. Successful portfolio management requires a combination of strategic asset allocation, risk management techniques, continuous learning, and adaptation to market dynamics.

By applying the principles discussed in this chapter and leveraging resources for ongoing education and improvement, investors can build resilient portfolios, achieve their financial goals, and navigate the complexities of the investment landscape with confidence and competence.

Chapter 12

FINANCIAL RATIOS AND METRICS

This chapter describes the intricate world of financial ratios and metrics, vital for evaluating companies' financial health, performance, and valuation. Investors and analysts can make informed decisions regarding investment opportunities, risk assessment, and strategic planning by analyzing critical financial indicators. This chapter will explore financial ratios and metrics, their significance, interpretation, and practical application in financial analysis. Whether you're a seasoned investor, financial professional, or someone looking to deepen their understanding of financial analysis, this chapter will provide valuable insights into the metrics that drive informed decision-making in finance.

Financial ratios and metrics are tools used to evaluate a company's financial performance and health. They provide insight into a company's liquidity, profitability, efficiency, and overall financial position. The chapter covers over 200 financial ratios and metrics that are informative and essential to investors.

1. CEO and Executive Team Metrics

Evaluating the performance of a company's CEO and executive team is crucial for understanding its overall effectiveness and potential for growth. Analysts and investors rely on various key ratios to assess this performance:

- **Return on equity (ROE):** This decisive metric measures how effectively management utilizes shareholders' equity to generate profits. A higher ROE signals exceptional management efficiency and profitability.
- **Return on assets (ROA):** This ratio indicates how efficiently a company uses its assets to produce earnings. A robust ROA reflects a management team that maximizes asset value to drive profit.
- **Return on investment (ROI):** This vital measure evaluates the profitability of a company's investments. A higher ROI indicates that management makes astute investment decisions that enhance shareholder value.
- **Earnings per share (EPS):** This ratio highlights the profit generated per share of stock. A rising EPS demonstrates effective management in increasing profitability.
- **Price-to-earnings (P/E) ratio:** This ratio compares a company's stock price to its earnings per share. A lower P/E suggests the stock may be undervalued relative to its earnings potential, indicating a possible investment opportunity. While these ratios are essential, it's important to remember that they are just one part of a comprehensive evaluation. They must be considered alongside other financial indicators—such as cash flow and balance sheets—along with industry trends and benchmarks. This holistic approach ensures we comprehensively picture a company's performance and management effectiveness, providing a more accurate assessment. The importance of these metrics cannot be overstated, particularly when assessing the catastrophic consequences of ineffective leadership. Companies like Circuit City, Radio Shack, Kmart, and Sears are stark reminders of how a lack of vision and competence at the CEO level and a complacent board of directors can precipitate significant

decline or even outright failure. Strong leadership is not merely desirable; it is critical for the success and sustainability of any organization.

2. Income Statement

An income statement, also known as a profit-and-loss statement (P&L), is a financial statement that reports a company's financial performance over a specific period, typically a quarter or a year. It summarizes a company's revenues, costs, and expenses and shows its net income or loss. The income statement typically starts with revenue, which is the total amount of money a company has earned from its operations during the reported period. This is then followed by the cost of goods sold (COGS), which represents the cost of the goods or services that the company has sold during the period. It subtracts COGS from revenue, which results in gross profit. Then, operating expenses, such as selling, general, and administrative expenses, are deducted from gross profit to arrive at operating income (also called earnings before interest and taxes [EBIT]), and then the interest and taxes are deducted from the operating income to arrive at the net income (also called net profit or net earnings). The income statement provides a picture of a company's performance over a specific period and can be used to identify trends in revenue, expenses, and net income. It is a useful tool for investors, analysts, and management to evaluate the company's financial performance and make informed decisions about its future.

3. Balance Sheet Statement

A balance sheet shows a company's financial position at a specific time. It is one of the three primary financial statements, as well as income and cash flow statements. The balance sheet has two main sections: assets and liabilities. The assets section lists the resources a company owns or controls that have monetary value, such as cash, accounts receivable, inventory, and property, plant, and equipment.

The liabilities section lists a company's debts and obligations, such as accounts payable, loans, and mortgages. The balance sheet also includes shareholders' equity, which is the amount of money left over if a company sells its assets and pays off all of its liabilities. Shareholders' equity can be further broken down into common stock, retained earnings, and treasury stock categories. The balance sheet helps understand a company's liquidity, which is its ability to meet short-term obligations, and its solvency, which is its ability to meet long-term obligations. It also helps identify trends in a company's assets and liabilities and evaluate its financial health.

4. Cash Flow Statement

A cash flow statement is a financial statement that shows the inflow and outflow of cash for a company over a specific period, such as a quarter or a fiscal year. It is one of the three primary financial statements, along with the balance sheet and income statement. The cash flow statement has three sections: cash flow from operating activities, cash flow from investing activities, and cash flow from financing activities. Cash flow from operating activities includes cash generated from a company's primary operations, such as sales, accounts receivable collections, and suppliers' payments. This section shows the company's ability to generate cash daily. Cash flow from investing activities includes cash generated or used in acquiring or disposing of long-term assets such as property, plant, and equipment. This section shows how much cash a company invests in future growth. Cash flow from financing activities includes cash generated or used in financing activities such as issuing new debt or equity, repaying debt, and paying dividends. This section shows how much cash a company obtains from investors or lenders and how much it returns to them. The cash flow statement helps understand a company's liquidity, ability to generate cash, and ability to invest in growth opportunities. It also helps identify a company's cash flow trends and evaluate its overall financial health. It's important to note that cash flow statements should be used with other financial statements, such as the balance sheet and income statement, to get a complete picture of a company's financial performance.

5. Value at Risk (VaR)

Value at Risk (VaR) is a risk management metric that measures the potential loss of an investment over a specified time horizon with a given level of confidence. It helps to identify the potential for loss under different scenarios, and financial institutions and investors commonly use it to measure and manage the risk of their portfolios. There are several methods to calculate VaR, but the most common is the Variance-Covariance method, which is based on the standard distribution assumption. The formula for VaR using this method is: VaR = - (Portfolio value) x (Standard deviation of portfolio returns) x (Inverse standard normal distribution function (confidence level)), Where: Portfolio value: the current value of the portfolio, Standard deviation of portfolio returns: the volatility of the portfolio returns over a specific period, Inverse standard normal distribution function: the inverse of the standard normal distribution function, used to determine the z-score for a given level of confidence. For example, if a portfolio has a VaR of $1,000,000 at a 95% confidence level, there is a 5% chance that the portfolio will lose more than $1,000,000 over the specified time horizon. The VaR is a statistical measure, and it does not take into account any extreme events. Also, it assumes that the portfolio returns are normally distributed, which is not always the case. Additionally, VaR is a backward-looking measure that does not consider future growth or market conditions.

6. Margin of Safety

The margin of safety is a principle used in investing and finance, which refers to the difference between the intrinsic value of an asset and its market price. It is the amount by which the market price of an asset is below its intrinsic value. The concept of margin of safety protects investors from potential losses and is a crucial principle of value investing. The margin of safety can be calculated by subtracting the intrinsic value of an asset from its market price. The intrinsic value can be calculated using various valuation methods such as discounted cash flow analysis, price-to-earnings ratio, and price-to-book ratio. The higher the margin of safety, the greater the potential for profit and the lower the risk of loss. A margin of safety of 30% or more is considered a good indication of an undervalued asset, which suggests that the asset has a good potential for future growth. The margin of safety is subject to interpretation, and different investors may have different opinions on the intrinsic value of an asset.

7. Sloan Ratio

The Sloan ratio, also known as the accruals ratio, is a financial metric that measures the quality of a company's earnings. It measures the proportion of a company's net income generated by non-cash items such as depreciation and amortization, as well as changes in working capital and deferred taxes. The Sloan ratio is named after Richard Sloan, a finance professor at the University of Southern California, who introduced the metric in the 1990s. The formula for the Sloan ratio is Sloan Ratio = (Net Income - Cash Flow from Operations) / Total Assets, Where Net Income = a company's net income as reported on its income statement, Cash Flow from Operations = a company's cash flow from operations as reported on its statement of cash flows Total Assets = a company's total assets as reported on its balance sheet. A high Sloan ratio indicates that a significant portion of a company's net income is generated by non-cash items, which may not be sustainable in the long term. This could be a red flag for investors, as the company's earnings may not be as robust as they appear. A low Sloan ratio, on the other hand, indicates that a company's net income is primarily generated by cash flow from operations, which is considered to be a more reliable indicator of a company's financial health. The Sloan ratio should be used with other financial metrics and analyses to understand a company's financial health better.

8. Piotroski F-Score

Piotroski F-Score is a financial scoring system used to evaluate the strength of a company's financial position. It was developed by accounting professor Joseph Piotrowski at Stanford University in 2000. Based on fundamental analysis, the F-Score is designed to assess a company's financial health and predict its future stock performance. The Piotroski F-Score is a numerical score ranging from 0 to 9 that evaluates a company's financial strength based on nine criteria. Each criterion is scored as either 1 (positive) or 0 (negative), resulting in a total score that indicates the company's overall financial health.

- Criteria: The F-Score assesses the following areas:

    1. Net Income: Positive net income.
    2. Return on Assets (ROA): Positive ROA.
    3. Operating Cash Flow: Positive operating cash flow.
    4. Quality of Earnings: Operating cash flow exceeds net income.
    5. Long-Term Debt: Lower long-term debt compared to the previous year.
    6. Current Ratio: Higher current ratio compared to the previous year.
    7. Shares Outstanding: No increase in the number of shares outstanding.
    8. Gross Margin: Higher gross margin compared to the previous year.
    9. Asset Turnover: Higher asset turnover compared to the previous year.

The F-Score is used to identify companies with strong financial performance and low risk. A higher F-Score suggests a company is financially healthy and may be a good investment, while a lower score indicates potential weaknesses. Investors use the Piotroski F-Score to screen for potential stock picks and to complement other financial analysis methods. The Piotroski F-Score is a practical tool for evaluating a company's financial health by considering various fundamental metrics, providing investors with insights into the company's stability and potential for future performance.

9. Altman-Z Score

The Altman Z-score is a financial metric used to predict the likelihood of a company going bankrupt. Edward I. Altman, a professor of finance at New York University, in 1968, developed it. The score is based on a combination of five financial ratios: working capital to total assets, retained earnings to total assets, earnings before interest and taxes (EBIT) to total assets, market value of equity to book value of total liabilities, and revenue to total assets. The formula for the Altman Z-score is: Z-score = 1.2A + 1.4B + 3.3C + 0.6D + 1.0E, Where: A = working capital / total assets B = retained earnings / total assets C = EBIT / total assets D = market value of equity / book value of liabilities E = revenue / total assets. The Altman Z-score is then compared to a set of predetermined thresholds to classify the company's credit risk as follows: A score of 2.99 or higher is considered safe; A score between 1.81 and 2.99 is regarded as a grey area, and A score of 1.81 or lower is considered a high risk of bankruptcy. The Altman Z-score is a backward-looking measure, and it does not consider any future growth or market conditions.

10. Beneish-M Score

The Beneish M-Score is a financial metric that is used to identify companies that may be engaging in earnings management. It was developed by Messod Beneish, a professor of accounting at Indiana University, in 1999. The M-Score is based on eight financial ratios that are calculated using a company's financial statements: Sales Growth, Days Sales in Receivables (DSR), Gross Margin, Asset Quality; Sales, General, and Administrative (SG&A) to Sales; Depreciation to Depreciation plus Amortization (DTA), Accruals to Sales, and

Leverage. The M-Score is calculated using a weighted average of these eight ratios, ranging from -4.84 to 9.07. A score greater than -2.22 indicates a higher likelihood of earnings management. The M-Score is a valuable tool for detecting red flags in earnings management. However, A high score does not necessarily mean that a company is engaging in fraudulent activities. The M-Score is a backward-looking measure and does not consider any future growth or market conditions. Therefore, it should be used with other financial analyses and research to make a well-rounded decision.

11. Risk/Return Ratios

Risk/return ratios are financial metrics used to measure an investment's risk and return. They evaluate the trade-off between the potential return on investment and the risk involved in achieving that return. There are several commonly used risk/return ratios, including the Sharpe Ratio: The Sharpe ratio measures the excess return per unit of risk. It is calculated by subtracting the risk-free rate from the return of an investment and then dividing it by the standard deviation of the investment's returns. A higher Sharpe ratio indicates a higher return for a given level of risk. Treynor Ratio: The Treynor ratio measures the excess return per unit of systematic risk. It is calculated by subtracting the risk-free rate from the return of an investment and then dividing it by the investment's beta. A higher Treynor ratio indicates a higher return for a given level of systematic risk; Jenson's Alpha: Jenson's Alpha is a risk-adjusted measure of performance. It measures the risk-adjusted return of an investment relative to a benchmark. A cheerful Jenson's Alpha indicates that the investment has performed better than expected, given its level of risk. Sortino Ratio: The Sortino ratio is similar to the Sharpe ratio, but it only considers downside deviation in the calculation. A higher Sortino ratio indicates a higher return for a given level of downside risk; and Information Ratio: The ratio measures the excess return per unit of active risk. It is calculated by subtracting a benchmark's return from an investment's return and dividing it by the tracking error. A higher information ratio indicates a higher return for a given level of active risk. Investors and financial analysts commonly use these ratios to evaluate the risk and return of an investment.

12. Expenses

Expenses refer to the costs incurred by a company to generate revenue. They are recorded on a company's income statement and subtracted from revenue to determine net income (profit). Expenses can be classified into several categories, including:

- **Cost of goods sold (COGS):** These are the direct costs of producing and selling a product, such as materials and labor.
- **Operating expenses:** These are the indirect costs of running a business, such as rent, utilities, and administrative expenses.
- **Selling, general, and administrative (SG&A) expenses:** These are the costs of selling and promoting a company's products or services and general expenses such as legal and accounting fees.
- **Depreciation and amortization:** These are noncash expenses that represent the reduction in the value of a company's assets over time, such as buildings and equipment. Interest expenses are the costs of borrowing money, such as interest on loans and bonds.
- **Income taxes:** These are the taxes that a company must pay on its net income. It's important to note that expenses can be fixed or variable. Fixed expenses are expenses that do not change regardless of the level of sales or production, such as rent, salaries, and insurance. Variable expenses change with the level of sales or production, such as the cost of goods sold.

To understand a company's profitability, it's essential to look at its net income or profit margin, which is calculated by dividing net income by revenue.

13. Return on Invested Capital (ROIC)

Return on Invested Capital (ROIC) is a financial ratio that measures a company's profitability to its invested capital. It evaluates a company's efficiency in generating profits for its investors. The formula for ROIC is ROIC = (Net Income / Invested Capital) x 100. ROIC expresses a company's net income as a percentage of its invested capital. Invested capital is the total amount of money investors have put into the company, including debt and equity. A higher ROIC indicates that a company generates more profit for its investors and is considered more efficient in using invested capital to generate income. A lower ROIC suggests that a company generates less profit for its investors and may be deemed less efficient in using invested capital to generate income. The ROIC is a profitability ratio that can be affected by factors such as changes in net income, invested capital, and industry averages. Additionally, ROIC can vary significantly depending on the industry and the type of business. Therefore, ROIC should be used with other financial metrics and analyses to understand a company's financial performance better. ROIC is commonly used by investors, analysts, and management to evaluate a company's profitability and efficiency and to compare it with industry peers. It also measures how effectively a company uses its invested capital to generate a profit. A high ROIC is generally considered a sign of a well-run company, as it indicates that it is generating a high return on the investors' funds.

14. Cash Return on Invested Capital (CROIC)

Cash Return on Invested Capital (CROIC) is a financial ratio that measures a company's cash flow about its invested capital. It is similar to Return on Invested Capital (ROIC) but uses cash flow from operations instead of using net income. CROIC evaluates a company's efficiency in generating cash flow for its investors. The formula for CROIC is CROIC = (Cash Flow from Operations / Invested Capital) x 100. CROIC expresses a company's cash flow from operations as a percentage of its invested capital. Invested capital is the total amount of money investors have put into the company, including debt and equity. A higher CROIC indicates that a company is generating more cash flow for its investors and is considered more efficient in using invested capital to generate cash flow. A lower CROIC suggests that a company is generating less cash flow for its investors and may be considered less efficient in using invested capital to generate cash flow. It's important to note that CROIC is a cash flow ratio that can be affected by various factors, such as changes in cash flow from operations, changes in invested capital, and changes in industry averages. Additionally, CROIC can vary significantly depending on the industry and the type of business. Therefore, CROIC should be used with other financial metrics and analyses to understand a company's financial performance better. CROIC is commonly used by investors and analysts to evaluate a company's cash flow generation efficiency and to compare it with industry peers. It also measures how effectively a company uses its invested capital to generate cash flow. A high CROIC is generally considered a sign of a well-run company, as it indicates that a company is generating a high return on the funds that investors have invested in terms of cash flow.

15. Gross Profitability Ratio

The Gross Profitability Ratio (Gross Profit Margin or GP Margin) is a financial ratio that measures a company's profitability before accounting for its operating expenses, taxes, and interest expenses. It is used to evaluate a company's efficiency in generating profits from its sales. The formula for GP Margin is GP Margin = (Gross Profit / Revenue) x 100. GP Margin expresses a company's gross profit as a percentage of its revenue. Gross Profit is calculated by subtracting the cost of goods sold (COGS) from income. A higher GP Margin indicates that a company generates more profit from its sales and is considered more efficient in managing its costs. A lower GP Margin suggests that a company generates less profit from its sales and may need to be more efficient in managing its costs.

It's important to note that GP Margin is a profitability ratio, and it can be affected by various factors such as changes in revenue, costs, and changes in industry averages. Additionally, GP Margin can vary significantly depending on the industry and the type of business. Therefore, GP Margin should be used with other financial metrics and analyses to better understand a company's financial performance. GP Margin is commonly used by investors, analysts and management to evaluate a company's efficiency in generating profit from its sales and to compare it with industry peers. It is also used to measure how effectively a company manages its costs, such as the cost of goods sold, to generate profit. A high GP Margin is generally considered a sign of a well-run company, as it indicates that it is generating a high return on its sales.

16. Sharpe Ratio

The Sharpe Ratio is a financial ratio that measures the risk-adjusted return of an investment. It is used to evaluate the performance of an investment by comparing its return to the risk-free rate of return, such as the return on a Treasury bond, and adjusting for the volatility of the investment's returns. The formula for the Sharpe Ratio is Sharpe Ratio = (Expected Return - Risk-Free Rate) / Standard Deviation of Returns. The Sharpe Ratio expresses the excess return per unit of volatility or risk. A higher Sharpe Ratio indicates that an investment has a better risk-adjusted return, while a lower Sharpe Ratio indicates that an investment has a worse risk-adjusted return. It's important to note that the Sharpe Ratio is a risk-adjusted performance measure commonly used to compare the returns of different investments with different risk profiles. However, the Sharpe Ratio does not account for skewness or kurtosis, which could give a distorted view of the risk-adjusted performance of the investment. Additionally, the risk-free rate used in the formula is an approximation, and the real risk-free rate can vary depending on the period and the country. Therefore, the Sharpe Ratio should be used with other financial metrics and analysis to better understand an investment's performance. The Sharpe Ratio is commonly used by investors and analysts to evaluate the risk-adjusted performance of an investment, such as a mutual fund, portfolio, or stock, and to compare it with other investments in the same category. It's also used as a measure of the excess return of an investment over the risk-free rate and how much risk an investor takes to achieve that return. A high Sharpe Ratio is generally considered a sign of a well-performing investment, as it indicates that an investment generates high returns while taking less risk.

17. Treynor Ratio

The Treynor Ratio is a financial ratio that measures the risk-adjusted return of an investment. It is similar to the Sharpe Ratio, but it uses beta, which is a measure of an investment's systematic risk, as a measure of risk instead of the standard deviation of returns. The formula for the Treynor Ratio is Treynor Ratio = (Expected Return - Risk-Free Rate) / Beta. The Treynor Ratio expresses the excess return per unit of systematic risk. A higher Treynor Ratio indicates that an investment has a better risk-adjusted return, while a lower Treynor Ratio suggests an investment has a worse risk-adjusted return. It's important to note that the Treynor Ratio is a risk-adjusted performance measure commonly used to compare the returns of different investments with different risk profiles. However, the Treynor Ratio only accounts for systematic risk, which means it doesn't account for unsystematic risk or the risk that can be diversified away. Additionally, the risk-free rate used in the formula is an approximation, and the real risk-free rate can vary depending on the period and the country. Therefore, the Treynor Ratio should be used with other financial metrics and analyses to understand an investment's performance better. The Treynor Ratio is commonly used by investors and analysts to evaluate the risk-adjusted performance of an investment, such as a mutual fund, portfolio, or stock, and to compare it with other investments in the same category. It's also used to measure an investment's excess return over the risk-free rate and how much systematic risk an investor takes to achieve that return. A high Treynor Ratio is generally considered a sign of a well-performing investment, as it indicates that an investment generates high returns while taking less systematic risk.

18. Sortino Ratio

The Sortino Ratio is a financial ratio that measures the risk-adjusted return of an investment. It is similar to the Sharpe Ratio but uses downside deviation, which measures the volatility of negative returns, as a measure of risk instead of the standard deviation of returns. The formula for the Sortino Ratio is Sortino Ratio = (Expected Return - Risk-Free Rate) / Downside Deviation. The Sortino Ratio expresses the excess return per unit of downside risk. A higher Sortino Ratio indicates that an investment has a better risk-adjusted return, while a lower Sortino Ratio indicates that an investment has a worse risk-adjusted return. It's important to note that the Sortino Ratio is a risk-adjusted performance measure commonly used to compare the returns of different investments with different risk profiles. However, the Sortino Ratio only accounts for downside risk, which means it doesn't account for upside potential. Additionally, the risk-free rate used in the formula is an approximation, and the real risk-free rate can vary depending on the period and the country. Therefore, the Sortino Ratio should be used with other financial metrics and analyses to understand an investment's performance better. The Sortino Ratio is commonly used by investors and analysts to evaluate the risk-adjusted performance of an investment, such as a mutual fund, portfolio, or stock, and to compare it with other investments in the same category. It's also used as a measure of the excess return of an investment over the risk-free rate, and how much downside risk an investor is taking to achieve that return. A high Sortino Ratio is generally considered a sign of a well-performing investment, as it indicates that an investment generates high returns while taking less downside risk.

19. Calmar Ratio and MAR Ratio

The Calmar Ratio and the MAR Ratio (also known as the Sterling Ratio) are similar financial ratios that measure the risk-adjusted return of an investment. Both ratios are used to evaluate the performance of an investment by comparing its return to the risk of the investment and adjusting for the volatility of the investment's returns. The Calmar Ratio is calculated as Calmar Ratio = (CAGR / Maximum Drawdown). The CAGR (Compound Annual Growth Rate) represents the average annual return of an investment over some time, while the Maximum Drawdown represents the most significant peak-to-trough decline in the value of an investment over a specific period. A higher Calmar Ratio indicates that an investment has a better risk-adjusted return, while a lower Calmar Ratio indicates that an investment has a worse risk-adjusted return. The MAR Ratio is calculated as MAR Ratio = (CAGR / Maximum Drawdown) x (252/ Holding period). The CAGR, Maximum Drawdown, and holding period are the same as the Calmar Ratio, but the MAR Ratio also considers the holding period. A higher MAR Ratio indicates that an investment has a better risk-adjusted return, while a lower MAR Ratio indicates that an investment has a worse risk-adjusted return. Investors and analysts commonly use both ratios to evaluate the risk-adjusted performance of an investment and compare it with other investments in the same category. A high Calmar Ratio or MAR Ratio is generally considered a sign of a well-performing investment, as it indicates that an investment is generating high returns while taking less risk. It's important to note that both ratios are only measures of risk-adjusted performance and should be used with other financial metrics and analyses to comprehensively understand an investment's performance.

20. Sterling Ratio

The Sterling Ratio, also known as the MAR ratio (Maximum Acceptable Return ratio), is a financial ratio that measures the risk-adjusted return of an investment. It is used to evaluate the performance of an investment by comparing its return to the risk of the investment and adjusting for the volatility of the investment's returns. The formula for the Sterling Ratio is Sterling Ratio = (CAGR / Maximum Drawdown) x (252 / Holding period). The Sterling Ratio is similar to the Calmar Ratio but also considers the holding period. CAGR (Compound Annual Growth Rate) represents the average annual return of an investment over a while. In contrast, the Maximum Drawdown represents the most significant peak-to-trough decline in the value of an investment over a specific period. Investors and analysts commonly use the Sterling ratio to evaluate the risk-adjusted performance of an investment and compare it with other investments in the same category. A high Sterling ratio is generally considered a sign of a well-performing investment, as it indicates that an investment generates high returns while taking less risk. It's important to note that the Sterling Ratio is only a measure of risk-adjusted performance. It should be used with other financial metrics and analyses to understand an investment's performance comprehensively. Additionally, a high ratio alone does not guarantee future performance, and past performance is not an indicator of future results.

21. Omega Ratio

The Omega Ratio is a financial ratio that measures the risk-adjusted return of an investment. It is used to evaluate the performance of an investment by comparing its return to the risk of the investment and adjusting for the probability of negative returns. The Omega Ratio is a generalization of the Sortino Ratio, which only considers downside risk and is defined as the expected return for a given level of tail risk, which is the risk of returns falling below a certain threshold. The formula for the Omega Ratio is Omega Ratio = (Expected Return - Target Return) / Tail Risk. The Omega Ratio expresses the excess return per unit of tail risk. A higher Omega Ratio indicates that an investment has a better risk-adjusted return, while a lower

Omega Ratio indicates that an investment has a worse risk-adjusted return. It's important to note that the Omega Ratio is a risk-adjusted performance measure, but it's commonly used to compare the returns of different investments with different risk profiles. Additionally, the target return used in the formula is a benchmark or a minimum acceptable return, which can vary depending on the investor's preference. Therefore, the Omega Ratio should be used with other financial metrics and analyses to better understand an investment's performance. Investors and analysts commonly use the Omega Ratio to evaluate the risk-adjusted performance of an investment and compare it with other investments in the same category. It's also used as a measure of the excess return of an investment over a target return and how much tail risk an investor takes to achieve that return. A high Omega Ratio is generally considered a sign of a well-performing investment, as it indicates that an investment generates high returns while taking less tail risk.

22. Market Capitalization

Market capitalization, also known as market cap, is a metric used to evaluate the size and value of a publicly traded company. It is calculated by multiplying the current stock price of a company by the number of shares outstanding. Market capitalization is used to classify companies into different market capitalization ranges, such as small-cap, mid-cap, and large-cap. Small-cap companies have a market capitalization of less than $2 billion, Mid-cap companies have a market capitalization between $2 billion and $10 billion, and Large-cap companies have a market capitalization greater than $10 billion. Market capitalization is an important metric because it gives investors an idea of how large a company is and how much it is worth. It can also compare companies within the same industry or sector.

23. Enterprise Value

Enterprise value (EV) is a metric used to evaluate the overall value of a publicly traded company. It is calculated by adding a company's market capitalization, the value of debt, and the value of preferred stock and minority interests and subtracting cash and cash equivalents. The formula for enterprise value is EV = Market Capitalization + Debt + Preferred Stock + Minority Interests - Cash and Cash Equivalents. Enterprise value is considered a more comprehensive measure of a company's value as it considers not only the market capitalization but also the company's debt and cash. It is a measure of the total value of a company if it were to be taken private, including all of its debt and cash. EV can be used to compare companies within the same industry or sector, regardless of their capital structure, and it is also useful when comparing companies with different capital structures. It can also be used as a basis for valuation methods such as EV/EBITDA (Enterprise Value over Earnings Before Interest, Taxes, Depreciation, and Amortization), which can be used as a proxy for the company's financial performance and its potential for future growth.

24. Revenue

Revenue is the income generated by a company from its business activities. It is the top line item on a company's income statement and is calculated by multiplying the number of units sold by the price per unit. Revenue is often used as a measure of a company's financial performance. It can be used to compare a company's performance over time or the performance of different companies in the same industry. There are various types of revenue, such as Net sales revenue, Which is the revenue generated from the sale of a company's products or services after deducting returns, allowances, and discounts; Gross revenue, Which is the revenue generated from the sale of a company's products or services, before deducting returns, allowances, and discounts; Recurring revenue: This is the revenue generated from ongoing or recurring sources, such as subscriptions, memberships, and license fees; and Non-recurring revenue: This is the revenue generated from one-time or non-recurring sources, such as the sale of a business or a one-time project. It's important to note that revenue is different from profit. A company can have high revenue but still only be profitable if its expenses are reasonable.

25. Insider Ownership

Insider ownership measures the percentage of a company's outstanding shares owned by its officers, directors, and other insiders. It is a way for investors to gauge the level of commitment and alignment of interests between the company's management and its shareholders. Insiders are considered to have a unique perspective on the company's performance and prospects, and a high level of insider ownership is generally seen as a positive sign, as it indicates that the company's management has a significant financial stake in the company's success. The percentage of insider ownership can be calculated by dividing the number of shares owned by insiders by the total number of outstanding shares. This information can be found in the company's annual report or on the company's website. It's important to note that Insider ownership is not a guarantee of a company's future performance. It's just one of the many factors to consider when evaluating a company. Also, it's important to remember that some insiders may hold shares for different reasons, such as personal financial planning, and not all of them are active in the company's management. It's crucial to analyze insider transactions, like buying or selling shares, and the role of the insider in the company.

26. Institutional Ownership

Institutional ownership refers to the percentage of a company's outstanding shares owned by institutional investors, such as mutual funds, pension funds, insurance companies, and other large financial institutions. Institutional ownership is a way for investors to gauge the level of interest and confidence that these large and sophisticated investors have in a particular company. A high level of institutional ownership can indicate that a company is considered a good investment opportunity by these large and professional investors. The percentage of institutional ownership can be calculated by dividing the number of shares owned by institutional investors by the total number of outstanding shares. It's important to note that Institutional ownership does not guarantee a company's future performance. It's just one of the many factors to consider when evaluating a company. Also, it's important to remember that some institutional investors may hold shares for different reasons, such as diversifying their portfolios. Not all of them have the same level of analysis or the same investment horizon.

27. Earnings and Adjusted Earnings

Earnings refer to a company's net income or profit. They are calculated by subtracting expenses from revenue on a company's income statement. Earnings are often used as a measure of a company's financial performance. They can be used to compare a company's performance over time or the performance of different companies in the same industry. Adjusted earnings, also known as pro forma earnings or non-GAAP earnings, are earnings that have been adjusted to exclude certain items that are not considered to be part of ongoing operations. These adjustments give a better picture of a company's underlying performance. Some standard adjustments include one-time charges or gains, such as legal settlements or gains from the sale of assets that are not considered part of ongoing operations. Stock-based compensation is the expense of granting stock options or restricted stock units to employees, which is not considered part of ongoing operations. Acquisition-related expenses: These are expenses related to acquiring another company, such as legal and accounting fees, which are not considered to be part of ongoing operations; and Depreciation and amortization: These are non-cash expenses that represent the reduction in value of a company's assets over time, such as buildings and equipment.

28. Earnings-Per-Share

Earnings per share (EPS) is a financial ratio that measures a company's profitability. It is calculated by dividing a company's net income by the number of outstanding shares of its common stock. EPS is often used as a measure of a company's financial performance, and it can be used to compare the performance of a company over time or to compare the performance of different companies in the same industry. There are two types of EPS: Basic EPS, Which is the EPS calculated using the number of outstanding shares of a company's common stock at the end of a period, and Diluted EPS, Which is the EPS computed using the number of outstanding shares of a company's common stock at the end of a period, including the potential shares that could be issued from the conversion of outstanding convertible securities, such as stock options and convertible bonds. EPS is an important ratio for investors because it gives an idea of how much of the company's profit is allocated to each share of stock. A higher EPS generally indicates that a company is more profitable and that the company's stock is likely to be more valuable.

29. Gross Margin

Gross margin is a financial ratio that measures a company's profitability. It is calculated by dividing gross profit by revenue. Gross profit is calculated by subtracting the cost of goods sold (COGS) from income. Gross margin measures a company's ability to generate revenue after covering the costs of producing and selling its products or services. A higher gross margin indicates that a company is generating more profit on its sales and more efficiently controlling its costs. Gross margin is a crucial indicator of a company's financial health and can be used to compare the performance of a company over time or to compare the performance of different companies in the same industry.

30. Operating Margin

Operating margin is a financial ratio that measures a company's profitability and efficiency. It is calculated by dividing operating income by revenue. Operating income is calculated by subtracting operating expenses from gross profit. Operating expenses include cost of goods sold (COGS), selling, general and administrative (SG&A) expenses, and depreciation. Operating margin measures a company's ability to profit after covering all its operating expenses. A higher operating margin indicates that a company is more efficient in controlling its costs and is more profitable. Operating margin is a crucial indicator of a company's financial health and can be used to compare the performance of a company over time or to compare the performance of different companies in the same industry.

31. Net Margin

Net margin, also known as net profit margin, is a financial ratio that measures a company's profitability and efficiency. It is calculated by dividing net income by revenue. Net income is calculated by subtracting all expenses from revenue, including cost of goods sold (COGS), selling, general, and administrative (SG&A) expenses, depreciation, and taxes. Net margin measures a company's ability to generate a profit after covering all its costs, including taxes. A higher net margin indicates that a company is more efficient in controlling its costs and is more profitable. Net margin is a crucial indicator of a company's financial health and can be used to compare the performance of a company over time or to compare the performance of different companies in the same industry.

32. Assets

Assets are resources that a company owns or controls and have economic value. They are recorded on a company's balance sheet and can be classified into several categories, including:

- **Current assets:** These are assets that are expected to be converted into cash or used up within one year, such as cash, accounts receivable, and inventory.
- **Fixed assets:** These are assets that are used in the production of goods or services, such as land, buildings, equipment, and vehicles.
- **Intangible assets:** These are assets that have no physical form, such as patents, trademarks, copyrights, and goodwill.
- **Long-term investments:** These are investments in securities, such as stocks and bonds, that are expected to be held for more than one year.
- **Other assets:** These are assets that do not fit into the categories above, such as prepaid expenses and deferred charges.

The value of a company's assets is vital in determining its net worth and its ability to generate revenue and cash flow. Additionally, the composition of a company's assets can provide important information about its operations and risk profile.

33. Current Assets

Current assets are expected to be converted into cash or used up within one year. They are recorded on a company's balance sheet and are vital to its liquidity and working capital. Some common types of current assets include cash and cash equivalents, which include cash on hand, as well as short-term investments that are highly liquid and can be easily converted into cash:

- **Accounts receivable:** These are amounts due to a company from customers for goods or services that have been provided but not yet paid for.
- **Inventory:** This includes raw materials, work-in-progress, and finished goods that are held for sale.
- **Prepaid expenses:** These are expenses that have been paid in advance, such as rent or insurance.
- **Short-term investments:** These are investments in securities, such as stocks and bonds, that are expected to be held for less than one year.

It's important to note that current assets are more liquid than long-term assets, which means they are more easily converted into cash. A company's current ratio, calculated by dividing current assets by current liabilities, often indicates its liquidity and ability to meet its short-term obligations. Additionally, companies with a high proportion of current assets relative to current liabilities may be more able to withstand economic downturns.

34. Fixed Assets

Fixed assets are long-term tangible assets that a company uses to generate revenue and are not intended for resale. They include property, buildings, machinery, equipment, and vehicles. Fixed assets are crucial for a company's operations and are typically subject to depreciation over time, reflecting their gradual loss of value due to wear and tear. Unlike current assets, which are expected to be converted into cash within a year, fixed assets provide long-term utility and value to a business. They are recorded at their purchase cost minus accumulated depreciation on the balance sheet.

35. Intangible Assets

Intangible assets are non-physical assets with value due to the rights or privileges they provide to a company. Unlike tangible assets such as property and equipment, intangible assets cannot be seen or touched. They include patents, trademarks, copyrights, brand recognition, and goodwill. Intangible assets are crucial for a company's competitive advantage and long-term value, as they often represent intellectual property, proprietary technologies, or established market positioning. They are typically amortized over their useful life on the balance sheet, reflecting their gradual loss of value over time.

36. Liabilities

Liabilities are obligations that a company owes to others. They are recorded on a company's balance sheet and can be classified into several categories, including:

- **Current liabilities:** These are obligations that are expected to be settled within one year, such as accounts payable, short-term debt, and taxes owed.
- **Long-term liabilities:** These are obligations that are likely to be settled after one year, such as long-term debt, leases, and pension obligations.
- **Contingent liabilities:** These are potential commitments that may or may not arise, such as pending lawsuits or debt guarantees.

A company's equity or debt typically finances liabilities, and their composition has an essential effect on its risk profile and creditworthiness. The balance between liabilities and assets is also crucial for investors, as a company's liabilities can affect its ability to generate cash flow and pay dividends.

37. Current Liabilities

Current liabilities are obligations that a company owes to others and are expected to be settled within one year. They are recorded on a company's balance sheet and are vital to its liquidity and working capital. Some common types of current liabilities include:

- Accounts payable, which are amounts that a company owes to its suppliers for goods or services that have been received but not yet paid for
- Short-term debt, which includes loans and other forms of borrowing that are due to be repaid within one year
- Accrued expenses, which are expenses that have been incurred but not yet paid, such as salaries and utilities
- Taxes owed, which includes all taxes that a company owes to the government, such as income tax and sales tax
- Dividends payable, which includes dividends that a company's board of directors has declared but not yet paid to shareholders.

Additionally, companies with a high proportion of current liabilities relative to current assets may have a higher risk of defaulting on their obligations.

38. Long-term Liabilities

Long-term liabilities are obligations a company owes to others and are not expected to be settled within one year. They are recorded on a company's balance sheet and are vital to its long-term debt and financial structure. Some common types of long-term liabilities include:

- Long-term debt, which provides for loans, bonds, and other forms of borrowing due to be repaid over more than one year
- Leases, which contain obligations for the rental of property or equipment for a period of more than one year
- Pension obligations, which consist of the company's obligations for employee pensions and other retirement benefits

- Post-retirement benefits, which include the company's obligations for employee benefits other than pensions, such as healthcare benefits
- Deferred taxes, which include taxes that a company has deferred paying until a later date

39. Contingent Liabilities

Contingent liabilities are potential obligations that may or may not arise and are not recorded on a company's balance sheet as a liability. They are considered uncertain and could have a material impact on a company's financial position. Some examples of contingent liabilities include:

- Legal proceedings, which include pending lawsuits, claims, and other legal actions that a company is involved in, which could result in financial settlements or judgements against the company
- Product warranties, which include obligations to repair or replace products that may be defective, which could result in additional expenses for the company.
- Environmental liabilities, which provide obligations to clean up or remediate contaminated property, which could result in significant costs for the company.
- Guarantees, which consist of any guarantees that a company has provided to others, such as guaranteeing loans or leases, which could result in the company being required to pay if the borrower defaults
- Contracts, which include any obligations that a company has under contracts, such as supply agreements or service agreements, that may become onerous and result in financial losses

40. Debt

Debt is a type of liability that a company owes to others and is the amount of money a company has borrowed. It is recorded on a company's balance sheet and can be classified into short-term and long-term debt. Short-term debt: This is debt that is due to be repaid within one year. Examples include short-term loans, commercial paper, and accounts payable. Long-term debt: This is debt that is due to be repaid over more than one year. Examples include bonds, long-term loans, and leases. Debt can finance a company's operations, expansion, or acquisition, fund research and development, or pay dividends to shareholders. However, carrying too much debt can also increase a company's risk of default and negatively impact its creditworthiness. It's important to note that debt can also affect a company's financial statements, as interest payments on debt are considered an expense, decreasing a company's net income and profitability. Additionally, the level of debt can also affect a company's ability to generate cash flow and pay dividends. Therefore, investors use several ratios to evaluate a company's debt, such as debt-to-equity ratio, debt-to-assets ratio, and debt-to-EBITDA ratio.

41. Equity

Equity, also known as shareholders' equity or owners' equity, is the residual interest in a company's assets after liabilities have been deducted. It represents the portion of a company's assets financed by shareholders and recorded on a company's balance sheet. Equity can be classified into several categories, including:

- Common stock, which represents the ownership interest of common shareholders in a company and is typically divided into shares of stock, which represent the ownership interest of preferred shareholders, who have priority over common shareholders in terms of dividends and liquidation

- Retained earnings, which represent the portion of a company's net income that is kept by the company instead of being distributed as dividends.
- Treasury stock, which represents the shares that a company has repurchased from its shareholders
- Additional paid-in capital, which represents the amount paid by shareholders in excess of the stock's par value.

Equity is important to a company's financial position and can affect its ability to raise capital and creditworthiness. Additionally, the composition of a company's equity can provide important information about its operations and risk profile. It's important to note that equity can be affected by changes in net income, dividends, and the number of shares outstanding. Additionally, the level of equity can also affect a company's ability to generate cash flow and pay dividends.

42. Capital Expenditures

Capital expenditures, or capex, are funds a company uses to acquire or upgrade long-term assets such as property, plant, and equipment (PP&E). These investments are intended to generate future income as opposed to being used for day-to-day operations. Capital expenditures can include:

- Building and construction, which consists of constructing new facilities or expanding existing ones
- Equipment and machinery, which consists of purchasing new or replacement equipment and machinery, such as computers, manufacturing equipment, and vehicles
- Technology, which includes investments in software, hardware, and IT systems that will be used in the company's operations
- Land and property, which consist of the purchase of land or property that will be used for the company's operations.

Capital expenditures are typically long-term investments and are expected to generate future income. They can also improve efficiency, reduce costs, and increase production capacity. It's important to note that capital expenditures can significantly impact a company's financial position, as they can result in increased debt or reduced cash flow. Therefore, it's important for investors to evaluate a company's capital expenditure plans and to understand the potential risks and benefits that they may pose. Additionally, capital expenditures are typically financed by debt, equity, or cash on hand; and their composition can also affect the company's risk profile and creditworthiness.

43. Operating Cash flow and Cash Flow from Operations

Operating cash flow, also known as cash flow from operations, is a measure of a company's cash flow generated by its core business operations. It is a key metric to evaluate a company's financial performance and ability to generate cash flow. Operating cash flow is calculated by taking cash inflows from sales and subtracting cash outflows for expenses and investments in working capital such as inventory and accounts receivable. Operating cash flow is a measure of a company's ability to generate cash from its normal business operations, and it is a key metric used to evaluate a company's financial performance and ability to generate cash flow. A favorable operating cash flow indicates that a company is generating more cash than it uses and can be used to pay dividends, reduce debt, and make investments. A negative operating cash flow, on the other hand, indicates that a company is using more cash than it is generating and may have difficulty meeting its financial obligations. It can also indicate a company's inability to generate enough revenue to cover its expenses or its inefficiency in managing its working capital. It's important to note that operating cash flow can be affected by various factors, such as changes in sales, costs, working capital requirements, and investment spending. Additionally, the industry and the type of business can significantly impact the operating cash flow.

44. Return on Assets (ROA)

Return on Assets (ROA) is a financial ratio that measures a company's profitability of its total assets. It evaluates a company's efficiency in generating profits from its assets. The formula for ROA is ROA = (Net Income / Total Assets) x 100, and ROA expresses a company's net income as a percentage of its total assets. A higher ROA indicates that a company is generating more profit from its assets and is considered more efficient in using its assets to generate income. A lower ROA indicates that a company is generating less profit from its assets and may be considered less efficient in using its assets to generate income. It's important to note that ROA is a profitability ratio, and it can be affected by various factors, such as changes in net income, changes in assets, and changes in industry averages. ROA can also vary significantly depending on the industry and the type of business, as a company with high leverage (high debt) may have a lower ROA but still be considered profitable.

45. Return on Equity (ROE)

Return on Equity (ROE) is a financial ratio that measures a company's profitability about its shareholders' equity. It evaluates a company's efficiency in generating profits for its shareholders. The formula for ROE is: ROE = (Net Income / Shareholders' Equity) x 100, and ROE expresses a company's net income as a percentage of its shareholders' equity. A higher ROE indicates that a company generates more profit for its shareholders and is considered more efficient in using shareholders' funds to generate income. A lower ROE indicates that a company generates less profit for its shareholders and may be considered less efficient in using shareholders' funds to generate income. It's important to note that ROE is a profitability ratio, and it can be affected by various factors, such as changes in net income, changes in shareholders' equity, and changes in industry averages. ROE can also vary significantly depending on the industry and the type of business. Therefore, ROE should be used with other financial metrics and analyses to understand a company's financial performance better. ROE is commonly used by investors, analysts, and management to evaluate a company's profitability and efficiency and to compare it with industry peers.

46. Trailing Price-to-Earnings (P/E) ratio

The Trailing Price-to-Earnings (P/E) ratio, also known as the "price multiple" or "earnings multiple," is a valuation ratio that compares a company's current stock price to its earnings per share (EPS) over the last 12 months. It is calculated by dividing the current stock price by the EPS for the previous 12 months. The Trailing P/E ratio determines how much investors will pay for each dollar of a company's earnings over the past year. The Trailing P/E ratio is commonly used to evaluate a stock. A high Trailing P/E ratio may indicate that a stock is overvalued, meaning that investors are willing to pay a premium for each dollar of earnings. A low Trailing P/E ratio may indicate that a stock is undervalued, meaning that investors are willing to pay less for each dollar of earnings. The Trailing P/E ratio should be considered in the context of the industry average and the company's historical P/E ratios. A P/E ratio significantly higher or lower than the industry average or the company's historical ratios may indicate that the stock is overvalued or undervalued.

47. Forward Price-to-Earnings (P/E) ratio

The Forward Price-to-Earnings (P/E) ratio is similar to the Trailing P/E ratio. Still, instead of using earnings per share (EPS) from the last 12 months, it uses estimated earnings per share for the next 12 months, also known as forward earnings. It is calculated by dividing the current stock price by the estimated EPS for the next 12 months. The Forward P/E ratio determines how much investors will pay for each dollar of a company's projected earnings. A high Forward P/E ratio may indicate that a stock is overvalued, meaning that investors are willing to pay a premium for each dollar of projected earnings. A low Forward P/E ratio may indicate that a stock is undervalued, meaning that investors are willing to pay less for each dollar of projected earnings. The Forward P/E ratio is based on estimates and projections, and it can be affected by many factors, such as changes in the economy and industry trends.

48. Price-to-Earnings-to-Growth (PEG Ratio)

The Price-to-Earnings-to-Growth (PEG) ratio is a valuation ratio that considers both the Price-to-Earnings (P/E) ratio and the company's growth rate. The PEG ratio is calculated by dividing the P/E ratio by the company's earnings growth rate, usually measured as the projected or estimated earnings per share (EPS) growth rate for the next few years. The PEG ratio is used to determine a stock's relative value by considering its current valuation and growth potential. A PEG ratio of one is supposed to be fair value, which means that the stock's P/E ratio is in line with its growth rate. A PEG ratio of less than one may indicate that a stock is undervalued, while a PEG ratio greater than one may indicate that a stock is overvalued. The PEG ratio is based on estimates and projections, and it can be affected by many factors, such as changes in the economy, industry trends, and the company's performance. Additionally, the PEG ratio does not consider other factors, such as dividends, debt, or cash flow, and should not be used in isolation when making investment decisions.

49. Price-to-Sales (P/S) ratio

The Price-to-Sales (P/S) ratio is a financial ratio that compares a company's current stock price to its revenue per share. It is calculated by dividing the current stock price by the revenue per share (total revenue divided by the number of shares outstanding). The P/S ratio determines how much investors will pay for each dollar of a company's revenue. A high P/S ratio may indicate that a stock is overvalued, meaning that investors are willing to pay a premium for each dollar of revenue. A low P/S ratio may indicate that a stock is undervalued, meaning that investors are willing to pay less for each dollar of revenue. The P/S ratio should be considered in the context of the industry average and the company's historical P/S ratios. A P/S ratio significantly higher or lower than the industry average or the company's historical ratios may indicate that the stock is overvalued or undervalued.

50. Price-to-Book (P/B) ratio

The Price-to-Book (P/B) ratio is a financial ratio that compares a company's current stock price to its book value (total assets minus liabilities). It is calculated by dividing the current stock price by the book value per share. The P/B ratio determines how much investors will pay for each dollar of a company's assets. A higher P/B ratio means that investors are willing to pay more for each dollar of the company's assets, indicating that they believe their assets are undervalued. On the other hand, a lower P/B ratio means that investors are willing to pay less for each dollar of the company's assets, indicating that they believe the company's assets are overvalued. The P/B ratio should be considered in the context of the industry average and the company's historical P/B ratios. A P/B ratio significantly higher or lower than the industry average or the company's historical ratios may indicate that the stock is overvalued or undervalued.

51. Enterprise Value/Revenue

The Enterprise Value to Revenue (EV/Revenue) ratio is a valuation ratio that compares a company's Enterprise Value (EV) to its revenue. It is calculated by dividing the company's Enterprise Value by its revenue. The EV/Revenue ratio determines how much investors are willing to pay for each dollar of a company's revenue. A high EV/Revenue ratio may indicate that a stock is overvalued, meaning that investors are willing to pay a premium for each dollar of revenue. A low EV/Revenue ratio may indicate that a stock is undervalued, meaning that investors are willing to pay less for each dollar of revenue. The EV/Revenue ratio should be considered in the context of the industry average and the company's historical EV/Revenue ratios. A significantly higher or lower ratio than the industry average or the company's historical ratios may indicate that the stock is overvalued or undervalued.

52. Enterprise Value/EBITDA

The Enterprise Value to Earnings Before Interest, Taxes, Depreciation, and Amortization (EV/EBITDA) ratio is a valuation ratio that compares a company's Enterprise Value (EV) to its Earnings Before Interest, Taxes, Depreciation, and Amortization (EBITDA). It is calculated by dividing the company's Enterprise Value by its EBITDA. The EV/EBITDA ratio determines how much investors will pay for each dollar of a company's earnings before interest, taxes, depreciation, and amortization. A high EV/EBITDA ratio may indicate that a stock is overvalued, meaning that investors are willing to pay a premium for each dollar of earnings. A low EV/EBITDA ratio may indicate that a stock is undervalued, meaning that investors are willing to pay less for each dollar of earnings. The EV/EBITDA ratio should be considered in the context of the industry average and the company's own historical EV/EBITDA ratios. A significantly higher or lower ratio than the industry average or the company's historical ratios may indicate that the stock is overvalued or undervalued.

53. Fiscal Year Ends

A fiscal year-end is a 12-month period a company or organization uses for accounting and budgeting purposes. It is not necessarily the same as the calendar year (January 1 to December 31) and can begin on any date. For example, a company's fiscal year could be from July 1 to June 30, from April 1 to March 31, or any other 12-month period. The company chooses the fiscal year, which is usually based on the company's business cycle, tax laws, or other factors that are relevant to the company's operations. The fiscal year-end can be different from one company to another. When comparing financial statements from different companies, it's essential to be aware of each company's fiscal year-end. Additionally, when comparing a company's financial statements over time, it's necessary to compare the same fiscal year.

54. Most Recent Quarter

The most recent quarter refers to the latest three-month period a company has reported its financial performance. This is typically referred to as the "current quarter" or the "latest quarter," and it is usually the quarter that ends closest to the current date. For example, if the current date is March 15, 2023, the most recent quarter would be the fourth quarter of the fiscal year 2022 (Q4FY22), which typically runs from October 1, 2022 - December 31, 2022. Companies regularly report their financial performance for the most recent quarter, usually once every three months. This is known as a "quarterly earnings report" or "quarterly financial statement," it includes financial information such as revenue, earnings, and cash flow for the quarter. The most recent quarter is considered a short-term period, and its results do not necessarily indicate the company's long-term performance.

55. Profitability

Profitability refers to a company's ability to generate a profit, or income, from its operations. It measures a company's financial performance and is typically expressed as a percentage of revenue. There are several ways to measure a company's profitability, including gross profit margin, which is the percentage of revenue a company keeps after subtracting the cost of goods sold (COGS). It is calculated by dividing gross profit (revenue minus COGS) by revenue. Operating profit margin: This is the percentage of revenue a company keeps after subtracting the cost of goods sold (COGS) and operating expenses (such as selling, general, and administrative expenses). It is calculated by dividing operating profit (revenue minus COGS and operating expenses) by revenue and Net profit margin: This is the percentage of revenue a company keeps after subtracting all expenses, including cost of goods sold (COGS), operating expenses, and taxes. It is calculated by dividing net profit (revenue minus all expenses) by revenue.

56. Operating Profit Margin

Operating Profit Margin is a financial metric measuring the percentage of revenue after covering operating expenses, excluding interest and taxes. It is calculated by dividing operating profit (or operating income) by total revenue and is expressed as a percentage. This margin indicates how efficiently a company is managing its core business operations and controlling costs. A higher operating profit margin suggests that a company is effectively generating profit from its operations, while a lower margin may indicate issues with cost control or pricing strategies. It provides insight into a company's operational efficiency and is a key indicator of financial health and profitability.

57. Gross Profit Margin

Gross Profit Margin is a financial ratio that measures the percentage of revenue remaining after subtracting the cost of goods sold (COGS). It is calculated by dividing gross profit by total revenue and expressing the result as a percentage. This margin reflects a company's efficiency in producing and selling its products. A higher gross profit margin indicates that a company effectively manages its production costs and pricing strategies, resulting in more profit from each dollar of revenue. Conversely, a lower margin may signal issues with cost control or pricing. Gross profit margin is a crucial indicator of a company's financial health and operational efficiency.

58. Revenue Per Share

Revenue per share (RPS) is a financial ratio that compares a company's revenue to the number of shares outstanding. It is calculated by dividing the company's total revenue by the number of shares outstanding. The resulting figure represents the amount of revenue generated per share. RPS helps evaluate a company's performance and its ability to generate revenue. It is beneficial when comparing companies with different capital structures, as it adjusts for the number of shares outstanding. A company with a higher RPS is generally considered more efficient in generating revenue. It's important to note that RPS should be viewed in the context of the company's industry and its competitors. Different industries have different revenue characteristics so that the RPS will vary considerably across various sectors. Additionally, RPS should not be considered in isolation when analyzing a company's performance and should be used in conjunction with other financial metrics such as net income per share, price-to-earnings ratio, and return on equity.

59. Index Rebalancing Metrics

Index rebalancing refers to the periodic adjustment of the components within a stock market index to maintain its intended structure and reflect the current market conditions. This process is crucial for ensuring an index accurately represents its underlying market or sector and remains a reliable investor benchmark. Understanding the metrics and methodologies behind index rebalancing is essential for both index providers and investors.

- Purpose of Rebalancing: Rebalancing is necessary to reflect changes in market capitalization, sector performance, and the economic landscape. Over time, some stocks may increase significantly in value, while others may decline or even be delisted. Rebalancing ensures that the index composition remains aligned with its investment strategy.

- Frequency of Rebalancing: Indexes may be rebalanced on a regular schedule, such as quarterly, semi-annually, or annually, depending on the rules set by the index provider. Some indexes also implement rules for ad hoc rebalancing based on significant market events or changes in individual securities.
- Methodologies: Different indexes utilize various methodologies for rebalancing, which may include Market Capitalization Weighting. This method, most commonly used, adjusts the weights of index constituents based on their market capitalizations. Equal Weighting: In this approach, each constituent has the same weight in the index, which requires more frequent rebalancing to maintain equal representation. Fundamental Weighting: This method considers fundamental metrics, such as revenue or earnings, to determine the constituents' weights, adjusting as these metrics change.
- Selection Criteria: Securities typically must meet specific criteria set by the index provider to be included in an index. Common factors include market capitalization, liquidity, sector classification, and financial performance. These criteria are reassessed during each rebalancing period to determine which securities remain in or are added to the index.
- Impact of Rebalancing: The rebalancing process can influence stock prices, particularly for heavily weighted stocks or those being added to or removed from an index. When security is added, demand increases as index-tracking funds and ETFs buy shares to replicate the index. Conversely, selling pressure may occur for securities removed from an index. The effects of rebalancing can lead to increased volatility around the rebalancing dates as market participants adjust their positions based on the anticipated changes.
- Tracking Error: Tracking error measures the divergence between an index's performance and that of a fund or ETF that seeks to replicate it. Frequent rebalancing can minimize

tracking error, ensuring that index funds closely follow the performance of their benchmark. Conversely, inadequate or infrequent rebalancing can lead to higher tracking errors.

Index rebalancing is vital for maintaining the integrity and reliability of stock market indexes. By periodically adjusting the composition of index constituents based on established criteria and methodologies, index providers ensure that the indexes accurately reflect current market conditions and sector dynamics. Understanding the metrics and implications of index rebalancing is crucial for investors who use these indexes as benchmarks for performance or as the basis for their investment strategies. Through effective rebalancing practices, market participants can navigate the complexities of investing in index-tracking funds and better manage their portfolios in alignment with market trends.

60. Seasonality Metrics

Seasonality metrics refer to statistical measures that analyze and quantify the regular and predictable changes in a financial asset's price or performance over specific periods, often influenced by seasonal factors. Understanding seasonality is crucial for investors and traders as it helps them make informed decisions based on historical patterns and trends.

Key Features of Seasonality Metrics

Definition and Importance: Seasonality refers to recurring patterns in asset prices or market performance at specific times of the year, month, or week. These patterns can arise from various factors, including weather conditions, holidays, consumer behavior, and economic cycles. Recognizing and utilizing seasonality can enhance trading strategies, risk management, and investment decisions. It allows investors to identify periods of expected strength or weakness in an asset's performance.

- Types of Seasonality:
  - Monthly Seasonality: This involves patterns that occur at specific months. For example, certain stocks may perform better in the fourth quarter due to holiday shopping, while others may experience declines during summer months when trading volumes typically decrease.
  - Weekly Seasonality: Certain days may exhibit consistent price patterns. For instance, the phenomenon known as the "Monday effect" suggests that stock prices may decline on Mondays.
  - Daily Seasonality: Price movements can also exhibit patterns throughout the trading day, often influenced by economic reports, earnings announcements, or market sentiment.

- Statistical Analysis:
  - Seasonality metrics are derived from historical price data, often utilizing statistical techniques to identify patterns. Common methods include:
  - Moving Averages: This technique smooths price data to reveal underlying trends, helping to highlight seasonal patterns.
  - Regression Analysis: This statistical method can be used to quantify the relationship between seasonal factors and price movements.
  - Seasonal Decomposition of Time Series (STL): This approach separates a time series into seasonal, trend, and residual components, enabling analysts to isolate and examine seasonal effects.

- Applications in Trading:
  - Trading Strategies: Investors can develop trading strategies based on seasonal trends. For example, a trader might buy a stock known to perform well during a particular season and sell it before the expected downturn.

  - Risk Management: Understanding seasonal patterns can aid in risk management by allowing investors to anticipate periods of volatility or downturns and adjust their portfolios accordingly.
  - Market Timing: Seasonality metrics can inform decisions about when to enter or exit positions, potentially enhancing profitability.

- Limitations:
  - While seasonality can provide valuable insights, it is essential to recognize its limitations. Seasonal patterns may not always hold true, particularly in volatile or rapidly changing market conditions.
  - External factors, such as economic shifts, geopolitical events, or changes in consumer behavior, can disrupt historical patterns, leading to unexpected outcomes.

- Examples of Seasonality in Financial Markets:
  - Retail Stocks: Retail companies often see increased sales and stock performance during the holiday season (November and December), driven by consumer spending.
  - Agricultural Commodities: Prices for agricultural products may exhibit seasonal patterns based on planting and harvest cycles.
  - Energy Sector: Energy stocks often show seasonal trends based on weather patterns, with increased demand for heating oil in winter and gasoline in summer.

Seasonality metrics are powerful tools that enable investors and traders to identify and capitalize on predictable patterns in asset prices. By analyzing historical data and recognizing seasonal trends, market participants can enhance their trading strategies, manage risks more effectively, and make informed investment decisions. While seasonality can provide valuable insights, it is crucial to remain aware of its limitations and the potential for changing market dynamics. By integrating seasonality analysis into a broader investment strategy, investors can navigate the complexities of financial markets with greater confidence and precision.

61. Quarterly Revenue Growth

Quarterly revenue growth is a financial metric that measures a company's revenue change over three months (a quarter). It is typically expressed as a percentage and compares the current quarter's revenue to the revenue of the same quarter in the previous year. To calculate quarterly revenue growth, you can use the formula: (Current quarter revenue - Same quarter revenue of the previous year) / Same quarter revenue of the previous year x 100. A positive quarterly revenue growth rate indicates a company's revenue is increasing, while a negative growth rate means revenue decreases. A higher growth rate is generally considered a positive sign for a company's financial performance. It's important to note that revenue growth should be viewed in the context of the company's industry and its competitors. Different industries have different growth characteristics so that the growth rate will vary considerably across various sectors.

62. EBITDA

EBITDA stands for Earnings Before Interest, Taxes, Depreciation, and Amortization. It is a financial metric used to assess a company's operating performance by focusing on its profitability from core business activities, excluding the effects of capital structure, tax rates, and non-cash accounting items. EBITDA is calculated by adding interest expenses, taxes, depreciation, and amortization to net income. It provides insight into a company's ability to generate cash from operations, making it a useful measure for comparing companies within the same industry, as it eliminates variables that can differ widely between firms. Investors and analysts often use EBITDA to evaluate a company's financial health and operational efficiency. EBITDA=Net Income+Taxes+Interest Expense+D&A or EBITDA=Operating Income+D&A where: D&A=Depreciation and amortization.

63. Interest

Interest is the cost of borrowing money; it is the amount of money a lender charges a borrower for the use of their money. Interest is typically expressed as a percentage of the amount borrowed and is usually paid regularly, such as annually, semi-annually, or monthly. Companies can borrow money in various forms, such as loans from banks, bonds, or lines of credit. The interest expense on these debts will be recognized in the company's income statement as an operating expense, decreasing the company's net income. Interest expense can significantly impact a company's financial performance, and it's essential to consider a company's interest expense in terms of its revenue, operating income, and net income. High-interest expenses could indicate that a company is heavily leveraged and is struggling to generate enough income to cover its debt payments. A company with lower interest expense, relative to its revenue, operating income, and net income, is generally considered to be in a better financial position.

64. Taxes

Taxes are a financial obligation imposed by governments on individuals and businesses. They are typically calculated as a percentage of a company's income or profits and are used to fund government operations and public services. Companies must pay taxes on their income, which is calculated based on their revenue, expenses, and other financial transactions. The tax expense on a company's income will be recognized in its income statement as an operating expense, decreasing the company's net income. Taxes can significantly impact a company's financial performance, and it's essential to consider a company's tax expense in terms of its revenue, operating income, and net income. A company with a lower tax rate relative to its revenue, operating income, and net income is generally considered to be in a better financial position. The tax expense is not the only measure of a company's financial performance. It should be considered with other financial metrics such as revenue growth, return on equity, and liquidity.

65. Depreciation

Depreciation is an accounting method used to spread the cost of an asset over its useful life. It is a non-cash expense, which means it does not involve any actual cash outflow. Depreciation is recorded as an expense on a company's income statement and is used to match an asset's expense with the revenue it generates. Depreciation is calculated by dividing the asset's cost by its useful life and then spreading that amount over the asset's life. For example, if a company bought a machine for $100,000 with a useful life of 5 years, the annual depreciation expense would be $20,000 ($100,000 / 5 years). Depreciation is significant because it allows companies to match an asset's cost with its revenue. It also helps companies to spread the cost of an asset over its useful life, which makes it easier to manage the company's cash flow. Additionally, it reduces the company's net income and taxes, which can be helpful in specific financial scenarios.

66. Amortization

Amortization refers to gradually repaying a debt or expensing an intangible asset over time. In the context of loans, amortization involves paying off a debt through regular payments over a specified period. Each payment includes both interest and principal repayment. Over time, the portion of the payment applied to interest decreases, while the portion applied to the principal increases until the debt is fully repaid. For intangible assets, such as patents or copyrights, amortization involves allocating the asset's cost over its useful life. This process spreads out the expense on the company's financial statements, reflecting the gradual consumption of the asset's value. Amortization helps businesses and individuals manage cash flow and provides a more accurate picture of expenses related to long-term obligations or assets. Amortization is calculated by dividing the intangible asset's cost by its useful life and spreading that amount over the asset's life. For example, if a company bought a patent for $50,000 with a useful life of 10 years, the annual amortization expense would be $5,000 ($50,000 / 10 years). Amortization is essential because it allows companies to match the cost of an intangible asset with its revenue. It also helps companies to spread the cost of an intangible asset over its useful life, which makes it easier to manage the company's cash flow. Additionally, it reduces the company's net income and taxes, which can be helpful in specific financial scenarios.

67. Net Income Avi to Common

Net income available to common shareholders, also known as net income attributable to common shareholders, is a financial metric that measures the portion of a company's net income available to be distributed to the company's ordinary shareholders. It is calculated by subtracting the preferred dividends from the net income. Preferred dividends are paid to the holders of preferred shares before common shareholders. Preferred shareholders have priority over common shareholders in receiving dividends, meaning they will be paid before common shareholders. Net income available to common shareholders is essential for evaluating a company's profitability. It shows the portion of the net income to be distributed to the common shareholders. It also calculates common shareholders' earnings per share (EPS). EPS is calculated by dividing the net income available to common shareholders by the number of outstanding common shares. The Net income available to common shareholders is not the only measure of a company's financial performance. It should be considered with other financial metrics such as revenue growth, return on equity, and liquidity.

68. Diluted EPS

Diluted Earnings Per Share (EPS) is a financial ratio that shows how much of a company's net income is attributable to each outstanding share of common stock. It considers the exceptional common shares and the potential dilution from exercising options, warrants, and convertible securities. The diluted EPS formula is calculated by dividing the net income available to common shareholders by the weighted average number of outstanding shares, including the common shares exceptional and the potential dilution from exercising options, warrants, and convertible securities. Diluted EPS is considered a more accurate measure of a company's earnings per share than essential EPS because it considers the potential dilution of the earnings per share if all the outstanding options, warrants, and convertible securities were exercised. The Diluted EPS is not the only measure of a company's financial performance, and it should be considered in conjunction with other financial metrics such as revenue growth, return on equity, and liquidity.

69. Quarterly Earnings Growth

Quarterly Earnings Growth is a financial metric measuring a company's net income change over three months (a quarter). It is typically expressed as a percentage and compares the current quarter's net income to the net income of the same quarter in the previous year. To calculate quarterly earnings growth, you can use the formula: (Current quarter net income - Same quarter net income of the previous year) / Same quarter net income of the previous year x 100. A positive quarterly earnings growth rate indicates that a company's net income is increasing, while a negative growth rate indicates that net income is decreasing. A higher growth rate is generally considered a positive sign for a company's financial performance. The quartely earnings growth should be viewed in the context of the company's industry and its competitors. Different industries have different growth characteristics, so the growth rate will vary considerably across different sectors.

70. Total Cash

Total cash is a financial metric representing the amount of cash and cash equivalents that a company has on hand at a specific time. Cash and cash equivalents are short-term, highly liquid assets easily converted into cash, such as cash on hand, savings accounts, money market funds, and marketable securities. Total cash is typically reported on a company's balance sheet and is an essential metric for evaluating a company's liquidity and financial flexibility. A company with a large amount of cash generally has a stronger financial position than a company with little or no cash.

71. Total Cash Per Share

Total cash per share is a financial metric representing the cash and cash equivalents a company has on hand per share of its common stock. It is calculated by dividing the company's total cash by the number of outstanding shares of common stock. Total cash per share is an essential metric for evaluating a company's liquidity and financial flexibility at the shareholder level. It gives an idea of how much cash each shareholder would receive if the company distributed its cash among the shareholders. A higher total cash per share is generally considered a positive sign for a company's financial position. The total cash per share should be viewed as a company's other financial metrics, such as its earnings per share (EPS) and price-to-earnings ratio (P/E), to get a complete picture of its financial performance.

72. Total Debt

Total debt is a financial metric representing the amount of money a company owes to its creditors, including short-term and long-term debt. It includes all forms of debt, such as bonds, loans, and leases.

Total debt is typically reported on a company's balance sheet. It is an essential metric for evaluating a company's financial leverage, which is using debt to finance its operations and growth. A high level of debt can increase a company's financial risk and make it more vulnerable to economic downturns and other adverse conditions. On the other hand, a low level of debt may indicate a solid financial position and a healthy balance sheet. To get a complete picture of its financial position, the total debt should be considered in a company's other financial metrics, such as total assets, equity, and cash flow from operations.

73. Total Debt/Equity

The Total Debt to Equity ratio (D/E) is a financial metric that compares a company's total debt to its total shareholders' equity. It is used to measure a company's financial leverage and assess the risk associated with its level of debt. The ratio is calculated by dividing the total debt by the total equity. A higher ratio indicates a greater degree of leverage and a greater level of risk. A lower ratio means a lower degree of leverage and a lower level of risk. A company with a high D/E ratio may be considered more risky because it has more debt than equity. This means that if the company were to experience financial difficulties, its creditors would be at a greater risk of not being repaid. However, a high D/E ratio can also indicate that a company uses leverage to its advantage and can generate a higher return on equity. It's important to note that the D/E ratio should be considered concerning a company's other financial metrics, such as its ability to generate cash flow, to get a complete picture of its financial position.

74. Current Ratio

The current ratio is a financial metric measuring a company's ability to pay its short-term liabilities with its assets. It is calculated by dividing a company's assets by its liabilities. Current assets are expected to be converted into cash or used up within one year, such as cash and cash equivalents, accounts receivable, and inventory. Current liabilities such as accounts payable, short-term loans, and taxes are expected to be paid off within one year. A ratio of one or higher is generally considered healthy and indicates that a company has enough liquid assets to meet its short-term liabilities. A ratio of less than one indicates that a company may have difficulty meeting its short-term obligations. The current ratio should be considered in the context of a company's industry and competitors. Different industries have different working capital needs so that the current ratio will vary considerably across different sectors.

75. Book Value Per Share

Book value per share is a financial metric representing the value of a company's assets after subtracting liabilities. It is calculated by dividing the shareholder's equity by the number of outstanding shares of common stock. Book value per share measures a company's net asset value and gives investors an idea of its worth based on its accounting values. It is considered a conservative estimate of a company's intrinsic value. A company with a high book value per share is generally considered to be in a stronger financial position than a company with a low book value per share. The book value per share does not consider a company's potential earnings. Therefore, it may not accurately measure a company's intrinsic value.

76. Intrinsic Value

Intrinsic value is a financial concept that refers to the inherent value of an asset, such as a stock, based on its underlying fundamentals, such as earnings, dividends, and growth prospects. It is often used in value investing, a strategy in which investors try to identify stocks trading at a price below their intrinsic value, expecting the market to recognize the stock's true worth, and the price eventually will increase. Several methods are used to estimate intrinsic value, such as discounted cash flow (DCF) analysis, dividend discount model, and relative valuation. DCF analysis estimates inherent value by projecting a company's future cash flows and discounting them to the present using a discount rate. The dividend discount model estimates intrinsic value by projecting a company's future dividends and discounting them to the present using a discount rate. Relative valuation compares a company's financials to its peers or industry averages to estimate its intrinsic value. The intrinsic value is subjective and can vary depending on the method used to calculate it and the assumptions made about the future.

77. Cash Flow from Operating Activities

Cash Flow from Operating Activities refers to the cash generated or used by a company's core business operations during a specific period. This measure is crucial for understanding a company's ability to generate cash from its regular business activities, excluding cash flows from investing and financing activities. Key components include customer Receipts for goods sold or services provided, payments to suppliers and employees for operating expenses, and interest and taxes paid related to the company's operating activities. Cash Flow from Operating Activities is typically calculated using either the direct method (where cash inflows and outflows are directly reported) or the indirect method (where net income is adjusted for changes in working capital and non-cash expenses). This metric is important for assessing the company's operational efficiency, liquidity, and overall financial health.

78. Cash Flow from Investing Activities

Cash Flow from Investing Activities represents the cash used for or generated from the company's investments in assets and other financial instruments. It reflects the cash inflows and outflows related to acquiring and disposing of long-term assets and investments. Key components include property, plant, equipment (PP&E) purchases and cash spent on developing or upgrading physical assets. Sales of PP&E: Cash received from selling physical assets. Investments in securities: Cash used to purchase or receive from the sale of investments in other companies or financial instruments. Loans made to other entities: Cash lent to others, which may be repaid over time. Cash Flow from Investing Activities helps assess how much cash is being invested in the company's growth and asset base and how much is being returned through asset sales or investment returns. It is an indicator of the company's strategic investment decisions and its capacity to fund future growth.

79. Cash Flow from Financing Activities

Cash Flow from financing activities represents the cash flows associated with raising and repaying capital. This section of the cash flow statement details how a company finances its operations and growth through various forms of capital. Key components include

- **Issuance of stock:** Cash received from issuing new shares of stock
- **Repurchase of stock:** Cash used to buy back shares from the market
- **Borrowings:** Cash inflows from taking on new debt or loans
- **Repayment of debt:** Cash outflows are used to pay back principal on borrowed funds
- **Dividend payments:** Cash paid out to shareholders as dividends

Cash flow from financing activities provides insights into a company's financial structure and how it manages its capital resources. It reflects the company's ability to raise funds to support operations and growth and its approach to managing debt and equity.

80. Levered Free Cash Flow

Levered free cash flow (LFCF) is a financial metric that measures a company's cash after accounting for capital expenditures and debt payments. It is calculated by subtracting capital expenditures and debt payments from the operating cash flow. LFCF is an essential metric for evaluating a company's ability to generate cash after accounting for the investments required to maintain and grow its operations and the necessary payments to service its debt. A positive LFCF indicates that a company generates more cash than it is spending and can fund its operations, pay dividends, and make investments. A negative LFCF suggests that a company spends more cash than it generates and may be in a difficult financial position. To get a complete picture of its economic performance, the LFCF should be considered concerning a company's other financial metrics, such as its net income.

81. Beta

Beta measures a stock's volatility to the overall market. It is a statistical measure that compares the volatility of a stock to that of a benchmark index, typically the S&P 500. A beta of one indicates that the stock's price will move with the market, while a beta less than one means it is less volatile than the market, and a beta greater than one indicates that the stock is more volatile than the market. A stock with a beta of one is considered as risky as the market, a stock with a beta of less than one is considered less risky, and a stock with a beta greater than one is considered riskier. A stock with a beta of less than one can be a good option for investors looking for a lower-risk investment, while a stock with a beta greater than one can be a good option for investors looking for a higher-risk investment with the potential for higher returns. The beta is not a measure of the stock's return but rather a measure of the stock's volatility.

82. 52-Week Change

The 52-week change is a financial metric that shows the percentage difference between a stock's current price and its price 52 weeks ago. It is calculated by subtracting the current stock price 52 weeks ago, then dividing the result by the price 52 weeks ago and multiplying it by 100 to get the percentage change. The 52-week change can be used as a quick way to gauge a stock's recent performance and to compare it to its performance over the past year. A positive 52-week change indicates that the stock's price has increased over the past year, while a negative 52-week change suggests that the stock's price has decreased over the past year. The 52-week change is historical and may not accurately predict future performance.

83. S&P500 52-Week Change

The S&P 500 52-week change is the percentage change in the value of the S&P 500 index over the past 52 weeks. The S&P 500 is a stock market index that comprises 500 of the largest publicly traded companies in the United States, and it is considered to be a broad measure of the overall performance of the U.S. stock market. The 52-week change in the value of the S&P 500 is calculated by taking the index's current level and subtracting the level from 52 weeks ago, then dividing the result by the level from 52 weeks ago and multiplying it by 100 to get the percentage change. A positive 52-week change in the value of the S&P 500 indicates that the index has increased in value over the past year, while a negative 52-week change suggests that the index has decreased in value. The S&P 500 52-week change can be used as a quick way to gauge the overall performance of the U.S. stock market and as a benchmark to compare the performance of individual stocks. The S&P 500 52-week change is historical and may not predict future performance accurately.

84. 52-Week Stock Price Range

52-week stock price range is a metric that measures the high and low prices of a stock over one year, or 52 weeks. Investors use this metric to gauge a stock's volatility and determine whether it is overvalued or undervalued compared to its historical price range. 52-week high: This is the highest price that a stock has reached in the past 52 weeks, and 52-week low: This is the lowest price that a stock has reached in the past 52 weeks. 52-week price performance: This measures the change in a stock's price over the past 52 weeks and can be expressed as a percentage or a dollar amount. Investors can use the 52-week stock price range as a reference point when determining whether a stock is currently trading at a premium or a discount to its historical price levels. If a stock is trading close to its 52-week high, it may be considered overvalued; if it is trading near its 52-week low, it may be regarded as undervalued.

85. 50-Day Moving Average

A 50-day moving average (50 DMA) is a technical analysis indicator that calculates the average closing price of a stock over the past 50 days. The 50 DMA is plotted on a stock chart and can measure a stock's short-term trend and momentum. A stock trading above its 50 DMA is generally considered to be in an uptrend, while a stock trading below its 50 DMA is considered to be in a downtrend. When a stock crosses above its 50 DMA, it can be seen as a bullish signal, indicating that the stock may have upward momentum. Conversely, when a stock crosses below its 50 DMA, it can be seen as a bearish signal, suggesting that it may have downward momentum.

86. 200-Day Moving Average

A 200-day moving average (200 DMA) is a technical analysis indicator that calculates the average closing price of a stock over the past 200 days. The 200 DMA is plotted on a stock chart and can measure a stock's long-term trend and momentum. A stock trading above its 200 DMA is generally considered in a long-term uptrend, while a stock trading below its 200 DMA is considered in a long-term downtrend. When a stock crosses above its 200 DMA, it can be seen as a bullish signal, indicating that the stock may have strong upward momentum. Conversely, when a stock crosses below its 200 DMA, it can be seen as a bearish signal, indicating that it may have downward momentum.

87. Margin calls

Margin call metrics refer to financial measures that provide information about the use of margin and the risk of a margin call for a stock. Here are a few examples of margin call metrics:

- **Margin debt:** This metric measures the amount of debt a stock investor has taken to purchase securities, using the value of those securities as collateral. It shows how much of the stock's value is financed by debt.
- **Margin utilization rate:** This metric measures the percentage of the investor's available margin used to purchase securities. It shows how close the investor is to a margin call.
- **Maintenance margin:** This metric is the minimum margin requirement the brokerage firm sets to keep a position open. A margin call will be issued if the investor's margin falls below this level.
- **Margin call level:** This metric is how a margin call is issued. It is usually defined as a percentage of the value of the securities purchased on margin.
- **Buying power:** This metric is the money an investor can use to make additional trades. It is the difference between the cash and securities the investor has in the account and the amount of margin debt.
- **Initial margin:** This metric is the amount of money or securities required to be deposited with a broker when buying

on margin. These metrics can help assess the risk of a margin call for a stock and the overall leverage of the stock portfolio.

88. Buying Power

Buying Power refers to the capital an investor can use to purchase securities or assets based on their available funds and any leverage or margin available in their brokerage account. It represents the total value of assets an investor can acquire with their current financial resources. Critical aspects of buying power include Cash Balance, which is the actual cash available in the investor's account, and margin, which is the additional funds that can be borrowed from the brokerage to buy securities based on the margin requirements set by the broker—total Available Funds: The sum of cash and margin available for investment. Buying power is crucial for investors as it determines how many shares or assets they can purchase. It can be influenced by account balance, leverage used, and ongoing trades or positions.

89. Vix Metrix

The VIX, or Volatility Index, is a widely recognized measure of market volatility, often called the "fear gauge." It was introduced by the Chicago Board Options Exchange (CBOE) in 1993 and is designed to reflect investor sentiment and expectations regarding future market volatility based on S&P 500 index options. The VIX is calculated using the prices of a range of S&P 500 options, specifically call and put options, with a range of expiration dates. It uses a weighted average of the implied volatilities of these options to derive a forward-looking estimate of expected volatility over the next 30 days. The VIX is expressed as an annualized percentage, indicating the anticipated movement of the S&P 500 index over the coming month. For example, a VIX reading 20 suggests an expected annualized volatility of 20%, translating to an anticipated move of approximately 1.15% for the S&P 500 index over the next month. A rising VIX typically indicates increasing investor fear or uncertainty regarding market conditions, often correlating with a declining stock market. Conversely, a falling VIX suggests a more stable market environment and rising investor confidence. Historically, the VIX tends to spike during market turmoil, such as economic crises or significant geopolitical events, making it a useful tool for gauging market sentiment. Trading the VIX: Investors can trade the VIX through various financial instruments, including VIX futures, VIX options, and exchange-traded products (ETPs) that track the index. These products allow investors to hedge against volatility or speculate on future market movements. The VIX is also commonly used by traders as part of broader risk management strategies, allowing them to make informed decisions based on expected market volatility.

While the VIX provides valuable insights into market expectations, it is important to note that it is not a direct measure of actual market volatility. The VIX reflects implied volatility based on option prices, which can be influenced by supply and demand dynamics rather than just market conditions. Additionally, the VIX can exhibit volatility, leading to rapid fluctuations that may not always correlate with actual market movements.

The VIX is a critical tool for investors and traders, offering a unique perspective on market sentiment and expectations of future volatility. By understanding the mechanics of the VIX and its implications for market conditions, investors can better navigate the complexities of financial markets, enhance their risk management strategies, and make informed decisions in their investment pursuits. As a barometer of fear and uncertainty, the VIX serves as an essential indicator for gauging market dynamics and anticipating potential shifts in investor behavior

90. Margin Debt

Margin Debt refers to the money borrowed from a brokerage firm to purchase securities, using the securities in the investor's account as collateral. It allows investors to leverage their investments by borrowing funds to buy more securities than they could with just their capital. Critical aspects of margin debt include Leverage: Margin debt increases an investor's buying power, enabling them to purchase more assets than their available cash would allow. Interest Costs: Interest is charged on the borrowed funds, which can impact overall returns. Margin Calls: If the value of the securities purchased declines, the investor may face a margin call, requiring them to deposit additional funds or sell assets to maintain the level of margin needed. Margin debt amplifies potential gains and losses, making it a high-risk strategy that requires careful management and understanding of the associated risks.

91. Margin Utilization Rate

Margin Utilization Rate is a financial metric that measures the proportion of an investor's margin account used to buy securities compared to the total margin available. It reflects how much of the available margin credit is utilized by the investor. Critical aspects of the Margin Utilization Rate include Calculation: It is calculated by dividing the total amount of margin debt (borrowed funds) by the total margin available in the account. For example, if an investor has $10,000 in margin debt and $20,000 in available margin, the margin utilization rate would be 50%. Leverage Indicator: A higher margin utilization rate indicates that the investor is using a more significant portion of their margin capacity, which can amplify potential returns and risks. Risk Management: Monitoring the margin utilization rate helps investors assess their leverage and manage the risk of margin calls, where they may need to add more funds or liquidate positions to meet minimum margin requirements.

92. Maintaining Margin

Maintaining Margin refers to the minimum amount of equity an investor must keep in their margin account to support their positions. It is a critical component in margin trading, ensuring that investors maintain a certain level of equity to cover potential losses. Vital aspects of Maintaining Margin include Requirement: Brokerage firms and regulatory bodies set the maintaining margin, representing the minimum equity that must be maintained in the margin account after a trade is executed. This margin is usually a percentage of the total value of the securities purchased on margin. Margin Calls: The investor will receive a margin call if the equity in the margin account falls below the maintaining margin requirement due to market fluctuations or losses. This requires the investor to deposit additional funds or sell securities to return the account to the required level. Purpose: Maintaining margin ensures a buffer against potential losses and protects the investor and the brokerage from excessive risk. It helps prevent situations where investors could lose more than their initial investment. Maintaining an adequate margin is crucial for managing risk in margin trading and avoiding margin calls that could force the liquidation of assets.

93. Volume

Volume measures the number of shares or contracts of a security that have been traded during a specific period, such as a day, a week, or a month. It is commonly used in the stock market but can also apply to other securities such as options, futures, and currencies. Volume is an essential indicator for several reasons: It can indicate the level of interest in a stock or other security. High volume suggests that many investors are buying and selling shares, indicating that the stock is attracting much attention and may be experiencing significant price movement. On the other hand, low volume may indicate that the stock is not attracting much interest and may be less volatile. It can indicate the validity of price movements: High volume during a price movement can indicate that the move is significant and may be more likely to continue, while low volume during a price movement may indicate that the move is not significant and may be more likely to reverse; and It can also be used in technical analysis: Many technical analysts use volume as a confirmation of a trend or pattern, such as a breakout or a trend reversal, this is because high volume is usually associated with solid momentum, while low volume is generally associated with weak momentum.

94. Average Volume

Average volume is a financial metric that measures the average number of shares of a stock traded over a certain period, typically over the past 30 or 60 days. It is used as a measure of a stock's liquidity and investor interest. A stock with a high average volume is considered liquid, meaning there is a high level of buying and selling activity. It can be easily bought or sold without significantly affecting the stock price. A stock with a low average volume is considered illiquid, meaning there is a low level of buying and selling activity, and it may be harder to buy or sell the stock without significantly affecting the stock price. Average volume can be used with other technical indicators, such as moving averages, to make buy or sell decisions. For example, if a stock is breaking out from a long-term trend and its volume is significantly above its average volume, it may indicate that a trend reversal is taking place. It's important to note that average volume is a historical measure and may not accurately predict future volume or liquidity.

95. 10-Day Average Volume

The 10-day average volume is a financial metric that measures the average number of shares of a stock that have been traded over the past ten days. It measures a stock's liquidity and investor interest, similar to the average volume, but with a shorter time frame. A stock with a high 10-day average volume is considered liquid, meaning a high buying and selling activity exists. It can be easily bought or sold without significantly affecting the stock price. A stock with a low 10-day average volume is considered illiquid, meaning there is a low level of buying and selling activity, and it may be harder to buy or sell the stock without significantly affecting the stock price. The 10-day average volume can be used with other technical indicators, such as moving averages and other volume indicators, to make buy or sell decisions. It can also detect sudden changes in the volume of a stock, which can indicate a shift in market sentiment or a potential buying or selling opportunity. It's important to note that the 10-day average volume is a historical measure and may not accurately predict future volume or liquidity.

96. 3-Day Average Volume

The 3-day average volume is a financial metric that measures the average number of shares of a stock that have been traded over the past three trading days. It measures a stock's liquidity and investor interest, similar to the average volume, but with a shorter time frame. A stock with a high 3-day average volume is considered liquid, meaning that there is a high level of buying and selling activity, and it can be easily bought or sold without significantly affecting the stock price. A stock with a low 3-day average volume is considered to be illiquid, meaning that there is a low level of buying and selling activity, and it may be harder to buy or sell the stock without significantly affecting the stock price. The 3-day average volume can be used with other technical indicators, such as moving averages and other volume indicators, to make buy or sell decisions. It can also detect sudden changes in the volume of a stock, which can indicate a shift in market sentiment or a potential buying or selling opportunity.

97. Shares Outstanding

Shares outstanding refer to the total number of shares of a company's stock currently held by investors, including standard and preferred shares. It's a critical metric that can be used to evaluate a company's equity and its market capitalization. Shares outstanding can be found in a company's balance sheet, and it's important to note that it's a static figure that can change over time due to various factors such as stock buybacks, new stock issuances, or stock dilution. When investors want to know a company's market capitalization, they multiply the current stock price by the number of shares outstanding. This will give them an idea of the overall value of a company. Shares outstanding can also be used to calculate other financial metrics such as the Earnings per share (EPS) and the Price-to-Earnings ratio (P/E). It can also compare a company's size and valuation with those in the same industry.

98. Implied Shares Outstanding

Implied shares outstanding is a financial metric that estimates the total number of shares of a company's stock currently held by investors, including standard and preferred shares. It is calculated by dividing a company's market capitalization by its current stock price. The difference between Implied shares outstanding and the actual shares outstanding is that the implied shares outstanding use the current stock price to estimate the shares outstanding. In contrast, the outstanding shares are a static number found on the balance sheet. Implied outstanding shares can be used to estimate the number of outstanding shares when a company has not yet reported its latest financial results or when the outstanding ones have not been updated recently. It can also compare a company's size and valuation with those in the same industry. It's important to note that implied shares outstanding are an estimate, and it may only be accurate if the stock price reflects the company's actual value.

99. Float

Float refers to the number of shares of a company's stock that are available for trading by the general public. It is calculated by subtracting the number of shares held by company insiders, such as officers, directors, and large shareholders, from the total shares outstanding. Float can be a valuable metric for investors as it gives an idea of the liquidity of a stock or how easily shares can be bought and sold in the market. A stock with a high float generally has more shares available for trading, making it more liquid and accessible to buy and sell. A stock with a low float may be more difficult to trade due to a lack of shares available, and it can be more susceptible to price volatility.

100. Percentage Held by Insiders

The percentage held by insiders is a financial metric that shows the percentage of a company's shares held by company insiders, such as officers, directors, and large shareholders. It is calculated by dividing the number of shares insiders held by the total outstanding shares. This metric can provide insight into the level of insider ownership of a company, and it's a way for investors to gauge the alignment of interests between the company's management and other shareholders. A high percentage of insider ownership can indicate that management is heavily invested in the company and is likely to make decisions that are in the best interest of shareholders. A low percentage of insider ownership can indicate that management does not have a significant stake in the company and may not be as invested in its success.

101. Percentage Held by Institutions

The percentage held by institutions is a financial metric that shows the percentage of a company's shares held by institutional investors, such as mutual funds, pension funds, and hedge funds. It is calculated by dividing the number of shares institutions hold by the total outstanding shares. This metric can provide insight into a company's institutional ownership level, and it's a way for investors to gauge the level of interest and support from professional investors. A high percentage of institutional ownership can indicate that the company is widely followed and respected by professional investors, and it may be seen as a sign of a solid financial position and growth prospects. A low percentage of institutional ownership can indicate that professional investors do not widely follow the company and may be considered a less attractive investment.

102. Shares Short

Shares short, also known as short interest, refers to the number of shares of a stock that have been sold short by investors. When investors sell shares short, they borrow shares from another investor and sell them, with the hope that the stock price will decrease, allowing them to buy back the shares at a lower price and make a profit. Shares short can be a valuable metric for investors as it can indicate the bearish sentiment toward a particular stock. A high number of short shares can suggest that many investors believe that a stock's price will decrease, while a low number of short shares can indicate that most investors believe that a stock's price will increase.

103. Short Ratio

The short ratio is a financial metric that compares the number of shares short to the average daily trading volume of a stock. It is calculated by dividing the number of shares short by the average daily trading volume. The short ratio can indicate the level of bearish sentiment towards a stock and provide insight into the potential level of buying pressure for a stock. A high short ratio can suggest that there are a large number of shares short relative to the average daily trading volume, which suggests that many investors believe that a stock's price will decrease. A low short ratio can indicate that fewer shares are short relative to the average daily trading volume, which suggests that most investors believe a stock's price will increase.

104. Short % of Float

Short % of float is a financial metric that shows the percentage of a company's float (shares available for trading by the general public) that have been sold short by investors. It is calculated by dividing the number of shares short by the float. This metric can provide insight into the level of bearish sentiment towards a particular stock and indicate the level of potential buying pressure for a stock. A high short % of the float can suggest that a large percentage of the shares available for trading have been sold short, which indicates that many investors believe that the stock's price will decrease. A low short % of the float can suggest that a small percentage of the shares available for trading has been sold short, which indicates that most investors believe that the stock's price will increase.

105. Short % of Shares Outstanding

Short % of shares outstanding is a financial metric that shows the percentage of a company's shares outstanding (the total number of shares of a company's stock that investors currently hold) that have been sold short by investors. It is calculated by dividing the number of shares short by the total shares outstanding. This metric can provide insight into the level of bearish sentiment towards a particular stock and indicate the level of potential buying pressure for a stock. A high short % of outstanding shares can suggest that a large percentage of the company's shares have been sold short, which indicates that many investors believe the stock's price will decrease. A low short % of outstanding shares can suggest that a small percentage of the company's shares have been sold short, which indicates that most investors believe the stock's price will increase.

106. Forward Annual Dividend Rate

The forward annual dividend rate is a financial metric showing the expected annual dividend per share a company will pay its shareholders. It is calculated by dividing the forward yearly dividend by the current stock price. This metric is used to estimate a stock's future dividend yield, which is the return investors can expect from the company's dividends. The forward annual dividend rate is often used to compare the expected future returns of different stocks and to assess the potential for income from dividends.

107. Forward Annual Dividend Yield

The forward annual dividend yield is a financial metric that shows the expected return investors can expect from dividends paid by a company based on the current stock price. It is calculated by dividing the forward annual dividend by the current stock price. It is often expressed as a percentage and used to compare the expected future returns of different stocks and assess the potential for income from dividends. A higher yield generally indicates that a stock is expected to pay a higher return in the form of dividends relative to its current stock price. The forward annual dividend yield is an estimate, and it may only be accurate if the stock price reflects the company's actual value or if the company's dividend policy changes in the future.

108. Trailing Annual Dividend Yield

The trailing annual dividend yield is a financial metric that shows the historical return that investors have received from dividends paid by a company over the last 12 months based on the current stock price. It is calculated by dividing the total dividends paid in the previous 12 months by the current stock price. It is often expressed as a percentage and used to compare the return that different stocks have provided in the form of dividends over the last year. A higher yield generally indicates that a stock has provided a higher return in dividends over the last year, relative to its current stock price. The trailing annual dividend yield is based on the company's past performance, and it may not be indicative of the future performance of the company or the dividends it will pay in the future.

109. Five Year Average Dividend Yield

The five-year average dividend yield is a financial metric that shows the average return investors have received from dividends paid by a company over the last five years based on the current stock price. It is calculated by dividing the total dividends paid over the last five years by the current stock price and then taking an average of the result for five years. It is often expressed as a percentage and used to compare the return that different stocks have provided in dividends over the last five years. A higher yield generally indicates that a stock has provided a higher return in dividends over the previous five years relative to its current stock price. The five-year average dividend yield is based on the company's past performance and may not indicate its future performance or the dividends it will pay.

110. Payout Ratio

The payout ratio is a financial metric showing the proportion of earnings a company pays out to shareholders as dividends. It is calculated by dividing the dividends paid to shareholders by the company's net income. The payout ratio can provide insight into a company's dividend policy and ability to maintain or grow its dividends in the future. A high payout ratio can indicate that a company is paying out a significant portion of its earnings as dividends, which may not leave enough earnings to reinvest in the business for future growth or to cover unexpected costs. A low payout ratio can indicate that a company is retaining a more significant portion of its earnings for reinvestment in the business or to build a cash reserve fundamental analysis of the company when evaluating the stock's performance and making investment decisions.

111. Dividend Date

Dividend date refers to the critical dates associated with a company's dividend payments. These dates are crucial for investors to understand when they will receive dividend payments and how they will impact the stock's price. Critical aspects of dividend date include:

- **Declaration date:** The date the company announces its intention to pay a dividend. This date consists of the dividend amount and the dates for the record and payment.
- **Ex-dividend date:** The date after which new stock buyers are not entitled to receive the declared dividend. Investors must purchase the stock before the ex-dividend date to qualify for the dividend.
- **Record date:** The date on which the company determines which shareholders are eligible to receive the dividend. Shareholders must be on the company's books to receive the dividend payment as of this date.
- **Payment date:** The date the dividend is paid out to eligible shareholders. This is when investors receive the cash dividend in their accounts or additional shares, as in the case of stock dividends.

Understanding these dates helps investors plan their trades and ensure they receive the dividends they are entitled to.

112. Ex-Dividend Date

The ex-dividend date is when a company's stock begins trading without the right to receive the upcoming dividend. The ex-dividend date is typically one business day before the record date when the company establishes its list of shareholders eligible to receive dividends. When a stock goes ex-dividend, the stock price is typically adjusted downward by the dividend amount. This is because the stock is trading without the right to receive the upcoming dividend, so the dividend amount reduces the value of the stock. Investors must pay attention to the ex-dividend date if they consider purchasing stock to receive the dividend. Investors who buy a stock before the ex-dividend date will receive the dividend, while investors who purchase a stock on or after the ex-dividend date will not receive the dividend. The ex-dividend date is subject to change and may be affected by various factors, such as a company's financial performance or changes in its dividend policy. The information about the ex-dividend date can be found in the company's annual report, on the company's website, or in the financial news.

113. Stock Buy Back metrics

Stock buyback (also known as share repurchase) is a strategy companies use to reduce the number of outstanding shares on the market by purchasing their shares from shareholders. This can have several effects on the company's stock price and financial performance, and as such, several metrics can be used to analyze stock buybacks. Key metrics include buyback amount, which is the total value or number of shares the company repurchases. This figure provides insight into the scale of the buyback program:

- **Buyback percentage:** The proportion of total outstanding shares repurchased. This number helps assess the buyback's impact on the company's capital structure.
- **Repurchase price:** The average price at which the shares were repurchased. This metric helps evaluate the cost-effectiveness of the buyback program.
- **Earnings per share (EPS) impact:** Stock buybacks can increase EPS by reducing the number of outstanding shares. Assessing the change in EPS before and after the buyback provides insight into its impact on shareholder value.
- **Return on equity (ROE) impact:** Buybacks can affect ROE by altering the company's equity base. Analyzing ROE trends helps assess the buyback's financial benefits.
- **Cash flow impact:** The amount of cash used for buybacks and its effect on the company's cash reserves or liquidity position. This metric highlights the buyback program's financial health and sustainability. These metrics help investors and

analysts gauge the effectiveness and strategic rationale behind a company's stock repurchase decisions.

114. Stock Split

A stock split is a corporate action in which a company increases the number of outstanding shares by issuing more to existing shareholders. The most common type of stock split is a 2-for-1 split, which doubles the number of outstanding shares and halves each share's price. Stock splits are typically done to make the stock more affordable to small investors and increase liquidity. Companies may also do a stock split to make their stock more attractive to institutional investors or to boost investor confidence and increase the stock's trading volume. During a stock split, a company's total market capitalization remains the same; it only increases the number of shares outstanding. The value of each share decreases by the same factor as the number of shares increases. Thus, the total market capitalization remains the same. A stock split does not impact a company's financial performance or underlying business. However, it can impact a company's stock price and liquidity, as well as the company's perception among investors. Stock splits are also subject to the approval of the company's board of directors and shareholders, and it may be affected by various factors such as a company's financial performance or changes in the company's dividend policy.

115. Reverse Stock Split

A reverse stock split is a corporate action in which a company reduces the number of shares outstanding by issuing fewer shares to existing shareholders. The most common reverse stock split is a 1-for-2 split, which halves the number of outstanding shares and doubles each share's price. Reverse stock splits are typically done by companies that have seen their stock price decline significantly, and they are used as a way to boost the stock price and maintain listing requirements on stock exchanges. This can benefit companies in danger of being delisted from an exchange due to their low stock price. During a reverse stock split, a company's total market capitalization remains the same; it only reduces the number of shares outstanding. The value of each share increases by the same factor as the number of shares decreases. Thus, the total market capitalization remains the same. A reverse stock split by itself has no impact on a company's financial performance or its underlying business. However, it can impact a company's stock price and liquidity, as well as the company's perception among investors. Reverse stock splits are also subject to the approval of the company's board of directors and shareholders, and they may be affected by factors such as a company's financial performance or changes in the company's dividend policy.

116. Last Split Date

The last Split Date refers to the most recent date a company executed a stock split. A stock split involves issuing additional shares to shareholders, increasing the total number of shares outstanding while proportionally reducing the share price. The last split date marks when this adjustment occurred and is essential for understanding the company's historical stock price adjustments and how they impact share value and shareholder equity.

117. Long Ratio

The Long Ratio is a metric that measures the level of bullish sentiment in a stock. It is calculated by dividing the number of shares held by investors who are betting that the stock will rise in value by the average daily trading volume. The formula for calculating the Long Ratio is Long Ratio = Number of Shares held by Long Investors / Average Daily Trading Volume. A high long ratio indicates that a significant number of shares have been held by investors betting the stock will rise, indicating a high level of bullish sentiment among investors. A low long ratio, on the other hand, can suggest that there is not much bullish sentiment among investors.

118. Price-to-Earnings ratio

The Price-to-Earnings (P/E) ratio is a commonly used valuation ratio that compares a company's current stock price to its earnings per share (EPS). It is calculated by dividing the current stock price by the EPS. The P/E ratio determines how much investors are willing to pay for each dollar of a company's earnings. A higher P/E ratio means that investors are willing to pay more for each dollar of earnings, indicating a higher confidence level in the company's future earnings potential. A lower P/E ratio, on the other hand, indicates that investors are willing to pay less for each dollar of earnings, which may suggest that they have a lower confidence level in the company's future earnings potential. However, a low P/E ratio could indicate a company's stock is undervalued. The P/E ratio should be considered in the context of the industry average and the company's historical P/E ratios. A P/E ratio that is significantly higher or lower than the industry average or the company's historical ratios may indicate that the stock is overvalued or undervalued

119. Debt-to-Equity ratio

The Debt-to-Equity (D/E) ratio is a financial ratio that compares a company's total debt to its total equity. It is calculated by dividing a company's total liabilities by its shareholders' equity. The D/E ratio is used to determine how much of a company's financing comes from debt versus equity. A higher D/E ratio means that a company has a higher level of debt relative to its equity, which may indicate that the company is highly leveraged and may be at risk of defaulting on its debt. On the other hand, a lower D/E ratio means that a company has a lower level of debt relative to its equity, which may indicate that the company is less leveraged and may be less risky. The D/E ratio should be considered in the context of the industry average and the company's historical D/E ratios. A D/E ratio significantly higher or lower than the industry average or the company's historical ratios may indicate that the company is overleveraged or underleveraged.

Additionally, D/E ratio does not take into account the company's earning potential and ability to generate cash flows, so it should not be considered in isolation when making investment decisions.

120. Dividend Yield

The Dividend Yield is a financial ratio that measures the income generated by a stock for its shareholders in the form of dividends. It is calculated by dividing a company's annual share dividend by its current stock price. The dividend yield is expressed as a percentage and is used to determine the income potential of a stock. A higher dividend yield means that a stock generates more income for its shareholders, while a lower dividend yield means that a stock generates less income. The Dividend Yield should be considered in the context of the industry average and the company's historical Dividend Yield ratios. A Dividend Yield significantly higher or lower than the industry average or the company's historical ratios may indicate that the stock is generating more or less income than its peers. Additionally, a high dividend yield may indicate that a stock is undervalued. Still, it could also mean the company is in financial distress, and the dividends are at risk of being cut. It's also important to note that a company may choose not to pay dividends at all or may have a fluctuating dividend payout, so the dividend yield ratio may not accurately indicate a stock's income potential. Additionally, a company's ability to continue paying future dividends depends on its earning potential and cash flow.

121. Debt capital

Debt capital refers to the funds a company raises by borrowing from lenders. This type of capital is used to finance operations, make acquisitions, or invest in new projects. When a company borrows money, it is typically required to pay interest on the loan and to repay the principal amount borrowed over a specific time. Debt can come in bonds, loans, or lines of credit. In this case, the lender is entitled to the interest payment and principal repayment as per the agreed terms but doesn't share ownership or control over the company. Debt capital is considered less risky for the lender, but it can be costly for the borrower if the interest rate is high. Debt capital is a common source of financing for companies, and it can be used in conjunction with equity capital to finance a company's operations.

122. Working Capital

Working capital measures a company's short-term liquidity and ability to meet its financial obligations. It is calculated as the difference between a company's current assets (cash, accounts receivable, and inventory) and its current liabilities (accounts payable, short-term loans, and other debts due within a year). A positive working capital indicates that a company has enough assets to cover its short-term obligations. In contrast, a negative working capital indicates that a company may have difficulty meeting its short-term obligations. Working capital is important because it shows a company's ability to pay its bills and meet its financial obligations in the short term. A company with positive working capital is considered financially healthy. In contrast, a company with negative working capital may have difficulty paying its bills and could be at risk of financial distress. Companies use different strategies to manage working capital, such as increasing sales, reducing expenses, or improving inventory management.

123. Debt Financing

Debt Financing is a method of raising capital in which a company borrows money from external sources and is obligated to repay the principal amount and interest over time. This type of financing involves issuing bonds, taking out loans, or entering into credit agreements. Key characteristics of debt financing include Interest Payments: Borrowers must pay interest on the borrowed amount, which represents the cost of the debt. The borrowed funds must be repaid according to a predetermined schedule, including principal and interest payments. Debt financing creates a fixed financial obligation, which must be fulfilled regardless of the company's economic performance. Unlike equity financing, debt financing does not dilute existing shareholders' ownership stake. Debt financing is often used to fund expansion, capital projects, or other significant expenditures. It can be advantageous for maintaining control and leveraging investments, but due to the obligation of repayment, it also increases financial risk.

124. Personal savings

Personal savings refer to an individual's money for future expenses or investments. Personal savings can be used for short-term or long-term goals, such as buying a house, paying for education, or saving for retirement. Personal savings can come in cash, savings accounts, CDs, stocks, bonds, and other investment vehicles. Having a savings plan and regularly setting aside money is essential for financial stability and security. It can help individuals to manage unexpected expenses, as well as to achieve long-term financial goals. Building up personal savings can also be beneficial in case of job loss or other unforeseen financial difficulties. There are different ways to save money, such as creating a budget, setting financial goals, reducing expenses, and increasing income. Many financial experts recommend saving at least 20% of one's income, and setting up automatic transfers to a savings account can be a simple way to make saving a habit. Additionally, opening a savings account or other savings vehicles with high interest rates can help an individual's savings grow faster.

125. Crowdfunding

Crowdfunding is raising money for a project or venture by soliciting small contributions from many people, typically through the Internet. Crowdfunding campaigns can raise money for various projects, including startups, creative projects, charitable causes, and personal expenses. There are different types of crowdfunding models, such as Reward-based crowdfunding. In this model, contributors receive a tangible reward, such as a product or service, in exchange for their support. This is commonly used for creative projects such as films, music albums, and video games. Equity-based crowdfunding: In this model, contributors receive equity in the company or project in exchange for support. This is similar to traditional venture capital but with a larger pool of investors. Debt-based crowdfunding: In this model, contributors loan money to the project or company and receive a return on their investment in the form of interest payments. Crowdfunding can be a valuable way for entrepreneurs, small business owners, and individuals to raise funds for their projects or ventures. It allows them to bypass traditional funding sources such as banks and enables investors to support projects they believe in.

126. Capital Gain

A capital gain refers to the increase in the value of an asset, such as a stock, bond, real estate, or other investment, over time. When an asset is sold for more than its purchase price, the difference between the sale and purchase prices is a capital gain. Capital gains are typically taxed at a lower rate than ordinary income, and the tax rate can vary depending on the type of asset and how long it was held. For example, if an individual buys a stock for $50 and sells it for $70, they have a capital gain of $20. If the stock is held for more than a year before it is sold, the capital gain would be taxed at the long-term capital gains tax rate, which is typically lower than the short-term capital gains tax rate. Capital gains can be generated by individuals, businesses, and even governments. Capital gains can be used to generate income and can play an essential role in an investment strategy.

127. Capital Loss

A capital loss refers to the decrease in the value of an asset, such as a stock, bond, real estate, or other investment, over time. When an asset is sold for less than its purchase price, the difference between the sale and purchase prices is a capital loss. Capital losses can offset capital gains and lower the overall tax liability. For example, if an individual buys a stock for $70 and sells it for $50, they have a capital loss of $20. If the stock is held for more than a year before it is sold, the capital loss would be considered a long-term capital loss. Long-term capital losses can be used to offset long-term capital gains, and if there are no capital gains to offset, up to $3,000 of capital losses can be used to offset ordinary income in a tax year

128. Capital Gains Ex-date

The Capital Gains Ex-Date is a crucial date related to capital gains distribution by mutual funds or other investment funds. It is when the shares of a mutual fund or investment fund begin trading without entitlement to the most recently declared capital gains distribution. On the ex-date, the price of the fund's shares typically drops by an amount roughly equivalent to the distribution. This adjustment reflects the fact that new investors buying shares on or after this date will not receive the upcoming capital gains payment. This date is essential for investors to know when they will or will not receive capital gains distributions. It helps them make informed decisions about buying or selling shares in the fund. If you purchase shares before the ex-date, you will receive the capital gains distribution. You will not receive the distribution if you purchase shares on or after the ex-date. Understanding the capital gains ex-date is crucial for investors managing their tax liabilities or optimizing their investment returns.

129. Capital Gains Long Term

Long-term capital gains refer to the increase in the value of an asset held for more than a year before it is sold. When an asset is held for more than a year before it is sold, and the sale price is higher than the purchase price, the difference between the sale price and the purchase price is considered a long-term capital gain. Long-term capital gains are taxed lower than short-term capital gains or ordinary income. The tax rate on long-term capital gains can vary depending on the investor's tax bracket. For example, as of 2021, long-term capital gains are taxed at 20% for taxpayers in the highest tax bracket, while for those in lower tax brackets, the tax rate is 0%. Long-term capital gains can be an essential source of income for investors, particularly for retirement savings or other long-term financial goals. However, it's important to note that long-term capital gains are not guaranteed, and the asset's value can decrease, resulting in a capital loss.

130. Capital Gains Reinvest NAV

Capital Gains Reinvest NAV (Net Asset Value) refers to the NAV of a mutual fund or investment fund calculated after the reinvestment of capital gains distributions. It is the net asset value of a fund per share, adjusted to include the reinvested capital gains distributions. Instead of receiving cash, investors can reinvest their capital gains into additional fund shares. This NAV reflects the increased number of shares held by investors who opted for reinvestment of their capital gains. The reinvestment typically occurs at the NAV calculated on the ex-date or shortly after. It allows investors to benefit from compounding growth by reinvesting their capital gains rather than taking them as cash. This can be beneficial for the long-term development of their investment portfolio. Reinvesting capital gains can increase an investor's shares without making an additional cash investment. The Capital Gains Reinvest NAV helps track the value of these additional shares and understand their effect on overall investment performance. Capital Gains Reinvest NAV is a crucial metric for investors who prefer to reinvest their capital gains, providing an accurate measure of the value of their investments after such reinvestments.

131. Capital Gains Short Term

Short-term capital gains refer to the increase in the value of an asset held for a year or less before it is sold. When an asset is held for a year or less before it is sold, and the sale price is higher than the purchase price, the difference between the sale price and the purchase price is considered a short-term capital gain. Short-term capital gains are typically taxed at a higher rate than long-term capital gains. This is because the IRS believes short-term gains are ordinary income taxed at the same rate as salary or wages. The tax rate on short-term capital gains can vary depending on the investor's tax bracket. Individuals, businesses, and even governments can generate short-term capital gains. The short-term capital gains are not guaranteed, and the asset's value can decrease, resulting in a capital loss. Additionally, it's essential to consult a tax professional to understand the tax implications of short-term capital gains. Short-term capital gains are not always negative; it's also possible to generate short-term capital gains by selling an asset that has been appreciated, but it's essential to consider the higher tax rate on short-term capital gains before making an investment decision.

132. Options Contract Ratios

Options contract ratios are financial metrics used to evaluate the sentiment of the options market for a particular stock or index. They are calculated by dividing the number of open options contracts for a given security by the total number of outstanding shares. An options contract is a financial contract that gives the holder the right, but not the obligation, to buy or sell a stock at a specific price (strike price) on or before a specific date (expiration date); A high options contract ratio indicates that there are a large number of open options contracts about the total number of outstanding shares, which suggests that there is a high level of interest in the stock or index among options traders; A low options contract ratio indicates that there are a small number of open options contracts about the total number of outstanding shares, which suggests that there is a low level of interest in the stock or index among options traders; Options contract ratios can be used to identify potential market turning points and to evaluate the risk and potential return of an investment in a stock or index. For example, a high options contract ratio may indicate that the market is overbought and that a correction is likely, while a low options contract ratio may suggest that the market is oversold and that a rally is likely. Options contract ratios can vary depending on the underlying stock or index and its volatility, as well as the expiration date of the options contracts. Options contract ratios should be used with other technical analysis tools such as trend analysis, price action, and indicators to understand market sentiment and potential price movement better. Overall, options contract ratios can provide insight into the level of interest in a particular stock or index among options traders, as well as the potential for market turning points.

133. FOMO

FOMO stands for Fear of Missing Out. It is a phenomenon where an individual feels compelled to make an investment decision based on the fear that they will miss out on potential gains if they don't take action. In the context of the stock market, FOMO can manifest in buying stocks that have recently gone up in value, even though the individual may not understand the stock or the underlying company well. FOMO can be a dangerous emotion when it comes to investing, as it can lead individuals to make impulsive and irrational decisions. It can cause people to invest in overpriced stocks or more than they can afford to lose. This is especially true with the rise of social media and online forums, where people can see others making money from a particular stock and feel compelled to join in, regardless of the stock's fundamentals or the company. To avoid FOMO, it's essential to have a well-thought-out investment strategy and to stick to it, even during periods of market volatility. It's also essential to do proper research and due diligence on any stock before investing and to invest only the amount one can afford to lose

134. Asset Allocation

Asset allocation divides an investment portfolio among asset categories, such as stocks, bonds, and cash. Asset allocation aims to balance risk and reward by investing in a mix of assets that can provide the highest return for a given level of risk. There are several approaches to asset allocation, but one standard method is using a combination of stocks, bonds, and cash. Stocks, also known as equities, tend to have higher potential returns, volatility, and risk. On the other hand, bonds have lower potential returns but also lower volatility and risk. Cash and cash equivalents, such as money market funds, have the lowest potential returns but also the lowest volatility and risk. The specific mix of appropriate assets for an individual or organization will depend on their investment goals, risk tolerance, and time horizon. For example, a young investor with a long time horizon and a high-risk tolerance might have a higher percentage of their portfolio allocated to stocks, while an older investor nearing retirement with a low-risk tolerance might have a higher percentage allocated to bonds. The asset allocation of an investment portfolio can be reviewed and adjusted periodically, considering the investor's goals, risk tolerance, and market conditions.

135. Asset Class

The asset class is a category of investments with similar characteristics and behave similarly in the market. The three main asset classes are stocks, bonds, and cash and cash equivalents. Stocks, also known as equities, represent ownership in a company and have the potential for higher returns but also higher volatility and risk. Bonds are debt securities issued by companies and governments. They typically pay a fixed or variable interest rate and have a maturity date. Bonds generally have lower potential returns than stocks and lower volatility and risk. Cash and cash equivalents, such as money market funds, are short-term, highly liquid investments with the lowest potential returns but also the lowest volatility and risk. Real estate is also an asset class that is considered an alternative asset class that is not correlated with the stock market. Other asset classes include commodities and precious metals and alternative investments, such as hedge funds and private equity. Each asset class has unique characteristics, risks, and return potentials, and investors can use a combination of different asset classes to create a diversified portfolio that aligns with their investment goals and risk tolerance.

136. Ticker

A ticker is a unique symbol or code used to identify a stock or other security traded on a stock exchange. Tickers are typically made up of one to four letters and refer to a specific stock or security. For example, the ticker for Apple Inc. is AAPL, for Ford Motor Company is F, and for General Electric Company is GE. Tickers are used by traders, investors, and financial analysts to identify and reference a specific stock or security quickly. They are also used by economic news and data providers to track and report on the performance of stocks and other securities. Tickers are unique to the stock exchange they are listed on; for example, ticker 'AAPL' is listed on NASDAQ, and ticker 'F' is listed on the New York Stock Exchange (NYSE). In addition, tickers are not just limited to stocks; other securities such as bonds, options, and futures also have ticker symbols. Tickets can be viewed on the stock exchange's website or other financial websites providing market data.

137. Sector

A sector groups companies or industries with similar characteristics or operating in the same general business area. The companies in an industry are typically engaged in similar business activities, have similar products or services, and are subject to identical market conditions and economic factors. Sectors are used to classify stocks and other securities for investment and analysis purposes. The sectors are usually grouped by the Global Industry Classification Standard (GICS), which MSCI and S&P developed. The GICS sectors are Energy, Materials, Industrials, Consumer Discretionary, Consumer staples, Health Care, Financials, Information technology, Communication Services, Utilities, and Real Estate. For example, companies such as ExxonMobil, Chevron Corporation, and ConocoPhillips would be classified in the Energy sector, while companies like Amazon, Netflix, and Disney would be in the Consumer Discretionary sector. Sectors can be affected by different factors, such as global economic conditions, political events, and technological advancements. Understanding the performance of a specific industry can provide insight into the economy's overall health and help investors and analysts identify trends and make informed investment decisions.

138. Standard Deviation

Standard deviation is a statistical measure of the dispersion of a data set from its mean. It measures the degree to which the data varies from the average. In finance, standard deviation measures the volatility of a stock's returns over a specific period. The formula for calculating the standard deviation of a set of returns is: Standard deviation = $\sqrt{((\Sigma(\text{Returns} - \text{Mean})^2)/\text{Number of observations})}$, Where: Returns = the individual returns of the stock over a specific period Mean = the average return of the stock over the same period Number of observations = the number of returns in the set. A lower standard deviation indicates that the returns of a stock are more consistent and less volatile, while a higher standard deviation indicates that the returns of a stock are more spread out and, therefore, more volatile. Standard deviation is a commonly used metric in finance and investment because it measures risk. A stock with a high standard deviation is considered more risky than one with a low standard deviation. It also calculates other risk metrics, such as the Sharpe Ratio. The standard deviation should be used with other metrics, such as the mean return, to understand the overall performance of the stock and make a well-rounded investment decision.

139. Maximum Drawdown

Maximum drawdown (MDD) is a financial metric that measures the most significant peak-to-trough decline of a portfolio or investment over a specified period. It is used to measure the risk of an investment, specifically the risk of losing a significant amount of value in a relatively short period. The drawdown is often expressed as a percentage of the peak value, and it represents the worst-case scenario for an investment, assuming the investment has not been liquidated. The formula for calculating the maximum drawdown is MDD = (Peak value - Trough value) / Peak value, where: Peak value = the highest value reached by the portfolio or investment Trough value = the lowest value reached by the portfolio or investment after the peak value. A higher maximum drawdown indicates a higher level of risk, as the investment can potentially lose a more significant percentage of its value. A lower maximum drawdown suggests a lower level of risk, as the investment is less likely to experience a substantial decline in value. The Maximum Drawdown is not a measure of expected loss but rather a measure of the worst-case scenario loss. It is a backward-looking measure that does not consider future growth or market conditions. Therefore, it should be used with other metrics, such as expected return and volatility, to make a well-rounded investment decision.

140. Information Ratio

The Information Ratio (IR) is a financial ratio that measures the risk-adjusted return of an investment relative to a benchmark. It is used to evaluate the performance of an investment by comparing its return to that of a benchmark, such as a market index, and adjusting for the volatility of the investment's returns. The formula for the Information Ratio is Information Ratio = (Expected Return - Benchmark Return) / Tracking Error. The Information Ratio expresses the excess return per unit of tracking error. A higher Information Ratio indicates that an investment has a better risk-adjusted return than the benchmark. In comparison, a lower Information Ratio indicates that an investment has a worse risk-adjusted return relative to the benchmark. The Information Ratio is a risk-adjusted performance measure. Still, it's commonly used to compare the returns of different investments with different risk profiles and to compare it with a benchmark. The benchmark return used in the formula is a benchmark or a market index, which can vary depending on the investor's preference. The tracking error measures the volatility of the return difference between the investment and the benchmark. Therefore, the Information Ratio should be used with other financial metrics and analysis to understand an investment's performance better. Investors and analysts commonly use the Information Ratio to evaluate the risk-adjusted performance of an investment relative to a benchmark and compare it with other investments in the same category. It's also used to measure an investment's excess return over a benchmark return and how much tracking error an investor takes to achieve that return. A high information ratio is generally considered a sign of a well-performing investment, as it indicates that an investment generates high returns relative to a benchmark while taking less tracking error.

141. Upside and Downside Capture Ratios

The Upside Capture Ratio and the Downside Capture Ratio are financial ratios that measure the performance of an investment relative to a benchmark. They are used to evaluate how well an investment performs compared to a benchmark, such as a market index, during market gains and losses, respectively. The Upside Capture Ratio is calculated as Upside Capture Ratio = (Investment Return during Up Markets / Benchmark Return during Up Markets). It measures the degree to which the investment's returns are aligned with the benchmark's returns during periods when the market is rising. A ratio greater than 100% indicates that the investment has outperformed the benchmark during up markets, while a ratio less than 100% indicates underperformance. The Downside Capture Ratio is calculated as Downside Capture Ratio = (Investment Return during Down Markets / Benchmark Return during Down Markets). It measures the degree to which the investment's returns are aligned with the benchmark's returns during periods when the market is falling. A ratio less than 100% indicates that the investment has outperformed the benchmark during down markets, while a ratio greater than 100% indicates underperformance. Investors and analysts commonly use both ratios to evaluate the performance of an investment relative to a benchmark during periods of market gains and losses. They are also used to determine if an investment is more or less volatile than the benchmark and how well it performs during different market conditions. It's important to note that both ratios are based on past performance and don't guarantee future results. Additionally, the chosen benchmark can impact the ratios, and it's essential to select a benchmark appropriate for the investment being analyzed.

142. Open Interest Metrics

Open interest is a metric commonly used in the futures and options markets to measure the number of outstanding contracts that have not been settled or closed. It is a crucial indicator of market activity, liquidity, and investor sentiment. Traders and investors commonly use several open interest metrics to analyze futures and options markets. Open interest measures market activity, liquidity, and investor sentiment.

- **Change in open interest:** The difference in the number of outstanding contracts from the previous trading day. It is a measure of market activity and liquidity and can be used to identify trends in market sentiment.
- **Open interest-to-volume ratio:** The ratio of open interest to trading volume. It is used to determine a market's liquidity level and identify market sentiment trends.
- **Open interest-to-open interest ratio:** The ratio of open interest in one contract to open interest in another. It compares the relative liquidity of different agreements and identifies market sentiment trends.
- **Put-call open interest ratio:** The ratio of open interest in put options to open interest in call options. It is used to identify market sentiment trends and determine whether investors are more bullish or bearish on a particular market. Open interest metrics can be used with other market analyses to identify trends in market activity and investor sentiment.

143. Dividend Payback Period

The Dividend Payback Period, also known as the Dividend Recovery Period, is a financial ratio that measures the years it takes for a company's dividends to pay back the initial investment made in the stock. It is used to evaluate a company's ability to generate cash flow and determine the level of income investors can expect from the company's dividends. The formula for a Dividend Payback Period is: Dividend Payback Period = (Initial Investment / Annual Dividend per share). The Dividend Payback Period is usually expressed in years. A shorter Dividend Payback Period indicates that a company pays more of its earnings as dividends. It takes less time to recover the initial investment. In contrast, a more extended Dividend Payback Period indicates that a company is paying out a lower proportion of its earnings as dividends. It takes more time to recover the initial investment. The Dividend Payback Period is historical and doesn't guarantee future dividends. Additionally, the Dividend Payback Period doesn't consider the potential for capital appreciation, so it should be used with other financial metrics to understand an investment's performance comprehensively. Investors and analysts commonly use the Dividend Payback Period to evaluate a company's stock's income-generating potential and compare it with other companies in the same sector or industry. It's also used to identify companies with a consistent history of paying dividends and to determine whether their dividends are a reliable source of income. A shorter Dividend Payback Period is generally considered a positive indicator of a company's ability to generate cash flow and pay dividends to its shareholders.

144. Yield on Cost

Yield on Cost (YOC) is a financial ratio that measures the annual dividend income from an investment relative to the cost of the investment. It is used to evaluate the performance of an investment over time and to determine the level of income investors can expect to receive from the investment. The formula for Yield on Cost is Yield on Cost = (Annual Dividends / Initial Investment Cost) x 100. The Yield on Cost is usually expressed as a percentage. A higher Yield on Cost indicates that an investment is generating a higher proportion of income relative to the cost of the investment. In comparison, a lower yield on cost indicates that an investment generates a lower proportion of income relative to the cost of the investment. The Yield on Cost is a historical measure that doesn't guarantee future dividends. Additionally, Yield on Cost doesn't consider the potential for capital appreciation, so it should be used with other financial metrics to understand an investment's performance comprehensively.

The Yield on Cost is commonly used by investors and analysts to evaluate the income-generating potential of an investment over time and to compare it with other investments in the same category. It's also used to identify investments that have a consistent history of paying dividends and to determine whether an investment is a reliable source of income. A higher Yield on Cost is generally considered a positive indicator of an investment's ability to generate income over time.

145. Dividend Discount Model

The Dividend Discount Model (DDM) values a company's stock by estimating the present value of all future dividends. It is based on the idea that a stock's value equals the present value of all future dividends the stock is expected to pay. The DDM is commonly used to value stocks of companies that pay dividends. There are two main versions of the DDM: the Gordon Growth Model and the Two-stage Dividend Discount Model. The Gordon Growth Model uses the following formula: Stock Price = Dividend per share / (Discount Rate - Dividend growth rate), where Dividend per share = the most recent annual dividend paid by the company, Discount Rate = the required rate of return for the stock Dividend growth rate = the expected annual rate of growth of the dividends. The two-stage dividend discount model is a variation of the Gordon Growth Model, which considers that the growth rate of dividends may change over time. It uses the following formula: Stock Price = (Dividend per share * (1 + g1)) / (r - g2) + (Dividend per share * (1 + g1)^2) / (r - g2)^2 + ... + (Dividend per share * (1 + g1)^n) / (r - g2)^n, Where: Dividend per share = the most recent annual dividend paid by the company g1 = the expected growth rate of dividends during the first period g2 = the predicted growth rate of dividends during the second-period r = the required rate of return for the stock n = the number of periods in the projection. It's important to note that the Dividend Discount Model is based on several assumptions, such as future dividends, growth rates, and required rate of return, which can be challenging to predict with certainty. Therefore, the results of DDM should be used in conjunction with other financial metrics and analyses to gain a comprehensive understanding of a company's stock value.

146. Dividend History

Dividend history refers to the record of dividends paid by a company to its shareholders over some time. This information is essential to investors and analysts as it provides insight into a company's ability to generate cash flow and determines the income level investors can expect from the company's dividends. Dividend history can be found in a company's financial statements, such as the income statement, and can also be found in financial databases and on financial websites. The dividend history typically includes the following information: The number of dividends paid per share; The date the dividends were paid; The frequency of the dividends (e.g., quarterly, semi-annually, annually); and The dividend yield (Annual dividends per share / Current stock price per share). Investors and analysts commonly use dividend history to evaluate a company's ability to generate cash flow and determine the income level investors can expect to receive from the company's dividends. It's also used to identify companies with a consistent history of paying dividends and determine whether a stock is overvalued or undervalued. Additionally, Dividend history can be used to predict a company's future dividends. For example, if a company has a history of increasing its dividends every year, it will likely continue to do so. A company's dividend history can also identify trends in its dividends, such as if they have been increasing or decreasing over time. This can provide insight into the company's financial health and prospects.

147. Arithmetic Growth Rate

The Arithmetic Growth Rate (AGR) is a financial metric that measures the rate at which a value has grown over time, using a simple arithmetic average of the growth rates. It is used to evaluate the growth of a company's financials, dividends, and other financial metrics over time. The formula for AGR is AGR = (Ending value - Beginning value) / Beginning value, Where: Ending value = the value at the end of the period being measured and Beginning value = the value at the start of the period being measured. The AGR is usually expressed as a percentage. A positive AGR indicates that the value has grown over the period, while a negative AGR indicates that the value has shrunk. The AGR is a historical measure that doesn't guarantee future growth. Additionally, AGR doesn't consider the potential for volatility, so it should be used with other financial metrics to understand a company's growth comprehensively. Investors and analysts commonly use AGR to evaluate the growth of a company's financials, dividends, and other financial metrics over time, such as sales, earnings, and dividends. It's also used to identify trends in a company's growth and compare its growth with other companies in the same sector or industry. A higher AGR is generally considered a positive indicator of a company's growth prospects.

148. Geometric Growth Rate

The Geometric Growth Rate (GGR) is a financial metric that measures the rate at which a value has grown over time, using the geometric average of the growth rates. It is used to evaluate the growth of a company's financials, dividends, and other financial metrics over time. The formula for GGR is GGR = (Ending value / Beginning value)^(1/n) – 1, Where: Ending value = the value at the end of the period being measured, Beginning value = the value at the start of the period being measured n = the number of periods in the measurement. The GGR is usually expressed as a percentage. A positive GGR indicates that the value has grown over the period, while a negative GGR indicates that the value has shrunk. The GGR is a historical measure that doesn't guarantee future growth. Additionally, GGR considers the compounding effect of growth over time, and it's more accurate than the AGR when the values change unevenly over time. Investors and analysts commonly use

GGR to evaluate the growth of a company's financials, dividends, and other financial metrics over time, such as sales, earnings, and dividends. It's also used to identify trends in a company's growth and compare its growth with other companies in the same sector or industry. A higher GGR is generally considered a positive indicator of a company's growth prospects.

149. Total Return

Total return is a measure of an investment's overall performance, including capital appreciation and income (dividends and interest). It is used to evaluate the overall performance of a stock, bond, or other investment and to compare the performance of different investments. The formula for total return is Total Return = (Ending Value - Beginning Value + Income) / Beginning Value, where: Ending value = the value of the investment at the end of the period being measured Beginning value = the value of the investment at the start of the period being measured Income = any dividends or interest received during the period. The total return is usually expressed as a percentage. A positive total return indicates that the value of the investment has grown and income has been received. In contrast, a negative total return indicates that the value of the investment has shrunk and no income has been received. The total return is a historical measure that doesn't guarantee future performance. Total return considers capital appreciation and income, making it a more comprehensive measure of an investment's performance than just looking at the price change. Total return is commonly used by investors and analysts to evaluate the overall performance of a stock, bond, or other investment and to compare the performance of different investments. It's also used to identify trends in an investment's performance over time and to determine whether an investment is overvalued or undervalued. A higher total return is generally considered a positive indicator of an investment's performance.

150. Survivorship Bias

Survivorship bias is a phenomenon that occurs when the performance of only those investments that have survived a certain period is evaluated. In contrast, the performance of those investments that have failed and been removed from the sample is ignored. This can lead to an overestimation of the performance of a particular investment strategy because the worst-performing investments are not included in the analysis. Survivorship bias can occur in various contexts, such as:

- **Mutual funds:** Only mutual funds that have survived and not closed or merged with another fund are included in the analysis of mutual fund performance, which leads to an overestimation of mutual fund performance.
- **Stock picking:** When evaluating the performance of a stock picker, the stocks that have failed and been sold are ignored, and only the profitable stocks are included in the analysis, which leads to an overestimation of the stock picker's performance.
- **Historical stock performance:** When evaluating historical stock performance, companies that have gone bankrupt or been acquired are not included in the analysis, which leads to an overestimation of stock market performance.

To avoid survivorship bias, it is important to include data on all investments, whether they have succeeded or failed. This can be done using a database that provides for closed funds and bankrupt companies, for example. Additionally, one can use backtesting to simulate the performance of an investment strategy over a period, which includes the investments that would have failed and been removed from the sample. In summary, survivorship bias can lead to an overestimation of a particular investment strategy or manager's performance and poor investment decisions. It's essential for investors and analysts to consider survivorship bias when evaluating an investment's performance and to use a comprehensive data set that includes all investments, whether they have succeeded or failed.

151. Previous Day Close Price Metrics

Previous day close price is a metric used to measure a stock's closing price on the previous trading day. This metric is commonly used to track short-term price movements of a stock and can help identify trends in the stock's performance. Several metrics are widely used in conjunction with the previous day's close price to analyze a stock, including:

- **Price change:** The difference between the current day's closing price and the previous day's closing price. It measures the stock's short-term price movement and can be used to identify trends in the stock's performance.
- **Price change percentage:** The percentage change in the stock price from the previous day's closing price. It is calculated by taking the difference between the current day's closing price and the previous day's closing price and then dividing that difference by the previous day's closing price.
- **Moving average:** A commonly used technical indicator calculated by taking the average of a stock's closing price over a specific number of days. A moving average can identify trends in a stock's price and determine whether a stock is in an uptrend, downtrend, or trading sideways.
- **Relative strength index (RSI):** A commonly used technical indicator that compares the magnitude of a stock's recent gains to its recent losses. The RSI can identify overbought or oversold conditions and determine whether a stock will likely experience a price reversal.
- **Bollinger Bands:** A commonly used technical indicator consisting of a simple moving average and two standard deviation lines plotted above and below the moving average. Bollinger Bands can identify trends in a stock's price and

determine whether a stock is in an uptrend, downtrend, or trading sideways. These metrics are commonly used to analyze a stock's performance and identify trends in the stock's price. They should be used in conjunction with other financial ratios and metrics to understand a company's performance and a stock's potential for investment.

152. Time Premium Metrics

Time premium is a metric used to measure an option's value based on the amount of time remaining until expiration. Precisely, it measures the value of an option above and beyond the intrinsic value. The inherent value of an option is the difference between the strike price and the underlying asset's current price, while the time premium reflects the value of an option in the future. Several metrics are commonly used to measure time premium, including Time Value, which is the difference between the price of an option and its intrinsic value. It represents the time premium of an option and is a measure of the value of an option based on the amount of time remaining until expiration. Implied Volatility: A measure of the expected volatility of the underlying asset, as implied by the price of an option. It measures the market's expectations for the underlying asset's volatility over the life of an option. Days to Expiration: The number of days remaining until an option expires. It measures the amount of time remaining until expiration and, thus, the amount of time premium included in an option's price. Interest Rate: The interest rate used to determine the value of an option. Higher interest rates increase the time premium of an option, while lower interest rates decrease the time premium of an option. Time premium is an essential concept in options trading, and traders and investors use these metrics to evaluate an option's value and determine the appropriate strategy for a given options trade. Time premium metrics can also be used by investors to determine whether an option is overpriced or underpriced and to adjust their positions in response to changes in market conditions.

153. Enterprise Value to Free Cash Flow

The Enterprise Value to Free Cash Flow (EV/FCF) ratio is a financial ratio that compares a company's enterprise value (EV) to its free cash flow (FCF). It is used to evaluate a company's ability to generate cash flow and to compare the value of different companies. The EV/FCF ratio formula is EV/FCF = Enterprise Value / Free Cash Flow, Where Enterprise Value = Market Capitalization + Debt - Cash and Cash Equivalents Free Cash Flow = Operating Cash Flow - Capital Expenditures. The EV/FCF ratio measures a company's financial performance and compares its enterprise value with its ability to generate cash flow after accounting for capital expenditures. A lower EV/FCF ratio is generally considered more favorable, as it indicates that the company has a lower level of debt relative to its cash flow. A higher EV/FCF ratio may suggest that the company has a higher level of debt relative to its cash flow and may be less financially healthy. The EV/FCF ratio is a relative measure and should be compared to the EV/FCF ratio of other companies in the same sector or industry. Additionally, the ratio can vary over time, especially in the short term, due to changes in market conditions and the company's financial performance. Investors and analysts commonly use the EV/FCF ratio to evaluate a company's ability to generate cash flow and compare different companies' values. It also identifies overvalued or undervalued companies based on their cash flow generation.

154. Price to Tangible Book Value

The Price-to-Tangible Book (P/TB) ratio is a financial ratio that compares a company's market capitalization to its tangible book value. It is used to evaluate a company's valuation and compare different companies' values. The formula for the P/TB ratio is P/TB Ratio = Market Capitalization / Tangible Book Value, Where Market Capitalization = the current market price of the stock multiplied by the number of outstanding shares Tangible Book Value = the value of a company's assets as stated on its balance sheet, after deducting its liabilities and intangible assets (such as patents, trademarks, and goodwill). A high P/TB ratio means that investors are willing to pay a higher price for each dollar of tangible book value, indicating that they believe the company's assets are undervalued. A low P/TB ratio means that investors are willing to pay less for each dollar of tangible book value, indicating that they believe the company's assets are overvalued. The P/TB ratio is a relative measure and should be compared to the P/TB ratio of other companies in the same sector or industry. Additionally, the P/TB ratio can vary over time, especially in the short term, due to changes in market conditions and the company's financial performance. The P/TB ratio is commonly used by investors and analysts to evaluate a company's valuation and to compare it with other companies in the same sector or industry. It's also used to identify overvalued or undervalued companies based on the value of their tangible assets. The ratio is considered a more conservative valuation measure as it excludes intangible assets, which can often be overstated or have uncertain values.

155. Modified Price to Earnings to Growth Ratio

The Modified Price-to-Earnings-to-Growth (MPEG) ratio is a variation of the traditional Price-to-Earnings-to-Growth (PEG) ratio. It is used to evaluate a company's valuation and compare different companies' values. The formula for MPEG ratio is MPEG Ratio = (P/E Ratio x (1 + G)) / (G), where: P/E Ratio = Current Stock Price / Earnings per Share G = The growth rate of a company's Earnings per Share over a specific period. Like the PEG ratio, the MPEG ratio compares a company's P/E ratio to its EPS growth rate. The main difference is that it includes an additional term, (1 + G) in the ratio numerator, which accounts for the compounding effect of the company's EPS growth rate. This extra term makes the MPEG ratio more sensitive to the EPS growth rate and more accurate in reflecting the stock's true value. The MPEG ratio is a relative measure and should be compared to the MPEG ratio of other companies in the same sector or industry. Additionally, the MPEG ratio can vary over time, especially in the short term, due to changes in market conditions and the company's financial performance. The MPEG ratio is less commonly used than the PEG ratio, but it is gaining popularity among investors and analysts as a more accurate measure of a company's valuation. It is used with other financial metrics and analysis to understand a company's financial performance and value comprehensively.

156. Shiller Price to Earnings Ratio

The Shiller Price-to-Earnings (P/E) ratio, also known as the Cyclically Adjusted Price-to-Earnings (CAPE) ratio, is a financial ratio that compares a company's current stock price to its average earnings over the past ten years. It is used to evaluate a company's valuation and compare different companies' values. The formula for the Shiller P/E ratio is Shiller P/E Ratio = Current Stock Price / (Average Earnings per Share over the past ten years), Where: Current Stock Price = the current market price of the stock Average Earnings per Share = the average of the company's earnings per share over the past ten years, adjusted for inflation. The Shiller P/E ratio is considered a more accurate measure of a company's valuation than the traditional P/E ratio because it uses an average of the company's earnings over the past ten years, which smooths out the impact of short-term fluctuations in earnings. A high Shiller P/E ratio means that investors are willing to pay a higher price for each dollar of earnings, indicating that they believe the company's earnings will grow. A low Shiller P/E ratio means that investors are willing to pay less for each dollar of earnings, indicating that they believe the company's earnings will not grow as much in the future. It's important to note that the Shiller P/E ratio is a relative measure, and it should be compared to the Shiller P/E ratio of other companies in the same sector or industry or to historical average ratios. Additionally, the ratio can vary over time, especially in the short term, due to changes in market conditions and the company's financial performance. The Shiller

P/E ratio is commonly used by investors and analysts to evaluate a company's valuation and to compare it with other companies in the same sector or industry. It's also used to identify overvalued or undervalued companies based on their historical earnings. However, it should be used in conjunction with other financial metrics and analyses to gain a comprehensive understanding of a company's financial performance and value.

157. Negative Enterprise Value

Enterprise value (EV) is a measure of a company's total value, including both its equity value and its debt. It is calculated by adding the market capitalization of the company, the outstanding debt, and any preferred shares and then subtracting the cash and cash equivalents. A negative enterprise value can occur when a company has more cash and cash equivalents than its market capitalization and debt combined. In other words, the value of a company's cash and cash equivalents is greater than the value of the company's liabilities and equity. A negative enterprise value is not a common occurrence, and it may indicate that the company is over-capitalized or has a large amount of cash on hand that is not being put to productive use. It can also suggest that the market is underestimating the company's future potential or that the company is a takeover target. A negative enterprise value does not mean that the company is not profitable or that it is not generating cash flow. It simply means that the company has more cash and cash equivalents than its market capitalization and debt combined. Investors should evaluate a company's negative enterprise value in conjunction with other financial metrics and analysis to gain a comprehensive understanding of a company's financial performance and value.

158. Discount to Net Current Asset Value

The Discount to Net Current Asset Value (NCAV) ratio is a financial ratio that compares a company's market capitalization to its net current assets. It is used to evaluate a company's valuation and to identify companies that may be undervalued. The formula for the NCAV ratio is NCAV Ratio = (Current Assets - Total Liabilities) / Outstanding Shares, Where Current Assets = the value of a company's assets that can be converted to cash within a year Total Liabilities = the value of a company's debts and other obligations Outstanding Shares = the number of shares of stock that investors currently hold. A company that trades at a discount to its NCAV is considered undervalued because its market capitalization is less than the value of its net current assets. The ratio is often used to screen for potential value investments. It's important to note that the NCAV ratio is a relative measure, and it should be compared to the NCAV ratio of other companies in the same sector or industry. Additionally, the ratio can vary over time, especially in the short term, due to changes in market conditions and the company's financial performance. Value investors commonly use the NCAV ratio to identify companies that may be undervalued based on the value of their net current assets.

159. Discounted Cash Flow

Discounted Cash Flow (DCF) is a method of valuing a company's future cash flows and determining its intrinsic value. It is based on the principle that the value of a company today is equal to the present value of its future cash flows. The formula for DCF is: DCF = CF1/(1+r)^1 + CF2/(1+r)^2 + ... + CFn/(1+r)^n, Where: CF1, CF2, ..., CFn = the cash flows generated by the company in year 1, year 2, ..., year n r = the discount rate, or the required rate of return that investors expect to earn on their investment n = the number of years over which the cash flows are projected. Investors and analysts widely use the DCF model to evaluate a company's intrinsic value, or its value if it were to be sold or liquidated today. To perform a DCF analysis, an investor must estimate a company's future cash flows and the discount rate that should be used to discount those cash flows. It's important to note that DCF is a relative measure, and it should be compared to the DCF of other companies in the same sector or industry. Additionally, the DCF can vary over time, especially in the short term, due to changes in market conditions, the company's financial performance, and the assumptions made in the model. DCF is a widely accepted company valuing method but has some limitations. It requires a lot of data and assumptions, is sensitive to the discount rate and the projections of cash flows, and relies heavily on the company's uncertain future performance. It should be used with other financial metrics and analyses to comprehensively understand a company's financial performance and value.

160. Earnings Yield

The Earnings Yield is a financial ratio measuring the return on investment an investor can expect to earn from a company's earnings. It is calculated by dividing a company's earnings per share (EPS) by its current stock price. The formula for the Earnings Yield is: Earnings Yield = Earnings per Share (EPS) / Current Stock Price. It's important to note that the Earnings Yield is the reciprocal of the Price to Earnings (P/E) ratio, a commonly used valuation metric. A high Earnings Yield means that the company is generating a high return on investment for its shareholders, indicating that the stock may be undervalued. On the other hand, a low Earnings Yield means that the company is generating a low return on investment for its shareholders, indicating that the stock may be overvalued. It's important to note that the Earnings Yield is a relative measure and should be compared to the Earnings Yield of other companies in the same sector or industry. Additionally, the Earnings Yield can vary over time, especially in the short term, due to changes in market conditions and the company's financial performance. Investors and analysts commonly use the earnings yield to evaluate a company's valuation and compare it with other companies in the same sector or industry. It also identifies overvalued or undervalued companies based on their earnings.

161. Magic Formula

The Magic Formula is a stock selection strategy developed by Joel Greenblatt, an American hedge fund manager and author. The approach is based on the idea that a company's financial performance can be measured by two key metrics: return on capital and earnings yield. The Magic Formula uses a ranking system to select stocks, with the highest-ranking stocks being the most attractive for investment. The formula is calculated as follows: Rank = (Earnings Yield x 1.5) + (Return on Capital x 2), Where: Earnings Yield = Earnings per Share (EPS) / Current Stock Price Return on Capital = (Earnings Before Interest and Taxes (EBIT) / (Total Assets - Current Liabilities)). The Magic Formula is essentially a value investing strategy to identify companies that are undervalued by the market and have strong financial performance. The strategy suggests investors should buy the companies with the highest ranking, hold them for one year, and repeat the process every year. It's important to note that the Magic Formula is a relative measure and should be compared to the Magic Formula of other companies in the same sector or industry. Additionally, the Magic Formula can vary over time, especially in the short term, due to changes in market conditions and the company's financial performance. The Magic Formula is widely used by investors and analysts to evaluate a company's valuation and to identify companies that may be undervalued based on their financial performance.

162. Net Net Working Capital

Net Net Working Capital (NNWC) is a financial ratio that measures a company's liquidity. It is calculated by taking the company's current assets minus its current liabilities and subtracting its total liabilities. The formula for NNWC is NNWC = (Current Assets - Current Liabilities) - Total Liabilities, Where Current Assets = the value of a company's assets that can be converted to cash within a year. Current Liabilities = the value of a company's debts and other obligations due within a year—total Liabilities = the value of a company's debts and other commitments. A positive NNWC value indicates that a company has more assets than liabilities and is financially healthy. A negative NNWC value indicates that a company has more liabilities than assets, indicating financial distress. The NNWC is a relative measure and should be compared to the NNWC of other companies in the same sector or industry. Additionally, the ratio can vary over time, especially in the short term, due to changes in market conditions and the company's financial performance. Investors and analysts commonly use the NNWC ratio to evaluate a company's liquidity and financial health. It is often used as a screening tool for value investing.

163. Shareholder Yield

Shareholder Yield is a metric that measures the total return to shareholders from a combination of dividends, buybacks, and debt reduction. It is calculated by adding the dividend yield, the buyback yield, and the debt reduction yield and dividing it by the company's market capitalization. The formula for Shareholder Yield is Shareholder Yield = (Dividend Yield + Buyback Yield - Debt Reduction Yield) / Market Capitalization, Where Dividend Yield = Annual Dividends per Share / Current Stock Price Buyback Yield = (Shares repurchased during the period / Outstanding shares) / Current Stock Price Debt Reduction Yield = (Reduction in debt during the period / Market Capitalization). The Shareholder Yield measures how much of a company's cash flow is returned to shareholders through dividends, buybacks, and debt reduction. A high Shareholder Yield indicates that a company is returning more cash to shareholders and may suggest that the market undervalues the company. The Shareholder Yield is a relative measure and should be compared to the Shareholder Yield of other companies in the same sector or industry. The Shareholder Yield can vary over time, especially in the short term, due to changes in market conditions, financial performance, and capital allocation strategy. Investors and analysts commonly use the Shareholder Yield to evaluate a company's capital allocation strategy and identify companies returning more cash to shareholders.

164. Graham Number

The Graham Number is a valuation metric developed by Benjamin Graham, widely considered the father of value investing. It determines the maximum price an investor should pay for a stock based on the company's financials. The formula for the Graham Number is Graham Number = (Earnings per Share (EPS) * 22.5) / Price to Earnings (P/E) ratio, Where Earnings per Share (EPS) = a company's net income divided by the number of outstanding shares Price to Earnings (P/E) ratio = the current market price per share divided by the earnings per share. The calculation's result is a number representing the maximum price at which an investor should buy a stock. If the stock's current market price is lower than the Graham Number, it may be considered undervalued. It's important to note that the Graham Number is a relative measure, and it should be compared to the Graham Number of other companies in the same sector or industry. Additionally, the Graham Number can vary over time, especially in the short term, due to changes in market conditions and the company's financial performance. The Graham Number is widely used by investors and analysts to evaluate a company's valuation and to identify companies that may be undervalued based on their financials.

165. Equity to Assets Ratio

The Equity to Assets Ratio (also known as the Equity Ratio) is a financial ratio that measures the proportion of a company's assets financed by shareholders' equity. It is calculated by dividing the company's total shareholders' equity by its total assets. The Equity to Assets Ratio formula is Equity to Assets Ratio = Shareholders' Equity / Total Assets, Where Shareholders' Equity = the value of a company's assets minus its liabilities Total Assets = the value of all assets owned by the company. A high Equity Assets Ratio indicates that a company has a more significant proportion of assets financed by shareholders' equity, which may suggest that the company is financially stable and has a lower level of leverage. On the other hand, a low Equity Assets Ratio indicates that a company has a more significant proportion of assets financed by debt, which may suggest that the company is more leveraged and has a higher level of risk. The Equity to Assets Ratio is a relative measure, and it should be compared to the Equity to Assets Ratio of other companies in the same sector or industry. Additionally, the ratio can vary over time, especially in the short term, due to changes in market conditions and the company's financial performance. Investors and analysts commonly use the Equity Assets Ratio to evaluate a company's financial stability and leverage, and it's often used in conjunction with other financial metrics such as the Debt-to-Equity Ratio.

166. Cash Flow to Debt Coverage Ratio

The Cash Flow to Debt Coverage Ratio (or the Debt Service Coverage Ratio) is a financial ratio that measures a company's ability to meet its debt obligations using its cash flow. It is calculated by dividing the company's cash flow by its total debt payments. The formula for the Cash Flow to Debt Coverage Ratio is Cash Flow to Debt Coverage Ratio = Cash Flow from Operations / Total Debt Payments, Where Cash Flow from Operations = the amount of cash generated by a company's core business operations Total Debt Payments = the amount of money a company uses to pay off its debt. A high Cash Flow to Debt Coverage Ratio indicates that a company can meet its debt obligations with its cash flow, which suggests that it is financially healthy. On the other hand, a low Cash Flow to Debt Coverage Ratio indicates that a company may have difficulty meeting its debt obligations, which suggests that it may be in financial distress. It's important to note that the Cash Flow to Debt Coverage Ratio is a relative measure, and it should be compared to the Cash Flow to Debt Coverage Ratio of other companies in the same sector or industry. Additionally, the ratio can vary over time, especially in the short term, due to changes in market conditions and the company's financial performance. The Cash Flow to Debt Coverage Ratio is commonly used by investors and analysts to evaluate a company's ability to meet its debt obligations, and it's often used in conjunction with other financial metrics such as the Interest Coverage Ratio.

167. Quick Ratio

The Quick Ratio (also known as the Acid-Test Ratio) is a financial ratio that measures a company's ability to meet its short-term obligations using its most liquid assets. It is calculated by dividing the company's current assets minus its inventory by its current liabilities. The formula for the Quick Ratio is Quick Ratio = (Current Assets - Inventory) / Current Liabilities, Where Current Assets = the value of a company's assets that can be converted to cash within a year, Inventory = the value of a company's goods that are available for sale, and Current Liabilities = the value of a company's debts and other obligations that are due within a year. A high Quick Ratio indicates that a company can meet its short-term obligations with its most liquid assets, which suggests that it is financially healthy. A low Quick Ratio, on the other hand, indicates that a company may have difficulty meeting its short-term obligations, which suggests that the company may be in financial distress. The Quick Ratio is a relative measure and should be compared to the Quick Ratio of other companies in the same sector or industry. Additionally, the ratio can vary over time, especially in the short term, due to changes in market conditions and the company's financial performance. Investors and analysts commonly use the Quick Ratio to evaluate a company's liquidity and short-term financial health, and it's often used in conjunction with other financial metrics, such as the Current Ratio.

168. Futures Metrics

Futures metrics are indicators used to evaluate the performance and risk of futures contracts. They provide insight into the price movements and volatility of the underlying asset and can be used to make informed trading decisions. Here are a few commonly used futures metrics: Open Interest: It is the total number of outstanding contracts that have not been settled by delivery; Volume: It is the number of contracts traded during a specified time; Basis: It is the difference between the futures price and the cash price of the underlying asset; Time Premium: It is the difference between the futures price and the intrinsic value of the underlying asset; Implied Volatility: It is a measure of the volatility of the underlying asset, as implied by the price of futures contracts; Carry: It is the difference between the interest income earned on the underlying asset and the cost of financing the underlying asset; Delta: It is the rate of change of the price of a futures contract concerning the price of the underlying asset; and Gamma: It is the rate of change of delta concerning the price of the underlying asset. It can be used to estimate the sensitivity of delta to changes in the underlying asset price. These metrics can provide insight into the price movements and volatility of the underlying asset, as well as the level of participation and liquidity in the market. They can be used to identify trends in supply and demand, market expectations, and the cost of financing and to evaluate a trade's risk and potential return.

169. Interest Coverage Ratio

The Interest Coverage Ratio (also known as the Times Interest Earned Ratio) is a financial ratio that measures a company's ability to meet its interest payments on its debt. It is calculated by dividing a company's earnings before interest and taxes (EBIT) by interest expenses. The formula for the Interest Coverage Ratio is Interest Coverage Ratio = Earnings Before Interest and Taxes (EBIT) / Interest Expense, Where Earnings Before Interest and Taxes (EBIT) = a company's income from its core operations before deducting interest and taxes Interest Expense = the amount of money a company pays in interest on its debt. A high-interest Coverage Ratio indicates that a company can meet its interest payments on its debt, which suggests that it is financially healthy. On the other hand, a low-interest Coverage Ratio indicates that a company may have difficulty meeting its interest payments, which suggests that it may be in financial distress. It's important to note that the Interest Coverage Ratio is a relative measure, and it should be compared to the Ratio of other companies in the same sector or industry. Additionally, the ratio can vary over time, especially in the short term, due to changes in market conditions and the company's financial performance. Investors and analysts commonly use the Interest Coverage Ratio to evaluate a company's ability to meet its interest payments, and it's often used in conjunction with other financial metrics such as the debt-equity ratio and the debt-to-capital ratio. However, it should be used with other financial metrics and analyses to understand a company's financial performance and risk comprehensively.

170. All-Time Range

The All-time range is a financial metric used to measure a stock's high and low price over its entire trading history. It is represented as two numbers separated by a dash, the first being the all-time high and the second being the all-time low. For example, if a stock had a high price of $100 and a low price of $50 over its entire trading history, its all-time range would be $100 - $50. The all-time range is a commonly used metric by investors and traders to gauge the volatility of a stock over a long period, such as decades, and to get an idea of the stock's historical price movement. A stock with a wide all-time range may be considered more volatile than one with a narrow all-time range. Additionally, it can be used to identify stocks that may be undervalued or overvalued relative to their historical price range. The all-time range is based on historical data, and it does not predict future performance.

171. Momentum

Momentum is a financial metric used to measure the rate of change in a stock's price over a specific period. A commonly used technical indicator helps investors and traders identify stocks trending in a particular direction. There are a few different ways to calculate momentum, but one of the most common methods is to use the relative strength index (RSI). The relative strength index (RSI) compares the magnitude of a stock's recent gains to its recent losses over a specified time. It is calculated by dividing the average increase of the stock over a certain period by the average loss of the stock over the same period. The resulting number is then plotted on a scale of 0 to 100, with readings above 70 indicating that a stock is overbought (likely to fall in price), and readings below 30 indicating that a stock is oversold (likely to rise in price). Another way to calculate momentum is to use the moving average, which can be calculated using the stock's closing prices over time, such as a 50-day or 200-day moving average. If the stock's current price is above its moving average, it is considered to have positive momentum, indicating that the stock is trending upward. If the stock's current price is below its moving average, it is considered to have negative momentum, indicating that the stock is trending downward. Momentum is a relative measure, and it should be used in conjunction with other financial metrics, analysis, and research to gain a comprehensive understanding of a company and its stock performance.

172. Simple Moving Average

Simple moving average (SMA) is a financial metric used to measure the average price of a stock over a specific period. It is calculated by adding the closing prices of a stock over a specified number of periods (such as days, weeks, or months) and then dividing that total by the number of time periods. For example, if you wanted to calculate a 50-day simple moving average for a stock, you would add up the closing prices for the stock over the past 50 days and then divide that total by 50. This would give you the average closing price for the stock over the past 50 days. The simple moving average is a commonly used technical indicator that helps investors and traders identify stock price trends. A stock's price above its moving average is considered to be in an uptrend, and a stock's price below its moving average is considered to be in a downtrend. Additionally, the distance between the stock's price and the moving average can indicate the stock's strength or weakness. A stock trading far above its moving average is considered strong, and a stock trading far below its moving average is considered weak. However, the SMA is a lagging indicator, which means it is based on past data and does not predict future performance. Therefore, it should be used with other financial metrics, analysis, and research to understand a company and its stock performance comprehensively.

173. Relative Strength Index (RSI)

The Relative Strength Index (RSI) is a technical indicator that measures the strength of a stock's price action. It compares the magnitude of a stock's recent gains to its losses over a specified time, typically 14 trading days. RSI is a momentum indicator; it oscillates between 0 and 100, where values above 70 are considered overbought, and values below 30 are considered oversold. The formula for calculating RSI is RSI = 100 - (100/(1 + RS)), Where RS = Average gain of the stock over the specified period / Average loss of the stock over the specified period. A stock with an RSI value above 70 is considered overbought, meaning that it has been trading at a high price for an extended period of time and may be due for a price correction. A stock that has an RSI value below 30 is considered to be oversold, meaning that it has been trading at a low price for an extended period and may be due for a price increase. The RSI is a widely used momentum indicator; traders and investors use it to identify overbought and oversold conditions and assess whether a stock is trending.

174. Average True Range

The Average True Range (ATR) is a technical indicator that measures the volatility of a stock. It determines the average range of a stock's price movements over a specified period, typically 14 trading days. The formula for calculating the ATR is ATR = [(Prior ATR x (n-1)) + TR] / n, Where: TR = True Range, it is the greatest of the following: * Current high minus current low * Absolute value of current high minus previous close * Absolute value of current low minus previous close; Prior ATR is the average true range of the last period; and n is the number of periods used in the calculation. Traders and investors commonly use the ATR to gauge the volatility of a stock. A stock with a high ATR is considered more volatile than one with a low ATR. Additionally, it can be used to identify stocks that may be undervalued or overvalued relative to their historical price range. The ATR is also a component of many volatility-based trading systems and strategies. The ATR is a relative measure, and it should be used in conjunction with other financial metrics, analysis, and research to gain a comprehensive understanding of a company and its stock performance.

175. Alpha

Alpha is a financial metric that measures the performance of an investment relative to a benchmark index or benchmark portfolio. It represents the excess return of an investment compared to what would have been expected given the level of risk taken. A positive alpha indicates that the investment has performed better than expected, while a negative alpha indicates that the investment has performed worse than expected. The formula for calculating alpha is: Alpha = (Return on Investment - Risk-free rate of return) - (Beta x (Market return - Risk-free rate of return)), Where: Return on Investment is the actual return on the investment; Risk-free rate of return is the return on a risk-free investment, such as a US Treasury bond; Beta is a measure of a stock's volatility to the overall market; and Market return is the return on the benchmark index or benchmark portfolio. Fund managers and investment professionals often use alpha to evaluate the performance of their portfolios or strategies. A positive alpha indicates that the portfolio has outperformed its benchmark, and a negative alpha indicates that it has underperformed its benchmark. It's important to note that alpha is a relative measure, and it should be used in conjunction with other financial metrics, analysis, and research to gain a comprehensive understanding of an investment and its performance.

176. Risk-Free Rate of Return

The risk-free rate of return is the theoretical rate of return of an investment with zero risk. In practice, it is represented by the return on a highly secure and liquid investment such as a short-term US Treasury bond. The risk-free rate is used as a benchmark to evaluate the performance of other investments. The most common use of the risk-free rate is in the Capital Asset Pricing Model (CAPM), a widely used financial model that helps determine an investment's expected return. In the CAPM, the risk-free rate is used as a baseline return against which the returns of risky investments can be compared. The risk-free rate also serves as a benchmark for evaluating the performance of other investments, such as stocks or bonds. For instance, if a stock has a return of 10% and the risk-free rate is 2%, the stock's excess return is 8%. The risk-free rate is theoretical, and the actual risk-free rate can vary depending on the period, currency, and other factors. Therefore, the risk-free rate used in financial models should be chosen carefully to ensure it is an appropriate benchmark for the evaluated investment.

177. Weighted Average Cost of Capital

The Weighted Average Cost of Capital (WACC) is a financial metric representing a company's average cost of capital. It is the blended cost of all the capital that a company has raised, including equity and debt. The WACC is used to determine the minimum return that a company needs to generate to meet the expectations of its investors and to cover its capital costs. The formula for calculating WACC is: WACC = (E/V x Re) + (D/V x Rd x (1-Tc)), Where: E = Market value of the company's equity, V = Total market value of the company's equity and debt, Re = Cost of equity, D = Total value of the company's debt, Rd = Cost of debt, and Tc = Corporate tax rate. The WACC is a widely used financial metric that evaluates the efficiency of a company's capital structure, the cost of capital for new projects, and the decision to make investments. A lower WACC indicates that a company is more efficiently using its capital and is better positioned to generate returns for its investors.

178. R-Squared

R-squared (R2) is a statistical measure representing the proportion of a stock's performance that the overall market or benchmark can explain. It ranges from 0 to 1, with one indicating that its benchmark can explain 100% of the stock's performance and 0 indicating that its benchmark can explain none. The formula for calculating R-squared is R2 = 1 - (Sum of Squared Residuals / Total Sum of Squares), Where the sum of Squared Residuals is the sum of the squared differences between the actual stock returns and the returns predicted by the benchmark and Total Sum of Squares is the sum of the squared differences between the actual stock returns and the average stock return. R-squared is often used to measure the goodness of fit for a linear regression model. It is commonly used in finance and economics to measure the degree to which a stock's returns are correlated with the returns of a benchmark or market index. A high R-squared value indicates that a stock's performance is closely related to the benchmark's performance. In contrast, a low R-squared value suggests a stock's performance is not closely associated with the benchmark's performance. The R-squared is a relative measure, and it should be used in conjunction with other financial metrics, analysis, and research to gain a comprehensive understanding of a company and its stock performance.

179. Active Share

Active Share is a measure used to assess the degree to which a portfolio's holdings differ from its benchmark index. It quantifies how actively a fund manager manages a portfolio compared to a passive investment strategy. Active Share is the percentage of a portfolio's holdings that differ from the benchmark index. A higher Active Share indicates a more significant deviation from the benchmark, suggesting a more active management style. Active Share is determined by comparing the weight of each holding in the portfolio to its weight in the benchmark index. The formula involves summing the absolute differences in weight for each holding and dividing by two. An active share of 0% indicates a portfolio that mirrors the benchmark exactly, which is typical of passive management. An Active Share of 100% signifies a portfolio that does not overlap with the benchmark, reflecting a fully active management approach. Active Share helps investors evaluate the effectiveness of fund managers. A high Active Share and strong performance can indicate that a manager successfully adds value through active management. While Active Share provides insights into management style, it should be considered alongside other metrics, such as tracking error and performance relative to the benchmark, to gain a comprehensive view of a fund's investment strategy. Active Share is a valuable metric for assessing the level of active management in an investment portfolio, helping investors understand how much a fund's holdings differ from its benchmark and the potential for value creation through active investment strategies.

180. Tracking Error

Tracking error (TE) measures how closely the returns of a mutual fund or portfolio match the returns of its benchmark index. It is the standard deviation of the difference in returns between the fund or portfolio and the benchmark, calculated as the annualized volatility of those differences. The formula for calculating Tracking Error is TE = sqrt(sum((Return of Fund or Portfolio - Return of Benchmark)^2) / n), Where: Return of Fund or Portfolio is the return of the fund or portfolio for each period, Return of Benchmark is the return of the benchmark index for each period, and n is the number of periods. Tracking error is commonly used to measure the level of deviation of a mutual fund or portfolio's returns from its benchmark index. The higher the tracking error, the more the fund or portfolio's returns deviate from the benchmark. A high tracking error indicates that a fund or portfolio manager makes many stock selections that differ from the benchmark. In contrast, a low tracking error indicates that the manager closely tracks the benchmark. Tracking errors are relative measures, and they should be used in conjunction with other financial metrics, analysis, and research to gain a comprehensive understanding of a fund or portfolio and its deviation from the benchmark.

181. Correlation

In the context of the stock market, correlation is used to measure the degree to which the returns of different stocks or stock indices are related to each other. It can be used to evaluate the risk of a portfolio by measuring the degree to which the returns of different stocks within the portfolio are related to each other. A high correlation between the stocks in a portfolio indicates that the portfolio has a high level of risk, as the stocks are likely to move in the same direction. In contrast, a low correlation suggests that the portfolio has a low level of risk, as the stocks are less likely to move in the same direction. Correlation can also be used to measure the relationship between different markets, such as the correlation between the returns of the U.S. stock market and the returns of the Chinese stock market. A high correlation between these two markets indicates that they are likely to move in the same direction, while a low correlation indicates that they are less likely to move in the same direction. Correlation can be used to evaluate the risk of investing in a particular stock or stock index relative to the overall market. A stock or index that has a high correlation with the overall market is likely to move in the same direction as the market. In contrast, a stock or index that has a low correlation with the overall market is less likely to move in the same direction as the market.

182. Owner's Earnings

Owner's Earnings, also known as "economic earnings" or "cash flow from assets," is a financial metric used to measure the cash flow that can be generated by a business that is available to the owners of the business. It is calculated by subtracting capital expenditures (the money a company spends on property, plant, and equipment) from its net income (earnings after taxes) and adding any non-cash charges such as depreciation. The formula for calculating Owner's Earnings is Owner's Earnings = Net Income + Depreciation - Capital Expenditures. Value investors often use this metric to estimate a company's cash flow after accounting for the money needed to maintain and grow the business. It is also used to calculate a company's intrinsic value, which is the company's value based on its fundamentals and financial performance. Investors can determine whether a stock is undervalued or overvalued by comparing the inherent value to the current market price. It's important to note that the Owner's Earnings are not an official financial statement, and all investors or analysts do not widely use it. It's just a way to calculate the cash flow available to the business's owners.

183. Funds from Operations (FFO)

Funds from Operations (FFO) is a financial metric used to measure the cash flow generated by a real estate investment trust (REIT) or real estate company. It is calculated by adding back non-cash charges such as depreciation and amortization to the company's net income. The formula for calculating FFO is: FFO = Net Income + Depreciation + Amortization. Many investors and analysts consider FFO a more accurate measure of a real estate company's performance than net income, as it removes the effects of non-cash charges that can distort the actual cash flow generated by the company. It also excludes any gains or losses on the property sale, which can affect the net income. REITs and real estate companies use FFO to measure their ability to generate cash flow from their properties and by investors and analysts to evaluate the company's performance and potential for growth. It's also used to estimate the company's intrinsic value by comparing the FFO to the current market price of its stock. It's important to note that FFO is not an official financial statement, and not all investors or analysts widely use it; it's just a way to calculate the cash flow that a real estate company generates.

184. Adjusted Funds from Operations (AFFO)

Adjusted Funds from Operations (AFFO) is a financial metric used to measure the cash flow generated by a real estate investment trust (REIT) or real estate company after accounting for maintenance capital expenditures and other non-recurring items. It is calculated by subtracting these expenses from Funds from Operations (FFO). The formula for calculating AFFO is AFFO = FFO - Maintenance Capital Expenditures - Non-recurring Items. Maintenance capital expenditures are the costs associated with maintaining and repairing the company's properties, such as painting, roofing, and landscaping. Non-recurring items are one-time expenses that do not reflect the company's ongoing operations, such as legal fees, accounting fees, and other miscellaneous costs. Many investors and analysts consider AFFO a more accurate measure of a real estate company's performance than FFO, as it removes the effects of non-recurring expenses and maintenance capital expenditures, which can affect the company's cash flow. REITs and real estate companies use AFFO to measure their ability to generate cash flow from their properties and by investors and analysts to evaluate the company's performance and potential for growth. It's also used to estimate the company's intrinsic value by comparing the AFFO to the current market price of the company's stock.

185. Cash Conversion Cycle

The Cash Conversion Cycle (CCC) is a metric that measures the length of time it takes a company to convert its investments in inventory and other resources into cash. It is calculated by adding the average collection period (the length of time it takes to collect payment from customers) to the average inventory period (the length of time it takes to convert inventory into cash) and then subtracting the average payment period (the length of time it takes to pay suppliers). The calculating CCC formula is CCC = Average Collection Period + Average Inventory Period - Average Payment Period. A lower CCC indicates that a company generates cash more quickly, which can be a positive sign of financial health. On the other hand, a high CCC can indicate that a company is having difficulty turning its investments into cash, which can pressure its liquidity and profitability

186. Days Sales of Inventory

Days Sales of Inventory (DSI) measures the number of days a company takes to sell its inventory. It is calculated by dividing the average inventory balance by the cost of goods sold (COGS) and multiplying by the number of days in a period. The formula for calculating DSI is DSI = (Average Inventory / COGS) x Number of Days in the Period. A lower DSI indicates that a company can sell its inventory more quickly, which can be a positive sign of efficient inventory management and strong demand for its products. On the other hand, a high DSI can indicate that a company is having difficulty selling its inventory, which can lead to higher carrying costs and potential inventory write-downs.

187. Days Sales Outstanding

Days Sales Outstanding (DSO) is a metric measuring the days a company takes to collect payment from its customers. It is calculated by dividing the average accounts receivable balance by the average net credit sales and multiplying by the number of days in a period. The formula for calculating DSO is DSO = (Average Accounts Receivable / Average Net Credit Sales) x Number of Days in the Period. A lower DSO indicates that a company can collect payment from its customers more quickly, which can be a positive sign of efficient credit and collections management and strong customer relationships. On the other hand, a high DSO can indicate that a company is having difficulty collecting payment from its customers, which can lead to cash flow issues and potential bad debt.

188. Days Payable Outstanding

Days Payable Outstanding (DPO) measures the days a company takes to pay its bills and other obligations to suppliers. It is calculated by dividing the average accounts payable balance by the average cost of goods sold (COGS) and multiplying by the number of days in a period. The formula for calculating DPO is DPO = (Average Accounts Payable / Average COGS) x Number of Days in the Period. A higher DPO indicates that a company is taking longer to pay its bills, which can be a positive sign of efficient working capital management and strong negotiation power with suppliers. A lower DPO, on the other hand, can indicate that a company is paying its bills more quickly, which can lead to potential cash flow issues and higher borrowing costs.

189. Inventory Turnover Ratio

The Inventory Turnover Ratio (ITR) is a metric that measures how often a company sells and replaces its inventory over a certain period. It is calculated by dividing the cost of goods sold (COGS) by the average inventory balance. The formula for calculating ITR is ITR = COGS / Average Inventory. A higher ITR indicates that a company is selling and replacing its inventory more quickly, which can be a positive sign of efficient inventory management and strong demand for its products. A lower ITR, on the other hand, can indicate that a company is having difficulty selling its inventory, which can lead to higher carrying costs and potential inventory write-downs.

190. Social Media Ratio

Social media ratios are measurements that can be used to evaluate the performance and engagement of content on social media platforms. They are computed by dividing one metric by another and can provide additional insights when used with other social media metrics. Here are a few examples of social media ratios: Engagement rate: The ratio of engagement (likes, shares, comments) to reach (number of unique users who have seen a piece of content); Click-through rate (CTR): The ratio of clicks to impressions (number of times a piece of content has been seen); Bounce rate: The ratio of users who leave a website after only viewing one page to the total number of users who visited the website; Follower-to-following ratio: The ratio of followers to the number of accounts the user is following; and Video completion rate: The ratio of the number of video views to the number of video starts. These ratios can be used to track the performance of company posts and overall account performance and compare it to competitors. Additionally, these ratios can be used to track competitors' performance and identify trends in audience engagement. These ratios may not provide a complete picture of a company's performance; other metrics, such as financial performance, sales, and customer satisfaction, should also be considered. Additionally, ratios can be interpreted differently depending on the industry, and it's crucial to consider the context and compare it with the industry benchmarks.

191. Cost of Revenue Ratio

The cost of revenue ratio, or the cost of goods sold (COGS) ratio, is a financial metric that compares the cost of the goods or services a company sells to its revenue. It measures the efficiency of a company's operations by calculating how much it costs to generate one dollar of revenue. The cost of revenue ratio is calculated by dividing the cost of goods sold (COGS) by total revenue. COGS includes all costs directly associated with producing and selling a product or service, such as raw materials, labor, and manufacturing overhead. A low cost-of-revenue ratio is generally considered desirable, as it indicates that a company can produce and sell its products or services at a low cost relative to revenue. On the other hand, a high cost-of-revenue ratio indicates that a company has high costs relative to revenue and might not be as profitable. The cost of revenue ratio can vary by industry and company size, and therefore it's best to compare a company's cost of revenue ratio to its peers and industry averages. It's important to remember that the cost-of-revenue ratio is just one of the many financial metrics that can be used to evaluate a company's performance. Other financial metrics such as gross profit margin, operating margin, and net profit margin should be considered to better understand a company's overall financial performance.

192. S&P 500 metrics

The S&P 500 (Standard & Poor's 500) is a stock market index that tracks the performance of 500 large publicly traded companies listed on the New York Stock Exchange (NYSE) and the NASDAQ. It is considered a benchmark for the overall stock market, and investors and financial analysts follow it widely. The S&P 500 can be used as an indicator of the overall stock market's performance. When the S&P 500 is rising, it can signal that the stock market is performing well, which can lead to increased profits and stock prices and boost investor confidence. Conversely, when the S&P 500 falls, it can signal that the stock market is performing poorly, leading to decreased profits and stock prices, reducing investor confidence. The S&P 500 is just one of many stock market indices and is not the only factor that drives the stock market. Other stock market indices, such as the Dow Jones Industrial Average (DJIA) and NASDAQ, provide a broader picture of the stock market and other sectors. Therefore, the S&P 500 is just one of the many indicators that can affect the stock market, and it's important to consider other stock market indices and the broader economic context when assessing the relationship between the S&P 500 and the stock market.

193. Dow Jones metrics

The Dow Jones Industrial Average (DJIA) is a stock market index that tracks the performance of 30 large publicly traded companies listed on the New York Stock Exchange (NYSE) and the NASDAQ. It is considered a benchmark for the overall stock market and one of the world's oldest and most widely followed indices. The DJIA can be used as an indicator of the overall stock market's performance. When the DJIA is rising, it can signal that the stock market is performing well, which can lead to increased profits and stock prices and boost investor confidence. Conversely, when the DJIA is falling, it can signal that the stock market is performing poorly, leading to decreased profits and stock prices and reducing investor confidence. It's important to note that the DJIA is just one of many stock market indices and is not the only factor that drives the stock market. Other stock market indices, such as the S&P 500 and NASDAQ, also provide a broader picture of the stock market and other sectors. Therefore, the DJIA is just one of the many indicators that can affect the stock market, and it's important to consider other stock market indices and the broader economic context when assessing the relationship between the DJIA and the stock market. Additionally, the DJIA is a price-weighted index, meaning that the weight of each stock in the index is based on its price per share, which can be affected by the company's financial performance and other factors. Therefore, the high or low performance of some expensive stocks in the DJIA could significantly impact the index more than other stocks with a lower price per share.

194. Consumer Index metrics

Consumer index metrics, such as the Consumer Price Index (CPI) and the Consumer Confidence Index (CCI), can provide insight into the economy's overall health and can therefore impact the stock market. The Consumer Price Index (CPI) measures the average price change over time for a basket of goods and services households consume. When the CPI increases, it can signal that inflation is rising, leading to higher interest rates, which can cause the stock market to decrease. Conversely, when the CPI is low, it can signal that inflation is low, leading to lower interest rates and a more favorable environment for the stock market. The Consumer Confidence Index (CCI) measures consumers' perceptions of current and future economic conditions, including their confidence in the labor market. When the CCI is high, it can indicate that consumers are optimistic about the economy, which can lead to increased consumer spending, boosting the stock market. Conversely, when the CCI is low, it can indicate that consumers are pessimistic about the economy, which can lead to decreased consumer spending and a decrease in the stock market.

195. Gross Domestic Product (GDP) metrics

Gross Domestic Product (GDP) measures the total economic activity within a country and is often used as an indicator of the economy's overall health. The stock market and GDP have a complex relationship; a strong and growing GDP is generally considered suitable for the stock market, as it indicates a strong and growing economy. Companies tend to perform better when the economy is strong, and this can lead to increased profits and stock prices. However, the relationship between GDP and the stock market is not linear nor the only factor that drives the stock market. When

GDP grows, it can signal that the economy is expanding, leading to increased business activity, higher employment, and increased consumer spending, which can all be positive for the stock market. Conversely, when GDP is shrinking, it can signal that the economy is contracting, leading to decreased business activity, higher unemployment, and decreased consumer spending, which can all be negative for the stock market. DP is also important in the sense that it provides an indication of the country's production and consumption, which reflects the country's economic performance. A strong GDP performance can indicate a robust economic performance, which can lead to increased investor confidence, which can boost the stock market. A weak GDP performance can indicate a weak economic performance, decreasing investor confidence and reducing the stock market. The GDP is just one of many indicators that can affect the stock market and is not the only factor that drives it. Economic indicators such as unemployment rate, interest rate, consumer price index, and global events also play a significant role. Therefore, GDP is just one of the many indicators that can affect the stock market, and it's important to consider other economic indicators, as well as the broader economic context, when assessing the relationship between GDP and the stock market.

196. Russel Indexes metrics

Russell Indexes are stock market indices created and maintained by Russell Investments. The Russell 2000 Index is a small-cap index that tracks the performance of the 2000 smallest publicly traded companies listed on the NYSE and Nasdaq. The Russell 1000 Index is a large-cap index that tracks the performance of the 1000 largest publicly traded companies listed on the NYSE and Nasdaq. The Russell 3000 Index is a broad-market index that tracks the performance of the 3000 largest publicly traded companies listed on the NYSE and NASDAQ. Like other stock market indices such as the S&P 500 and Dow Jones Industrial Average, the Russell indexes can be used as an indicator of the overall stock market performance. When the Russell indexes are rising, it can signal that the stock market is performing well, which can lead to increased profits and stock prices and boost investor confidence. Conversely, when the Russell indexes are falling, it can signal that the stock market is performing poorly, leading to decreased profits and stock prices, which can reduce investor confidence. The Russell indexes are just one of many stock market indices and are not the only factor that drives the stock market. Other stock market indices such as the S&P 500, Nasdaq, and Dow Jones Industrial Average also provide a broader picture of the stock market and other sectors. Therefore, the Russell indexes are just one of the many indicators that can affect the stock market, and it's important to consider other stock market indices and the broader economic context when assessing the relationship between the Russell indexes and the stock market.

197. NASDAQ metrics

The Nasdaq (National Association of Securities Dealers Automated Quotations) is a stock market index that tracks the performance of over 3,000 publicly traded companies listed on the Nasdaq stock exchange. It is considered a benchmark for technology and internet-based companies but includes companies from other sectors. The Nasdaq can be used as an indicator of the performance of technology and internet-based companies and the overall stock market. When the Nasdaq is rising, it can signal that technology and internet-based companies are performing well, which can lead to increased profits and stock prices, boosting investor confidence and leading to a rising stock market. Conversely, when the NASDAQ is falling, it can signal that technology and internet-based companies are performing poorly, decreasing profits and stock prices, reducing investor confidence, and leading to a falling stock market. The Nasdaq is just one of many stock market indices and is not the only factor that drives the stock market. Other stock market indices such as the Dow Jones Industrial Average (DJIA) and S&P 500 also provide a broader picture of the stock market and other sectors. Therefore,

Nasdaq is just one of the many indicators that can affect the stock market, and it's important to consider other stock market indices, as well as the broader economic context when assessing the relationship between Nasdaq and the stock market. Additionally, the Nasdaq is a market capitalization-weighted index, meaning that the weight of each stock in the index is based on its market capitalization, which can be affected by the company's financial performance and other factors. Therefore, some big companies' high or low performance on the Nasdaq could significantly impact the index more than that of other companies with smaller market capitalization.

198. Stock Ipos Metrics

Stock IPO (Initial Public Offerings) metrics are indicators used to evaluate the performance and risk of newly public companies. They provide insight into the valuation and market reception of the stock and can be used to make informed investment decisions. Here are a few commonly used Stock IPO metrics: First-day return is the percentage change in the stock price from the offer price to the closing price on the first day of trading. It indicates the market's initial reaction to the stock and can be used to evaluate the success of the IPO. Underpricing is the difference between the offer price and the first-day closing price. It reflects the degree to which the stock was undervalued at the time of the IPO and can be used to evaluate the pricing strategy of the IPO. Insider buying and selling: It is the buying and selling activity of the company's insiders, such as its officers and directors, in the stock. It reflects the company's insiders' confidence in the stock and can be used to evaluate its growth potential. These metrics can provide insight into the valuation and market reception of the stock, as well as the company's potential for growth. They can be used to identify trends in market sentiment, pricing strategies, and the company's financial performance and to evaluate the risk and potential return of an investment in the stock.

199. Fair value Ratios

Fair value ratios are financial metrics used to evaluate the relative value of a stock or index. They are calculated by comparing a stock or index's current market price to its intrinsic value, which estimates its true worth based on various financial factors such as earnings, dividends, and growth prospects. Here are a few things to know about fair value ratios: The most common fair value ratio is the price-to-earnings ratio (P/E ratio), which compares a stock or index's market price to its earnings per share (EPS). A high P/E ratio indicates that the stock or index is overvalued, while a low P/E ratio indicates that it is undervalued. Another standard fair value ratio is the price-to-book ratio (P/B ratio), which compares a stock or index's market price to its book value, which is the value of the company's assets minus its liabilities. A high P/B ratio indicates that the stock or index is overvalued, while a low P/B ratio indicates that it is undervalued. A third fair value ratio is the price-to-sales ratio (P/S ratio), which compares a stock or index's market price to its sales per share. A high P/S ratio indicates that the stock or index is overvalued, while a low P/S ratio indicates that it is undervalued. Other fair value ratios include price-to-cash flow ratio (P/CF ratio), which compares a stock or index's market price to its cash flow per share, and Dividend yield ratio (DY ratio), which compares a stock or index's current dividend per share to the market price per share; Fair value ratios can be used to identify potential buying opportunities and to evaluate the risk and potential return of an investment in a stock or index. For example, a stock or index with a low P/E ratio and high DY ratio may be considered undervalued and a good buying opportunity. Fair value ratios can vary depending on the underlying stock or index, the sector it belongs to, and its industry. Fair value ratios should be used with other technical and fundamental analysis tools, such as trend analysis, price action, and indicators, to understand market sentiment and potential price movement better. Overall, fair value ratios can provide insight into the relative value of a stock or index and the potential for buying opportunities.

200. Poison Pill Metrics

A poison pill is a defensive measure companies can use to make their shares less attractive to potential acquirers. It is a type of stock dilution strategy that companies use to deter hostile takeovers. A poison pill typically involves issuing new shares of stock at a discounted price, which dilutes the value of existing shares and makes it more expensive for an acquirer to buy a controlling stake in the company. Here are a few things to know about poison pill metrics: Poison pills are typically triggered when a single investor or group of investors acquires a certain percentage of a company's shares, usually around 10-20%. Once the trigger is activated, the company issues new shares at a discounted price, which dilutes the value of existing shares and makes it more expensive for the acquirer to buy a controlling stake in the company. Poison pills are controversial because they can make it more difficult for shareholders to sell their shares and can also make it more difficult for companies to acquire. They are also seen as a way for management to entrench themselves and protect their positions. Poison pills can be challenging to detect, and companies may not disclose whether they have implemented one. Some investors and analysts may look at metrics such as insider buying and selling and company capital structure changes to detect whether a poison pill has been implemented. Poison pills are not always successful in deterring hostile takeovers. Some acquirers may be willing to pay a premium for a company despite the dilution caused by a poison pill; poison pills are not always the only or the best defense against a hostile takeover. Companies can also use other defensive measures, such as a "golden parachute" provision providing generous severance packages to executives if the company is acquired or a "white knight" provision encouraging friendly bidders to come forward. Overall, poison pills are a defensive measure companies can use to make their shares less attractive to potential acquirers. It is a type of stock dilution strategy that companies use to deter hostile takeovers.

201. Hostile Takeover Metrics

A hostile takeover is when one company tries to acquire another without the support or approval of the target company's management or board of directors. Hostile takeovers can be difficult and complex, typically involving significant negotiation and legal maneuvering. Here are a few things to know about metrics related to hostile takeovers:

- **Shareholder ownership:** One metric that can indicate a company is vulnerable to a hostile takeover is a high percentage of shares held by a small group of shareholders. This can make acquiring a controlling stake in the company easier for an acquirer.
- **Stock price performance:** A company with a consistently underperforming stock price may be seen as a more attractive target for a hostile takeover.
- **Debt-to-equity ratio:** A high debt-to-equity ratio can indicate that a company is financially vulnerable and may be more susceptible to a hostile takeover.
- **Earnings per share (EPS):** A company with consistently low EPS may be seen as a more attractive target for a hostile takeover.
- **Insider trading activity:** Insider buying and selling can indicate potential hostile takeover activity. If executives or significant shareholders buy or sell large amounts of stock, they may be aware of a possible takeover attempt.
- **Merger and acquisition activity:** A company in the process of or has recently completed a merger or acquisition may be more likely to be targeted for a hostile takeover.
- **Short interest:** A high level of short interest (shares sold short as a percentage of shares outstanding) can indicate that investors believe a company's stock price will decrease in the future, making it a more attractive target for a hostile takeover

- **Market capitalization:** A company with a relatively lower market capitalization than its peers may be more susceptible to a hostile takeover. Hostile takeovers can be complex and challenging, involving significant negotiation and legal maneuvering. Shareholder ownership, stock price performance, debt-to-equity ratio, earnings per share, insider trading activity, merger and acquisition activity, short interest, and market capitalization are some metrics that can indicate a company's vulnerability to a hostile takeover.

202. Market Capital/Employee Ratios

The market capitalization per employee (market cap/employee) ratio is a metric that compares a company's market capitalization to its number of employees. It is calculated by dividing a company's market capitalization by its number of employees. This ratio can be used to compare companies within the same industry or sector and the productivity of different companies. A company with a high market cap/employee ratio may be considered more productive or efficient than a low one. This can be due to various factors, such as automation, a high-skilled workforce, or lower labor costs. A company with a high market cap/employee ratio may also be considered more valuable per employee than a low ratio. However, this ratio should be used cautiously because it can be affected by factors such as the company's industry, business model, and accounting practices. For example, a company with a high market cap/employee ratio in a capital-intensive industry such as mining or energy may not be as efficient as a company with a lower ratio in a labor-intensive industry such as retail or restaurant. Additionally, a company with many part-time or contract employees may have a lower ratio than a company with fewer full-time employees, even if the former is more efficient.

203. Delta Metrics

Delta is a metric commonly used in options trading to measure the rate of change of an option's price concerning the underlying asset's price. It measures the rate of change of the option's price concerning a $1 change in the underlying asset's price. It can be used to measure the sensitivity of an option's price to changes in the price of the underlying asset. Traders and investors commonly use several delta metrics to analyze options markets, including delta, which is the rate of change of an option's price concerning a $1 change in the underlying asset's price. It measures an option's price sensitivity to changes in the underlying asset's price.

- **Gamma:** The rate of change of an option's delta concerning a $1 change in the underlying asset's price. It measures the sensitivity of an option's delta to changes in the underlying asset's price.
- **Theta:** The rate of change of an option's price concerning the passage of time. It measures an option's price sensitivity to changes in the time remaining until expiration.
- **Vega:** The rate of change of an option's price concerning a 1% change in the underlying asset's volatility. It measures the sensitivity of an option's price to changes in the underlying asset's volatility.

Delta, *gamma*, *theta*, and *vega* are the four most commonly used Greek letters in options trading and are known as the Greeks. They are used to measure the sensitivity of an option's price to changes in underlying asset price, time, volatility, and other market conditions. Traders and investors use the Greeks to evaluate the risk and potential return of an options trade and can also use them to adjust their positions in response to changes in market conditions.

204. Day's Range Ratios

Day's Range Ratios are financial metrics that assess a security's volatility and price movement over a single trading day. They provide insights into how much a stock's price fluctuates within that day, helping investors gauge potential risk and trading opportunities. For instance, a Higher ratio indicates greater volatility and price movement relative to the opening or closing price, suggesting that the security may be more active or unpredictable. On the other hand, a lower ratio signifies less volatility, indicating more stable price action within that trading day. Day's Range Ratios can be a useful tool for day traders looking to capitalize on short-term price fluctuations and volatility, as they provide valuable insights into a security's intraday volatility and price dynamics, aiding investors in making informed trading decisions based on price movements within a single trading day.

205. Call/Put Ratios

Call/put ratios are financial metrics used to evaluate the sentiment of the options market for a particular stock or index. They are calculated by dividing the number of open call options contracts by the number of open put options contracts for a given security call option is a contract that gives the holder the right, but not the obligation, to buy a stock at a specific price (strike price) on or before a specific date (expiration date). A put option is a contract that gives the holder the right, but not the obligation, to sell a stock at a specific price (strike price) on or before a specific date (expiration date). A high call/put ratio indicates that there are more open call options contracts than put options contracts, which suggests that the market is bullish on the stock or index. A low call/put ratio indicates that there are more open put options contracts than call options contracts, which suggests that the market is bearish on the stock or index. Call/put ratios are considered a leading indicator of market sentiment, as options traders tend to buy calls when they are bullish and buy puts when they are bearish on a stock. Call/put ratios can be used to identify potential market turning points and to evaluate the risk and potential return of an investment in a stock or index. For example, a high call/put ratio may indicate that the market is overbought and that a correction is likely. In contrast, a low call/put ratio may suggest that the market is oversold and that a rally is expected. Call/put ratios can vary depending on the underlying stock or index and its volatility, as well as the expiration date of the options contracts.

206. Options Contract Ratios

Options contract ratios are financial metrics used to evaluate the sentiment of the options market for a particular stock or index. They are calculated by dividing the number of open options contracts for a given security by the total number of outstanding shares. An options contract is a financial contract that gives the holder the right, but not the obligation, to buy or sell a stock at a specific price (strike price) on or before a specific date (expiration date). A high options contract ratio indicates that there are a large number of open options contracts about the total number of outstanding shares, which suggests that there is a high level of interest in the stock or index among options traders. A low options contract ratio indicates a small number of open options contracts about the total number of outstanding shares, which suggests a low level of interest in the stock or index among options traders. Options contract ratios can be used to identify potential market turning points and to evaluate the risk and potential return of an investment in a stock or index. For example, a high options contract ratio may indicate that the market is overbought and that a correction is likely. In contrast, a low options contract ratio may suggest that the market is oversold and that a rally is expected.

207. Earnings Estimate Metrics

Earnings estimate metrics are financial metrics that estimate a company's future financial performance and earnings per share

(EPS). These estimates are typically provided by analysts who follow the company and are based on various factors, including past performance, industry trends, and the overall economic environment. Here are a few things to know about earnings estimate metrics: EPS is a measure of a company's profitability and is calculated by dividing the company's net income by the number of outstanding shares of stock. A company with a high EPS is generally considered more profitable and attractive to investors. Earnings estimates are typically provided for the current quarter and the next four quarters, as well as for the current fiscal year and the next fiscal year. These estimates are usually updated regularly as new information becomes available. Analysts use various methods and sources to generate earnings estimates, including company financial statements, guidance provided by management, and industry trends. They also consider external factors such as interest rates, exchange rates, and overall economic conditions. Earnings estimates can be a valuable tool for investors and analysts to evaluate a company's future performance, but they do not guarantee future results. Actual earnings can differ significantly from the estimates due to various factors, such as changes in the economic environment, unexpected events, or company-specific factors. Investors and analysts also use earnings estimate metrics to assess the relative value of a stock by comparing the company's expected earnings to its current stock price. Earnings estimate metrics should be used with other technical and fundamental analysis tools and interpreted with caution. Overall, earnings estimate metrics are financial metrics that estimate a company's future financial performance.

208. Earnings History Metrics

Earnings history metrics are financial measures that provide information about a company's past performance. Here are a few examples of earnings history metrics: Earnings per share (EPS): This metric represents the amount of a company's profit allocated to each outstanding share of common stock. It is calculated by dividing a company's net income by its number of outstanding shares. EPS is a commonly used metric to measure a company's profitability. Earnings growth rate: This metric measures the rate at which a company's earnings have grown over a certain period. It is calculated by comparing a company's current period earnings to those from the same period in the previous year. A high earnings growth rate is generally seen as a positive sign for a company's future performance. Earnings surprise: This metric measures how much a company's reported earnings deviate from analysts' expectations. A positive earnings surprise is when a company's reported earnings are higher than analysts' expectations, and a negative earnings surprise is when a company's reported earnings are lower than analysts' expectations. Earnings yield: This metric represents the ratio of a company's earnings to its current market price. It is calculated by dividing the company's earnings per share by its current market price. A high earnings yield is generally seen as a positive sign for a company's future performance. Earnings consistency: This metric measures a company's ability to generate earnings consistently. It is calculated by comparing a company's earnings over a certain period (e.g., the past five years) and determining their consistency. Overall, earnings history metrics provide insight into a company's past performance and can be used to predict its future performance. It is essential to make informed investment decisions to consider a company's earnings history along with other financial metrics and information, such as its revenue, cash flow, and debt levels.

209. Historical Price Metrics

Historical price metrics are financial measures that provide information about a stock's past performance, precisely its price. Here are a few examples of historical price metrics: Price-to-earnings ratio (P/E ratio): This metric compares a stock's current price to its earnings per share (EPS). It is calculated by dividing the stock's current price by its EPS. A high P/E ratio generally indicates that the market is optimistic about the stock's future growth prospects and willing to pay a higher price. Price-to-sales ratio (P/S ratio): This metric compares a stock's current price to its revenue per share. It is calculated by dividing the stock's current price by its revenue per share. A high P/S ratio may indicate that the stock is overvalued, as it suggests that the market is paying a high price for the stock's revenue. Price-to-book ratio (P/B ratio): This metric compares a stock's current price to its book value per share. It is calculated by dividing the stock's current price by its book value per share. A low P/B ratio may indicate that the stock is undervalued, as it suggests that the market is paying a low price for the stock's book value. Historical price-to-earnings growth ratio (PEG ratio): This metric compares a stock's P/E ratio to its earnings growth rate. It is calculated by dividing the P/E ratio by the earnings growth rate. A low PEG ratio may indicate that the stock is undervalued, as it suggests that the market is paying a low price for the stock's earnings growth. 52-week high and low: This metric represents the highest and lowest price a stock has traded in the past 52 weeks. It can be used to gauge a stock's volatility and to identify potential buying or selling opportunities. Overall, historical price metrics provide insight into a stock's past performance and can be used to predict its future performance.

210. Stock Chart Metrics

Stock chart metrics are financial measures that provide information about a stock's historical performance and are represented visually in a stock chart. Here are a few examples of stock chart metrics: Moving averages: A moving average is a trend-following indicator that smooths out price fluctuations by calculating the average price of a stock over a certain period, such as 50 days or 200 days. The most commonly used moving averages are the 50-day moving average and the 200-day moving average. These moving averages can be used to identify trends, such as uptrends and downtrends, and to spot potential buying or selling opportunities. Relative strength index (RSI): The RSI is a momentum indicator that compares the magnitude of recent gains to recent losses to determine an asset's overbought and oversold conditions. The RSI is typically plotted on a scale of 0 to 100. A stock is considered overbought when its RSI is above 70 and oversold when its RSI is below 30. Bollinger Bands: Bollinger Bands are a volatility indicator that consists of a moving average and two standard deviation lines plotted two standard deviations away from the moving average. Bollinger Bands can be used to identify potential buying or selling opportunities and spot possible stock trends. Volume: Volume refers to the number of stock shares traded over a certain period. Volume can be used to identify buying and selling pressure and to confirm trends. Candlestick Chart: It's a way to represent a stock's price action over time. It's composed of a "body" representing the range between the opening and closing prices and "shadows" above and below the body representing the highest and lowest prices. It's a valuable tool to identify patterns and trends, such as bullish or bearish signals.

211. Sector Metrics

Sector metrics refer to the various financial and economic indicators that are specific to a particular industry sector. These metrics help investors and analysts assess the overall health and performance of companies within a sector and make informed investment decisions. Some standard sector metrics include Sector performance: This metric measures the overall performance of a sector in terms of stock price returns and growth and can be expressed as a percentage. Sector earnings: This metric measures companies' earnings within a sector and can indicate the sector's financial health. Sector revenue: This metric measures the total revenue generated by companies within a sector and suggests the sector's size and growth potential. Sector P/E ratio: This metric measures the price-to-earnings ratio of companies within a sector and indicates the sector's valuation compared to its earnings growth. Sector dividend yield: This metric measures the dividend yield of companies within a sector and suggests the sector's potential for income generation. Sector volatility: This metric measures the amount of price fluctuations and volatility within a sector and indicates the sector's risk profile. Investors and analysts can use sector metrics to compare the performance of different sectors and make informed investment decisions based on their goals, risk tolerance, and investment time horizon

212. Dark pools Metrics

Dark pool metrics are indicators used to measure the activity and performance of dark pools, which are private stock exchanges where large institutional investors can trade securities with minimal market impact and improved price discovery. Some standard dark pool metrics include Volume, The total number of shares traded in a dark pool during a given period; Order book depth, The number of shares available to trade at different price levels, which is a measure of liquidity; Execution quality: The average difference between the execution price and the mid-market price, which measures the effectiveness of price discovery in the dark pool; Fill rate: The percentage of orders that are executed fully or partially in the dark pool; Latency: The time it takes for an order to be executed in the dark pool, from the time it is submitted; Cancel rate: The percentage of orders that are canceled before they are executed in the dark pool; Participation rate: The percentage of total trading volume that occurs in the dark pool, compared to other exchanges; and Market share: The percentage of total trading volume that occurs in a specific dark pool, compared to other dark pools. These metrics help traders and investors understand the level of activity and performance of different dark pools and can be used to make informed decisions about where to trade.

In conclusion, this chapter has comprehensively explored financial ratios and metrics, essential tools for analyzing a company's financial health, performance, and operational efficiency. These ratios serve as critical indicators that help investors, analysts, and stakeholders make informed decisions regarding investments, valuations, and corporate strategies. Throughout the chapter, we examined various categories of financial ratios, including liquidity ratios, profitability ratios, leverage ratios, efficiency ratios, and market valuation ratios. Each category offers unique insights into a company's financial performance, providing practical guidance for making investment decisions.

Liquidity Ratios: These ratios, such as the current and quick ratios, are crucial for assessing a company's ability to meet its short-term obligations. Understanding liquidity is not only important but vital for evaluating a firm's financial stability and operational efficiency, making it a key aspect of financial analysis.

Profitability Ratios: Metrics like the gross profit margin, operating profit margin, and return on equity (ROE) provide insights into a company's ability to generate profits relative to its revenues and equity. These ratios are crucial for assessing overall profitability and operational effectiveness.

Leverage Ratios: The debt-to-equity and interest coverage ratios measure a company's financial risk and ability to manage debt. Understanding these metrics allows investors to gauge the firm's financial leverage and risk exposure.

Efficiency Ratios: Metrics like inventory turnover and asset turnover are not just numbers; they are indicators of how effectively a company utilizes its resources to generate sales. High efficiency ratios don't just show efficiency, they indicate strong operational performance and effective asset management, making them crucial for financial analysis.

Market Valuation Ratios: Price-to-earnings (P/E) and price-to-book (P/B) provide insights into how the market values a company relative to its earnings and book value. These ratios are essential for making comparative assessments across companies and industries.

In addition to these categories, we discussed the importance of contextualizing financial ratios within industry benchmarks and historical performance. Ratios should not be viewed in isolation; instead, they should be analyzed by peers and historical trends to provide meaningful insights. Furthermore, we explored the limitations of financial ratios, including the potential for manipulation, the impact of accounting practices, and the influence of economic conditions. Recognizing these limitations is crucial for conducting thorough financial analysis and avoiding misleading conclusions.

Chapter 12 emphasizes that financial ratios and metrics are indispensable tools for evaluating a company's financial performance and making informed investment decisions. By mastering these ratios, you can analyze and compare companies effectively, understand their operational strengths and weaknesses, and assess potential investment opportunities with greater confidence. As you continue your journey in investing and finance, the insights gained from this chapter will empower you to make more informed and strategic decisions, ultimately enhancing your financial understanding and investment success.

CONCLUSION

Mastering the Stock Market: A Comprehensive Guide to Investing and Trading offers a holistic and in-depth exploration of the intricate world of financial markets. It provides readers with a comprehensive toolkit to navigate the complexities of investing and trading. Each chapter builds a solid foundation of knowledge and skills to empower readers to make informed investment decisions.

Starting with the 'History of the Stock Market', we explored the evolution of financial markets, gaining insights into how past events shape contemporary practices. Understanding this historical context equips investors with a perspective on market behavior and trends that can inform future strategies.

In the chapter on 'Stock Market Exchanges', we learned about the various platforms where securities are bought and sold, including their structures and functionalities. This knowledge is crucial for understanding how trading operates, including the significance of liquidity and price discovery.

The chapter on 'Understanding the Basics' laid the groundwork for fundamental concepts essential for all investors. We demystified terminology, trading mechanics, and the various types of assets available, ensuring you are well-prepared to engage with the market confidently.

'Getting Started' provided practical steps for setting investment goals, choosing the right brokerage, and understanding how to buy and sell stocks. This chapter emphasizes the importance of strategic planning and execution in your investment journey.

We then delved into 'Fundamental and Technical Analysis', two pivotal investment evaluation approaches. Fundamental analysis allowed us to assess a company's intrinsic value, while technical analysis provided tools to interpret market trends and price movements. Mastering both methods equips you to analyze potential investments from multiple perspectives.

The chapter on 'Trading Strategies' introduced various approaches to investing, including long-term and short-term strategies. This diverse toolkit lets you align your trading style with your financial goals and market conditions.

In 'Risk Management and Psychology', we discussed the critical role of emotional discipline and risk mitigation in achieving long-term success. Recognizing behavioral biases and implementing sound risk management techniques are essential for navigating the inevitable ups and downs of the market.

As we ventured into 'Advanced Topics', we explored sophisticated trading strategies and instruments, including options trading strategies, how to buy and sell stock options, futures and derivatives, leveraged trading and margin accounts, algorithmic trading, high-frequency trading, and artificial intelligence (AI). Understanding these advanced concepts expands your potential for returns and enhances your ability to adapt to a rapidly changing market environment.

The 'Global Markets and International Investing' chapter highlighted the opportunities and challenges of investing beyond domestic borders. By embracing global diversification, you can enhance your portfolio's resilience and tap into growth potential in emerging markets.

In 'Putting It All Together', we synthesized the knowledge gained throughout the book, reinforcing the interconnectedness of the concepts discussed. This holistic view empowers you to develop a cohesive investment strategy that aligns with your objectives and risk tolerance.

Finally, the 'Financial Ratios and Metrics' chapter provided over 200 tools for evaluating a company's financial health, enabling you to make informed decisions based on quantitative analysis. These metrics are invaluable for assessing potential investments and comparing companies within the same industry.

In summary, *Mastering the Stock Market: A Comprehensive Guide to Investing and Trading* has equipped you with a comprehensive understanding of the fundamental principles, strategies, and tools necessary for successful investing and trading. As you move forward in your financial journey, remember that continuous learning and adaptation are crucial to thriving in the ever-evolving landscape of the stock market. By applying the insights gained from this guide, you are well-prepared to navigate the complexities of investing confidently, make informed decisions, and work towards achieving your financial goals. Embrace the journey ahead with curiosity and diligence and may your investing endeavors be both rewarding and fulfilling.

ACKNOWLEDGMENTS

In recognition of their extraordinary contributions to the stock market, I sincerely thank the following thirty individuals for their visionary leadership and profound impact on Wall Street. These esteemed investors have left indelible marks on the financial world, serving as beacons of inspiration for countless others in the investment community. Their exceptional insight, strategic foresight, and unwavering dedication to investment excellence have shaped the financial landscape and inspired generations of investors to strive for excellence and pursue success in the dynamic world of finance.

1. **Carl Icahn:** Carl Icahn is a renowned American investor, activist shareholder, and business magnate. Born on February 16, 1936, in Queens, New York, Icahn has established himself as one of the most influential figures in finance and corporate governance. Icahn gained prominence for his aggressive investing style and knack for restructuring companies to unlock shareholder value. He often takes large stakes in undervalued companies and then pushes for management, operations, or corporate structure changes to boost stock prices.

Icahn has been involved in numerous high-profile corporate battles and acquisitions. His successful investments include taking significant positions in companies like TWA, Texaco, and RJR Nabisco. He is also known for investing in technology, particularly in companies like Apple, Netflix, and Dell.

Beyond his investment activities, Icahn is a vocal advocate for shareholder rights and corporate governance reforms. He has pushed for changes in executive compensation, board composition, and overall corporate accountability.

Icahn's investing prowess and bold activism have earned him a reputation as a Wall Street titan and a force to be reckoned with in finance. His strategies, successes, and controversies have made him a prominent figure in investment circles and a source of inspiration for aspiring investors and enterprises.

2. Peter Lynch: Peter Lynch is a legendary American investor and mutual fund manager who succeeded remarkably at Fidelity Investments. Born on January 19, 1944, Lynch is widely acclaimed for his ability to generate exceptional returns and straightforward investing approach. Lynch's investment philosophy revolves around 'investing in what you know'. He believed individual investors could gain an edge by focusing on companies and industries they understand well. This approach led him to invest in companies with simple business models and competitive advantages.

One of Lynch's most notable achievements was managing the Fidelity Magellan Fund from 1977 to 1990. Under his stewardship, the fund delivered an average annual return of around 29%, significantly outperforming the S&P 500 index and establishing Lynch as one of the most successful fund managers of his time. Lynch is also known for his best-selling book *One Up on Wall Street*, where he shares his investment strategies and insights in an accessible and engaging manner. He emphasizes the importance of thorough research, patience, and long-term thinking in the investment process. After retiring from Fidelity, Lynch continued to be active in the investment community as a consultant, author, and speaker. He remains a highly respected figure in the financial world, with his investment principles continuing to influence and inspire investors globally.

Overall, Peter Lynch's track record of consistent outperformance and his down-to-earth approach to investing have cemented his legacy as one of the most successful and influential investors ever. His contributions to finance continue to resonate with investors seeking to achieve long-term success in the stock market.

3. **Warren Buffett:** Warren Buffett is regarded as one of the most successful and influential investors ever. Born on August 30, 1930, in Omaha, Nebraska, Buffett has built an unparalleled reputation for his value investing approach and exceptional long-term investment track record. Buffett's investment philosophy is grounded in fundamental analysis. He focuses on businesses with strong economic moats, competent management, and attractive valuations. He is known for his patience, discipline, and ability to identify undervalued companies with significant growth potential.

One of Buffett's most notable achievements is his stewardship of Berkshire Hathaway, a conglomerate holding company he took control of in the 1960s. Under his leadership, Berkshire Hathaway has grown into one of the largest and most successful companies globally, with a diverse portfolio of businesses spanning various industries. Buffett is also renowned for his annual letters to shareholders, where he shares his investment insights, principles, and wisdom gained over decades of investing experience. His letters are widely read and studied by investors around the world.

Beyond his investment prowess, Buffett is known for his philanthropy. He has pledged most of his wealth to charitable causes through the Bill & Melinda Gates Foundation and encourages other billionaires to follow suit through the Giving Pledge initiative.

Buffett's investment insight, integrity, and humility have earned him the nickname 'The Oracle of Omaha' and made him a role model for investors seeking long-term success in the stock market. His timeless investment principles, such as 'Be fearful when others are greedy and greedy when others are fearful', continue to guide and inspire generations of investors globally.

4. **George Soros:** George Soros is a prominent Hungarian American investor, philanthropist, and author known for his successful finance career and active involvement in political and social causes. Born

on August 12, 1930, in Budapest, Hungary, Soros is considered one of the most successful and influential investors of his time. Soros gained fame for his investment prowess, mainly his speculative trades in the currency and financial markets. He is known for his theory of reflexivity, which posits that investor sentiment and market fundamentals can influence each other in a feedback loop, leading to market inefficiencies and opportunities for profit.

One of Soros's most famous trades occurred on September 16, 1992, when he famously shorted the British pound, earning him approximately $1 billion daily and the nickname 'The Man Who Broke the Bank of England'. This trade showcased Soros's ability to analyze macroeconomic trends and make bold investment decisions.

In addition to his investment activities, Soros is a well-known philanthropist and political activist. Through his Open Society Foundations, Soros supports democracy, human rights, and social justice causes around the world. He has been involved in initiatives to promote education, healthcare, and economic development in various countries.

Despite controversy and criticism surrounding some of his political activities, Soros remains highly respected in the financial and philanthropic communities. His insights on global economics, financial markets, and political dynamics continue to be widely followed and studied by investors, policymakers, and academics. George Soros's legacy extends beyond his financial success, as he has used his wealth and influence to advocate for positive social change and make a lasting impact on the world.

5. John Templeton: John Templeton was a renowned American-born British investor, fund manager, and philanthropist known for his exceptional investment insight and global perspective. Born on November 29, 1912, in Winchester, Tennessee, Templeton is widely regarded as one of the pioneers of international investing and value-oriented strategies.

Templeton's investment philosophy was deeply rooted in value investing principles. He emphasized the importance of buying undervalued assets with solid growth potential and believed in conducting thorough research and analysis. He often looked for opportunities in overlooked or distressed markets around the world.

One of Templeton's most significant achievements was founding the Templeton Growth Fund in 1954, which averaged growth of over 15% annually for 38 years. It became known for its successful track record of investing in global equities. His approach to seeking bargains in international markets, particularly during market pessimism, yielded substantial returns for investors. Templeton's investment success was not limited to equities; he also made profitable investments in bonds, currencies, and commodities, showcasing his versatility and ability to adapt to changing market conditions.

Beyond his investment prowess, Templeton was a dedicated philanthropist. He established the John Templeton Foundation, which supports research and initiatives related to science, religion, and human well-being. His philanthropic efforts have impacted various fields, including healthcare, education, and spirituality. Templeton's legacy continues to inspire investors and philanthropists worldwide. His disciplined approach to investing, focus on long-term value creation, and commitment to giving back serve as timeless lessons for those seeking success in finance and philanthropy.

6. **Benjamin Graham:** Benjamin Graham was a renowned economist, investor, and author known as the father of value investing and one of the most influential figures in the world of finance. He was born on May 9, 1894, in London, England. Graham's investment philosophy laid the foundation for modern value investing principles. Graham's approach to investing emphasized the importance of fundamental analysis, margin of safety, and long-term perspective. He believed in investing in undervalued stocks with robust financial fundamentals, aiming to buy assets below their intrinsic value to achieve a margin of safety and reduce risk.

One of Graham's most famous works is the book *Security Analysis*, co-authored with David Dodd and first published in 1934. This seminal work introduced the concept of value investing and laid out principles for evaluating stocks based on their underlying business fundamentals rather than market trends or speculation.

Graham's investment philosophy influenced generations of investors, including notable disciples such as Warren Buffett, who credited Graham as his mentor and guide. Graham's teachings on risk management, diversification, and emotional discipline remain fundamental to successful investing. In addition to his contributions to investment theory, Graham had a distinguished career as an educator and investment manager. He taught at Columbia Business School and managed the Graham-Newman Corporation, where he applied his value investing principles to achieve impressive investment returns. Graham's legacy continues to shape the investment landscape, with value investing remaining a cornerstone of sound investment practices. His emphasis on rationality, thorough analysis, and discipline in investment decisions is a timeless guide for investors seeking to navigate the complexities of financial markets.

7. **Ray Dalio:** Ray Dalio is a prominent American investor, hedge fund manager, and philanthropist known for founding Bridgewater Associates, one of the world's largest and most successful hedge funds. Born on August 8, 1949, in Queens, New York, Dalio is renowned for his innovative investment strategies and deep understanding of economic cycles. Dalio's investment philosophy is based on 'radical transparency' and 'radical truth', emphasizing open communication, rigorous analysis, and learning from mistakes. He believes in diversification across asset classes, geographic regions, and economic environments to manage risk effectively.

One of Dalio's notable contributions to investment theory is his concept of the economic machine, which he explains in his book *Principles: Life and Work*. He views the economy as a complex system driven by cycles of inflation, deleveraging, and reflation and seeks to position his investments accordingly.

Under Dalio's leadership, Bridgewater Associates has achieved significant success, generating solid returns for its investors while navigating various market conditions and economic cycles. The firm is known for its data-driven approach, systematic investment strategies, and risk management practices. In addition to his achievements in finance, Dalio is an active philanthropist. He has pledged to donate most of his wealth to charitable causes and has supported education, healthcare, and economic development initiatives.

Dalio's insights on investing, leadership, and decision-making have earned him widespread recognition and influence in the financial industry. His principles-based approach to investing and focus on continuous learning and improvement are valuable lessons for investors and leaders seeking long-term success.

8. **Michael Burry:** Michael Burry is an American investor, hedge fund manager, and physician known for his contrarian investment approach and successful bets against the subprime mortgage market leading to the 2008 financial crisis. Born on June 19, 1971, Burry gained fame for his early recognition of the housing bubble and profitable investment strategies. Burry's investment philosophy centers around deep value investing and fundamental analysis. He is known for his meticulous research and willingness to go against popular market sentiment. One of his notable investment strategies is finding undervalued assets overlooked or misunderstood by the market, often taking contrarian positions.

Burry gained widespread attention for predicting the collapse of the subprime mortgage market in the mid-2000s. He famously bet against mortgage-backed securities through credit default swaps, a move that earned him substantial profits and was later depicted in the book and film *The Big Short*.

Even though he faced skepticism and criticism at the time, Burry's foresight and conviction in his investment thesis proved highly lucrative. His success in identifying and capitalizing on market inefficiencies showcased his analytical prowess and risk management skills. In addition to his investment career, Burry is known for his background as a medical doctor. He earned a degree in medicine and practiced neurology before transitioning to full-time investing.

Burry's contrarian approach to investing and ability to identify undervalued opportunities have made him a respected figure in the investment community. His story reminds us of the importance of independent thinking, thorough research, and disciplined risk management in achieving investment success.

9. David Tepper: David Tepper is an American billionaire hedge fund manager, investor, and philanthropist known for his successful finance career and contrarian investment strategies. Born on September 11, 1957, in Pittsburgh, Pennsylvania, Tepper founded Appaloosa Management, a hedge fund known for its significant returns and risk-adjusted performance. Tepper's investment philosophy is characterized by his ability to identify undervalued assets and distressed opportunities. He is known for his contrarian bets and willingness to invest in assets others may avoid or overlook. Tepper often uses market dislocations and volatility to generate alpha for his investors.

One of Tepper's most famous investment moves was during the global financial crisis of 2008 and 2009, where he made substantial profits by investing in distressed assets such as financial stocks and bonds. His ability to navigate turbulent market conditions and capitalize on opportunities earned him recognition as one of his time's top-performing hedge fund managers. Beyond his investment acumen, Tepper is also known for his philanthropic efforts. He has donated significant sums to charitable causes, including education, healthcare, and poverty alleviation. Tepper is also a signatory of the Giving Pledge, committing to donate most of his wealth to philanthropy during his lifetime.

Tepper's success in the financial industry and his generosity and commitment to social causes have made him a respected figure in the investment community and the broader public. His story inspires aspiring investors and philanthropists alike, showcasing the potential for achieving financial success while positively impacting society.

10. Steven A. Cohen: Steven A. Cohen is an American billionaire, hedge fund manager, investor, and philanthropist known for his exceptional success in the financial industry and significant contributions to charitable causes. Born on June 11, 1956, in Great Neck, New York, Cohen founded Point72 Asset Management and was previously the founder of S.A.C. Capital Advisors, one of the most successful hedge funds in history. Cohen's investment approach is characterized by his deep understanding of market dynamics, rigorous research process, and ability to identify lucrative investment opportunities. He is known for his focus on fundamental analysis, risk management, and long-term value creation.

One of Cohen's notable achievements was consistently generating high returns for investors at S.A.C. Capital Advisors. His fund was renowned for its strong performance and innovative trading strategies, often including long and short positions across various asset classes. Cohen's career has been subject to controversy, as S.A.C. Capital Advisors faced legal scrutiny and regulatory issues related to insider trading allegations. However, Cohen was never charged with wrongdoing, and he settled with authorities that involved paying significant fines and transforming his firm into a family office, Point72 Asset Management.

In addition to his financial success, Cohen is actively involved in philanthropy. Through the Cohen Veterans Network, he supports mental health services for military veterans and their families. His charitable foundation also contributes to various educational, healthcare, and cultural initiatives. Cohen's impact on the financial industry, combined with his philanthropic efforts, has solidified his reputation as one of the most influential and respected figures in finance. His career trajectory inspires aspiring investors and entrepreneurs, showcasing the potential to succeed while giving back to society.

11. Esther Dyson: Esther Dyson is an American investor, entrepreneur, and philanthropist known for contributing to the technology and healthcare industries. Born on July 14, 1951, in Zürich, Switzerland, Dyson has made significant strides in venture capital, emerging technologies, and space exploration. Dyson's career began in journalism, where she gained recognition as a technology writer and analyst. She later transitioned into venture capital and angel investing, focusing on early-stage startups in the healthcare, information technology, and aerospace sectors.

One of Dyson's notable achievements is her role as an early investor in several successful tech companies, including Flickr, Evernote, and 23andMe. Her expertise in identifying promising startups and hands-on approach to mentoring entrepreneurs have contributed to her reputation as a successful investor and advisor. In addition to her investment activities, Dyson is passionate about healthcare innovation. She has been involved in various healthcare initiatives and startups, particularly those focused on leveraging technology to improve patient care, healthcare delivery, and medical research.

Dyson's interest in space exploration led her to become a board member of several space-related organizations, including Space Adventures, a company that arranges space tourism flights. She is also a member of the advisory board for the XPRIZE Foundation, which promotes breakthrough innovations in science and technology. Apart from her business ventures, Dyson is actively involved in philanthropy. Through her charitable contributions and advocacy work, she has supported education, entrepreneurship, and global health initiatives.

Dyson's multifaceted career, spanning technology, venture capital, healthcare, and space exploration, reflects her diverse interests and entrepreneurial spirit. Her impact on the tech and investment communities and commitment to social causes have earned her recognition as a prominent figure in the intersection of technology, business, and philanthropy.

12. Tim Draper: Tim Draper is a prominent American venture capitalist and entrepreneur known for investing in technology startups and advocating cryptocurrency and blockchain technology. Born on June 11, 1958, in California, Draper comes from a family with a venture capital and entrepreneurship history. Draper founded Draper Associates, a venture capital firm that has invested in numerous successful startups, including Skype, Tesla, Hotmail, and Coinbase. He is known for his early investments in internet companies during the dot-com boom era, which helped solidify his reputation as a successful venture capitalist.

One of Draper's notable investments was in Bitcoin, a pioneering cryptocurrency and blockchain technology. He purchased significant Bitcoin in 2014 and has been a vocal advocate for its potential to revolutionize finance, governance, and various industries.

In addition to his investment activities, Draper is an entrepreneur and founder of Draper University, a school for aspiring entrepreneurs and innovators. He is a strong proponent of entrepreneurship and has actively promoted startup ecosystems worldwide. Draper's impact extends beyond investing and entrepreneurship. He is known for his bold predictions and visionary outlook on technology and society. He has advocated decentralizing power and decision-making, citing blockchain technology as a catalyst for positive change.

Draper's contributions to the technology and investment industries, forward-thinking vision, and advocacy for innovation have earned him recognition as a leading figure in Silicon Valley and the global tech community. His investments and initiatives continue to shape the landscape of technology and entrepreneurship, inspiring future generations of innovators and disruptors.

13. Seth Klarman: Seth Klarman is a highly respected American investor, hedge fund manager, and author known for his value investing approach and disciplined investment strategy. Born on May 21, 1957, Klarman is the founder and CEO of The Baupost Group, one of the most successful hedge funds renowned for its long-term value-oriented investment philosophy. Klarman's investment style is deeply rooted in the principles of value investing pioneered by Benjamin Graham and Warren Buffett. He seeks to invest in undervalued securities with a margin of safety, focusing on fundamental analysis, risk management, and capital preservation.

One of Klarman's fundamental principles is patience, emphasizing the importance of long-term thinking and resisting short-term market noise. He advocates for thorough research, independent analysis, and maintenance of a contrarian mindset to identify investment opportunities that others may overlook. Throughout his career, Klarman has generated consistently solid returns for his investors by investing in a diversified portfolio of equities, distressed debt, real estate, and other asset classes. His disciplined approach to investing has earned him a reputation as a prudent and astute investor, often called a super investor in value investing circles.

In addition to his investment activities, Klarman is known for his insightful writings on investing and financial markets. His book *Margin of Safety*, published in 1991, is considered a classic in value investing literature and has become a sought-after collector's item due to its limited availability. Klarman's contributions to the investment community, adherence to value investing principles, and track record of success have made him a highly regarded figure in the finance industry. His insights and wisdom continue to influence investors and shape the landscape of value investing globally.

14. Bill Miller: Bill Miller is an American investor and fund manager known for his successful track record in the financial industry, particularly his tenure as the portfolio manager of the Legg Mason Capital Management Value Trust. Born on April 15, 1950, Miller gained prominence for his investment strategies and impressive performance during his career. One of Miller's most notable achievements was his record-breaking streak of beating the S&P 500 index for 15 consecutive years from 1991 to 2005. His ability to consistently outperform the market attracted widespread attention and earned him a reputation as one of the most skilled investors of his time.

Miller's investment approach is characterized by his focus on value investing principles, including identifying undervalued stocks with growth potential and maintaining a long-term investment horizon. He is known for his deep research and analysis of companies, sectors, and macroeconomic trends, allowing him to make informed investment decisions. In addition to his success as a fund manager,

Miller is recognized for his philanthropic efforts. He has made significant contributions to charitable causes, including education, healthcare, and environmental conservation, demonstrating his commitment to giving back to society.

Despite facing challenges during the global financial crisis of 2008, Miller's investment acumen and resilience have allowed him to navigate volatile markets and continue delivering solid results for investors. His insights and strategies have influenced many aspiring investors and fund managers, solidifying his legacy as a prominent figure in the investment community.

15. Peter Thiel: Peter Thiel is a renowned American entrepreneur, venture capitalist, and author known for co-founding PayPal, serving as the first outside investor in Facebook, and founding Palantir Technologies. Born on October 11, 1967, in Frankfurt, Germany, Thiel has made significant contributions to the technology industry and has been a prominent figure in Silicon Valley. Thiel co-founded PayPal in 1998 and played a pivotal role in the company's growth and success as a leading online payment platform. Following PayPal's acquisition by eBay, Thiel became one of the earliest investors in Facebook, providing crucial funding and strategic guidance during its formative years.

As a venture capitalist, Thiel co-founded Founders Fund, a venture capital firm that has invested in numerous successful startups, including SpaceX, Airbnb, Spotify, and Lyft. He is known for his contrarian investment approach, focusing on disruptive technologies and companies with high growth potential. Thiel's influence extends beyond his investments. He is also a prolific author and thinker, publishing books such as *Zero to One: Notes on Startups or How to Build the Future*, where he shares insights on entrepreneurship, innovation, and how to build successful businesses. In addition to his work in technology and investing, Thiel is known for his advocacy of libertarian and conservative viewpoints. He has been involved in political activism, supporting causes related to individual freedom, technology innovation, and national security.

Thiel's impact on the technology industry, venture capital, and entrepreneurship has been profound. His strategic investments, visionary thinking, and contributions to shaping the startup ecosystem have solidified his reputation as a leading figure in technology and innovation.

16. David Dreman: David Dreman is a prominent American investor, author, and financial expert known for his contrarian investment approach and contributions to value investing literature. Born on August 19, 1936, Dreman has had a successful career in the finance industry and is widely respected for his insights into stock market behavior and investment strategies. Dreman is the founder and chairman of Dreman Value Management LLC, an investment firm known for its contrarian investment philosophy. He is renowned for his research on investor psychology, market inefficiencies, and the principles of value investing.

One of Dreman's critical contributions to the investment community is his concept of contrarian investing, which involves buying undervalued stocks that are out of favor with the market and selling overvalued stocks that are overhyped. He believes market overreactions and emotional biases create opportunities for disciplined investors to profit from mispriced assets.

Dreman has authored several books on investing, including *Contrarian Investment Strategies: The Next Generation* and *The New Contrarian Investment Strategy.* In these books, he outlines his contrarian approach to investing, emphasizing the importance of fundamental analysis, patience, and long-term thinking. Throughout his career, Dreman has emphasized the significance of focusing on the intrinsic value of companies, avoiding market speculation, and maintaining a diversified portfolio. His research and writings have influenced many investors and fund managers, shaping their investment philosophies and approaches.

In addition to his investment management and writing work, Dreman has been actively involved in philanthropy and educational initiatives. He has supported charitable causes related to education, healthcare, and community development. Dreman's contributions to value investing, contrarian strategies, and investor psychology have earned him recognition as a leading figure in the finance industry. His insights continue to be studied and applied by investors seeking to navigate financial markets with a disciplined and rational approach.

17. Cathie Wood: Cathie Wood is a highly respected American investor, entrepreneur, and founder of Ark Invest, an investment management firm focused on disruptive innovation. Born on November 22, 1955, Wood has gained prominence for her forward-thinking investment strategies and expertise in identifying transformative technologies and trends. Wood's investment approach revolves around investing in innovative companies at the forefront of disruptive technologies, such as artificial intelligence, robotics, genomics, blockchain, and renewable energy. She believes in the long-term potential of these technologies to revolutionize various industries and create substantial value for investors.

As the CEO and chief investment officer of Ark Invest, Wood oversees the firm's investment strategies, research, and portfolio management. Ark Invest is known for its thematic investing approach, with actively managed exchange-traded funds (ETFs) focused on disruptive innovation themes, including ARK Innovation ETF (ARKK) and ARK Genomic Revolution ETF (ARKG). Wood gained widespread attention for her bullish stance on companies like Tesla, which she identified early as a leader in electric vehicles and sustainable energy. Her conviction in disruptive innovation has led to impressive returns for Ark Invest's funds and garnered a loyal following among investors and industry professionals. In addition to her investment prowess, Wood is known for her thought leadership and public speaking engagements, where she shares insights on emerging technologies, market trends, and investment opportunities. She has become a prominent voice in the investment community, advocating for innovation-driven investing and challenging traditional investment paradigms.

Wood's contributions to the finance industry, her visionary

approach to investing in disruptive technologies, and her track record of success have cemented her reputation as one of her generation's most influential and innovative investors. Her insights continue to shape the investment landscape and inspire investors worldwide.

18. Chris Sacca: Chris Sacca is a prominent American venture investor, entrepreneur, and former lawyer known for his successful investments in technology startups and appearances as a guest shark on the television show *Shark Tank*. Born on May 12, 1975, Sacca has made significant contributions to the startup ecosystem and is recognized for his early investments in companies like Twitter, Uber, and Instagram. Before becoming an investor, Sacca worked as a lawyer at Fenwick & West and as an associate at the Silicon Valley law firm of Gunderson Dettmer. He later joined Google in 2003, where he led special initiatives and played a vital role in developing Google's advertising platforms.

In 2006, Sacca left Google to start his venture capital fund, Lowercase Capital, which focused on early-stage investments in technology companies. He quickly gained attention for his successful investments in Twitter, Instagram, and Uber, among others, establishing himself as one of Silicon Valley's most successful and influential investors. Sacca is known for his hands-on approach to investing, providing strategic guidance and mentorship to the companies he invests in. His investment philosophy emphasizes the importance of disruptive innovation, strong leadership, and market potential.

In addition to his investment activities, Sacca is a well-known philanthropist and advocate for social causes. He has been involved in environmental conservation, education, and entrepreneurship initiatives, using his resources and influence to drive positive societal change. Sacca's contributions to the tech industry, keen eye for promising startups, and entrepreneurial spirit have earned him a reputation as a leading figure in venture capital and startup investing. His insights and advice inspire entrepreneurs and investors alike, shaping the future of innovation and technology.

19. Sam Zell: Sam Zell is a prominent American businessman, real estate investor, and entrepreneur known for his expertise in the real estate industry and successful investments across various sectors. Born on September 28, 1941, Zell has made significant contributions to the business world and is widely recognized for his entrepreneurial spirit and investment acumen. Zell is the founder and chairman of Equity Group Investments (EGI), a private investment firm focused on real estate, energy, logistics, and other industries. He gained prominence for his contrarian investment approach and ability to identify undervalued assets with significant growth potential.

One of Zell's most notable achievements is his role in transforming the real estate investment trust (REIT) industry. In the 1960s and 1970s, he pioneered modern REITs, allowing individual investors to access real estate investments through publicly traded companies. This innovation revolutionized the real estate market and opened up new investor opportunities. Zell has been involved in numerous high-profile transactions and investments throughout his career. He has a reputation for taking calculated risks and capitalizing on market opportunities, earning him the nickname 'the Grave Dancer' for his ability to profit from distressed assets. In addition to his real estate investments, Zell has been involved in various other businesses, including energy, manufacturing, and media. He has served on multiple companies' boards and has been recognized for his contributions to entrepreneurship and business leadership.

Zell's entrepreneurial achievements, investment success, and contributions to the real estate industry have earned him widespread respect and recognition. His insights into market trends, risk management, and investment strategies continue to inspire investors and entrepreneurs worldwide.

20. Martin Zweig: Martin Zweig was a prominent American investor, financial analyst, and author known for his insightful market commentary, investment strategies, and role in the financial industry. Born on July 2, 1942, Zweig made significant contributions to investment management and is widely regarded for his market-timing techniques and analysis.

Zweig gained recognition for his forecasting abilities and use of technical and fundamental analysis to make investment decisions. He is perhaps best known for his Zweig Forecast, a market timing indicator based on interest rates, market breadth, and investor sentiment. His accurate predictions and market insights earned him a reputation as a top market strategist.

As an author, Zweig wrote several influential books on investing, including *Winning on Wall Street* and *Martin Zweig's Winning with New IRAs*. These books provided valuable insights into his investment philosophy, emphasizing the importance of thorough research, market timing, and disciplined risk management. Zweig was also known for his role as the founder of Zweig-DiMenna Associates LLC. This hedge fund management firm utilized its investment strategies to achieve impressive client returns. His investment success and analytical approach made him a highly sought-after commentator and speaker in the financial community.

In addition to his investment career, Zweig was an active philanthropist and supporter of charitable causes related to education and medical research. His legacy continues to impact the investment industry, with many investors and professionals studying his strategies and insights for navigating financial markets.

Zweig's contributions to investment analysis, market forecasting, and financial education have solidified his reputation as a legendary figure in the world of finance. His innovative approaches and dedication to excellence inspire investors and analysts worldwide.

21. Charlie Munger: Charlie Munger was born in Omaha, Nebraska, on January 1, 1924. Growing up in a family that valued education and intellectual curiosity, Munger developed an early interest in business and investing. He attended the University of Michigan and later served in the U.S. Army during World War II. After the war, he returned to academics, earning a law degree from Harvard Law School without ever completing an undergraduate degree, showcasing his exceptional intellect and determination. Munger is best known for his long-standing partnership with Warren Buffett, the chairman and CEO of Berkshire Hathaway. He joined the company as vice chairman in 1978 and played a pivotal role in shaping its investment philosophy and strategies. Munger's focus on rational decision-making, value investing, and a long-term perspective complements Buffett's approach, creating a powerful synergy that has driven Berkshire Hathaway's remarkable success.

Like Buffett, Munger adheres to the principles of value investing, seeking undervalued companies with solid fundamentals. He emphasizes the importance of buying high-quality businesses at reasonable prices. Munger advocates for a long-term investment horizon, believing that patience and discipline are crucial for achieving substantial returns. He encourages investors to keep quality investments rather than frequently buy and sell. Munger is a proponent of using diverse mental models to make better investment decisions. He draws from various disciplines, including psychology, economics, and mathematics, to analyze situations and assess risks effectively. Munger advises against speculative investments and emphasizes the importance of understanding the underlying business before making investment decisions. He believes that investors should only invest in companies they comprehend thoroughly. Munger, a lifelong learner, encourages investors to expand their knowledge and understanding continuously. He believes that staying curious and informed is essential for making sound investment decisions.

Munger's influence extends beyond his partnership with Buffett. He is a sought-after speaker and writer known for his wit, wisdom, and straightforward approach to investing. His speeches and writings often reflect his belief in ethics and business integrity, emphasizing character's importance in investment decisions. Munger's impact is also evident in his role as the chairman of the Daily Journal Corporation, where he has applied his investment philosophy to drive the company's growth. His insights and perspectives have shaped the investment community and continue to inspire seasoned investors and newcomers.

In addition to his investment endeavors, Munger is known for his philanthropic efforts. He has made significant contributions to education and healthcare, reflecting his commitment to giving back to society. His donations have supported various institutions, including the University of California, Santa Barbara, and the University of Michigan. Charlie Munger is a great investor and visionary thinker whose principles and philosophies have left an indelible mark on finance. His partnership with Warren Buffett and role at Berkshire Hathaway have solidified his status as a legendary figure in investing. Through his emphasis on value investing, long-term thinking, and ethical business practices, Munger continues to influence and inspire future investors. His legacy is of intellect, integrity, and a relentless pursuit of knowledge, making him a true icon in the investment community.

22. Jerry Buss: Jerry Buss was a prominent American businessman, real estate investor, and sports executive known primarily for owning the Los Angeles Lakers basketball team. Born on January 27, 1933, Buss made significant contributions to the sports and entertainment industry, leaving a lasting legacy as one of the most successful and influential team owners in professional sports. Buss acquired the Los Angeles Lakers in 1979, along with the Los Angeles Kings hockey team and the Forum sports arena, in a landmark transaction that reshaped the landscape of sports ownership. Under his leadership, the Lakers became one of the most successful franchises in NBA history, winning numerous championships and cultivating a culture of excellence and innovation.

Buss's key contributions to the Lakers' success were his strategic vision and commitment to assembling talented teams on and off the court. He hired exceptional coaches and front-office personnel, including legendary figures like Pat Riley and Jerry West, who played instrumental roles in the team's championship runs. Beyond his achievements in sports, Buss was also a successful entrepreneur and real estate investor. He had a keen eye for business opportunities and was involved in various ventures outside of sports, including real estate development and investment.

Buss's impact extended beyond the basketball court and business world. He was known for his philanthropic efforts and charitable contributions, supporting causes related to education, healthcare, and youth development. Throughout his career, Buss earned widespread respect and admiration for his leadership, innovation, and dedication to excellence. His legacy as the Lakers owner inspires sports executives, team owners, and fans worldwide, cementing his position as a sports industry visionary.

23. Howard S. Marks: Howard S. Marks is a highly regarded American investor, author, and co-founder of Oaktree Capital Management, a global investment firm specializing in alternative investments. Born on April 23, 1946, Marks is widely recognized for his expertise in distressed debt, value investing, and risk management. Marks began his career in finance in the early 1970s, working for Citibank and later joining TCW Group, where he focused on high-yield debt and distressed debt investments. In 1995, Marks and his colleagues Bruce Karsh and others founded Oaktree Capital Management, which has grown into one of the world's leading alternative investment firms, managing billions of dollars for institutional and individual investors.

Marks is known for his contrarian investment approach, emphasizing the importance of risk management, market cycles, and patience in investing. He has authored several books on investing, including *The Most Important Thing*, which discusses crucial investment principles and strategies for achieving long-term success in financial markets. As an investor, Marks has a reputation for identifying undervalued assets and opportunities in distressed markets. His insights into market trends, macroeconomic factors, and investor psychology have earned him a loyal following among investors and industry professionals.

In addition to his investment activities, Marks is an influential thinker in the finance industry, frequently sharing his views on market conditions, investment strategies, and economic trends through memos and public appearances. His writings and speeches are highly regarded for their wisdom, clarity, and practical advice for investors. Marks's contributions to the investing field, his focus on risk management, and his dedication to investor education have made him a respected figure in the investment community. His insights continue to guide investors and shape how professionals approach financial markets.

24. Al Waleed bin Talal Al Saud: Prince Al-Waleed bin Talal bin Abdulaziz Al Saud is a prominent Saudi Arabian businessman, investor, and philanthropist known for his significant contributions to the global business world and charitable initiatives. Born on March 7, 1955, Prince Al-Waleed is a member of the Saudi royal family and holds various positions in investment companies and organizations. As the founder and chairman of Kingdom Holding Company, Prince Al-Waleed has built a diversified investment portfolio spanning multiple sectors, including finance, real estate, technology, entertainment, and hospitality. He is known for his strategic investments in global companies such as Citigroup, Twitter, Apple, and Disney.

Prince Al-Waleed is recognized for his entrepreneurial vision, astute investment strategies, and ability to identify lucrative opportunities in emerging markets. His investments and business initiatives have played a key role in promoting economic growth and development in Saudi Arabia and the broader Middle East region. In addition to his business ventures, Prince Al-Waleed is actively involved in philanthropy and charitable work. He has established various foundations and initiatives to support education, healthcare, youth empowerment, and disaster relief efforts. His philanthropic contributions have made a positive impact on communities and individuals across the globe.

Prince Al-Waleed's leadership, business acumen, and commitment to social responsibility have earned him recognition and respect in Saudi Arabia and internationally. His contributions to the business world and philanthropic endeavors have solidified his reputation as a prominent figure in global business and philanthropy.

25. Kenneth Fisher: Kenneth Fisher is an esteemed American investor, author, and philanthropist, recognized for his significant contributions to the investment industry and expertise in financial markets. Born on November 29, 1950, Fisher is the founder and chairman of Fisher Investments, one of the largest independent wealth management firms globally. Fisher's career in finance began in the early 1970s when he joined his father's investment advisory firm, Fisher & Co. He later founded Fisher Investments in 1979, building it into a renowned investment management firm that serves institutional and individual clients worldwide.

As an investor, Fisher is known for his contrarian approach, focusing on identifying undervalued assets and opportunities in market inefficiencies. He has authored several books on investing, including *Super Stocks* and *The Only Three Questions That Count*, where he shares his investment philosophy and strategies for achieving long-term success in financial markets. Fisher's insights into market trends, behavioral finance, and economic cycles have earned him a reputation as a thought leader in the investment community. He regularly contributes to financial publications and media outlets, commenting on market conditions, investment strategies, and economic outlooks. In addition to his professional accomplishments, Fisher is actively involved in philanthropy and charitable initiatives. He has supported various causes related to education, healthcare, and wildlife conservation, demonstrating his commitment to giving back to society.

Fisher's contributions to the investment industry, his innovative approach to investing, and his dedication to investor education have made him a respected figure in finance. His insights continue to guide investors and shape how professionals approach financial markets.

26. Mario Gabelli: Mario Gabelli is a highly respected American investor, money manager, and philanthropist known for his value investing expertise and contributions to the financial industry. Born on June 19, 1942, in The Bronx, New York, Gabelli is the founder, chairman, and CEO of GAMCO Investors Inc., a leading investment management firm. Gabelli's career in finance began in the 1960s, and he quickly gained recognition for his analytical skills and investment prowess. Mario J. Gabelli is the chairman and chief executive officer of GAMCO Investors Inc., the firm he founded in 1977 focusing on a value-oriented investing approach emphasizing fundamental analysis, financial research, and long-term value creation.

Gabelli is an investor known for his deep understanding of financial markets, corporate governance, and strategic investment opportunities. He has built a reputation for identifying undervalued companies and investment themes across various sectors, including media, telecommunications, consumer goods, and energy. Beyond his investment activities, Gabelli is actively involved in philanthropy and charitable initiatives. He has supported educational institutions, healthcare organizations, and cultural programs, demonstrating his commitment to giving back to society and promoting social welfare.

Gabelli's contributions to the investment industry, his value-oriented investment philosophy, and his dedication to philanthropy have earned him widespread respect and admiration. He continues to be a prominent figure in the financial community, influencing investment strategies and inspiring future generations of investors.

27. Geraldine Weiss: Geraldine Weiss was a prominent American investment analyst, author, and pioneer in the field of dividend investing. Born on November 20, 1926, Weiss became known for her analytical skills, financial acumen, and investment research and education contributions. Weiss gained recognition for her work in dividend investing, which focuses on selecting stocks based on their dividend payments and historical dividend growth. She co-founded the Investment Research Institute in 1966 and published the investment newsletter *Investment Quality Trends* (*IQT*) in 1966, which became widely respected in the investment community.

As an investment analyst, Weiss emphasized the importance of fundamental analysis, financial strength, and dividend stability when evaluating potential investments. She developed the dividend-value approach, which involves identifying undervalued stocks with solid dividend yields and favorable growth prospects. Weiss's investment strategies and insights influenced the dividend investing philosophy and guided investors to select quality stocks for long-term wealth accumulation. Her work inspired many investors and analysts to adopt a disciplined approach to investing based on fundamental analysis and value investing principles.

Weiss authored several books on investment strategies throughout her career, including *Dividends Don't Lie* and *The Dividend Connection*. She was also a frequent speaker at investment conferences and seminars, sharing her expertise and knowledge with aspiring investors. Geraldine Weiss's legacy in the investment world continues to be celebrated for her pioneering work in dividend investing, dedication to educating investors, and lasting impact on investment research and analysis.

28. Bill Ackman: William 'Bill' Ackman is a prominent American hedge fund manager, investor, and philanthropist known for his influential role in the financial industry and investment strategies. Born on May 11, 1966, in New York City, Ackman is the founder and CEO of Pershing Square Capital Management, a hedge fund known for its activist investing approach. Ackman gained recognition for his successful investments and activist campaigns targeting underperforming companies. He is known for conducting thorough research and analysis to identify undervalued assets and opportunities for value creation. Ackman has made significant investments in companies across various sectors, including consumer goods, healthcare, technology, and real estate.

One of Ackman's notable investment successes was his involvement in the turnaround of Canadian Pacific Railway Limited (CP Rail), where he played a crucial role in appointing a new CEO and implementing operational changes that led to improved performance and shareholder value. In addition to his investment activities, Ackman is actively involved in philanthropy and charitable initiatives. He has supported educational institutions, healthcare organizations, and social causes, demonstrating his commitment to giving back to society.

Ackman's investment strategies, leadership in activist investing, and contributions to the financial industry have earned him widespread recognition and respect. He continues to be a prominent figure in the investment community, influencing market trends and investor sentiment through his actions and insights.

29. David Einhorn: David Einhorn is a renowned American hedge fund manager, investor, and author known for his value investing approach and insightful analysis of financial markets. Born on November 20, 1968, in New Jersey, Einhorn is the founder and president of Greenlight Capital, a hedge fund known for its contrarian investment strategies. Einhorn gained prominence in the investment community for his astute stock picks, deep research, and keen understanding of market trends. He is known for identifying undervalued companies with solid growth potential and taking substantial positions in them.

One of Einhorn's notable investment successes was his early recognition of the financial risks posed by the subprime mortgage market before the 2008 financial crisis. He famously shorted several financial institutions heavily exposed to subprime mortgages, earning significant profits for his fund during the crisis. Einhorn is also known for his activism in corporate governance and shareholder rights. He has been vocal about advocating for changes in company management, capital allocation, and transparency, often engaging in public debates and shareholder meetings to drive his agenda. In addition to his investment activities, Einhorn is an author and philanthropist. He has written books on investing, including *Fooling Some of the People All of the Time*, where he shares his experiences as an investor and lessons learned from his investment journey.

Einhorn's investment acumen, principled approach to investing, and contributions to the financial industry have earned him respect and recognition as one of the most influential investors of his generation. He remains a prominent figure in the investment community, sharing his insights and perspectives on market trends and investment opportunities.

30. Walter Schloss: Walter Schloss was a renowned American investor and money manager known for his value investing philosophy and remarkable track record in the financial markets. Born on August 28, 1916, in New York City, Schloss began his career in finance in the 1930s and gained recognition for his disciplined approach to investing. Schloss's investment strategy was heavily influenced by Benjamin Graham, the father of value investing, who also served as his mentor. He focused on buying undervalued stocks trading below their intrinsic value, with a keen eye on financial fundamentals and low price-to-book ratios.

One of Schloss's fundamental principles was to invest in companies with solid balance sheets, consistent earnings, and a history of profitability. He believed in conducting thorough research and analysis, often delving into financial statements and company reports to uncover hidden opportunities. Schloss was known for his patient and long-term investment approach, often holding on to stocks for many years. His conservative investment style and emphasis on value and margin of safety served him well, enabling him to navigate various market cycles and deliver consistent returns for his clients.

Despite his low-key persona and avoidance of media attention, Schloss earned a stellar reputation in the investment community for his integrity, humility, and exceptional results. He managed money for over five decades, achieving impressive compounded returns and leaving a lasting legacy as one of the great value investors of his time. Walter Schloss's investment philosophy and success inspire value investors and financial professionals, emphasizing the importance of discipline, patience, and a deep understanding of economic fundamentals in achieving long-term investment success.

Milton Keynes UK
Ingram Content Group UK Ltd.
UKHW020646211124
3009UKWH00018B/25/J

9 798369 432907